Video Game Design

Composition

Software Design Guide

D. Michael Ploor, MBA
National Board Certified Teacher
STEM Curriculum Integration Specialist
School District of Hillsborough County
Tampa, Florida

Publisher
The Goodheart-Willcox Company, Inc.
Tinley Park, Illinois
www.g-w.com

Cover illustration: Bertrand Benoit/Shutterstock.com

Introduction

Video Game Design Composition provides students with an advanced understanding of the technological and creative aspects of video game design in an easy-to-follow format. This Software Design Guide (SDG) provides the hands-on application of the theory presented in the textbook.

Video Game Design Composition presents content in 13 chapters, with each chapter acting as a building block that supports the next skill learned. This allows students to learn the objective of each lesson, practice the corresponding skill, and lay the foundation on which to acquire the next skill set.

Software Design Guide

In this Software Design Guide, students will participate in a simulation of a real video game design team, seeing each project from origination to fruition. This provides a valuable lesson in team building that can be applied to any other aspect of the technology and engineering industries in real-life future careers.

The chapters in this SDG are correlated to the textbook chapters. After learning the theory of video game design in a textbook chapter, the corresponding SDG chapter applies the theory. This hands-on approach allows students to apply the theory in an environment of a simulated video game design team.

The capstone project is a culmination of all advanced knowledge and skills obtained in the course. Students will design an original game from scratch, starting with a concept that must be approved by a simulated Board of Directors. Students must create and follow a budget and time schedule. Evaluation of the final build is based on critical individual and peer reviews.

Game Engine Software

The game builds in this Software Design Guide use 001 Game Creator or Multimedia Fusion 2. These game engines are provided with this teaching package. In addition, some activities make use of common software, such as Microsoft PowerPoint or Excel, freeware software, or demo software.

001 Game Creator

The 001 Game Creator software from Engine 001 is a flexible game engine designed to create role-playing games, as well as a variety of other games. It offers easy graphical scripting, making it ideal for constructing story-based games. The 001 Game Creator software is included with the purchase of this Software Design Guide. The 001 Game Creator software runs under Windows.

Multimedia Fusion 2

Multimedia Fusion 2 from Clickteam is an intuitive, easy-to-use game engine. It uses a point-and-click and drag-and-drop interface to assemble game frames, program logic statements, and create a functioning game application. This software is an excellent tool for teaching video game design.

Multimedia Fusion 2 is free for school use. It may be downloaded, installed, and used on computers owned or leased by the educational institution. For information on downloading the free school-use software, contact Goodheart-Willcox Publisher or Clickteam.

Multimedia Fusion 2 runs under Windows. It will also run under Mac OS using Parallels. To run Multimedia Fusion 2 under Linux, use a Windows emulator, such as Wine (www.winehq.org), or one of the other Windows emulators available for Linux.

Table of Contents

Chapter 1
Design Composition

Objectives

After completing this chapter, you will be able to:

- Brainstorm game concepts.
- Create a high-concept document.
- Design a marketing brochure.
- Create a presentation for a game concept.
- Develop a plan for using social media to promote a game and company.

Goodheart-Willcox Publisher;
brochures courtesy of www.posimotion.com

macrovarro/Shutterstock.com

Goodheart-Willcox Publisher

Bellwork

Day	Date	Activity	Response
1		Complete the anticipation guide and the K and W columns of the KWL chart for this chapter.	
2		Why are some types of digital entertainment considered toys and not games?	
3		State your favorite genre of games, and list two reasons why you like it.	
4		Which member of game design team is responsible for creating the story, plot, and characters?	
5		List the five Ps of video game publishing.	
6		What is a USP, and why is it important to have one in a game?	
7		Define *asset*.	
8		Define *subroutine,* and describe how a subroutine is used in game programming.	
9		Define *GUI,* and list three elements that are part of the GUI.	
10		What is a PERT diagram? How is it used to help in the game design process?	
11		How can a game-design project be fast tracked?	

Day	Date	Activity	Response
12		List the main duties remaining for the design team once an alpha version of a game is available.	
13		What is a bug report?	
14		Define *porting*.	
15		What is a channel of distribution?	
16		How can a patch be distributed without the customer knowing it was an error?	
17		Define *jailbreak,* and describe why a person may jailbreak his or her smartphone.	
18		List four types of business ownership.	
19		How are indie developers able to compete with major corporations in the app marketplace?	
20		How is stock used in the ownership of a corporation?	
21		Which type of business ownership would you most likely create if you yourself created a game app and sold it on iTunes? Why?	
22		Complete the L column of the KWL chart and the After Reading column of the anticipation guide with what you learned from this chapter.	
23		Speculate why functionality testing can be done by a computer while playability testing is done with people.	

Anticipation Guide

Directions

Before reading the chapter, read each statement in the table below. In the column titled Before Reading, write the letter *T* if you agree with the statement or *F* if you disagree with the statement. After reading the chapter, reread each statement in the table below. In the column titled After Reading, write the letter *T* if you agree with the statement or *F* if you disagree with the statement. Be prepared to justify your answers in a class discussion.

Before Reading	Statement	After Reading
	The drawings and other art for a game project are stored in the art bible.	
	Provisional approval means the team has approval to build the game to the final version.	
	A video game publisher will oversee the entire process of bringing the game to market.	
	The quality assurance team completes game testing.	
	Quick time is the point in game design when time begins to run short and decisive action is required.	

KWL Chart

Directions

Before reading the chapter, fill in what you already know about the topic in the K column and what you want to learn in the W column. After reading the chapter, review what you know and wanted to learn about the topic. Reflect on what you have studied and completed in this chapter. Fill in what you learned in the L column. Be prepared to justify your answers in a class discussion.

Topic: Video Game Design Jobs		
K What you already *know*	**W** What you *want* to learn	**L** What you *learned*

Activity 1-1

Concept Composition

Objectives

Students will brainstorm ideas for a game concept. Students will make ideas conform to marketing requirements such as audience and gameplay specifications. Students will perform authentic research on mechanical processes and synthesize alternative approaches to each mechanical system.

Situation

The process of designing a video game is not just the glamour and glitz of cool artwork, characters, and gameplay. Before any of those things are created, the details of the design must be created. The Really Cool Game Company has been approached by a juice-box manufacturer to create a game that will play on smartphones, tablets, and its website. Your team will submit a concept document, brochure, and presentation for your unique version of the game. The game should appeal to a young audience, ages 8 to 12, and showcase the cartoon fruit characters the manufacturer uses in television and print advertising.

How to Begin

1. Research the machines and processes used in manufacturing and distributing juice boxes.
2. Brainstorm ideas on how gameplay can be created to use the company's cartoon fruit characters, shown in **Figure 1,** to manufacture and distribute the juice boxes. Record all brainstormed ideas in the Idea column of the Brainstorming Document on the next page. The process of brainstorming must be an open format for ideas to flow and develop without evaluation. All ideas are important as they may lead to better ideas in the next step.
3. After all brainstormed ideas are recorded, go back through the document and mark each idea as shown in **Figure 2.**
4. Add to the document and rate any new ideas you came up with during the review.
5. Record comments on the document so you can remember how each idea relates to the others.
6. Review the ideas with your team to help refine a single concept.

Symbol	Meaning
✔	Good idea; can work on its own as a concept component.
+	Good idea, but not a complete concept component; could be used as part of the gameplay or other part of the game.
×	Not a good idea for this concept.

Figure 2   Goodheart-Willcox Publisher

Name: _____

Date: _____

Class: _____

Brainstorming Document

	Sort (✔, +, or ✕)	Idea (record all ideas without evaluating them)	Comments and Possible Uses
1			
2			
3			
4			
5			
6			
7			
8			
9			
10			
11			
12			
13			
14			
15			

Name: _____

Date: _____

Class: _____

Activity 1-2

High-Concept Document Composition

Objectives

Students will summarize ideas to form a coherent game concept. Students will format a word processing document, including font changes, margins, spacing, and layout. Students will compose paragraphs and sentences to form complete thoughts following established language arts principles.

Situation

The Really Cool Game Company requires a one-page document to review the ideas for the concept you have developed. Using software such as Microsoft Word or Adobe InDesign, create a document to the specifications outlined in this activity. Keep in mind that this is a professional document. Correct grammar and spelling rules must be applied; *no* texting language is allowed. Choose words to show excitement in persuading the decision makers to take a closer look at your concept.

How to Begin

1. Using the software, create a new document and save it in your working folder as *LastName*_HighConceptDocument.

2. Set the margins to 1″ on the top, bottom, right, and left. **Figure 1** shows how to do this in Microsoft Word.

3. Enter a title for the document and format it as 22 point type, bold, and underlined. See **Figure 2.**

4. For the body of the document, use 12 point type and the font Times New Roman.

5. Write the concept following the five essential questions and rules presented in textbook Chapter 1:

   ◦ What is the game going to be about (genre type, basic idea)?
   ◦ Who is going to play this game (audience, age, target market, desired ESRB rating)?
   ◦ Who is the player, or protagonist, going to be in this game (player role, character types)?
   ◦ What will the player do in the game (victory condition, obstacles, opponents)?
   ◦ What will the world look like in the game (settings, levels, backgrounds, perspectives)?

6. Do not exceed one page in length. Edit the sentences in the document as needed to fit on a single page. You may *not* change the point size of the type, increase the margins, or reduce space between lines or paragraphs to gain additional room for text.

7. Proofread the document for errors, including any spelling and grammar errors. Errors make the document look unprofessional.

8. Save the document and submit it for review and approval by your instructor.

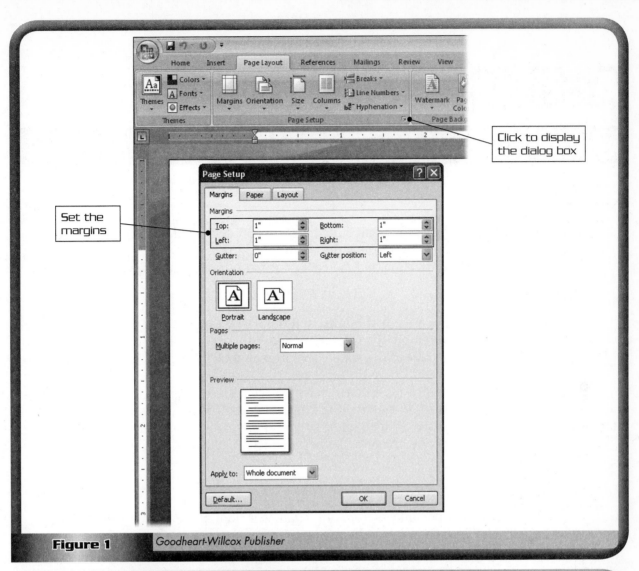

Set the margins

Click to display the dialog box

Figure 1 *Goodheart-Willcox Publisher*

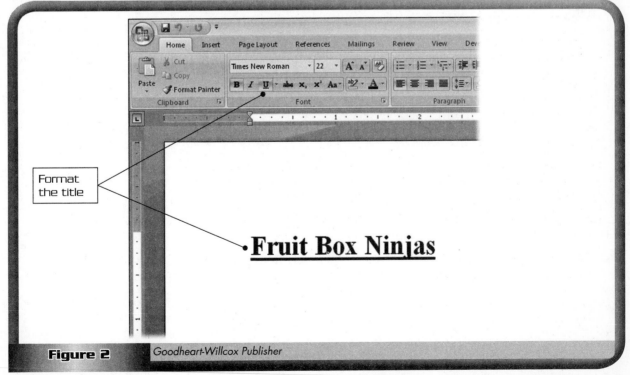

Format the title

Fruit Box Ninjas

Figure 2 *Goodheart-Willcox Publisher*

Activity 1-3

Game Treatment Document Composition

Objectives

Students will format and publish a marketing brochure. Students will determine important market factors and present summary information to fit a brochure format. Students will evaluate demographic and statistical information and match a concept to fit market parameters.

Situation

The game concept has passed the first hurdle, and the Really Cool Game Company needs a game-treatment document in the form of a trifold brochure. A trifold brochure has two folds to create six panels, three on each side of the paper. This format allows for many different layouts to present the information.

Creating a trifold brochure requires efficient use of space and information. Display your design and layout skills by placing the most eye-catching information on the two panels that are visible when the brochure is closed. Place detailed information on the panels that are visible when the brochure is open. This will give the brochure the best chance of making it through to the next step for concept presentation.

How to Begin

1. Research game-treatment documents from other games including the pitch documents for *Bioshock*, which can be found by searching on the Internet.

2. Use Microsoft Word, Microsoft Publisher, Adobe InDesign, or other software with a brochure template to create a trifold brochure to promote your game. **Figure 1** shows selecting a trifold brochure template in Microsoft Word.

3. Be sure to address the eight common items found in a game-treatment document:
   - game introduction
   - genre and target market
   - platform
   - game description and plot overview
   - concept art or sketches
   - USP
   - legal issues
   - reasons why your team is the best one to design the game

4. Include original sketches, clipart, or other artwork to add interest. See **Figure 2.** The artwork should reflect the style you are attempting to create for the game. You *must* cite all sources of artwork.

5. Save the work as *LastName*_GameTreatmentDocument in your working folder, and submit it for review and approval by your instructor.

Name: _____

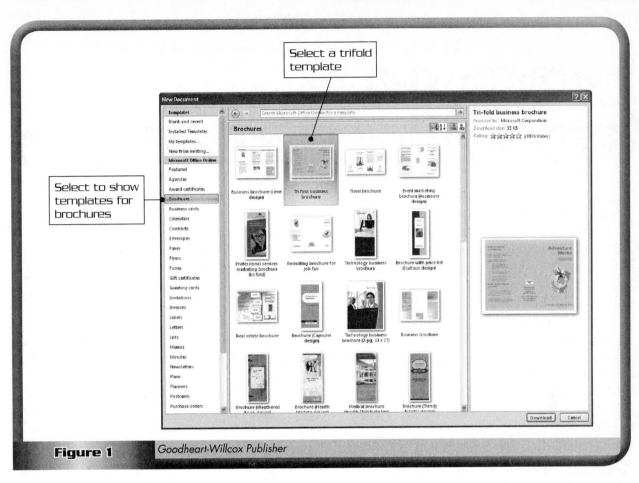

Select a trifold template

Select to show templates for brochures

Figure 1   Goodheart-Willcox Publisher

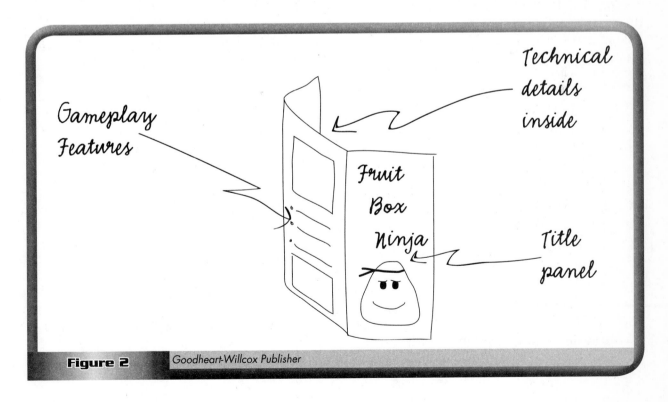

Technical details inside

Gameplay Features

Fruit Box Ninja

Title panel

Figure 2   Goodheart-Willcox Publisher

Activity 1-4

Concept Presentation Composition

Objectives

Students will publish a visual presentation. Students will create a narrated audiovisual presentation to communicate information to the audience. Students will incorporate sound, animation, transitions, and other effects in a digital media presentation.

Situation

In addition to the game-treatment document, the Really Cool Game Company is requiring a PechaKucha-style presentation before the board of directors of the juice box company. PechaKucha style allows 20 slides per presentation and each slide appears for only 20 seconds. The presenter must be energetic and fast-paced to keep up with the automatically advancing slides. Plan the presentation well and rehearse to ensure your great ideas will be conveyed to the audience.

Take the information contained in the high-concept and game-treatment documents, and create a visual presentation. The purpose of the presentation is to convey information, not to dazzle the viewer with animations and sound effects. Use animations and sound effects as appropriate, but be sure they do not distract from the message. Remember, the message is how the game best meets the needs of the client.

As this presentation is to be an aid to the delivery of information, it must meet the 6 × 6 requirement. A 6 × 6 presentation requirement restricts the amount of text on each slide to six talking points per slide and six words per talking point. Each talking point should contain summary information; complete sentences are not required. Pictures and titles are encouraged as these do not count against the limits.

How to Begin

1. Launch the presentation software, such as Microsoft PowerPoint.

2. Using the information from the high-concept and game-treatment documents, create a 15-slide presentation for the game concept following the 6 × 6 requirement. The remaining five slides will be added in the next activity.

3. Add images and other assets that will help effectively present the information in a quick and energetic manner.

4. Set the slide transition to automatically advance each slide after 20 seconds. **Figure 1** shows how to do this in PowerPoint.

5. Prepare for and practice presenting the concept to the class. Be ready to defend your decisions in creating the concept.

6. Save the presentation as *LastName*_ConceptPresentation in your working folder, and submit it for review and approval by your instructor.

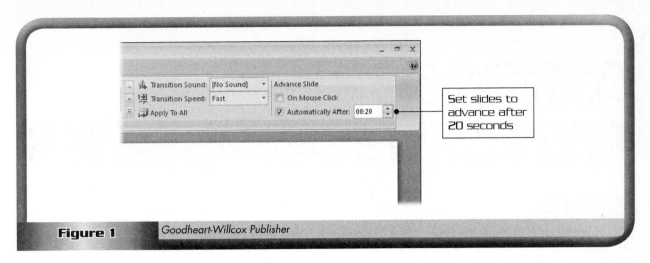

Figure 1   *Goodheart-Willcox Publisher*

Activity 1-5

Social Media Plan Composition

Objectives

Students will research social media and develop a plan to use social media to market and offer online playing of a video game. Students will synthesize research to create a social media marketing proposal and incorporate the proposal into a presentation.

Situation

Incorporating social media such as Facebook, Twitter, and YouTube is a requirement for all marketing and distribution plans. Social media is a great way to connect with loyal fans and others that like the company's products. With this in mind, the Really Cool Game Company requires all presentations to include considerations for social media. The client, the juice box manufacturer, really likes the idea of incorporating some social media aspects to the game similar to games like *FarmVille, CityVille, The Sims Social,* and *Words with Friends.* Your job is to think of ways to connect the game to social media, blogs, bulletin boards, chat rooms, forums, and video sites and add these ideas to the PechaKucha-style concept presentation. The game concept can include social media content such as the ability to buy, sell, and trade game assets.

How to Begin

1. Research social media and social marketing. Try to determine how other games have benefited from social media marketing and gameplay.

2. Think about ways that social media and social marketing can be applied to your game concept.

3. Open the concept presentation from Activity 1-4.

4. Save the presentation as *LastName*_SocialPresentation in your working folder. This allows content to be added without altering the original concept presentation.

5. Add five slides to the end of the presentation.

6. On the five new slides, discuss social marketing for the game. Be specific and list the type of content and possible examples of how the Internet, handheld devices, and social media will be used to generate interest in the game. Include examples of social marketing used by existing games.

7. Set transitions to advance every 20 seconds to keep with the PechaKucha style.

8. Save your work.

9. Be prepared to present the concept to the class and defend your decisions.

Activity 1-6

Packaging Prototype

Objectives

Students will use digital design software to create a folded-sheet insert for a video game case. Students will create a decorative cover prototype that will attract attention and convey information.

Situation

As an added bonus, the client wants to include a CD of the game in its six-pack juice box packaging. The hope is that the customers will buy the multipack item to get the game and quickly connect to the social media sites to get more involved. The CD will need to be enclosed in decorative packaging since it will be visible through the shrink-wrap of the six-pack packaging. Your job is to create the decorative packaging to give to the client during the presentation. Do a great job; the Really Cool Game Company is counting on you!

How to Begin

1. Launch the digital design software, such as Adobe InDesign, Microsoft Publisher, or similar software. Alternatively, this project can be easily completed with PowerPoint or Word.
2. Set the paper size to 9.5″ wide by 4.75″ tall or restrict the printable area to these dimensions. Alternately, draw a rectangle of those dimensions centered on the page. You will print on a standard letter-size paper (8.5″ × 11″). The image will be cut out and the sheet will be folded to create a pocket for the CD to fit inside.
3. Draw a line 4.75″ from the edge to create a front and back panel to the game cover. See **Figure 1.**
4. Place decorative text on the front cover for the name of the game.
5. Use artwork to decorate the front cover. The artwork should represent your concepts for the game.
6. Include text for **Designed by** *your name* and **Published by The Really Cool Game Company**.
7. Format the design so all text is readable and the design has appropriate color use.
8. Save the file as *LastName*_**Packaging** in your working folder.
9. Print the document and assemble the packaging. Use clear tape on the edges of the trimmed sheet to create a pocket for a CD.
10. Turn in completed design for grading.

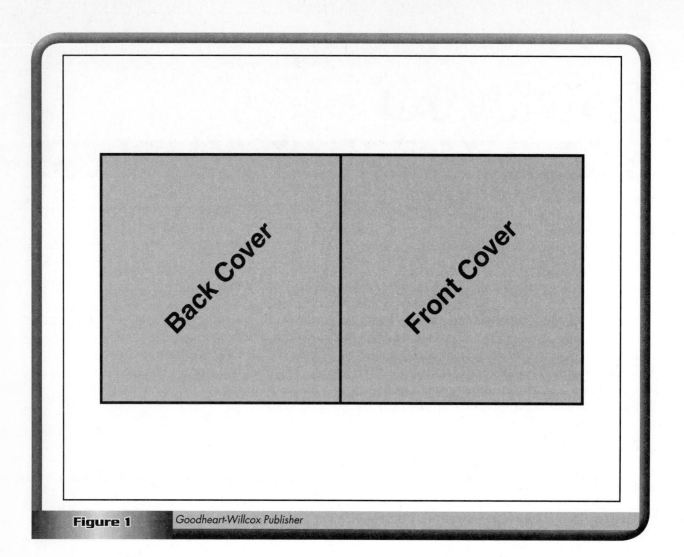

Figure 1   *Goodheart-Willcox Publisher*

Chapter 2
Character Composition

Objectives

After completing this chapter, you will be able to:
- Use an online character-creation tool.
- Develop character descriptions.
- Define a hero archetype character.
- Develop a character profile.
- Synthesize a gameplay-attributed character.
- Discuss the value of cultural differences in a team.

Algol/Shutterstock.com

YorkBerlin/Shutterstock.com

marcovarro/Shutterstock.com

Bellwork

Day	Date	Activity	Response
1		Complete the anticipation guide and the K and W columns of the KWL chart for this chapter.	
2		List three of your favorite video game characters and the games in which they are featured.	
3		How does the "Once upon a time..." fairy tale line help develop the main character of the story?	
4		List three video games containing memorable characters that have helped define a genre.	
5		Compare and contrast perks and upgrades.	
6		What is Sanskrit?	
7		What is a gaming handicap? Give two examples.	
8		Define *MMO* and describe how these games can have millions of unique characters.	
9		What is the purpose of having neutral NPCs?	
10		What is a swarm?	
11		How can a swarm be a good game design?	

Day	Date	Activity	Response
12		Describe how a tangible feature differs from an intangible feature.	
13		List the four main intangible features for character design.	
14		What are cultural values?	
15		List three ways game designers convey character attributes.	
16		Describe contextual clues in a conversation that you might use to convey the character of a popular teenager.	
17		Describe how a level-up changes a character's status, abilities, appearance, speech, and movement attributes.	
18		Describe how old cowboy movies used semiotics to help the audience know who were good guys and bad guys.	
19		What is an alter ego? Give one example.	
20		Which character archetype do you feel best describes you? Why?	
21		What is the purpose of expression sketches?	
22		Complete the L column of the KWL chart and the After Reading column of the anticipation guide with what you learned from this chapter.	
23		Speculate why building a character mockup would help in the final design.	

Anticipation Guide

Directions

Before reading the chapter, read each statement in the table below. In the column titled Before Reading, write the letter *T* if you agree with the statement or *F* if you disagree with the statement. After reading the chapter, reread each statement in the table below. In the column titled After Reading, write the letter *T* if you agree with the statement or *F* if you disagree with the statement. Be prepared to justify your answers in a class discussion.

Before Reading	Statement	After Reading
	Stories are about characters and what they do.	
	The literal, original meaning of *avatar* is the human form of a god or deity.	
	Game characters and avatars are only human-shaped beings.	
	Characters that are controlled by the game programming are called other player characters (OPCs).	
	Universal characters that are easily identifiable by any culture are known as archetypes.	

KWL Chart

Directions

Before reading the chapter, fill in what you already know about the topic in the K column and what you want to learn in the W column. After reading the chapter, review what you know and wanted to learn about the topic. Reflect on what you have studied and completed in this chapter. Fill in what you learned in the L column. Be prepared to justify your answers in a class discussion.

Topic: Character Development		
K What you already *know*	**W** What you *want* to learn	**L** What you *learned*

Name: _____

Date: _____

Class: _____

Activity 2-1

Contextual Clues

Objectives

Students will be able to understand and apply aesthetic characteristics and semiotics to design character features. Students will be able to interpret and decode contextual clues for characters. Students will perform a screen capture. Students will navigate and use two separate software programs in a multitasking environment.

Situation

The Really Cool Game Company is looking for a set of cartoon characters for a story-based game. The art director has assigned you the task of creating a set of characters for a cartoon family. The family will need a dad, mom, and three children. Your job is to use the company's stock art to begin developing the prototype characters.

How to Begin

1. Launch presentation software, such as Microsoft PowerPoint.
2. Add a new blank slide or delete all text boxes from the default slide.
3. Save the presentation as *LastName*_ContextalClues in your working folder.
4. Launch the Internet browser. You must be connected to the Internet for this activity.
5. Navigate to a character-creation website as indicated by your instructor.
6. Select the option on the website to create or become a character.
7. Use the tools on the website to assemble a character. Be sure to apply contextual clues that a player could use to identify the type of character or its purpose.

Capturing the Character

8. Press the [Print Screen] key on the keyboard. This feature creates an image of whatever is on your screen, which is called a screen capture, and stores it on your computer's clipboard.
9. Switch to the slide presentation software. The blank presentation started earlier should be displayed.
10. Use the **Paste** function, either with the [Ctrl][V] key combination or the button in the software, to place the screen capture on the slide. If the pasting does not work, switch to the Internet browser and try creating the screen capture again.
11. Save the presentation file.

Basic Image Editing

12. Start the **Crop** function in the slide presentation software. This function can be used to remove the extra screen material and leave just the character. The image remains rectangular.
13. Move the cursor over the image. When the cursor is over a cropping handle, the cursor changes to indicate the handle can be dragged to remove content. You may need to zoom out to see the entire screen capture.

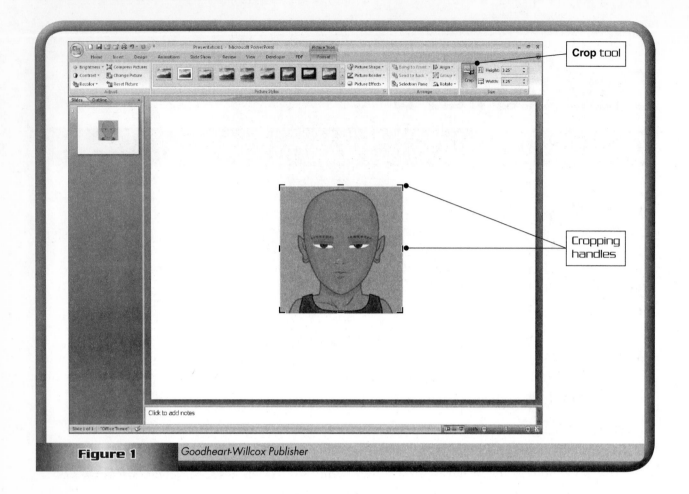

Crop tool

Cropping handles

Figure 1   *Goodheart-Willcox Publisher*

14. Crop all sides of the image so only the character is left. **Figure 1** shows this done in Microsoft PowerPoint.

15. End the **Crop** function. Depending on the software, this is usually done by clicking the tool button to turn it off or by pressing the [Esc] key.

16. Select the character image to display the resizing handles.

17. Click a corner sizing handle, and drag to enlarge or reduce the image. This proportional resizes the image, which maintains the ratio of length to width (called the aspect ratio). In some software, the [Shift] or [Ctrl] key must be held down to proportionally resize the image.

18. Proportionally resize the image until it fills most of the slide. Leave some blank space at the bottom for a name, which will be added next.

19. Save the presentation file.

Naming the Character

20. Insert a text box below the image.

21. Enter a name as the text. For example, if this character is the mom, the name might be Mommy, Mrs. Martian, Sandy Snow, or something else that relates to the character you created.

22. Center align the text.

23. Select the text, and change the font to one that will, if possible, provide a contextual clue to the character, as shown in **Figure 2.** For example, if the family is from Mars, you may select a font that communicates outer space or science fiction.

24. Choose a color for the font that matches the character or background.

25. Save the presentation file.

Name: _____

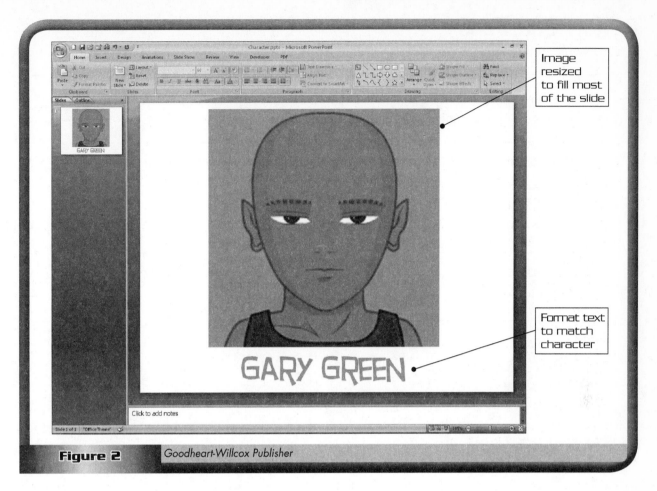

Image resized to fill most of the slide

Format text to match character

GARY GREEN

Figure 2   *Goodheart-Willcox Publisher*

Customizing the Characters

26. Add four new slides to the presentation, one for each remaining member of the cartoon family.

27. Switch to the Internet browser with the character-creation website loaded.

28. Create another character. Apply character attributes as context clues to the character.

29. Create a screen capture, add it to the next slide in the presentation, crop the image, and add a name for the character.

30. Create the remaining characters for the family.

31. Add a title slide as the first slide in the presentation. The main title should be Cartoon Family and the subtitle should be your name, class information, and date.

32. Add a slide to the end of the presentation.

33. Copy each individual character image and paste it on the final slide to create a family portrait.

34. Resize each image in the family portrait to an appropriate size. The scale of each image should provide contextual clues to which characters are the parents, which characters are the children, and the relative ages of the children.

35. Save the presentation file. Submit a copy of the file for grading.

Review Questions

1. Describe how to create a screen capture.

   _____

   _____

2. What is the key combination for the **Paste** function in Windows?

   _____

3. Which function is used to trim excess parts of an image while keeping the image rectangular?

   _____

4. What consideration should be given when selecting a font for the character's name?

   _____

   _____

5. Briefly describe how images were moved between slides to create a family portrait.

   _____

   _____

Activity 2-2

Character Description

Objectives

Students will be able to format text and paragraphs using word processing software. Students will be able to demonstrate creative writing skills and synthesize original content for characters. Students will be able to import images into a document and apply text wrapping.

Situation

The Really Cool Game Company liked the concept characters you created in the previous lesson. It would like a brief description for each character to show to the client. Use word processing software to create a document that describes each character of the cartoon family. The company would like you to use Microsoft Word to complete the assignment.

How to Begin

Header

1. Launch Microsoft Word. These instructions are based on Office 2007/2010.

2. Click the **Header** button on the **Header & Footer** panel of the **Insert** tab in the ribbon. A drop-down menu is displayed.

3. Click **Blank (Three Columns)** in the drop-down menu. The document is displayed in page view, and three text boxes are displayed in the header area of the page, as shown in **Figure 1.**

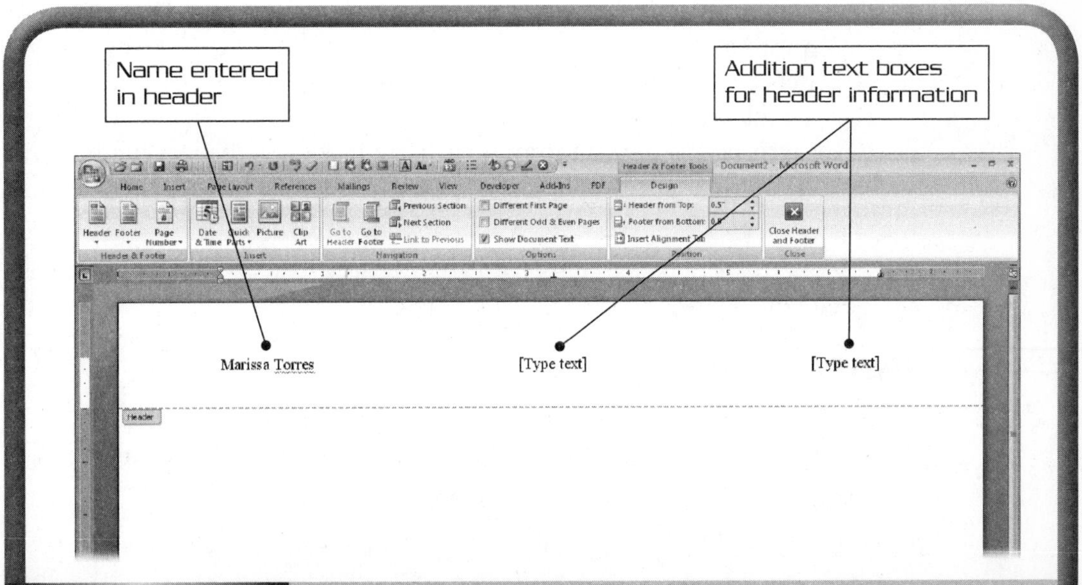

Name entered in header

Addition text boxes for header information

Marissa Torres   [Type text]   [Type text]

Header

Figure 1   *Goodheart-Willcox Publisher*

4. Click the left-hand text box. The default [Type Text] is highlighted. Enter your name to replace the default text.

5. In the middle text box, enter today's date.

6. In the right-hand text box, enter the class period.

7. Double-click on the page below the header. The words in the header turn gray to indicate the main part of the document is active for editing.

8. Enter Cartoon Family in the document.

9. Select the words Cartoon Family.

Font

10. Click the **Font** drop-down button on the **Font** panel of the **Home** tab on the ribbon, and click **Arial** in the drop-down list. This changes the font to Arial.

Font Size

11. Click the **Font Size** drop-down button on the **Font** panel of the **Home** tab on the ribbon, and click **20** in the drop-down list. This changes the size to 20 points.

Center

12. Click the **Center** button in the **Paragraph** panel of the **Home** tab in the ribbon. This center aligns the text.

13. Click at the end of the first line to deselect the text.

14. Press the [Enter] key two times to have one blank line between the title and the next line of text to be entered.

15. Enter the word DAD, left align the text, and change the font size to 12.

16. Save the file as *LastName*_Characters in your working folder.

Left

Descriptions

17. Next to the word DAD, add a colon (:) and a space.

18. Enter the name you gave the father character.

19. Press the [Enter] key to start a new line.

20. Write a four- to five-sentence description of the dad character. Include the following points. See **Figure 2** for an example.
    - age
    - where born and raised
    - amount of education (high school or college grade completed)
    - employer or school
    - hobbies or activities the character likes to do
    - name of spouse (for mom and dad) or boyfriend/girlfriend (for children, if age appropriate)
    - pets
    - secret wish

21. After writing the description, press [Enter] twice to leave a blank between descriptions, and write the description of the mom character. Include the same points outlined above.

22. Similarly, write a description for the oldest child, middle child, and youngest child

23. Save your work.

Image Importing

24. Keep the Word document open, and launch PowerPoint.

25. Open the presentation file *LastName*_ContextClues created in Activity 2-1.

26. Locate the image of the dad character.

27. Right-click on the image, and select **Copy** from the shortcut menu.

Name: _____

Name _____ Date _____ Class _____ Period _____

Cartoon Family

DAD: Martin Martian
Martin is 36 years old. He was born and raised on Mars. He graduated from Interstellar Astro University and now works for VistaTech as a cryogenic systems engineer. His favorite hobby is collecting Earth rocks, and he likes traveling to Earth's moon to ride moon buggies. Martin is married to Madeline Martian, and they have three children named Mick, Mary, and Mitzy. He has a prized pet otter imported from Earth. His secret wish is to visit the rings of Neptune.

MOM: Madeline Martian
Madeline is 37 years old. She was born and raised on Mars' largest moon, Phobos. She graduated from Interstellar Astro University and now works for Red Dust Ranges as a marketing manager. Her hobbies include collecting traditional Martian folk art and listening to contemporary Terran music. Madeline is married to Martin Martian, and they have three children named Mick, Mary, and Mitzy. She tolerates Martin's pet otter. Her secret wish is to spend a month camping in the Martian highlands with Martin.

Figure 2   *Goodheart-Willcox Publisher*

Paste

Text Wrapping

28. Leave PowerPoint open, and switch to Word.

29. Left-click after the name of the dad character. Anything inserted will be placed at this point.

30. Click the **Paste** button in the **Clipboard** panel on the **Home** tab of the ribbon. The image for the dad character is inserted into the document. However, the image is too large, and the alignment of the text is now incorrect.

31. Click the image to select it, and then click the **Picture Tools** tab in the ribbon.

32. Click **Text Wrapping** in the **Arrange** panel to display a drop-down list, and then click **Square** in the list. You may not see a difference at this point due to the size of the image.

33. The image should still be selected and the sizing handles displayed. If not, click the image to select it.

34. Hold down the [Shift] key and drag one of the corner sizing handles to proportionally resize the image until it is only as tall as the paragraph describing the dad character.

35. Drag the image to the right margin. Notice how the words wrap around the image, as shown in **Figure 3.**

36. Similarly, insert images for each of the other characters in the family.

37. Save the Word file. Submit a copy of the file for grading.

Name _____ Date _____ Class _____ Period _____

Cartoon Family

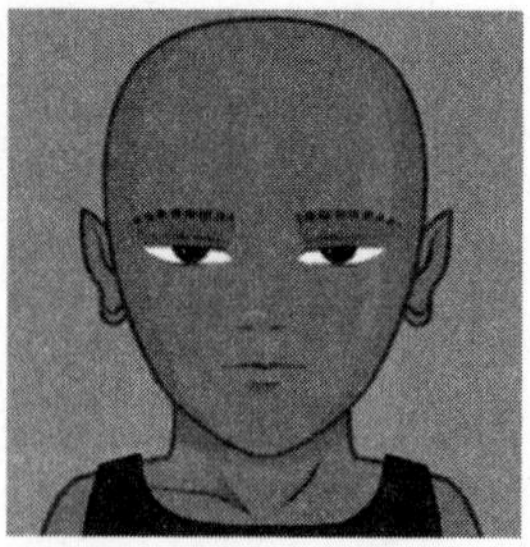

DAD: Martin Martian
Martin is 36 years old. He was born and raised on Mars. He graduated from Interstellar Astro University and now works for VistaTech as a cryogenic systems engineer. His favorite hobby is collecting Earth rocks, and he likes traveling to Earth's moon to ride moon buggies. Martin is married to Madeline Martian, and they have three children named Mick, Mary, and Mitzy. He has a prized pet otter imported from Earth. His secret wish is to visit the rings of Neptune.

MOM: Madeline Martian
Madeline is 37 years old. She was born and raised on Mars' largest moon, Phobos. She graduated from Interstellar Astro University and now works for Red Dust Ranges as a marketing manager. Her hobbies include collecting traditional Martian folk art and listening to contemporary Terran music. Madeline is married to Martin Martian, and they have three children named Mick, Mary, and Mitzy. She tolerates Martin's pet otter. Her secret wish is to spend a month camping in the Martian highlands with Martin.

Figure 3   *Goodheart-Willcox Publisher*

Review Questions

1. Which function is used to add a header to a document?

   _____

2. Describe where the commands to center or left align a paragraph are located in Microsoft Word.

   _____

   _____

3. What would the font size setting be if you wanted the title Cartoon Family twice as large as was specified in the activity?

   _____

4. Describe how to take an image from PowerPoint and place it into a Word document.

   _____

   _____

   _____

   _____

5. Which function allows the text of a paragraph wrap around an image?

   _____

Activity 2-3

Hero Character

Objectives

Students will create a hero archetype using classic comic-book and game attributes. Students will apply RGBA color model. Students will demonstrate creativity and cultural expression in character design. Students will explain design elements.

Situation

The Really Cool Game Company needs ideas for a cast of characters for a new superhero adventure game. It has issued a contest to all employees to make suggestions. Each employee is encouraged to design and submit an original hero character. Submissions will be judged on aesthetics and semiotics. The only restrictions are the hero must be appropriate for younger children and cannot carry a weapon.

How to Begin

1. As directed by your instructor, launch the Internet browser, and navigate to www.heromachine.com/educators/heromachine.htm or launch the installed version of Hero Machine on your machine.

2. Locate the section labeled **1. Choose slot, then genre**, click the drop-down arrow, and click **Pose** in the drop-down list.

3. In the window showing various poses, click the pose on which to base the character, as shown in **Figure 1**. The **Pose Loading Options** dialog box is displayed. This dialog box is only displayed once per session.

Click and select an attribute

Select a pose

Drag to scroll through the selections

Figure 1   *Goodheart-Willcox Publisher*

4. Click the **Complete** button. This loads all available features for the selected character pose. If the Internet connection is slow, you may wish to click the **Partial** button instead. When all features and attributes have loaded, a preview of the character is displayed on the left.

5. Click the drop-down arrow next to the **1. Choose slot, then genre** label, and click **Hair** in the drop-down list. The options for hair are displayed in the selection window.

6. Scroll through the list of options, and click a hairstyle for the character. The preview of the character is immediately updated.

7. Locate the section labeled **3. Color Items**. This section contains two color swatches and a color palette.

8. Click the color swatch labeled **1** to make it active. The active color swatch has a blue border.

9. Click a color in the palette to set the first color. The hair color on the preview is changed. Notice how the red, green, and blue (RGB) values and the alpha value for the color are displayed to the right of the color palette. The scale is 0 to 255.

10. Depending on the selected hairstyle, a second color may be assigned to the hair. Click the color swatch labeled **2** to make it active.

11. Click a color in the palette to set the second color. If the preview does not change, the selected hairstyle does not have a second color.

12. If you like, adjust the alpha value for one or both colors. An alpha value, or alpha channel, sets transparency for the color, with 100 opaque and 0 transparent. Any other value creates a semitransparent color.

13. Use the drop-down list in the section labeled **1. Choose slot, then genre** to select a different element, then select a design for that element and change the colors to suit you.

14. Continue building your character. Put careful thought into each attribute so it will convey contextual clues to and semiotics about your character. You will need to defend your choices and explain your character.

15. Click the **Character Name** label in the preview. Enter a name for the character.

16. Press the [Print Screen] key on the keyboard. This creates a screen capture and places it on the operating system clipboard.

17. Launch PowerPoint.

Page Setup

18. Click the **Page Setup** button on the **Page Setup** panel of the **Design** tab in the ribbon.

19. In the **Page Setup** dialog box, click the **Portrait** radio button in the **Slides** area. This changes the orientation of the slide to tall instead of wide. Click the **OK** button to apply the change.

Text Box

20. In the text boxes on the default slide, enter your name, class information, and date. If needed, insert text boxes by clicking the **Text Box** button on the **Text** panel of the **Insert** tab in the ribbon.

21. Insert a second slide by clicking the **New Slide** button on the **Slides** panel of the **Home** tab in the ribbon.

New Slide

22. On the second slide, paste the hero image, crop it to show just the hero, and proportionally resize the image to fill the slide.

23. Add a third slide, paste the hero image, crop it, and proportionally resize it so the image is about one-quarter of the slide. Place the image in the center of the slide.

Shapes

24. Click the **Shapes** button in the **Illustrations** panel of the **Insert** tab in the ribbon to display a drop-down menu. Click **Arrow** in the **Lines** area of the menu.

25. Draw a leader (line with an arrowhead) that points to a feature that is a contextual clue or semiotic for the hero, as shown in **Figure 2**.

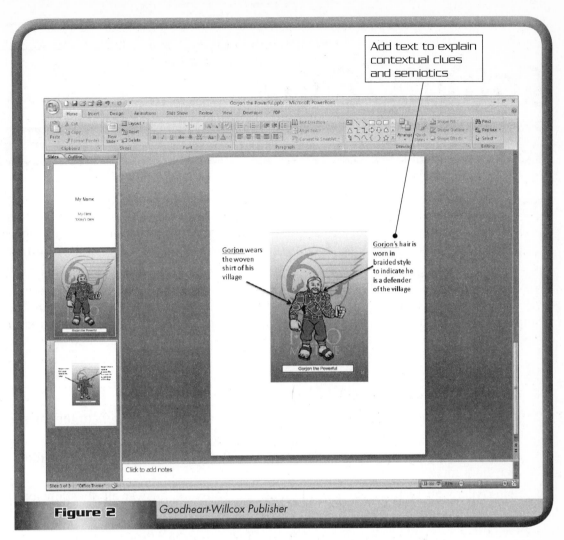

Figure 2 Goodheart-Willcox Publisher

26. Add a text box at the end of the leader, and enter a brief explanation of the feature and how it is a contextual clue or semiotic.

27. Save the PowerPoint file as *LastName*_Hero in your working folder.

Review Questions

1. What is the first attribute that must be selected when defining a character in Hero Machine?

_____

2. Which three color values are used to define a color in the Hero Machine color palette?

_____

3. What does the alpha color, or alpha channel set?

_____

4. Which page orientation creates a slide that is taller than it is wide?

_____

5. What is the process called when an image is made smaller by trimming the edges?

_____

Activity 2-4

Character Background

Objectives

Students will develop literary character attributes and apply them to a hero design. Students will create a background character document. Students will produce a character profile for a hero.

Situation

The Really Cool Game Company has placed your hero character in the finals of the competition. As such, you will need to provide more details. All finalists are required to complete a character profile and write a backstory for their heroes.

How to Begin

1. Form into groups as directed by your instructor.

2. Examine your hero image from Activity 2-3, and think about answers to the questions in the Character Profile Questionnaire sheet at the end of this activity.

3. Discuss ideas with the group. Consider how well your answers fit with the context clues of your hero image.

4. Using Microsoft Word or other word processing software, answer all questions on the Character Profile Questionnaire. Your answers will help to develop your hero and an alter ego.

5. Save the document as *LastName*_Hero Background in your working folder.

Backstory

Now that you have a firm grasp on the background of your hero, it is time to develop the backstory and motivation for the character. The *backstory* is the story of how the character arrived at the point where the player first sees the character.

6. Using Microsoft Word or other word processing program, format the document as outlined in **Figure 1.** Save the document as *LastName*_Hero Backstory in your working folder.

7. Write a backstory to describe your hero character. The backstory should be written in narrative style (storytelling) and must describe how the character became a hero and the character's motivation.

Margins	1.0" all margins
Header	Your name, class information, and date in the upper-right corner
Footer	Page numbers center aligned
First line of document	Title of Hero Backstory in a font of your choice, centered, bold, and size 20 points
Remainder of the document	Arial font, size 12 points, left aligned, each paragraph indented 1", double spaced

Figure 1   *Goodheart-Willcox Publisher*

8. Detail each of the character archetypes the hero represents and how each influences the hero. Include any of the seven archetypes you feel are important to the backstory, but not all need to be included. A character typically is only one archetype, but may have traits of more than one.

9. Discuss the backstory with your team to help refine ideas. Make certain the backstory develops character motivation, purpose, methodology, and a system of values.

10. Save your work.

Join a League

With each team member's hero character fully developed, it is time to create a league for all of the characters. The league will be an organization that the hero characters use to organize their actions against their enemies.

11. Working with your group, define a League of Heroes composed of all hero characters in your group. Start by cooperating and compromising as a team to decide which archetype each character represents. The league should have no more than one of each archetype.

12. Launch PowerPoint, enter a name for the league name as the title on the first slide, and the names of the group members as the subtitle.

13. Insert one slide for each hero in the league.

14. Use Hero Machine to create an image for each character archetype in the league.

15. Paste the image of each character archetype on the individual slides. Add brief notes to each slide as needed to help describe the character archetype.

16. Prepare notes to discuss each archetype during the class presentation.

17. Save the file as *LeagueName*_Archetypes in your working folder.

18. Decide which team member will lead the class presentation. All team members will need to participate in the presentation, but one member will lead the presentation.

19. Conduct the class presentation.

20. Each group member must present his or her hero and read the hero's backstory.

21. As a team, discuss and the archetypes represented by the characters in the league.

Review Questions

1. What is an alter ego?

   _____

   _____

2. Define *backstory*.

   _____

   _____

   _____

   _____

3. For the character developed in this activity, what four things should the backstory explain?

   _____

4. What is a narrative style of writing?

   _____

5. What are the seven major character archetypes?

   _____

Rubrics

Backstory Rubric

Item	Max Points	Score
Margins at 1″	10	
Header correct	10	
Footer correct	10	
Title formatting	10	
Body formatting	10	
Paragraphs indented 1″	10	
Paragraphs double spaced	10	
File saved properly	5	
Written in narrative style	25	
Total	100	

League Rubric

Item	Max Points	Score
Title slide contains league name and all member names	5	
Image for each member's hero displayed	20	
Description for each member's hero	20	
Image for each archetype	20	
Description for each archetype	20	
Presentation Style	15	
Total	100	

Name: _____

Character Profile Questionnaire

Enter the answers to these questions in a word-processing document to help define the hero character.

1. What is the character's name and alter ego?

2. What is the character's age?

3. What is the character's gender, ethnicity, and species (if not human)?

4. What is the characters body type? (husky, skinny, elflike, etc.)

5. How tall is the character?

6. What color are the characters hair, skin, and eyes?

7. Describe the character's physically aesthetic appearance. (beautiful, homely, etc.)

8. What is the character's temperament? (easygoing, angry, logical, emotional, etc.)

9. Is the character introverted or extroverted?

10. Describe the character's general health. (fit, sickly, prone to infections, etc.)

11. How intelligent is the character, or what level of education has the character obtained?

12. What is the character's moral attitude? (good or evil, kind or mean, etc.)

13. What is the character's philosophical attitude? (religious beliefs, family values, political beliefs, etc.)

14. What are the character's major talents or skills?

15. What is the character's favorite saying?

16. What does the character typically wear as the hero?

17. What does the character typically wear as the alter ego?

18. What method of transportation does the character typically use?

19. Describe the character's financial status, social class, and economic situation.

20. In what time period does the character exist?

21. From where is the character? (city, country, region, etc.)

22. Describe the character's place of living. (house, apartment, cave, etc.)

23. Does the character have a pet, and if so what?

24. Who is the character's best friend?

25. What is the character's favorite food?

26. Does the character have a hobby, and if so what?

27. Who is the character's spouse or mate, or if there is not one, why not?

28. Where are the character's parents?

29. Does the character have any siblings or children?

30. What job does the character do as the alter ego?

Activity 2-5

Gameplay-Attributed Characters

Objectives

Students will design a character to fit a theme and gameplay. Students will use a game engine to create physical characteristics and behavioral characteristics to match a character's abilities and role in game.

Situation

The Really Cool Game Company has purchased new game engine software that helps designers quickly build a game. You and your team have been assigned to use this software to create some prototype characters for a role-playing game for iPhone, iPad, and Android devices. Complete the character attributes tutorial below, and develop prototype characters to match your archetypes. For this task, you are not creating a fully functioning game, rather demonstrating prototype characters. This step is important in assessing the usability of the software to develop the characters needed to match the story.

How to Begin

1. Launch 001 Game Creator.
2. In the **New/Open Game** dialog box that appears, click the **New Folder** button.
3. In the **New Folder** dialog box that appears, enter your first and last name or other folder name as specified by your instructor.
4. Click the **OK** button to create the folder. The folder is now listed in the **New/Open Game** dialog box. All assets of the game will be saved in this folder so the game will compile correctly.
5. Double-click on the folder just created to open it, and then click the **New** button. The **New Game** dialog box is displayed, as shown in **Figure 1**.
6. Click the **Action/RPG (Pro)** entry in the list on the **Templates** tab.
7. Click in the **Name of Project:** text box, and enter *LastName*_Character Prototypes.
8. Click the **OK** button. The software loads the template.

Game Map

Currently displayed is a standard game map that will be used to build the game. Later, you will use the game map and programming features of 001 Game Creator to design a custom game. For this activity, you are designing prototype characters, so a standard map is acceptable.

Actor

9. Click the **Actor** button on the toolbar at the top of the map area below the main toolbar. All characters are called *actors* in the 001 Game Creator software.
10. Move the mouse over the game map in the middle of the screen. Notice a green box moves with the mouse to indicate where the asset will be placed.

Name: _____

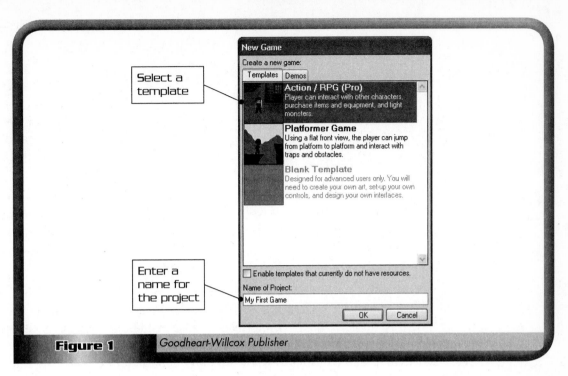

Select a template

Enter a name for the project

Figure 1 *Goodheart-Willcox Publisher*

11. Click in the top-left corner of the game map. The actor is dropped at that spot on the map, and the **Pick Actor Template** dialog box is displayed, as shown in **Figure 2.** Within this dialog box is a list of actor templates organized in a tree format.

12. Expand the tree, and select the Magma Spider template. Then, click the **OK** button. The **Actor: Magma Spider** dialog box is displayed.

13. Accept the default settings by clicking the **OK** button. The actor is placed on the game map.

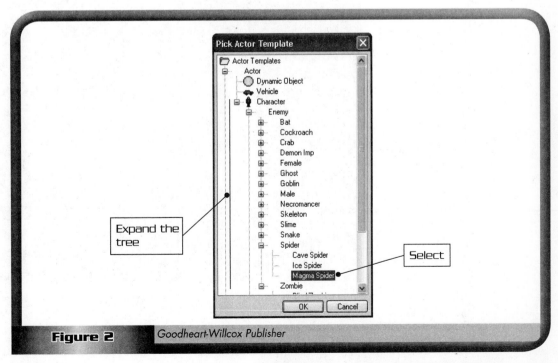

Expand the tree

Select

Figure 2 *Goodheart-Willcox Publisher*

On the game map, the spider actor is displayed behind a generic actor icon. This generic icon helps the designer recognize that the object is an actor. The actor icon will not be displayed when the game is played or tested.

14. The tool for adding actors is still active. Click in the top-right corner of the game map.

15. In the **Pick Actor Template** dialog box, select the Ice Spider template.

16. In the **Actor: Ice Spider** dialog box, click the **OK** button to accept the default settings. Notice that the character attributes (colors, etc.) are different for the ice spider and the magma spider to match the theme of each environment for each type of spider.

Test Map

17. Click the **Test Map** button on the toolbar at the top of the map area below the main toolbar. Before you can test play the game, you are asked to place a character on the map.

18. Click in the top-middle of the game map. This is a safe place for the character to start this game. Once you click, the **Test Script** window appears.

19. Click the **Save** button in the **Test Script** window to compile the game.

After the game is compiled, it is displayed in a window, as shown in **Figure 3.** Notice the keyboard controls for the user interface are displayed on the left side of the screen. This message only displays in test mode. It will not be displayed during normal gameplay.

20. Use the interface controls to walk the player character down to the middle of the game map. Do not move left or right under a spider or it will attack! Each spider is programmed with artificial intelligence (AI) and will attach the player character if it moves directly in front of the spider.

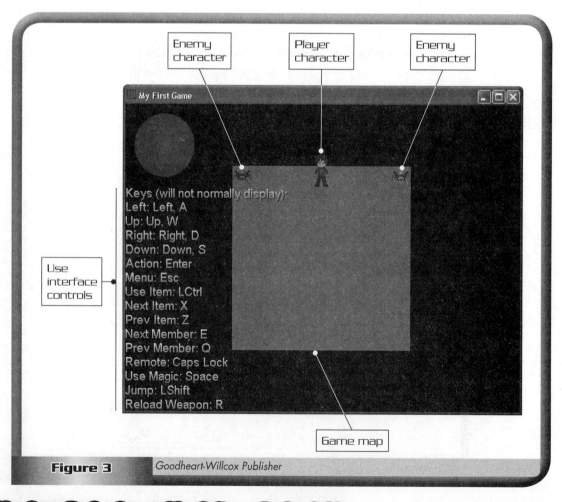

Figure 3   *Goodheart-Willcox Publisher*

21. Move the character left and right to see how the spiders react. When they attack the player character, the character will quickly lose health points and the game will end.

22. Click the **X** in the top-right corner of the window to close it and return to the 001 Game Creator window.

Removing Characters

Actor

23. Click the **Actor** button. Notice that an asset list is displayed in the top-left corner of the screen. Current actor (character) assets are Magma Spider 0 and Ice Spider 0. This is a convenient reference, especially for large maps.

24. Right-click on the magma spider actor on the game map, and click **Delete** from the shortcut menu. The actor (character) is removed.

25. Remove the ice spider. The map is now blank.

Custom Characters

Actor

Template characters like the spiders do not allow for any customization. As you saw, the player had little chance of evading the spiders for more than a few seconds. New characters need to be created that will work better on this small game map.

26. Click the **Actor** button if it is not already on (depressed), then click in the bottom-left corner of the game map. The **Pick Actor Template** dialog box is displayed.

27. In the **Pick Actor Template** dialog box, locate the NPC branch in the tree.

28. Click on the NPC branch to select it, and click the **OK** button. The **Actor: NPC** dialog box is displayed, as shown in **Figure 4.**

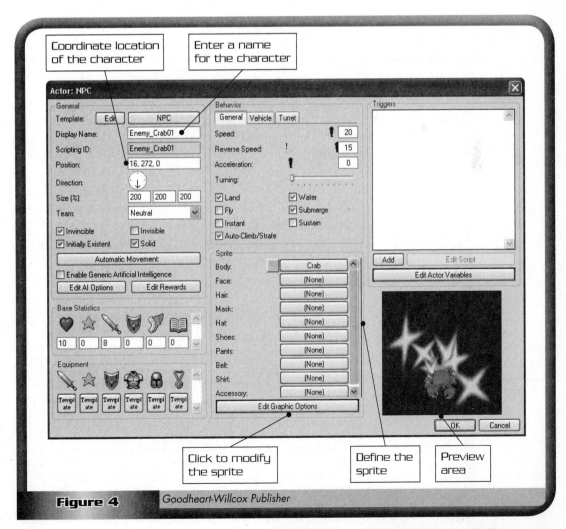

Figure 4   *Goodheart-Willcox Publisher*

29. In the **Sprite** area of the dialog box, click the **Body:** button, which is currently labeled **(Male)**. The **Pick Sprite** dialog box is displayed.

30. In the **Pick Sprite** dialog box, make sure the Body folder is selected, and then click Crab. Click the **OK** button to select the body type. The preview in the **Actor: NPC** dialog box is updated to show an animated crab.

31. Click in the **Display Name:** text box, and enter Enemy_Crab01.

A *naming convention* should be used to help identify all game assets, including characters. In this case, the character is identified as a crab and is the first one added to the game. This clearly differentiates it from all other crab characters that may be added to the game.

The display name and scripting name do not need to match, but it is a good idea so the asset has the same reference in the script. The scripting name should be set for each asset before any scripting is associated with the asset. Changing the name after scripting is associated with the asset may cause the game programming to fail.

32. Click in the **Scripting ID:** text box, and enter Enemy_Crab01. As soon as a character is entered, a warning appears asking to confirm the action. Click the **Continue** button and enter the name.

33. Click the **Direction:** wheel, and drag it to set the orientation of the character. Set the crab to be facing downward.

34. Change value in each of the **Size (%):** text boxes to 200. From left to right, these text boxes control the size of the character in the X, Y, and Z directions. The Z direction is not a size setting, rather an elevation above the ground.

Sprite Modification

35. Click the **Edit Graphic Options** button. The **Graphic Options** dialog box is displayed, as shown in **Figure 5**.

36. Click the **Tint/Opacity:** slider, and drag it one tick mark to the left. This makes the character semitransparent, so the crab will appear translucent.

37. Click the **Glow:** color swatch, and in the **Color** dialog box that is displayed, click the red color swatch and the **OK** button. This sets the glow to red. Glow is applied to the sprite as a whole.

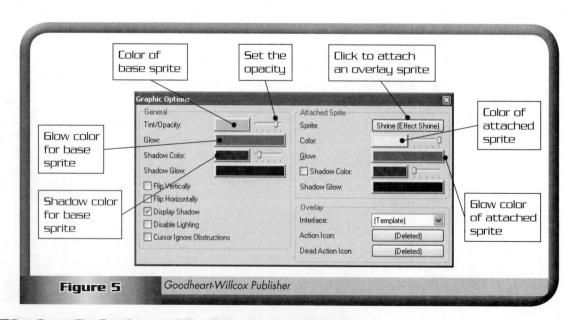

Figure 5   *Goodheart-Willcox Publisher*

38. Click the **Sprite:** button in the **Attached Sprite** area, which is currently labeled **(None)**. The **Pick Sprite** dialog box is displayed.

39. Make sure the Body folder is selected, and then click Shrine. Click the **OK** button to select the body type. The additional sprite, which is a series of animated stars, is layered onto the existing character sprite.

By layering a sprite, or attaching it, onto the base sprite, visually interesting characters can be created. You will be able to see the attached sprite in preview in the **Actor: NPC** dialog box once the **Graphic Options** dialog box is closed. For now, leave the **Graphic Options** dialog box open, and continue as follows. Keep in mind that you will not immediately see the attached sprite or the changes made to it.

40. In the **Attached Sprite** area, click the **Color:** swatch, select a yellow color in the palette, and click the **OK** button to close the palette. This sets the basic color of the sprite, which in this case is the inner color of the stars.

41. In the **Attached Sprite** area, click the **Glow:** color swatch, select a red color in the palette, and click the **OK** button to close the palette. The glow around the stars will now be red. The yellow stars with a red glow fit with the volcano theme. The stars will denote this character as a boss.

42. Click the close button (**X**) to close the **Graphic Options** dialog box and return to the **Actor: NPC** dialog box. The preview now shows the translucent red crab with animated stars around it.

Basic Statistics

43. In the **General** area of the **Actor: NPC** dialog box, check the **Invincible** check box. This means the character cannot be defeated after it has respawned. The setting must be turned off for the character to be defeated.

44. Make sure the **Invisible** check box is not check. If checked, the opacity of the character is set to zero, and the character will not be visible on the map.

45. Make sure the **Initially Existent** check box is checked. This makes the character show up when the map is loaded. When unchecked, programming must be added to make the character show in the game.

46. Make sure the **Solid** check box is checked. This makes it so the player cannot pass through solid objects. If unchecked, the player would be able to pass through the character as if it were a cloud.

47. In the **Base Statistics** area, click in the **HP** (heart icon) text box, and enter 10. This assigns ten health points to the character. Attacks by the player or other characters remove health points. If the health points are reduced to zero, the character is defeated.

48. Click in the **Attack** (sword icon) text box, and enter 8. This number is a relative measure of points of damage the character delivers with each attack. In other words, the higher this number, the greater the number of health points removed from an opponent when the character attacks it.

Now, this crab character can withstand up to ten points of damage before it is defeated. It also delivers eight points of damage with each attack. These attributes are generically called the character's *statistics*. During gameplay, a character can add to its statistics by collecting items and completing quests. The statistics that can be set for a character in the "actor" dialog box are described in **Figure 6.**

49. Click the **OK** button to close the **Actor: NPC** dialog box.

50. Click **Save Starting Map** from the **File** pull-down menu. Later you will rename the first map of the game, and after that "starting map" will change to reflect that name.

 **47**

Icon	Statistic	Meaning	Description and Use in Game Design
♥	HP	Health Points	Health of the character. Attacks by others reduces health points. If health reaches zero, the character is destroyed.
★	MP	Magic Power	Magic strength of character. If the character engages in a magic attack, MP will be reduced. Setting is also the power of the character's magic attack.
🗡	Attack	Attack Power	How many health points will be removed from an opponent with each hit from the character.
🛡	Defense	Defense Power	Each attack on the character must be above the defense power for the attack to reduce the character's health points. Think of defense power as a shield that blocks hits.
🪽	Agility	Skill Power	Determines the characters ability to use items. All items have a certain agility requirement. Increasing agility may unlock different moves or weapons for a character. Commonly, when the character levels up, its agility level is increased.
📖	Wisdom	Learned Power	Certain items or elements may have a wisdom requirement. For example, if a portal is programmed with a wisdom level of five, only players with a wisdom statistic of five or higher can pass. Commonly, increases in wisdom are used to unlock game items or allow passage to the next level.

Figure 6   *Goodheart-Willcox Publisher*

Visible Attributes and Tangible Features

You will now add another character to the map. This character will be based on a template, and then modified to create a unique character.

Actor

51. Click the **Actor** button if it is not already on (depressed), then click in the top-center of the game map. The **Pick Actor Template** dialog box is displayed.

52. In the **Pick Actor Template** dialog box, locate the Female branch in the tree.

53. Click on the Female branch to select it, and click the **OK** button. The **Actor: Female** dialog box is displayed.

54. Click in the **Scripting ID:** text box, and enter Enemy_Princess01. When the warning about scripts is displayed, click the **Continue** button.

55. Click the **Edit** button in the **Actor: Female** dialog box. The dialog box changes to display options similar to the NPC options seen earlier, as shown in **Figure 7**.

56. In the **Sprite** area, click the **Body:** color swatch. The standard **Color** dialog box is displayed.

57. Click in the **Red:** text box, and enter 96.

58. Click in the **Green:** text box, and enter 191.

59. Click in the **Blue:** text box, and enter 0. The preview swatch displays a medium-dark green.

60. Click the **Add to Custom Colors** button. The color is added to the **Custom colors:** palette at the bottom of the dialog box. By adding a custom color to the palette, it can be quickly reused for other color attributes.

61. Click the **OK** button to close the **Color** dialog box. The character preview is updated to reflect the new green skin color.

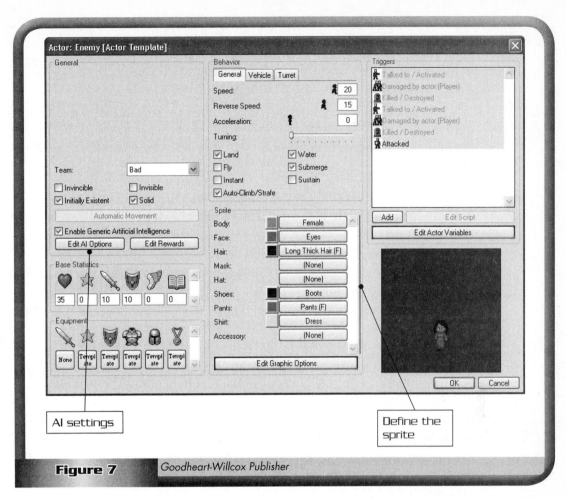

Figure 7   *Goodheart-Willcox Publisher*

62. Adjust the character attributes in the **Sprite** area as shown in **Figure 8.** To change the setting, click the button and select the setting in the dialog box displayed. This is similar to selecting the crab body earlier. To change the color, click the color swatch and select the new color in the **Color** dialog box. Most of these attributes apply only to humanoid (human shaped) characters and have no effect on characters like the big boss crab created earlier.

Attribute	Setting	Color
Body	Female	Medium-dark green
Face	Eyes	Red
Hair	Long thick hair	Black
Mask	None	—
Hat	None	—
Shoes	Boots	Black
Pants	Pants	Red
Shirt	Dress	Light blue
Accessory	None	—

Figure 8   *Goodheart-Willcox Publisher*

63. Click the **OK** button to return to the first page of the dialog box. You have successfully changed the basic female into an alien princess!

64. Click the **OK** button to save the changes to the character and return to the game map.

Equipment

Actor

A character can be edited after it has been placed on the map. With the **Actor** button selected, click the alien princess character you just created. The **Actor: Female** dialog box is redisplayed. Any of the attributes can be changed as needed to update the character.

It is time to give the character some equipment. A character can be given weapons, magic, a shield, armor, a helmet, and accessories like a necklace. Most of these items will only display on humanoid characters. They can be assigned to nonhumanoid characters, like the crab, but will not display.

65. Click the **Edit** button in the **Actor: Female** dialog box to display the details page.

66. In the **Equipment** area, click the **Weapon** (sword icon) button. The **Pick Item/Magic** dialog box is displayed.

67. Browse through the weapon set, click Energy Sword, and click the **OK** button to assign the weapon. The Weapon button now displays an icon of the energy sword, and the character preview shows the character carrying the weapon.

68. Edit the remaining attributes in the **Equipment** area as shown in **Figure 9.** For those listed as "none," select the None entry in the **Pick Item/Magic** dialog box. Some items will not be shown in the preview, like the necklace.

The energy sword has a damage value of 30. The weapon damage and character attack value are added to create a more powerful action. For example, if the character has an attack value of 10 and is carrying the energy sword, then the total attack damage is 40. The actual calculation in the programming is a bit more complex than that, but the general idea is the better equipment a character carries, the more damage it can inflict.

Behavior

69. Click the **General** tab in the **Behavior** area of the **Actor: Female** dialog box. This tab contains performance attributes for the character.

70. Click in the **Speed:** text box, and enter 50. Notice the walking icons next to the text box are now moving very quickly, as is the preview of the character.

71. Enter 10 in the **Speed:** text box. This is a more reasonable speed for the character.

72. Click in the **Reverse Speed:** text box, and enter 7. This makes the character a bit slower when moving backward than when moving forward.

Item	Setting
Weapon	Energy sword
Magic	None
Armor	None
Helmet	Winged helmet
Accessory	Necklace

Figure 9   *Goodheart-Willcox Publisher*

73. Click in the **Acceleration:** text box, and enter 2. This adds a bit of acceleration to the character's movement.

74. Click the **Turning:** slider and drag it to the middle. This will allow the character to turn more quickly to see other NPCs and the player.

NPC Type

As discussed in the textbook, an NPC can function by itself or as part of a party or troop. This is controlled by the **Team:** setting. Options include None (acting alone), Good (cooperative NPC), Bad (competitive NPC), and one of several "bad" groups. Click the **Team:** drop-down list in the **General** area of the **Actor: Female** dialog box, and select **Bad Group 1** in the list. This assigns the character to the group of actors named Bad Group 1. An NPC must also have some artificial intelligence set. This will program how the NPC will react to the character in the game.

Artificial Intelligence

75. In the **General** area of the **Actor: Female** dialog box, make sure the **Enable Generic Artificial Intelligence** check box is checked. This feature will automatically set enemy (Bad) characters to attack the player character when they see it. Good characters can be set to follow or scripted to join your troop. Neutral characters do not attack you or join you.

76. Click the **Edit AI Options** button. The **AI Options** dialog box is displayed, as shown in **Figure 10.**

77. Drag the **Weapon Speed:** slider to the third tick mark from the left. This controls how quickly the character can attack with its weapon.

Since this character appears early in this game, a slower speed is good to allow the player to build skill to defeat it. In later levels, the weapon speed setting can be increased to make the character a more powerful enemy.

The field of vision defines what the character can "see" or sense in the game world. It is like a triangle in front of the character. If the base of the triangle is widened, the character can see more, as shown in **Figure 11.**

78. Drag the **Field of View:** slider to the third tick mark from the left. Increasing this setting widens the vision for the character. If the slider is fully to the right, a circular vision pattern is created all the way around the character.

79. Click in the **Visual Distance:** text box, and enter 100. This sets the distance the character can see, or the depth of the field of vision triangle.

80. Click the close button (**X**) to close the **AI Options** dialog box and return to the **Actor: Female** dialog box.

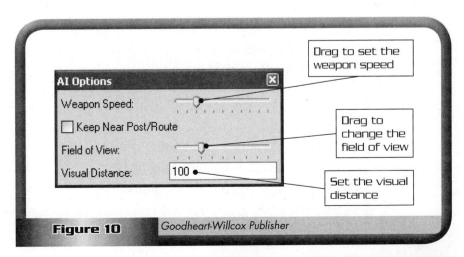

Figure 10   Goodheart-Willcox Publisher

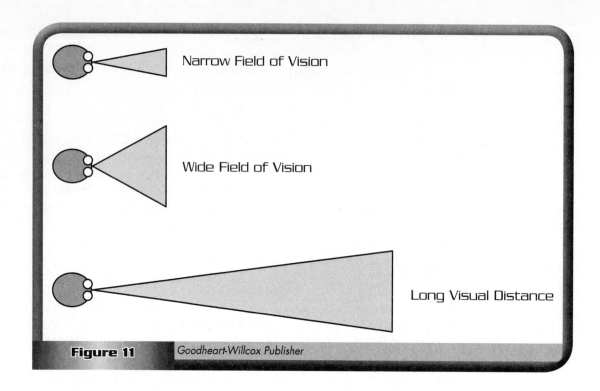

Narrow Field of Vision

Wide Field of Vision

Long Visual Distance

Figure 11   *Goodheart-Willcox Publisher*

81. Click the **OK** button to return to the main page of the **Actor: Female** dialog box, then click the **OK** button again to close the dialog box to return to the map.

Test

Test Map

82. Click the **Test Map** button.

83. Click in the bottom-middle of the game map.

84. Click the **Save** button in the **Test Script** window to compile the game.

85. Slowly walk up to the princess character.

The princess character does not move until the player character enters its field of view. Once the player character is within the field of view for the princess character, the NPC attacks the PC since its artificial intelligence is programmed as an enemy. The crab character has not been programmed with AI, so it remains stationary in the corner of the map and cannot inflict damage on the PC. Click the **X** in the top-right corner of the window to close it and return to the 001 Game Creator window. Instead of the generic artificial intelligence settings, the character can be set to face or move in a set direction. Continue as follows.

Actor

Actor

86. Click the **Actor** button, and click the princess character icon to open the **Actor: Female** dialog box.

87. Click the **Edit** button to display the details page of the dialog box.

88. Uncheck the **Enable Generic Artificial Intelligence** check box.

89. Click the **Automatic Movement** button that is now enabled. The **Auto-Movement** dialog box is displayed, as shown in **Figure 12.** Options are available for multiple directions for the character to either face, move, or both.

90. Check the **Move** and **Face** check boxes. The direction options are enabled.

91. Click the **Towards Player(s)** radio button.

92. Check the **Ignore Collision Detection** check box.

93. Click the close button (**X**) to close the **Auto-Movement** dialog box.

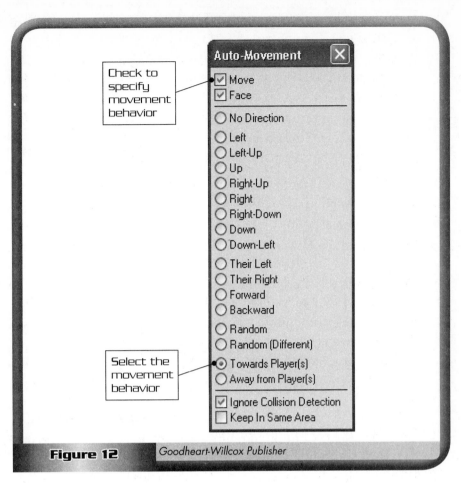

Figure 12   Goodheart-Willcox Publisher

When the **Ignore Collision Detection** check box is checked, enemy characters will not start the battle when it touches the player character. When unchecked, as soon as the enemy character touches the player character, the battle starts. In early stages of the game, this setting should be checked so the player has time to get a weapon, prepare for the battle, and strike the first blow.

94. Click the **OK** button. A warning appears indicating the character is set as an enemy (in one of the "bad" groups), but does not have AI enabled.

95. Click the **Cancel** button in the warning.

96. Click the **Team:** drop-down list, and click **Neutral** in the list. This sets the character as a neutral NPC.

97. Click the **OK** button to return to the main page of the **Actor: Female** dialog box, then click the **OK** button again to close the dialog box to return to the map.

98. Test play the game. The princess character now follows the player character, but does not attack it. Additionally, since the **Face** check box was checked, the NPC also turns so it is always facing the PC.

Test Map

Rewards and Status

99. Click the **Actor** button, and click the princess character icon to open the **Actor: Female** dialog box.

Actor

100. Click the **Edit** button to display the details page of the dialog box.

101. Click the **Team:** drop-down list, and click **Bad** in the list. The character becomes an enemy (competitive NPC).

102. Check the **Enable Generic Artificial Intelligence** check box. Notice that the **Automatic Movement** button is disabled, but still specifies movement toward the player. Even though the button is disabled, the setting is still active. The setting must be manually disabled, but leave it enabled for this character.

103. Click the **Edit Rewards** button. The **Rewards** dialog box is displayed, as shown in **Figure 13.** This dialog box is used to specify what the player character will receive when the enemy character is defeated. For every action in a game, the player must receive an appropriate reward for taking the risk of the quest or battle.

104. Click in the **Reward EXP:** text box, and enter 10. This will increase the player's experience points by ten when the player defeats this character.

105. Click in the **Reward Money:** text box, and enter $50. This is the amount of money added to the player's total when the player defeats this character.

106. Click in the **Reward Points:** text box, and enter 30. This is the number of points added to the player's score when the player defeats this character.

107. Click the **Add** button. The **Pick Item/Magic** dialog box is displayed.

108. Scroll through the list, select the energy sword, and click the **OK** button. The weapon is added to the list at the bottom of the **Rewards** dialog box. Anything that appears in this list will be left on the map when the player defeats the character. The player can recover and use the items.

109. Click the close button (**X**) to close the **Rewards** dialog box.

110. Click the **OK** button to return to the main page of the **Actor: Female** dialog box, then click the **OK** button again to close the dialog box to return to the map.

111. Test play the game to see if this character attacks and performs properly. You will not be able to test the rewards at this point because the player character does not have any way to defeat the princess.

112. Save your work.

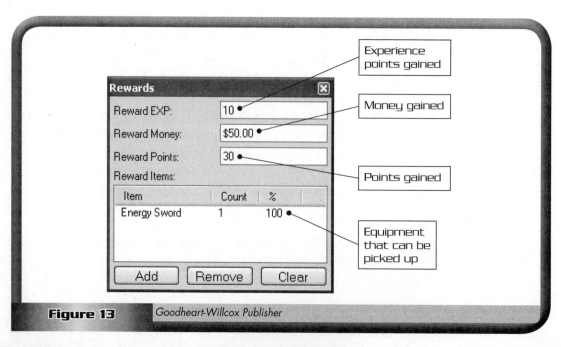

Figure 13   *Goodheart-Willcox Publisher*

Items

Game objects do not need to be characters. In the 001 Game Creator engine, *items* are objects with which the player can interact, like a treasure chest to receive a reward or a weapon to deliver damage to an enemy character. Just as with characters, items must match the theme and setting of the game.

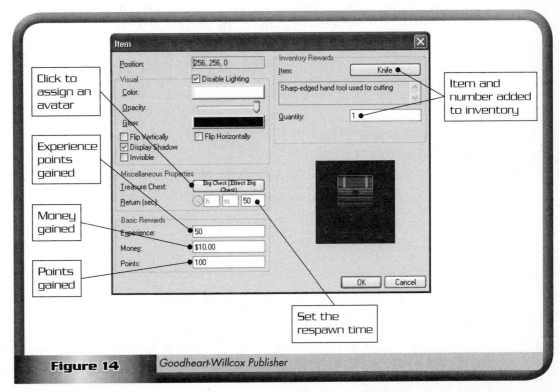

Item

Item Pick-Up

113. Click the **Item Pick-Up** button on the toolbar at the top of the map area below the main toolbar.

114. Click in the bottom-right corner of the game map to place the item. The **Item** dialog box is displayed, as shown in **Figure 14.**

115. Click in the **Experience:** text box in **Basic Rewards** area of the dialog box, and enter 50. This is the number of experience points that will be added to the player's total when the player collects the item.

116. Click in the **Money:** text box, and enter $10. This is the amount of money that will be added to the player's total when the player collects the item.

117. Click in the **Points:** text box, and enter 100. This is the number of points that will be added to the player's score when the player collects the item.

118. Click the **Item:** button, which is currently labeled **(None).** The **Pick Item/Magic** dialog box is displayed.

119. Scroll through the list, click the knife, and click the **OK** button. The button is now labeled with the name of the item, and additional options are displayed in the **Inventory Rewards** area, as shown in **Figure 14.**

120. Click in the **Quantity:** text box, and enter 1. This is the number of the inventory item that will be awarded to the player when the item object is collected.

121. Click the **Treasure Chest:** button in the **Miscellaneous Properties** area. The **Pick Sprite** dialog box is displayed, which is similar to the **Pick Item/Magic** dialog box.

122. Scroll through the list, click the small chest, and click the **OK** button. The sprite is assigned to the item, and the preview is updated.

Figure 14 *Goodheart-Willcox Publisher*

123. Click in the right-hand **Return (sec):** text box, and enter 20. This will respawn the treasure chest after twenty seconds, which is a very short time. Usually, reward items should respawn after a very long time or never. Otherwise, the player could stand in front of the chest and keep gathering the rewards.

124. Click the **OK** button to close the **Item** dialog box.

125. Save your work.

Testing

Before you test play the game, plan what is being tested. In this case, you need to test that the:

- player can activate the treasure chest by walking to it and pressing the [Enter] key;
- treasure chest opens and gives you the correct rewards (press the [Enter] key to dismiss the message);
- knife inventory item can be made active by pressing the [X] key;
- player can battle the NPC by pressing the left-hand [Ctrl] key;
- health points for the player and the NPC are reduced with each successful attack;
- player receives the reward items from the defeat of the NPC; and
- chest returns after twenty seconds (closes), and the player can collect additional rewards.

Test Map

Test play the game, and run through this sequence of tests. Try to defeat the NPC and collect the rewards. If needed, edit the NPC character to make it move slower.

As the game is played, the health for the player character is displayed as a red circle in the top-left corner of the screen. When the player character is damaged, the red-shaded portion of the circle is reduced. When all red is gone, the player character is defeated. During a battle, damage values appear as red numbers above the character to show how much damage was done on each attack. When an item in inventory is made current, such as the knife, it is displayed in the top-right corner of the screen. The avatar also changes to display the character carrying the item. Save your work.

Tuning

126. Edit the female NPC. Disable the automatic movement settings. To do so, first turn off generic AI to enable the button, then turn off the **Move** and **Face** options, and finally turn on generic AI. This prevents the NPC from tracking down the player character as soon as the game starts.

Actor

Test Map

127. Test play the game to see how the field of vision settings work. The NPC should attack when the player gets close to it from the left, right, or front, but not from the back. It may take several edits to get this set correctly.

128. Save your work.

129. Close 001 Game Creator.

Custom Composition

Launch 001 Game Creator, and start a new action/RPG game. Apply the skills you learned in this activity to create these prototype characters:

- Shadow
- Sidekick
- Two types of minions
- Boss
- Big Boss

Place each character on the game map. Save your work.

Character Development

130. Launch PowerPoint. You will create a presentation with a title slide and two slides for each prototype character created.

131. In 001 Game Creator, take a screen capture of the actor settings for the first character.

132. In PowerPoint, paste and crop the screen capture on the second slide (the first slide is the title slide).

133. On the third slide, change the slide layout to Title and Content. Refer to **Figure 15.**

134. In the title section, enter the character's name and the role of the character.

135. In the contents section, insert a table with two columns and five rows.

136. Label the right-hand column Character Element.

137. Label the left-hand column Description.

138. In the Character Elements column, enter with System of Evaluation, Methodology, Purpose, and Motivation.

139. Write a brief description for each character element for the character you created.

140. Similarly, add screen captures and description slides for the remaining prototype characters.

141. Save the presentation as *LastName*_Prototype Info.

142. Present the slide show to the class.

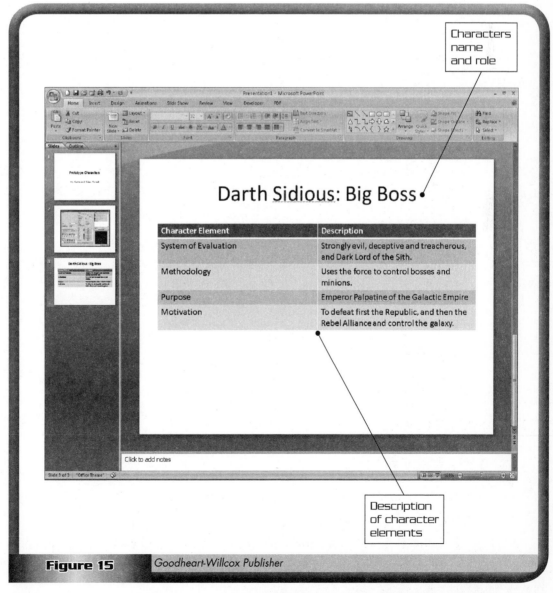

Figure 15   *Goodheart-Willcox Publisher*

Review Questions

1. What is the term for a character in 001 Game Creator?

   _____

2. Briefly describe how to add a character to the game map in 001 Game Creator.

   _____

   _____

   _____

3. Why should a naming convention be used to name all game assets?

   _____

   _____

4. What happens when a character's health points are reduced to zero during gameplay?

   _____

   _____

5. If a character is carrying a weapon with an attack value of 34, what is the effect on the character's attack?

   _____

   _____

Activity 2-6

Multicultural Expo

Objective

Students will explore the value of cultural differences. Students will use Internet to research. Students will use a digital camera and insert a digital picture into a project. Students will actively engage others in relating their personal cultural backgrounds.

Situation

The Really Cool Game Company celebrates the cultural diversity of its workforce. It believes that part of the strength of a team is the opinions of those with different backgrounds and cultural perspectives. The company holds an annual showcase called a Multicultural Expo. Each employee creates a single slide that displays a personal picture and some cultural information. The slides are displayed for all to view. Employees are also encouraged to bring in cultural objects and food to share with others.

How to Begin

1. Launch Microsoft PowerPoint.
2. Create one slide using PowerPoint word art, PowerPoint clipart, pictures from the Internet, and pictures from a digital camera, **Figure 1**.

Figure 1   *Goodheart-Willcox Publisher*

3. Produce a cultural representation of yourself. You may include multiple nationalities to describe yourself, if you desire. You must include:

    A. Flag of your ancestral country of origin.

    B. Map of the nation.

    C. Picture of something unique to that culture.

    D. Your name, photograph, and the name of any pictured nationality or culture.

    E. List the unit of currency and the value compared to the US dollar.

4. Print the slide on a single sheet of paper.

5. Post your slide printout on the wall of the classroom, as designated by your instructor.

6. View other students work and comment on at least five using the student response sheet.

Student Response Sheets

Complete five reviews of an expo sheet of a student in your class. Positive comments *only!*

Student name on slide: *Malik Holmes*

Cultures shown: *African*

Comments: *Great map picture. I did not know about the South African flag, as illustrated on your slide.*

Student name on slide: _____

Cultures shown: _____

Comments: _____

Student name on slide: _____

Cultures shown: _____

Comments: _____

Student name on slide: _____

Cultures shown: _____

Comments: _____

Student name on slide: _____

Cultures shown: _____

Comments: _____

Student name on slide: _____

Cultures shown: _____

Comments: _____

Chapter 3
Story Composition

Objectives

After completing this chapter, you will be able to:
- Create a storyboard.
- Develop a comprehensive story outline for a video game.
- Design a tile-based video game world.
- Implement dialogue and story into a role-playing video game.

Barone Firenze/Shutterstock.com

Inq/Shutterstock.com

Goodheart-Willcox Publisher;
image: DarkGeometryStudios/Shutterstock.com

Bellwork

Day	Date	Activity	Response
1		Complete the anticipation guide and the K and W columns of the KWL chart for this chapter.	
2		Define *story*.	
3		Describe how an audience is defined by the story told in the game.	
4		Define *brainstorming*. Why is it important not to judge responses during brainstorming?	
5		Define *moral*. Why would myths and legends include morals?	
6		Compare and contrast round and flat characters.	
7		List three chemicals or compounds that will be limited in or excluded from an environmentally friendly computer.	
8		Define *plot*.	
9		Describe how rising action, a climax, and falling action are used to move the story.	
10		Contrast the structure of a linear story with a branching story.	
11		What is a foldback event?	

Name: _____

Day	Date	Activity	Response
12		Describe the structure of a hub-and-spoke game.	
13		Determine the structure of the game *The Sims,* an open game where the player can move without restriction. List three reasons why you selected that structure.	
14		Compare and contrast a storyboard and a comic strip.	
15		Describe how atomic challenges are arranged to create missions.	
16		Describe how a color palette influences mood in game art.	
17		Describe how suspense, tension, and conflict are used to create dramatic action.	
18		Define *GUI.*	
19		Why is it important to include HUD design in planning a video game?	
20		Complete the L column of the KWL chart and the After Reading column of the anticipation guide with what you learned from this chapter.	
21		Speculate how design documents could be used to obtain financing to build a game.	

Name: _____

Date: _____

Class: _____

Anticipation Guide

Directions

Before reading the chapter, read each statement in the table below. In the column titled Before Reading, write the letter *T* if you agree with the statement or *F* if you disagree with the statement. After reading the chapter, reread each statement in the table below. In the column titled After Reading, write the letter *T* if you agree with the statement or *F* if you disagree with the statement. Be prepared to justify your answers in a class discussion.

Before Reading	Statement	After Reading
	Games with story always follow a linear format.	
	Resolution is used to build emotional interest in the story.	
	A foldback event is a place in the story where the action is repeated.	
	Storyboards are panels of action that describe the game and how the action will unfold.	
	Items like buildings, roads, and clothing are used to visually display the setting of a game.	
	Nontrivial tasks are important to keeping the player interested in the game.	

KWL Chart

Directions

Before reading the chapter, fill in what you already know about the topic in the K column and what you want to learn in the W column. After reading the chapter, review what you know and wanted to learn about the topic. Reflect on what you have studied and completed in this chapter. Fill in what you learned in the L column. Be prepared to justify your answers in a class discussion.

Topic: Adventure Stories		
K What you already *know*	**W** What you *want* to learn	**L** What you *learned*

Activity 3-1

Storyboarding

Objectives

Students will construct a storyboard to show action sequencing. Students will produce a storyboard sheet in electronic format. Students will print a storyboard in handout format.

Situation

The Really Cool Game Company is considering you for promotion to lead designer. Before your interview, it wants you to submit a storyboard to detail your morning activities. First, you will create a basic storyboard to describe how to make a peanut butter–and–jelly sandwich to learn the techniques of storyboarding. Then, you will create a storyboard to display your morning routine. Both storyboards will be created in electronic format.

How to Begin

1. Launch PowerPoint. These instructions are based on PowerPoint 2007/2010. For other versions of PowerPoint or other slide show presentation software, you may need to adjust the instructions.

2. Save the presentation as *LastName*_PBandJ in your working folder.

3. Create a title slide that includes your name and the title How to Make a Peanut Butter–and–Jelly Sandwich. You will add artistic elements to this title slide, including an image of the completed sandwich and the components needed to make the sandwich.

Creating Artwork Objects

Shapes

4. Click the **Shapes** button in the **Illustrations** panel on the **Insert** tab of the ribbon, and click the **Heart** button in the drop-down menu.

Heart

5. Click and drag on the slide to draw a heart shape. Later, this shape will be combined with a rectangular shape to create a slice of bread.

Shape Fill

6. Click the **Shape Fill** button in the **Shape Styles** panel on the **Format** tab of the ribbon, and click **Texture** in the drop-down menu to display a cascading menu. Click the Stationery texture in the cascading menu, as shown in **Figure 1.**

Shapes

7. Using the **Shapes** button in the **Illustrations** panel on the **Insert** tab of the ribbon, draw a rectangular shape that overlaps the heart shape. The two shapes together should look like the shape of a slice of bread.

8. Change the texture of the rectangular shape to match the heart shape.

9. Select both shapes by holding the [Shift] key and clicking each shape.

Shape Outline

10. Click the **Shape Outline** button in the **Shape Styles** panel on the **Format** tab of the ribbon, and click **No Color** in the drop-down menu. This removes the outline color from both shapes.

11. With both shapes selected, right-click on either shape and select **Group > Group** in the shortcut menu. The two shapes will now act as a single object.

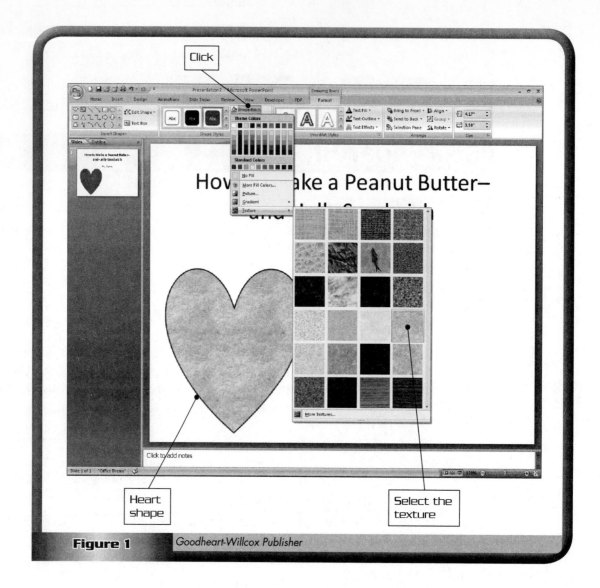

Click

How ... ake a Peanut Butter–

Heart shape

Select the texture

Figure 1   *Goodheart-Willcox Publisher*

12. Copy the grouped objects using the [Ctrl][C] key combination, and paste three copies using the [Ctrl][V] key combination. There should be a total of four grouped objects.

13. Select one of the grouped objects, and change the fill color to purple.

Shape Fill

14. Select a different grouped object, and change the fill color to a brown similar to the color of peanut butter.

15. Construct the sandwich by putting the bread, peanut butter, and jelly layers in order. Do this by right-clicking on each grouped object and selecting either **Bring to Front** > **Bring Forward** or **Send to Back** > **Send Backward** from the shortcut menu. You may need to do this more than once to get each grouped object in the proper order.

16. Move the grouped objects to stagger the layers so the edge of each layer can be seen, as if you are looking at the sandwich from a slight angle.

17. Using what you have learned, create artwork for a jar of peanut butter, a jar of jelly, a plate, and a butter knife. Refer to **Figure 2**.

18. Create the jars with a transparency fill to simulate a glass or plastic container. A transparency fill can be achieved in PowerPoint by clicking the **Shape Fill** button on the **Shape Styles** panel of the **Format** tab in the ribbon, and then clicking **More fill colors...** in the drop-down menu. In the **Colors** dialog box that is displayed, use the **Transparency:** slider to create a transparent color, as shown in **Figure 3**.

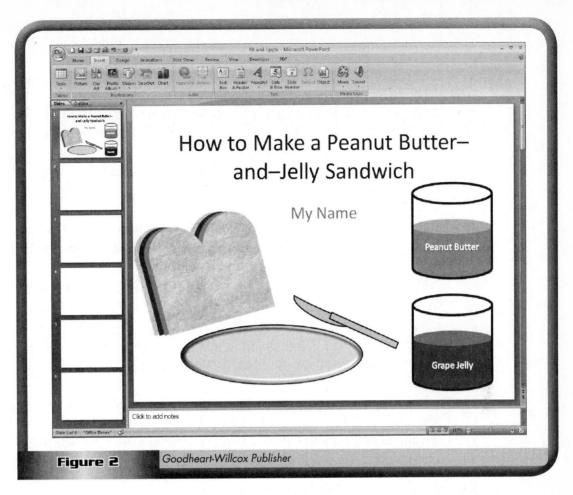

Figure 2   *Goodheart-Willcox Publisher*

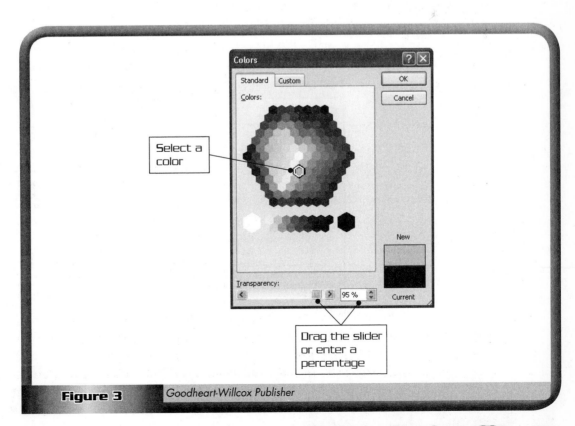

Figure 3   *Goodheart-Willcox Publisher*

19. Include text on the jars to indicate which one is peanut butter and which one is jelly. Be creative. Use shapes, colors, and textures to provide contextual clues.

20. Save your work.

Creating and Printing the Storyboard

21. Add five new blank slides. The storyboard will consist of five slides plus the title slide. Each of the slides just added will illustrate a key, or major action, of making a peanut butter–and–jelly sandwich.

22. On each blank slide, insert a text box (**Insert > Text Box**) at the bottom of the slide. Use this text box to write the description of the action shown on the slide (storyboard panel).

23. Decide on the five actions needed to make a peanut butter–and–jelly sandwich.

24. Using what you have learned, insert shapes on each slide and change the color or texture to visually depict the major actions.

25. In the text box at the bottom of each slide, describe the action needed to get to the next action frame.

26. Save your work.

27. Press the [Ctrl][P] key combination to open the **Print** dialog box. Do *not* click the **Quick Print** button. To create a hardcopy storyboard, all six slides must be printed on a single sheet of paper.

28. Click the **Print what:** drop-down list, and click **Handouts** in the list, as shown in **Figure 4.** The options in the **Handouts** area are enabled.

29. Click the **Slides per page:** drop-down list, and click **6** in the list.

30. Click the **OK** button to print your storyboard.

Morning Activities Storyboard

31. Determine the actions you take from the time you wake up to the time when you arrive in your first class on a typical school day.

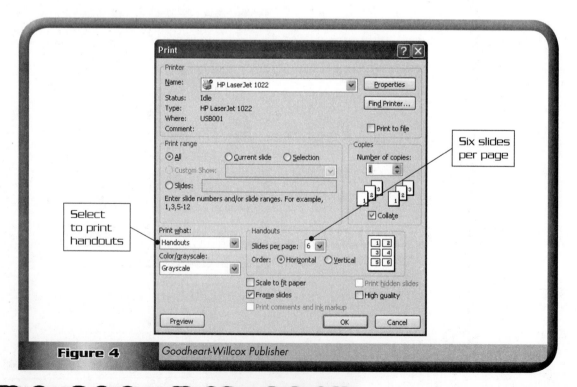

Figure 4   Goodheart-Willcox Publisher

32. Create a storyboard to describe your morning activities. Use as many slides as needed to fully describe the process. Quality and completeness count!

33. Save the PowerPoint file as *LastName*_Morning Activities in your working folder.

34. Print the storyboard with six slides per page.

35. Submit both storyboards for grading.

Review Questions

1. Which standard shape is used to create the top of a slice of bread in this activity?

   _____

2. How is a texture added as a fill color for an object?

   _____

   _____

3. How do you change the front-to-back order of objects in PowerPoint?

   _____

   _____

4. How is a transparency fill color created in PowerPoint?

   _____

   _____

5. Describe how to print six slides per page.

   _____

   _____

Activity 3-2

Story Development

Objectives

Students will brainstorm new game story ideas. Students will develop the central premise of a story from a brainstormed idea. Students will synthesize story elements of plot, conflict, climax, resolution, setting, and thematic elements. Students will align story elements to in-game action. Students will develop the atomic challenges and sub missions needed to lead to the final story resolution. Students will develop methods for the player to interact with the story through game actions.

Situation

The Really Cool Game Company has announced a competition for all staff members and teams to develop a new RPG concept. The winning game concept will go into production and be released to the public. The staff member or team that submits the winning concept will take a leadership role in the creative direction of the game and share in the profits of the game. Working with your concept team members, create the required predevelopment documentation to prepare the presentation for your game pitch.

How to Begin

1. Form into groups as directed by your instructor.
2. Write all names of the group members on one side of a note card or blank sheet of paper.
3. As a group, brainstorm ideas for a group name based on the letters RPG, such as Red Peacock Group. Record all ideas on the opposite side of the note card or paper.
4. Select a group name, and write it above the group member names. Turn in the note card or paper to your instructor.
5. Review all documents included at the end of this lesson before continuing.

Brainstorming Story Ideas Document

6. Review The Hero's Journey case study in textbook Chapter 3.
7. With your group, brainstorm story ideas for a role-playing game.
8. Record all ideas on the Brainstorming Story Ideas Document. Remember to record all suggestions without any argument as to validity. The process of brainstorming must be an open format for ideas to flow and develop without criticism or rejection. All ideas are important as they may lead to better ideas in the next step.

Concept Refinement

9. Discuss each idea on the Brainstorming Story Ideas Document as a group. Evaluate each idea based on the ability to fully develop a large-scale RPG that fits the model of The Hero's Journey. Combine all elements that fit best to be able to discuss a story idea with the creative director (your instructor).
10. On the Brainstorming Story Ideas Document, place a check mark in the Sort column next to ideas that can be developed into a game concept.

11. Place a plus in the Sort column next to ideas that can be part of a level, action sequence, or other part of a bigger game concept.

12. Place an X in the Sort column next to ideas that the group has fully discussed and decided will not work for the game concept. Do not quickly dismiss any idea without fully discussing how it could be developed or become part of a bigger game concept. Do *not* erase any idea.

13. Schedule a time with the creative director to review your brainstorming activities. Be prepared to defend all selected ideas and discarded ideas.

14. Review the Brainstorming Story Ideas Document with the creative director.

Central Premise and Plot Document

15. As a group, discuss any comments made during the meeting with the creative director and how the team can put together the best game concept.

16. Choose a single idea as the team's game concept.

17. Discuss the concept and how the story can begin and end.

18. Complete the Central Premise and Plot Document.

19. Review the completed Central Premise and Plot Document with the creative director before proceeding.

Journey Planning Document

20. Review the questions on the Journey Planning Document with the group.

21. Answer all the questions related to a heroic journey. This is a cooperative task, and all members of the group must agree on the answers.

22. In words, sketch out the basic story that will appear in the game. Use a word processor, and be as specific as needed to tell the story.

Level Layout Chart

With all elements of plot recorded in the planning documents and the basic story outlined in words, it is time to produce sketches and charts to refine these ideas. These sketches are required before moving the game concept into the construction phase.

23. Determine the game progression and layout by organizing the scenes from the story into rooms.

24. Use paper, PowerPoint, or other method to sketch a layout of the story in each level, similar to what is shown in Figure 3-11 in the textbook.

25. Name each room in each level, and record the name on the layout. Use a naming convention that can also be used during programming.

Story Design Document

26. Use paper, PowerPoint, or other method of creating a storyboard for each room in the level layout chart created above. The storyboard should be a minimum of six panels.

27. Write story details to describe the actions of the scene depicted in each storyboard panel.

28. Check the Central Premise and Plot Document and Journey Planning Document to make sure all specified details are included in the storyboard.

Environmental Illustrations

29. Refer to the thematic elements listed on the Central Premise and Plot Document, and select thematic elements for the game.

30. Start a blank PowerPoint presentation.

31. Create a title slide with the title of Environmental Illustrations and subtitle of the team's name.

32. Add slides as needed for environmental elements. Organize the slides either by scene or by element. For example, one slide could illustrate all trees in the game, or one slide could illustrate all elements in scene 2.

33. Use clip art, free-use images from the Internet, drawing shapes, and other sources to illustrate all thematic elements. All possible thematic elements should be illustrated, even if not used in the game, to help ensure all elements are matched to the theme.

34. Save the presentation as *TeamName*_Environment in your working folder.

Concept Art

35. Use Hero Machine, a sketch, or other method to prototype the major characters and archetypes in the story. Match character and background to your game setting.

36. Transfer all concept art to a PowerPoint presentation named *TeamName*_Concept.

37. Present the team's concept art and storyboard to the class. Explain all elements of the game design.

#	Sort (✓, + or X)	Idea — Write all ideas without evaluating them	Submitted By:	Comments and Possible Uses
1				
2				
3				
4				
5				
6				
7				
8				
9				
10				
11				
12				
13				
14				
15				

Brainstorming Story Ideas Document

Name: _____

Central Premise and Plot Document

Central Premise (30 words maximum)

What if _____

_____

_____

Primary Conflict

_____

_____

_____

_____

Dramatic Tension Needed from Conflict to Climax

_____

_____

_____

_____

Setting

Time _____

Place _____

Mood _____

Thematic Elements

Protagonist Name and Motivation

_____

_____

_____

_____

Other Archetypes

Archetype	Round or Flat	Name	Motivation

Method of Obtaining Resolution

_____

_____

_____

_____

What will occur at the climax to give the character purpose to resolve the conflict?

_____

_____

_____

How will the player interact with the story?

_____

_____

_____

_____

How will the player challenges and obstacles be achieved? Use skill, learning, or problem solving, not chance.

Challenge or Obstacle	Action (skill, learning, problem solving, etc.)

Name: _____

What strategies will be used to engage player emotion and immersion?

Emotion or Immersion	Strategy

List at least four items of player support that will appear in the game.

Describe why the conflict is important to the player.

_____

_____

_____

_____

Describe how the resolution is sufficient to end the story.

_____

_____

_____

_____

List twelve atomic challenges for the character or story.

List the player missions and explain how each mission leads to the final resolution.

Journey Planning Document

Answer the following questions. If more space is needed, enter the answers into a word processing document.

1. How is the player introduced to the hero?

_____

_____

2. How is the preliminary quest introduced to the hero?

_____

_____

3. What is the hero's final quest?

_____

_____

4. How will the hero meet the mentor?

_____

_____

5. What will the mentor teach the hero?

_____

_____

6. How will the hero later apply the skill learned from the mentor?

_____

_____

7. Who will be the allies and helpers for the hero?

_____

_____

8. How will the hero meet the helpers?

_____

_____

9. What enemies will the hero meet?

_____

_____

10. How will enemies be encountered to build skill before meeting the big boss?

_____

_____

11. How does the hero get acquainted with the world or community of the quest?

_____

_____

12. What side quests or activities will engage the player while learning from the community?

_____

_____

Name: _____

13. How do the hero and other characters learn of the final quest?

_____

_____

14. What is the heavy resistance that the hero will encounter? Will there be a boss, army, minions, etc.? At this stage, the resistance is not the heaviest resistance the hero will encounter.

_____

_____

15. What motivates the hero to keep going through the heavy resistance, or will the hero turn back?

_____

_____

16. What is the reward the hero will collect if successful in overcoming the heavy resistance?

_____

_____

17. How will the mentor leave the hero so the hero can become the master?

_____

_____

18. What side quests will the character undertake as soul searching or personal growth?

_____

_____

19. With the goal in sight, what evil force (heaviest resistance) will the hero find?

_____

_____

20. How is the evil force more powerful than the lower-ranking enemies?

_____

_____

21. How is the evil force revealed, or does the true identity stay mysterious and hidden?

_____

_____

22. What is the relationship of the evil force to the hero (closer than expected, unknown)?

_____

_____

23. How will the evil force take the hero to near defeat?

_____

_____

24. How does the hero gather strength at the lowest point and find a way to defeat the evil force?

_____

_____

25. How has the training from the mentor been applied during the battle?

_____

_____

26. What reward does the hero collect for victory?

_____

_____

27. What quests will the hero take on the return journey?

_____

_____

28. How will the hero pass some knowledge to helpers and youngsters along the journey home?

_____

_____

29. How will the hero protect the reward during the journey home?

_____

_____

30. What final resistance, if any, will the hero meet just before reaching home that will prove the hero has changed internally?

_____

_____

31. Will the hero be accepted home when returning, or will the hero be hard to recognize on return, and how has the hero changed?

_____

_____

32. What high honor will the hero receive at home to end the journey?

_____

_____

Activity 3-3

World Design for a Tile-Based RPG

Objectives

Students will build a scene on a tile-based game map. Students will use layers to assemble a scene. Students will program interactivity between the player character and in-game objects.

Situation

The Really Cool Game Company is impressed with your work designing story elements. It wants you to begin learning how to transfer story ideas into a playable game. The company uses a tile-based game engine to quickly and easily build RPG and platform games. Your first task is to learn how to use the software, building on skills you acquired in Chapter 2. When you are ready, you will create the dialogue and interactions needed to tell your story through the game.

How to Begin

1. Launch 001 Game Creator.
2. In the **New/Open Game** dialog box, double-click the folder with your name to open that folder.
3. Click the **New** button to begin a new game.
4. In the **New Game** dialog box, click **Action/RPG (Pro)**, enter the project name as *LastName_*Story01, and click the **OK** button to open the new game map. The sprites and game assets are loaded, and after that a game map appears in the workspace.

Map Properties

Your previous experience with 001 Game Creator in Chapter 2 focused only on the character attributes. This activity explores other features to build a scene and construct a quest for The Hero's Journey.

Locate the asset tree in the **Maps** tab at the bottom-left corner of the screen. The asset tree is a visual organization of how the files, folders, and game assets are arranged. Just like a real tree, it starts with a trunk folder, spreads out with folder branches, and on the end of the branches are twig folders or file leaves. Currently, the maps asset tree displays one folder called Story01 and one leaf called Starting Map, as shown in **Figure 1**.

5. Right-click the Starting Map leaf and click **Properties** in the shortcut menu. The **Map Properties** dialog box is displayed, as shown in **Figure 2**.
6. Click in the **Display Name:** text box, and enter Level 1. This is the name of the leaf that appears in the asset tree.
7. Click in the **Scripting ID/Filename:** text box, and enter Level 1. Dismiss the warning when it is displayed. It is always a good idea for the scripting ID to match the name.
8. Click in the **Width:** text box, and enter 20. Click in the **Height:** text box, and enter 20. Click in the **Depth:** text box, and enter 5. These settings yield a map that is 640 pixels wide and 640 pixels high.

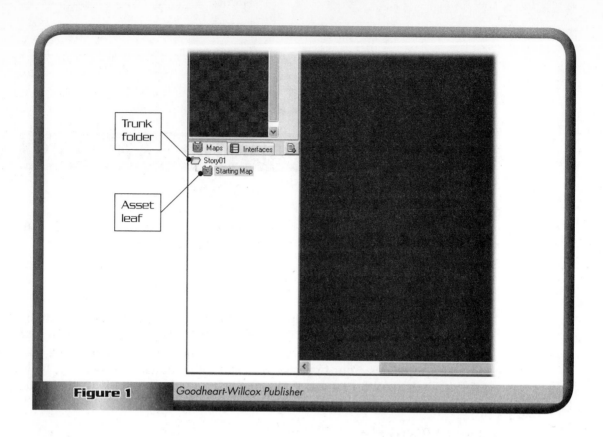

Trunk folder

Asset leaf

Figure 1   *Goodheart-Willcox Publisher*

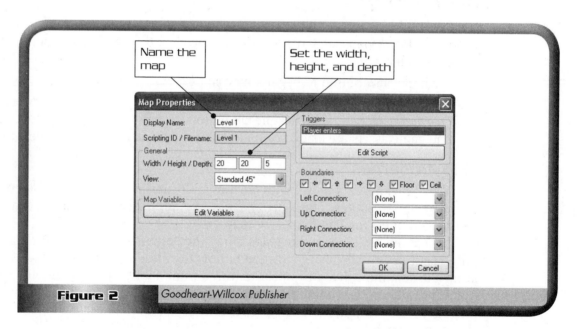

Name the map

Set the width, height, and depth

Figure 2   *Goodheart-Willcox Publisher*

The map size dimensions are in tiles. The 001 Game Creator game engine uses square tile images to build the map features. These tiles are 32 pixels wide and 32 pixels high. To find the overall map size in pixels, simply multiply each dimension by 32.

9. Click the **OK** button to close the **Map Properties** dialog box and update the map. Notice how the map size has changed. A black area appears to the right and below the original game map because no image tiles have been associated with this new area.

10. Save your work.

Tiles

The brown area on the map is default tiles, which is for ground or dirt. The game-map tiles are organized by layers and image group sets. These include the floor, lower objects, upper objects, and walls. The tile library panel is located on the left of the screen, as shown in **Figure 3**. At the top of the tiles panel are four tabs, one for each of the layers. Some layers have multiple image group sets. The tiles in the active group set are displayed below the tabs. Adding a tile from a group set places it on the corresponding layer of the game map.

11. Click the **Floor** tab to make it active. This also sets the layer.

12. Move the cursor over the image subsets, and click Tiled Floor set.

13. Move the cursor over the tiles in the library, and click the Wooden Floor tile. The selected tile appears with crosshatching to indicate it is active.

Flip Horizontally

14. Click the **Flip Horizontally** button. Notice how all tiles flip, but in this case only the checkerboard tile is noticeably different. The other tools along the side of the tile library are explained in **Figure 4**.

15. Click the **Fill** button.

Fill

16. Click once in the black area of the map. The area is filled with the wooden floor tile.

17. Click once in the area currently filled with dirt tiles. The dirt tiles are replaced with wooden floor tiles.

Scene Design

Now, the game map consists of a wooden floor. Next, you will place other tiles to create a scene for the game.

18. Click the **Walls** tab. There is only one image subset, and it is automatically selected.

19. Click the Wooden Wall tile. Notice that a new tool, a slider, appears in the tools in the tile library. This slider is used to adjust the height of the walls. The lowest setting is for walls one tile high. Each tick mark above that is one additional tile high.

20. Set the wall height to the second tick mark. This will create short walls so the player is visible behind the walls.

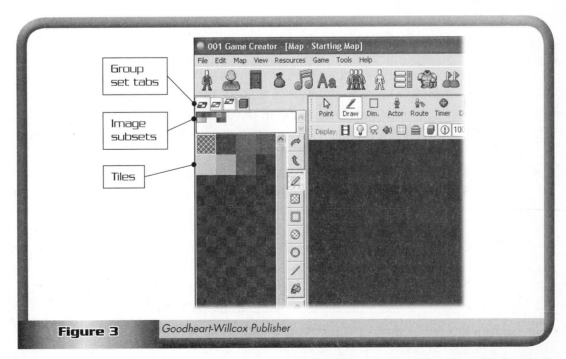

Figure 3   *Goodheart-Willcox Publisher*

Tool Icon	Tool Name	Function
	Flip Horizontally	Flips the entire tile set horizontally (left to right).
	Flip Vertically	Flips the entire tile set vertically (top to bottom).
	Pencil	Places individual tiles, or click and drag to place lines of the same tile.
	Filled Rectangle	Draws a rectangle and fills it with the selected tile.
	Rectangle	Draws a rectangle of the selected tiles; not filled.
	Filled Circle	Draws an oval and fills it with the selected tile.
	Circle	Draws an oval of the selected tile; not filled.
	Line	Draws a line of the selected tile; differs from click and drag with the **Pencil** tool as the line is previewed.
	Fill	Replaces all adjoining tiles of the same type with the selected tile.
	Eraser	Deletes single tiles, or click and drag to delete multiple tiles.

Figure 4   *Goodheart-Willcox Publisher*

Rectangle

21. Click the **Rectangle** button.
22. Move the cursor to the top-left corner of the map. Notice the coordinate display in the toolbar at the top editor, as shown in **Figure 5.** The first set of coordinate values is the pixel location of the cursor. The second set of coordinate value, which is in parentheses, is in units of tiles.
23. Click in tile (0,0,0) and drag to the opposite corner (19,19,0) to create a 640 × 640 box. This will build a short wooden wall around the map. Also notice there are shingles for a roof on top of the wall.
24. Click the **Line** button.
25. Click in tile (6,0,0), drag down to tile (6,4,0), and release the mouse button. Notice the preview of the line as you drag. When the mouse button is released, the line (wall) is drawn.

Line

26. Click the **Pencil** button, and add wall sections at tile (1,4,0), (2,4,0), and (5,4,0). This creates a small room.

Pencil

27. Using the **Line** button, draw a wall from tile (1,9,0) to tile (18,9,0).

Line

28. Draw a wall from tile (9,8,0) and to tile (9,19,0).
29. Draw a wall from tile (11,8,0) and to tile (11,19,0).

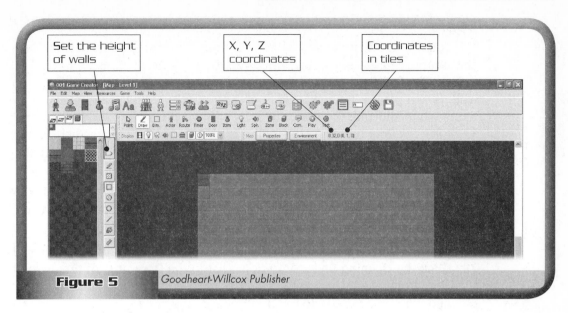

Figure 5   *Goodheart-Willcox Publisher*

Eraser

30. Click the **Eraser** button. Notice that the **Eraser** and **Line** buttons are both selected. This means that you will be erasing using the pencil. The **Eraser** tool must be used with a selection tool such as **Pencil**, **Rectangle**, or **Fill**.

31. Single-click at tile (10,9,0). This erases the wall at that tile to create a hallway, as shown in **Figure 6**.

32. Save your work.

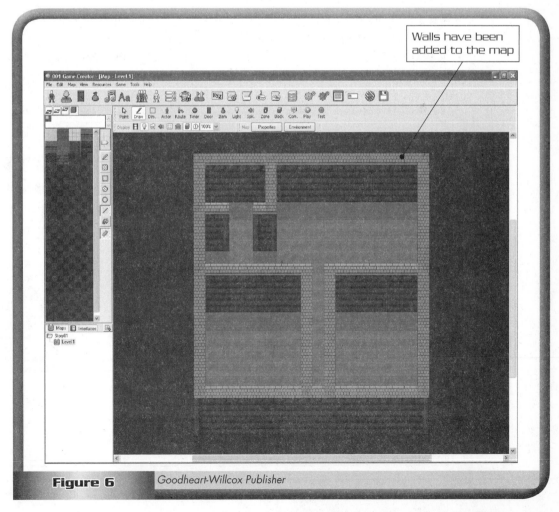

Figure 6   *Goodheart-Willcox Publisher*

Doors

You are in the process of creating a simple cottage for this scene. The exterior and interior walls are in place. However, there are no openings into the cottage or its rooms. The 001 Game Creator game engine comes with animated doors to add to a wall. When placed in a wall, the door acts as an opening. That keeps the roof section intact while allowing the player to pass through the wall.

Door

33. Click the **Door** button on the toolbar at the top of the map area below the main toolbar.

34. Click in tile (10,18,0) as the location to place the door. The **Door** dialog box is displayed, as shown in **Figure 7**.

35. In the **Tile** area of the dialog box, click the right-hand image. Notice the preview shows a wooden door with iron braces. This door matches the cottage theme for the scene.

36. Click in the **Display Name:** text box, and enter Door_Outside01.

37. Click in the **Scripting ID:** text box, and enter Door_Outside01. Dismiss the warning.

38. Click the **Opening Style:** drop-down list in the **Door** area of the dialog box, and click **Rotate Left (Up Only)** in the list. This setting specifies how the door will open and close and is reflected in the preview.

39. Click the **OK** button. The door is added to the map.

40. Click in tile (4,8,0) to add another door.

41. In the **Door** dialog box, click the door image second from the left.

42. Enter a display name and a scripting ID of Door_Bedroom01.

43. Click the **Color:** swatch in the **Visual** area of the dialog box, and in the **Color** dialog box that is displayed, select a brown. This sets the overall color of this door, and is reflected in the preview.

44. Click the **Opening Style:** drop-down list in the **Door** area of the dialog box, and click **Rotate Left (Down Only)** in the list.

45. Click the **Required Key:** drop-down list, and click **ID Keycard** in the list. This setting determines what item the character must be carrying to open the door.

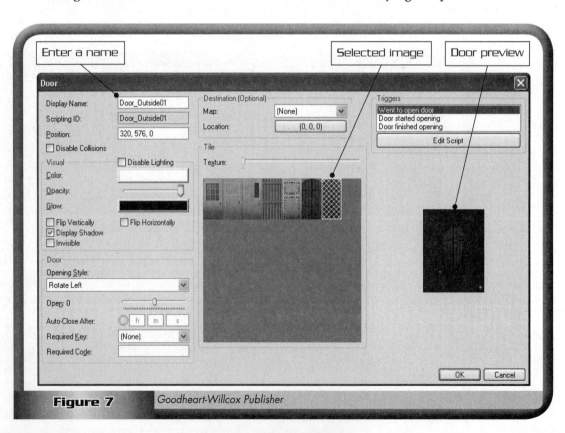

Figure 7 — *Goodheart-Willcox Publisher*

46. Click the **OK** button. The door is added to the map.

47. Right-click on the tile containing Bedroom_Door01, and click **Copy** in the shortcut menu. Many times, it is more efficient to copy and paste objects rather than adding new objects from scratch.

48. Right-click in tile (15,8,0), and click **Paste** in the shortcut menu. Notice the list of objects in the panel to the left of the map area lists three doors: Door_Outside01, Door_Bedroom01, and Door_Bedroom02. Using this naming convention allows for automatic sequential numbering of similarly named objects.

49. Click Door_Bedroom02 in the map area to open the **Door** dialog box for that object.

50. In the **Door** dialog box, click the **Required Key:** drop-down list, and click **Elixir** in the list.

51. Close the **Door** dialog box to update the object.

52. Click the **Item Pick-Up** button on the toolbar.

Item Pick-Up

53. Click in tile (4,1,0).

54. In the **Item** dialog box, click the **Treasure Chest:** button, and select **Chest (Effect Chest)**. Also click the **Item:** button, and select **Elixir** in the Common folder. Then close the **Item** dialog box.

Test Map

55. Test play the game. Place the player character in the empty room in the top-right section of the map. See **Figure 8.**

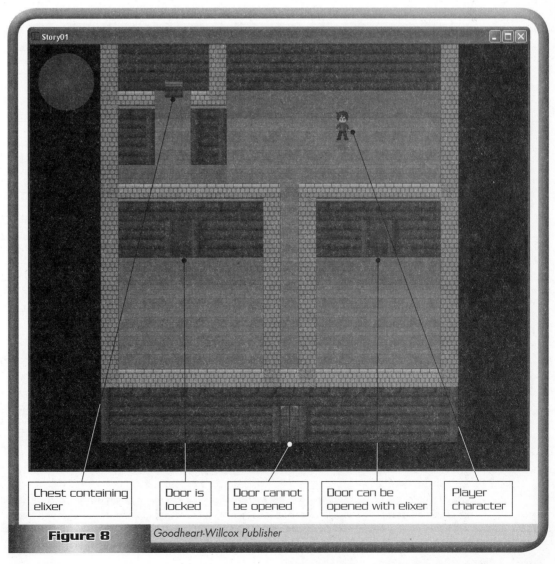

| Chest containing elixer | Door is locked | Door cannot be opened | Door can be opened with elixer | Player character |

Figure 8 *Goodheart-Willcox Publisher*

56. Check if the doors work properly by walking up to each door and pressing the [Enter] key. Door_Bedroom02 should be the only door that will open, and only after you have collected the elixir from the chest.

57. Save your work.

Thematic Elements

A basic level has been created as a cottage containing rooms and doors. Next, you need to add some objects to the scene, such as furniture, to serve as thematic elements.

58. Click the **Draw** button on the toolbar.

Draw

59. Click the **Lower Objects** tab, and select the Containers image group set.

60. Click the Wood Barrel with Metal Supports image. Notice that this image is larger than one tile. To select the entire image, drag over all tiles for the image. In this case, the image spans two tiles.

61. Click the **Pencil** button, and then click in tile (18,1,0) on the map.

Pencil

62. Using similar techniques, place the items shown in **Figure 9.** Be creative; use these items or choose ones of your own. Notice how objects placed on the upper layer are "above" objects on the lower layer.

Layer Tab	Image Group Set	Item	Tile
Lower Objects	Decoration	Big Blue Rug	(12,2,0)
		Suit of Armor	(18,9,0)
	Furniture 1	Bed	(1,9,0)
		Wooden Drawers	(9,0,0)
		Wooden Table	(13,9,0)
			(8,0,0)
	Furniture 2	Bookcase	(16,8,0)
	Containers	Wood Barrel	(5,0,0)
		Filled Crate	(2,0,0)
Upper Objects	Decorations	Shield	(5,0,0)
		Clock	(13,9,0)
		Large Cup	(18,1,0)
	Pictures	Large Picture	(1,8,0)
	Signs	Items Sign	(3,9,0)
			(1,0,0)
		Weapons Sign	(8,0,0)
		Armor Sign	(18,8,0)
	Windows	Six Part Window with Curtains	(4,18,0)
			(15,18,0)

Figure 9   *Goodheart-Willcox Publisher*

(Continued)

63. Click the **Lower Objects** tab, select the Furniture 1 image group set, and locate the Wood Counter image. Notice how this image spans multiple tiles in an irregular shape. This object must be placed on the map in two stages.

64. Select the bottom six tiles of the image.

65. Place this selection by clicking in tile (11,4,0). The intent is to match the width of the rug, but the image does not quite match.

66. In the tile library, select only the two tiles that make up the middle-center edge of the bottom of the counter.

67. Click in tile (13,4,0) and (14,4,0) to extend the counter. You can select as little as one tile of an item to build it to any dimension needed.

68. In the tile library, select only the two tiles that make up the right-hand end of the bottom of the counter.

69. Click in tile (15,4,0) to add the end to the counter at the edge of the rug.

70. Add the top part of the counter to the map so the counter is L-shaped.

71. Click the **Upper Objects** tab and select the Decorations image group set. Add the Open Book near the upper-left corner of the L-shaped counter, and add the Checkerboard anywhere on top of the counter.

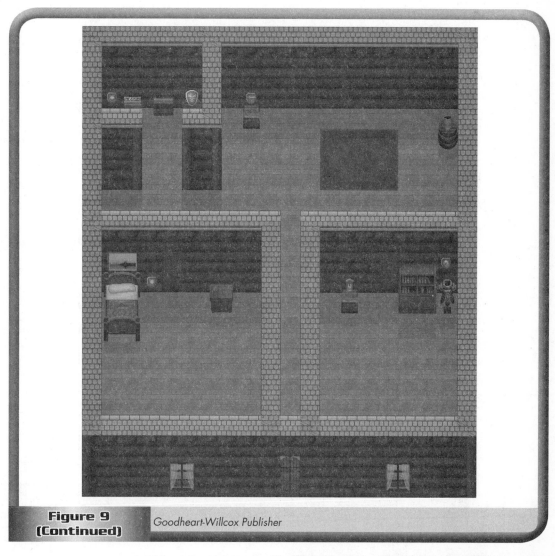

**Figure 9
(Continued)**

Goodheart-Willcox Publisher

When placing items, you may have noticed how it is not possible to add items hanging at the top of the top wall. That portion of the wall is actually beyond the edge of the map. If your game design requires an item to be placed at the top of the wall, the wall must be placed so it does not extend past the edge of the map.

Test Map

Test play the game. Make sure the player cannot walk through solid objects such as the barrel or counter. Also try jumping on top of the counter. Press the left [Shift] key to jump, and use the arrow keys to move while in the air. Notice how the 3D effect is achieved. Also notice how the character can walk through the checkerboard and open book on the counter. This is an error in how objects are stacked. You may also notice the door at the bottom does not fully render. Limitations such as these must be considered when designing levels.

Interactivity Zones

You may have noticed that the player character cannot get very close to the treasure chest. This object has a preset interactivity zone that is much larger than the item itself. The *interactivity zone* defines the area in which the player character can interact with the object. Zones are specified in half-tile increments for best fit. For the other items in the scene, you will now construct custom interactivity zones to improve the gameplay. In the process of doing this, you will see how 001 Game Creator is used to build scripts, or programming.

Zone

72. Click the **Zone** button on the toolbar.

73. Click on the tile at the top-left corner of the checkerboard (in front of the counter), and drag down one half-tile space and over three half-tile spaces. The zone should be over the checkerboard object and extend beyond the edges of the counter. The coordinate display should read 64 × 32 when you release the mouse button. The **Zone** dialog box is displayed, as shown in **Figure 10.**

74. Click in the **Display Name:** text box, and enter Zone_ID Keycard.

75. Click in the **Scripting ID:** text box, and enter Zone_ID Keycard. Dismiss the warning. Since you will be adding programming, it is important to change the ID now, not after the programming is created.

76. In the **Triggers** area, click the Collided with actor entry that shows an icon of a person and states Player.

77. Click the **Edit Script** button. The **Zone Script** dialog box is displayed.

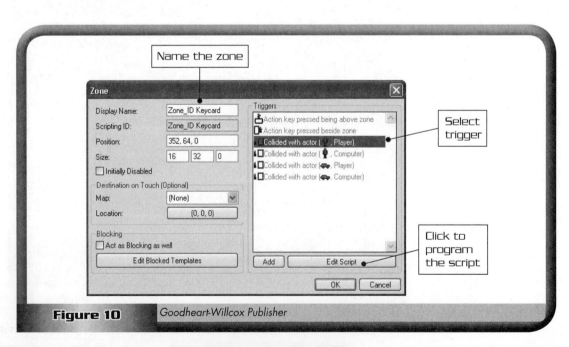

Figure 10 *Goodheart-Willcox Publisher*

The **Zone Script** dialog box is used to create the programming for this zone. The dialog box should look familiar as a similar scripting dialog box is displayed before test playing the game. This is the logic statement that needs to be programmed: **IF** the player collides with the zone named Zone_ID Keycard, **THEN** add one ID keycard object to the player character's inventory.

78. In the list in the **Zone Script** dialog box, double-click the **Add/Remove Item** command in the **Actors** group. The **Add/Remove Item** dialog box is displayed, as shown in **Figure 11.**

79. In the **Actor:** area of the **Add/Remove Item** dialog box, click Level 1 and (Main). The (Main) selection specifies the player character.

80. Make sure the **Only In Selected Map** check box is checked. This will allow the zone to work only on the Level 1 map.

81. Click the **Number of Items (Inventory Only):** button. In the **Pick Item/Magic** dialog box that is displayed, select the ID Keycard in the Common folder. Close the **Pick Item/Magic** dialog box.

82. In the **Number:** drop-down list, make sure **Add** is selected and 1 is entered as the quantity.

83. Click the **OK** button to close the **Add/Remove Item** dialog box and return to the **Zone Script** dialog box.

Notice that 001 Game Creator converts the information from the settings you made into a programming block, as shown in **Figure 12.** The programming blocks are attached to each with lines, or threads, to indicate the flow through the program. Hover the cursor over the Add/Remove Item block. The block expands so you can read all of the information in the block.

84. Click the **OK** button to close the **Zone Script** dialog box.

85. Click the **OK** button to close the **Zone** dialog box. Notice the zone on the map now has a comment providing information about the programming. This allows the designer to quickly see how the zone interactions are constructed for each level.

Test

Test Map

86. Test play the game.

Make sure each door will open. You must get the elixir to open the first door, and get the ID keycard to open the second door. In order to see if you have collected the ID keycard, press the [Esc] key to show the game menu, and click the **Items** link. All collected items will be listed. To return to the game, press the [Esc] key twice.

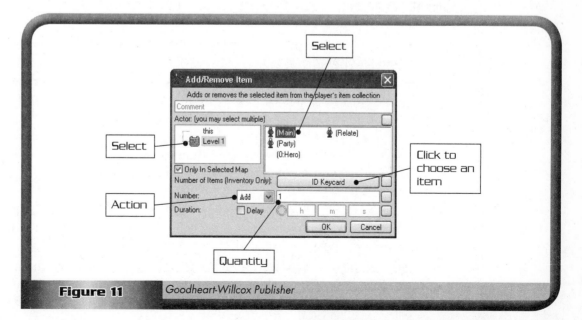

Figure 11   *Goodheart-Willcox Publisher*

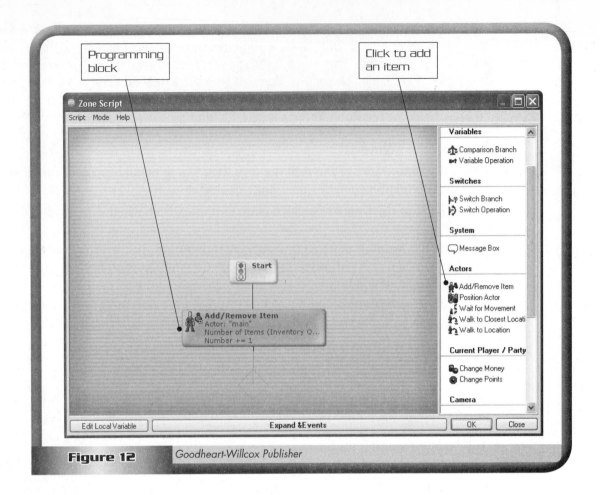

Figure 12   *Goodheart-Willcox Publisher*

Tuning

What would happen in the game if the player did not check inventory after walking next to the checkerboard (into the zone)? There would be no way to know that the ID keycard had been collected. Clearly, this interaction is not what players expect. At this tuning stage, you will edit the zone and associated programming to provide a better gameplay experience for the player.

Zone

87. Click the **Zone** button, and click anywhere in the Zone_ID Keycard zone on the map. The **Zone** dialog box is displayed.

88. Make sure the correct trigger is highlighted, and click the **Edit Script** button to open the **Zone Script** dialog box.

89. Double-click the **Message** command in the **System** group. The **Message Box** dialog box is displayed, which is used to provide information to the player on interaction with the zone.

90. In the **Message:** text box, enter You found a key to the other door!, as shown in **Figure 13.** This tells the player not only that an item has been found, but also its use. Without this information, the player would not know to check the second door. Messages like this help the player navigate the game.

91. Click the **OK** button to close the **Message Box** dialog box. Notice that a programming block for the message has been added and is attached to the Add/ Remove Item block by a thread.

92. Click and drag the Message Box block to the right. Notice that the thread follows the block. This allows blocks to be moved to quickly organize programming.

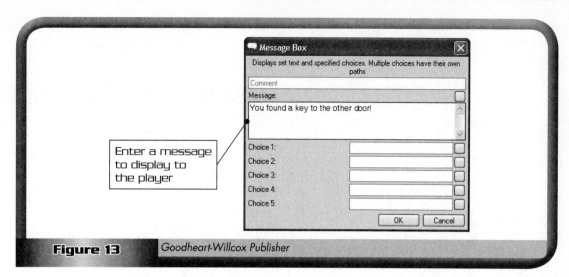

Enter a message to display to the player

Figure 13   *Goodheart-Willcox Publisher*

93. Move the cursor over the node at the bottom of the Add/Remove Item block. The node turns into a black triangle when the cursor is over it.

94. Right-click on the node to cut the thread between the Add/Remove Item block and the Message Box block.

95. Move the cursor over the node at the bottom of the Add/Remove Item block, and click and hold on the node. The node turns red, which means you can draw a thread from this block.

96. Drag the thread to the top of the **Message Box** block, and release the mouse button to draw the thread. This reconnects the two programming blocks.

97. Click the **OK** button to close the **Zone Script** dialog box.

98. Click the **OK** button to close the **Zone** dialog box.

99. Test play the game. Make sure the message is displayed when the player character interacts with the zone.

Test Map

Choices

Recall that signs were added to the map. Two item signs were added to rooms, an armor sign was added to one room, and a weapons sign was added by the counter. These signs are used to indicate to the player that items, weapons, or armor can be found. However, right now, the signs are just images. The programming needs to be added to allow the player to pick up the corresponding objects.

100. Draw a zone in front of the armor.

Zone

101. Enter the display name and scripting ID as Zone_Armor.

102. Select the trigger for interacting with the player, edit the script, and create a message box.

103. In the **Message Box** dialog box, enter You have found Leather Armor. Would you like to take it? in the **Message:** text box.

104. Click in the **Choice 1:** text box, and enter Yes, take it, as shown in **Figure 14.**

105. Click in the **Choice 2:** text box, and enter No, leave it. Close the **Message Box** dialog box.

Notice that the Message Box programming block has two connection nodes on the bottom of the block instead of one node as you have seen so far. Hover the cursor over the left-hand node, and help text appears that states picked "Yes, take it".

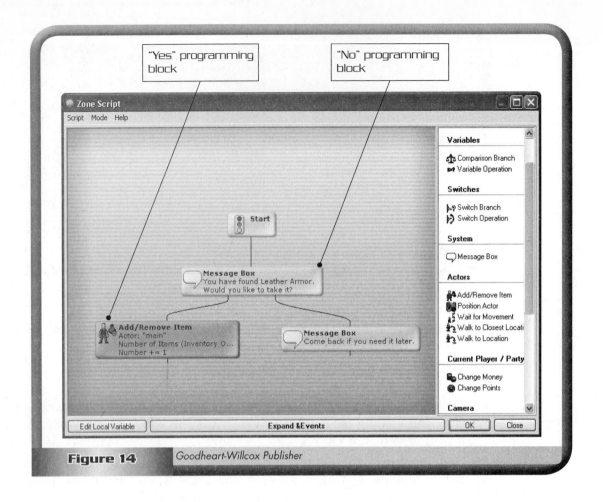

"Yes" programming block

"No" programming block

Figure 14   Goodheart-Willcox Publisher

The right-hand node will display picked "No, leave it." These are the two choices entered in the programming.

106. Click the left-hand node ("yes") so the next command will be attached to it.

107. Double-click the **Add/Remove Item** command in the **Actors** group. Use what you know to add programming to give the player character one leather armor item.

108. Click the right-hand node ("no") so the next command will be attached to it.

109. Add a message that tells the player Come back if you need it later. The programming blocks should now look like **Figure 14.** If the threads did not connect correctly, right-click on the bottom node to cut the thread, and draw a new thread as needed.

110. Close the **Zone Script** and **Zone** dialog boxes.

Player Information and Starting Location

As the designer, you know what to do when playing the game. The player does not have the same advantage. The player requires navigational aids to understand what to do in the game. You will now add elements to the game that will help the player understand how to play the game.

111. Create a zone over the open book object. The zone should extend beyond the edges of the counter, just as you did for the zone over the checkerboard. Name the zone Zone_Book.

112. In the **Zone** dialog box, select the trigger Action key pressed beside zone, and click the **Edit Script** button.

Zone

Zone

113. Add programming for a message box that states:

> Welcome to my cabin. This is the starting point for your journey. The journey is long and filled with danger. Hidden in this cabin are six items to assist you on your journey. When finished, meet my friend outside for more information on your quest.

114. Close the **Zone Script** and **Zone** dialog boxes.

115. Click **Game Settings** in the **Game** pull-down menu. The **General Settings** dialog box is displayed, as shown in **Figure 15.** In this dialog box, you can set the starting location for the player character at the beginning of the game.

116. In the **Game** area of the dialog box, click the **Starting Map:** drop-down list, and click **Level 1** in the list. This will be the map on which the game begins.

117. Click the **Starting Location:** button. The **Pick Location** dialog box is displayed. This dialog box displays a miniature version of the map, as shown in **Figure 16.**

118. Click at the bottom of the hallway near the door. When the player starts the game, it will appear as if he or she has just entered the cabin door.

119. Click the **OK** button to close the **Pick Location** dialog box and return to the **General Settings** dialog box. The **Starting Location:** button now displays the coordinates of the location where the player will start.

120. Click the **OK** button to close the **General Settings** dialog box.

121. Test play the game by clicking the **Test Game** button, not the **Test Map** button.

Test Game

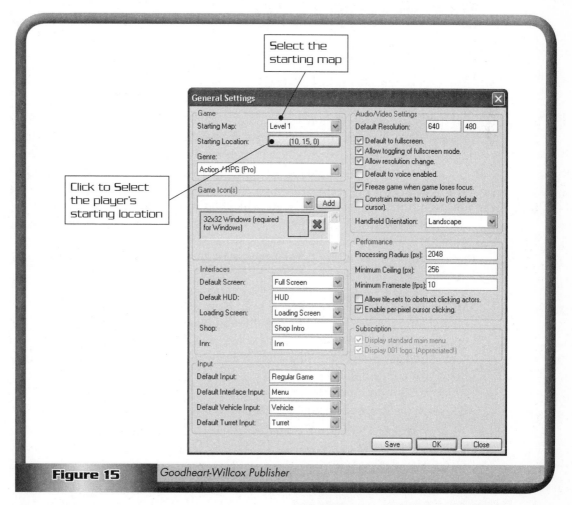

Figure 15   *Goodheart-Willcox Publisher*

Chapter 3   Story Composition   **93**

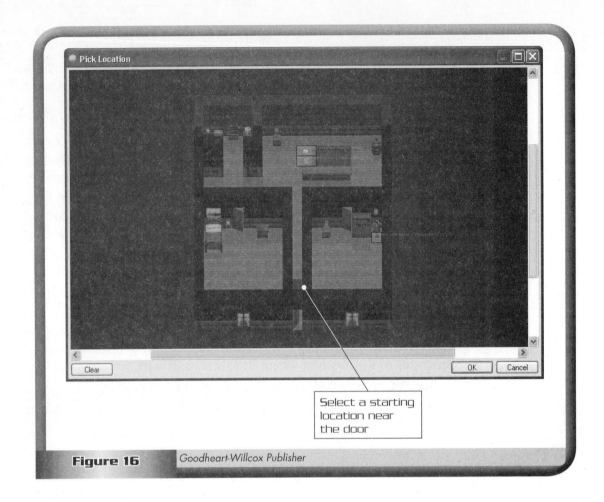

Pick Location

Clear

OK   Cancel

Select a starting
location near
the door

Figure 16   *Goodheart-Willcox Publisher*

Inventory

Apply the skills you have learned to create zones for the items shown in **Figure 17**. Do not put a zone next to a door if the zone requires pressing the action button. If you do, the game will not know whether to open the door or activate the zone.

Be sure to test play each script before moving on to the next script. If you test each one by one, then any errors can be easily found. If you try to test multiple scripts at the same time, it may not be clear which script is causing an error.

Test

Test Map

Test Game

After all scripts are programmed and functioning correctly, test play the game. Collect all items, and try using them. Try shooting all of the charges in the wand, and then go back to get more. Remember to press the [Z] key to select the weapon and the left [Ctrl] key to fire it.

Limiting Rewards

As you have been test playing the game, you may have noticed that you could keep going back to get more charges for the wand or more of any other item. In some cases, such as in a very difficult level, a reward such as ammo may be unlimited so the player can continually replenish to defeat the strong enemy. However, in most cases, the player should be limited to receiving a reward only once.

Zone

Zone

122. Click the **Zone** button, and then click on the zone for the wand (Zone_WeaponSign01).

123. In the **Zone** dialog box, make sure the correct trigger is selected, and click the **Edit Script** button.

124. In the **Zone Script** dialog box, right-click the thread from the bottom of the Start block to cut it.

Zone Location	Name	Interaction	Message	Choices	Add Item
Near weapons sign in upper-right room	Zone_WeaponSign01	Press action key beside zone	You have found a wand with ten charges. Would you like to take the wand?	Yes / No	One wand and ten charges*
Near item sign in upper-left room	Zone_ItemSign01	Press action key beside zone	Would you like to carry this winged helmet?	Yes / No	Winged helmet
Near item sign in bedroom (lower-left room)	Zone_ItemSign02	Press action key beside zone	You have found one potion. Would you like to take it?	Yes / No	Potion

*The wand and the charges are programmed as two separate Add/Remove Item blocks, and the charges are located in the Common folder in the **Pick Item/Magic** dialog box.

Figure 17   *Goodheart-Willcox Publisher*

125. Drag the Start block higher to make space between it and the Message Box block.

126. Click the node below the Start block to activate it as the attachment point.

127. Double-click the **Once Branch** command in the **Structure** group. The Once Branch block is added to the script layout.

128. Click the left-hand node ("first time") on the bottom of the Once Branch block, and drag the thread to the top of the Message Box block.

129. Click the right-hand node ("every other time") to activate it as the attachment point.

130. Add the programming to include a message box that displays the message There is nothing here. The script layout should look like **Figure 18.**

131. Test play the game to check that this script is functioning properly.

132. Edit the zones for all other items that can be picked up so the player can only collect each item once.

Test Game

Background Music Element

Music in a game can help not only set the mood, but also create dramatic tension. You will now incorporate background music into the game. The music will play while the player is exploring the cabin.

Environment

Environment

133. Click the **Environment** button on the toolbar. The **Map Environment** dialog box is displayed.

134. Click the **Change Music:** button in the **General** area. The **Pick Sound/Music** dialog box is displayed.

135. In the **Pick Sound/Music** dialog box, select the **Town 1** music file, and click the **OK** button to return to the **Map Environment** dialog box. Music should be playing through the computer speakers.

136. Make sure the **Change Music:** check box is checked, and click the **OK** button to close the **Map Environment** dialog box. The music will stop playing when the dialog box is closed.

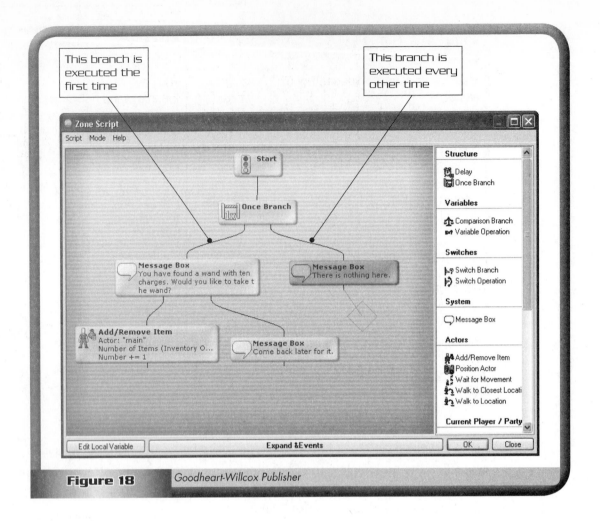

This branch is executed the first time

This branch is executed every other time

Figure 18   *Goodheart-Willcox Publisher*

Challenge Element

So far, the player can walk around the cabin and collect items. While these actions may be needed for the overall story, there is not much challenge. To add a bit of danger and challenge to this level, you will add a surprise monster to battle.

Actor

137. Click the **Actor** button.

138. Place the actor behind the counter in the corner of the L.

139. Create an NPC hiding ghost named NPC_Ghost01, and give it a knife.

140. Set the characteristics of the ghost so it is not initially existent and not solid.

141. Assign the ghost to the Bad group.

142. Set the speed, health points, and attack of the ghost low. This is needed so the player will be able to learn on this level and build skill.

143. Add a reward of five experience points, ten dollars, and fifteen reward points.

144. Program the ghost for auto movement to move toward the player.

145. Set the AI to keep the ghost near its post or route.

146. Close the actor dialog box, and save your work.

The ghost will not be visible when the game is started. It must be programmed to appear. In this case, the player should find the wand before the enemy is activated. Finding the wand will activate the enemy, and this programming is added in the next section.

Spawning the NPC

Zone

147. Edit the Zone_WeaponSign01 zone, and edit the script.

148. Select the node on the bottom of the last Add/Remove Item block, the block that adds the wand and charges, to make that node active.

149. Click the **Expand & Events** button at the bottom of the **Zone Script** dialog box. This will display all available interaction events, as shown in **Figure 19.**

150. Click **Actors** in the list on the left. This narrows the options to only those that apply to actors. Remember, the ghost is an actor.

151. Double-click the **Change Existence** option in the list on the right. The **Change Existence** dialog box is displayed, as shown in **Figure 20.** This option allows for programming the ghost from nonexistent to existent.

152. In the **Change Existence** dialog box, select Level 1 and NPC_Ghost01 in the **Actor:** area.

153. In the **State:** area, click the **Existent** radio button. This specifies the ghost will appear.

154. Click the **OK** button to close the **Change Existence** dialog box. The Change Existence programming block is added.

155. Click the **OK** button in the **Zone Script** dialog box, and click the **OK** button in the **Zone** dialog box.

156. Test play the game, and see how the ghost is spawned. Be quick with that new wand you collected!

Test Game

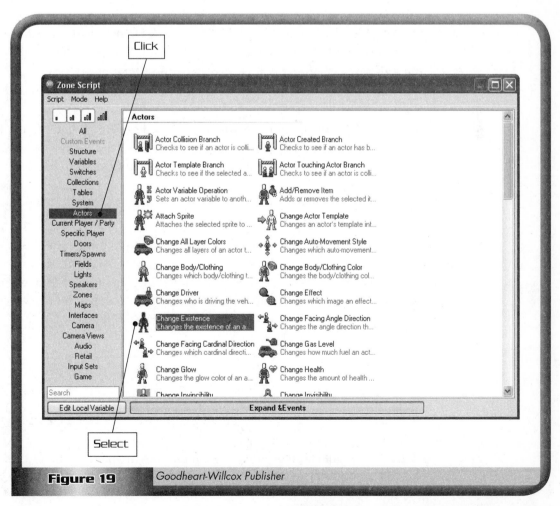

Figure 19   *Goodheart-Willcox Publisher*

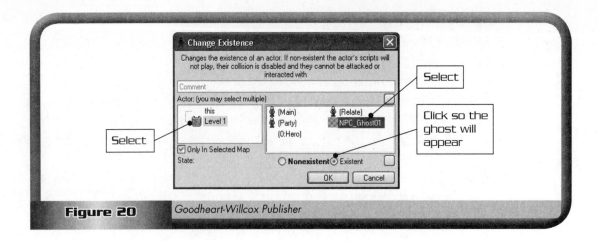

Figure 20   *Goodheart-Willcox Publisher*

Dramatic Music Element

When the ghost attacked, the background music did not change. The mood should change when the enemy appears. One way to achieve this is by changing the music that is played. When the player is engaged in combat, the music should communicate excitement, tension, and speed. Then, when the combat is concluded, the music should return to a normal, soothing ambient sound.

Actor

157. Edit the NPC_Ghost01 actor, and click the **Template: Edit** button in the **Actor: Hiding Ghost** dialog box.

158. On the details page of the **Actor: Hiding Ghost** dialog box, click the **Add** button in the **Triggers** area. The **Add Triggers** dialog box is displayed.

159. In the **Add Triggers** dialog box, select **Existence Changed** in the **State** area, and click the **OK** button. The **Existence Changed** dialog box is displayed.

160. In the **Existence Changed** dialog box, click the **State:** check box, and click the **Existent** radio button. Then, click the **OK** button. The **Actor Script** dialog box is displayed, which is the familiar scripting window.

161. Double-click **Play Music** in the **Audio** area. The **Play Music** dialog box is displayed.

162. Click the **Song:** button in the **Play Music** dialog box, and in the **Pick Sound/Music** dialog box that is displayed, click Boss 4 and the **OK** button.

163. Click the **OK** button to close the **Play Music** dialog box, and click the **OK** button to close the **Actor Script** dialog box. This trigger now appears in the **Triggers** area of the **Actor: Hiding Ghost** dialog box.

164. Similarly, add a new trigger for killed/destroyed and change the music back to Town 1.

Test Game

165. Test play the game. Test every aspect of the game, including the new music when the ghost is attacking. Note how the attack music changes the overall mood of the game, and when the ghost is defeated the mood changes again.

166. Fix any errors found during testing.

167. Save your work

Building the Game

168. Click **Build Game...** in the **Game** pull-down menu. The **Build Game** dialog box is displayed, as shown in **Figure 21.**

169. Click in the **Output Directory** text box, and enter the path of the output folder, as specified by your instructor.

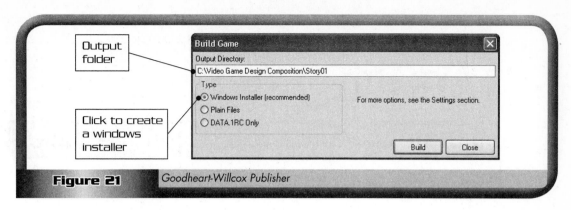

Figure 21   *Goodheart-Willcox Publisher*

170. Click the **Windows Installer** radio button.

171. Click the **Build** button.

172. Locate the setup EXE file in the output folder, and submit it for grading according to the directions provided by your instructor.

Review Questions

1. Describe how the asset tree in 001 Game Creator has a structure similar to a real tree.

   _____

   _____

   _____

   _____

2. Describe how game-map tiles are organized in 001 Game Creator.

   _____

   _____

3. What element is used to allow a player to pass through a wall?

   _____

   _____

4. How is the game programmed so the player does not get to access the reward more than one time?

   _____

   _____

5. Describe the purpose of changing music when an enemy appears and when it is defeated.

   _____

   _____

Activity 3-4

Dialogue and Story for a Tile-Based RPG

Objectives

Students will use a tile-based game to create player interaction that includes dialogue. Students will program player choices to create the story elements of a game. Students will program player movement between game maps. Students will program non-player character (NPC) entities.

Situation

The Really Cool Game Company has reviewed the first game level created in the last activity. It would like to have a complete game that begins in the cabin on the first level and branches out to many different adventures and quests. Your task now is to add game maps, levels, and objectives to the game created in the last activity.

How to Begin

It is not going to be much of a story if the player never gets to leave the cabin. The first step in creating a larger game is to add a new game map.

1. Launch 001 Game Creator.

2. Open the *LastName*_Story01 file from Activity 3-3.

New

3. Click the **New** button next to the asset tree. Make sure the Story01 folder is selected, not the Level 1 branch, before clicking the button. The **Map Properties** window is displayed, as shown in **Figure 1**.

4. Click in the **Display Name:** text box, and enter Yard_Front.

5. Click in the **Scripting ID/Filename:** text box, and enter Yard_Front.

6. In the **General** area of the dialog box, change the size to 21 × 20 × 8.

7. Leave the trigger as the preset Player enters. This specifies the map will begin when the player enters it.

8. Click the **OK** button to render the new map and add it to the asset tree below the Story01 folder; it should not be below the Level 1 branch. All tiles in the map are currently black.

Draw

9. Click the **Draw** button, and using skills you have learned, fill the map with light-colored grass on the floor layer.

10. Using the Dirt image tile, draw a path from tile (10,0,0) to tile (10,19,0).

11. Draw another path from tile (0,11,0) to tile (20,11,0).

12. Using the right-hand Wooden Floor image tile, draw a floor from tile (4,0,0) to tile (16,1,0). This is a filled rectangle 416 pixels by 64 pixels.

13. Using the Wooden Wall image tile set to three tiles high, draw a wall from tile (4,1,0) to tile (16,1,0). The wall will cover the floor, but the floor must be added so it can be seen through the door after that has been added.

14. Using the Six Part Window with Curtains image tile, add windows at tile (6,0,0) and tile (13,0,0).

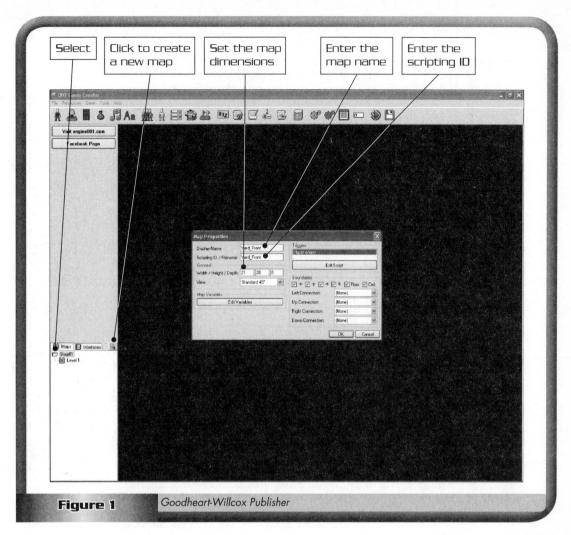

Figure 1   *Goodheart-Willcox Publisher*

15. Using the Well with Roof image tile in the Outside–Decoration image group set, add a well at tile (19,12,0).

16. Using the Sign image tile in the Outside–Decoration image group set, add a sign at tile (19,8,0).

17. Explore the other image group sets, and select some trees, bushes, and rocks to add more thematic elements to the scene.

Door

18. Add a wooden door with iron braces at tile (10,0,0). Enter the name and scripting ID for the door as Door_Outside01. The left-to-right location of the door is important so the player feels as if he or she has walked out of the cabin. The basic scene of the outside of the cabin is complete, as shown in **Figure 2.**

19. Save your work.

Teleporting

Teleporting moves the character from one location to another without the movement between points being seen by the player. In this case, the player character needs to be teleported from the cabin interior to the front yard. Keep in mind the immersion of the game. The character should not be teleported to just any location in the yard. The character will enter the yard by going through the door on the cabin, so it should be teleported to a location by the door in the front yard.

20. Click Level 1 in the asset tree. That map is made current and displayed.

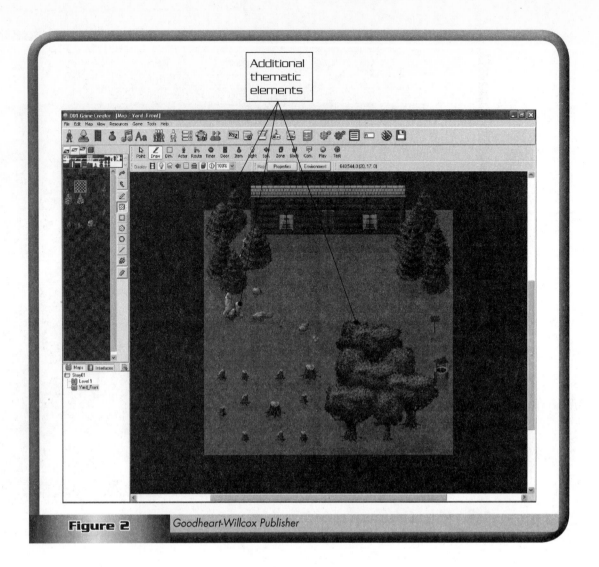

Additional thematic elements

Figure 2   *Goodheart-Willcox Publisher*

Door

21. Click the **Door** button, and click the Door_Outside01 door to edit it.

22. Select Went to open door in the **Triggers** area of the **Door** dialog box, and click the **Edit Script** button.

23. In the **Door Script** dialog box, double-click the **Position Actor** command in the **Actor** group. The **Position Action** dialog box is displayed, as shown in **Figure 3.**

24. In the **Actor:** area, click Level 1 and Main.

25. In the **Map:** area, click Yard_Front.

26. In the **Change Direction:** area, click the **Yes** radio button.

27. In the **Direction:** area, click the six o'clock position. This will make it look as though the player character just walked out of the cabin.

28. Click on the preview map to display the **Pick Location** dialog box.

29. In the **Pick Location** dialog box, click two tiles down in front of the cabin door. This location will allow the player to feel as if the character just walked through the door to the outside.

30. Click the **OK** button to close the **Pick Location** dialog box.

31. Click the **OK** button to close the **Position Actor** dialog box.

32. Click the **OK** button to close the **Door Script** dialog box.

33. Click the **OK** button to close the **Door** dialog box.

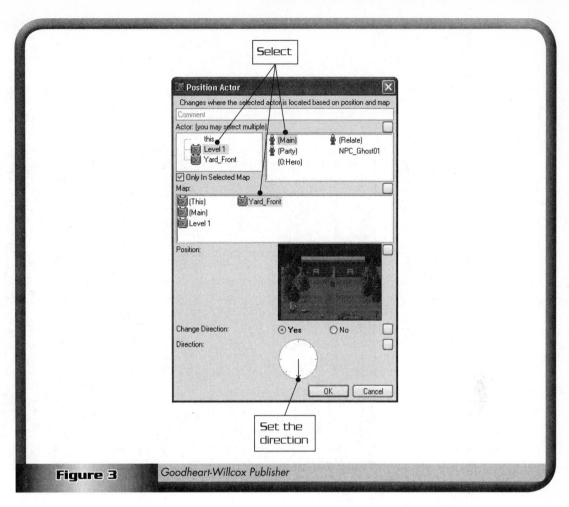

Select

Set the direction

Figure 3 *Goodheart-Willcox Publisher*

34. Save your work.

35. Test play the game. The game should start on Level 1 (inside the cabin). Check to see if the character is teleported to the front yard when you press the [Enter] key at the cabin's front door.

Test Game

Reentry

What happened when you test played the game? You could exit the cabin, but you could not get back into it. You programmed the game to teleport the character outside the cabin, but you have not programmed a way for the character to reenter it. Teleporters do not need to be doors. A zone can be programmed to teleport a character just as easily. A teleporting zone will be used to get the player character back into the cabin.

36. Click Yard_Front in the asset tree to make that map current.

37. Click the **Visualize Layers** button on the toolbar. Items on the topmost layer are shaded dark green. Any items that were hidden by the top layer are now visible.

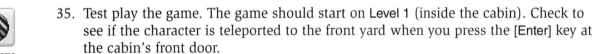

Visualize Layers

38. Click the **Visualize Layers** button again. The top and middle layers are hidden, which reveals the wooden floor behind the cabin walls and door, as shown in **Figure 4.** Clicking the button again will restore all layers, but leave the top and middle layers hidden for now.

Zone

39. Draw a zone 32 × 32 pixels in size from tile (10,0,0). Placing the zone just behind the top of the door allows the player to open the door and walk the character through before being teleported into the cabin.

40. Name the zone Zone_CabinEntry.

Click to change layer visibility

Only the lowest layer is visible

Zone is added

Figure 4   Goodheart-Willcox Publisher

41. In the **Destination on Touch** area of the **Zone** dialog box, click the **Map:** drop-down list, and click Level 1 in the list.

42. In the same area, click the **Location:** button, and in the **Pick Location** dialog box, click just inside the door of the cabin. Click the **OK** button to close the **Pick Location** dialog box.

43. Click the **OK** button to close the **Zone** dialog box.

44. Test play the game. Check that you can go in and out of the cabin. Check several times, and you just might find an error.

Test Game

Tuning

While testing the game, you should have noticed that the door to the cabin on the Level 1 map stays open. This means you cannot walk outside to the Yard_Front map more than once. The door only transports the player character when the door is being opened. This is fine if the player can never return to the map, but since the player should be able to go back and forth between the inside and outside of the cabin, the teleporter needs to be done as a zone instead of attached to the door.

Door

45. On the Level 1 map, edit Door_Outside01, and remove the teleporter programming from it. This is done by editing the script, right-clicking on the programming block, and selecting **Delete** from the shortcut menu.

Zone

46. Add a zone named Zone_CabinExit in front of the cabin door that teleports the player character to the Yard_Front map. Change layer visibility as needed to help.

Test Game

47. Test play the game. You should be able to walk in and out of the cabin flawlessly. Debug the game as needed. Note, however, because of the zone in front of the door inside the cabin, the player will not be able to activate the opening of the door.

NPC Dialog

The player gets most information for a quest from interactions with game objects and from dialogue with other characters. Interaction with the book in the Level 1 map stated that there would be someone outside the cabin to provide more information to the player. In this section, you will construct the basic dialog structure and control the conversation between the player and the NPC the player meets outside the cabin.

Actor

48. Add an NPC actor next to the cabin on the Yard_Front map. Name the actor Friend_01. Be creative in designing the appearance of the NPC, but make sure the actor is assigned to the Good group.

49. Add a **Talked to/Activated** trigger.

50. In the **Actor Script** dialog box, add a Once Branch block. Then, add the remaining programming as illustrated in **Figure 5.** This programming creates the basic dialogue between the player character and the NPC. Notice that two **No** nodes lead to the same Message Box block. The message in this block will help direct the player action to the well even if the quest is refused.

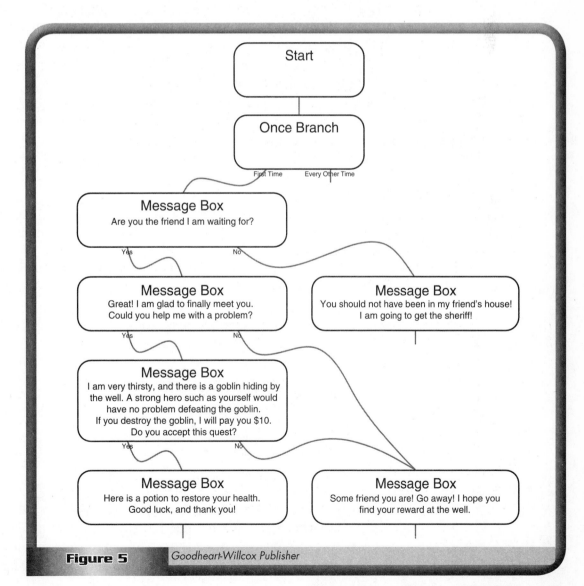

Figure 5   *Goodheart-Willcox Publisher*

51. Click the bottom node of the "here is a potion" **Message Box** block to make the node active.

52. Click the **Expand & Events** button at the bottom of the **Actor Script** dialog box.

Specifics

53. At the top of the **Actor Script** dialog box, click the **Specifics** button. This displays all commands in the dialog box.

54. Click in the search box at the bottom of the dialog box, and enter health. This limits the command displayed to only health-related commands. There should be two commands displayed.

55. Double-click the Change Health command. The **Change Health** dialog box is displayed, as shown in **Figure 6.**

56. In the **Actor:** area, select this and 0:Hero. The command will be applied only in the current map and only to the hero.

57. Click the **Health:** drop-down list, and click **Set** in the list.

58. Next to **Health:** drop-down list is a text box followed by an option button. Click the option button to display the **Use Value** dialog box.

59. In the **Use Value** dialog box, expand the Actor branch of the tree, select the Maximum Health leaf, and click the **Select** button. The **Maximum Health** dialog box is displayed.

60. In the **Maximum Health** dialog box, select this and 0:Hero, and click the **OK** button. The **Change Health** dialog box is redisplayed. Notice the programming code that now appears in the **Health:** text box. An explicit number could be entered, but having the game engine find the maximum health value and automatically set the character's health back to that amount is the correct way to do this.

61. Click the **OK** button to close the **Change Health** dialog box.

62. Click the **OK** button to close the **Actor Script** dialog box. There is more programming that needs to be added to the NPC, but this will be done later.

63. Click the **OK** button to close the **Actor: NPC** dialog box.

64. Save your work.

Goblin Objective

The dialogue with the NPC will lead the player to the well, even if the player does not accept the quest. The NPC dialog also indicated a goblin will be defending the well. The goblin NPC needs to be added to the game.

65. Place a goblin NPC on top of the well. Create it as described in **Figure 7.** Be creative with the other character attributes.

Actor
Actor

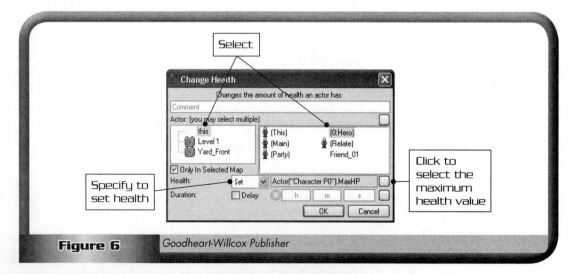

Figure 6   *Goodheart-Willcox Publisher*

Name	Direction	Attack	Weapon	Team	Initially Existent
Goblin_01	Up	3	Knife	Bad	No
Figure 7		*Goodheart-Willcox Publisher*			

Zone

66. Create a zone named Zone_Well to completely cover the well. In this way, when the player gets close to the well from any direction the zone will be activated.

67. In the **Zone** dialog box, select the first Collided with Actor in the **Trigger** area, and then click the **Edit Script** button.

68. In the **Zone Script** dialog box, click the **Expand & Events** button, and search for existence.

69. Double-click the **Change Existence** command in the **Actor** area.

70. In the **Change Existence** dialog box that is displayed, select this and Goblin_01, click the **Existent** radio button, and click the **OK** button, as shown in **Figure 8**.

71. Close the **Zone Script** dialog box and the **Zone** dialog box.

Testing

Test Game

Before you continue, test play the game. Check that the goblin, well zone, and health restoration work properly. To correctly test all of these elements, you will need to:

- collect the wand in the cabin;
- attack the ghost and let it take some health from you;
- exit the cabin;
- talk to the NPC by pressing the [Enter] key, and see if your health is restored to maximum;
- go to the well; and
- see if the goblin appears.

Debug the game as need if you find any errors.

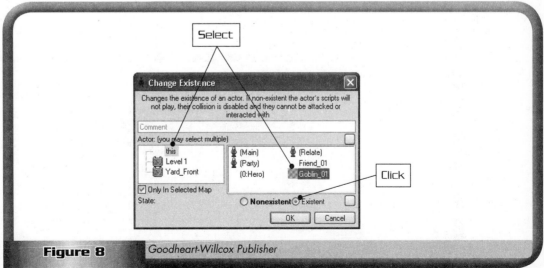

Figure 8	*Goodheart-Willcox Publisher*

Switches

Switches in programming are just like the light switches you have in your home. However, instead of turning on or off lights, they turn on or off scripts. When programming a quest, you can use a switch so an NPC will know when the quest is complete. In this game, the friend NPC should know when the goblin is defeated so the player can return and get paid the ten dollars.

Actor

72. Edit the Goblin_01 actor, and add a new trigger for killed/destroyed.

73. In the **Actor Script** dialog box, double-click the Switch Operation command in the **Switches** area.

74. In the **Switch Operation** dialog box that is displayed, click the **Switch: Edit** button. The **Switches** dialog box is displayed, which is where a new switch is created, as shown in **Figure 9.**

75. Click in the first **Name:** text box, and enter Quest_Well. Close the **Switches** dialog box. This creates a new switch called Quest_Well.

76. In the **Switch Operation** dialog box, click the **Switch:** drop-down list, and click **Quest_Well** in the list.

77. In the **Action:** area, click the **Turn ON** radio button. This sets the state to which the switch will be set.

78. Click the **OK** button to close the **Switch Operation** dialog box.

79. Close the **Actor Script** dialog box.

80. Close the **Actor: NPC** dialog box.

Switch Dialogue

The friend NPC can now be programmed to recognize when the goblin is destroyed. This is done by having the game engine check if the Quest_Well switch is on (goblin is dead) or off (goblin is alive).

Actor

81. Edit the Friend_01 actor.

82. Edit the Talked to/Activated script.

83. Select the Every Other Time node on the bottom of the Once Branch block.

84. Double-click on the **Switch Branch** command in the **Switches** area.

85. In the **Switch Branch** dialog box, click the **Switch:** drop-down list, and click **Quest_ Well** in the list. Click the **OK** button to close the dialog box. The Switch Branch block is added, and there are two nodes below it, one for on and one for off.

86. Click the "on" node, and add a Message Box block that includes the message Thank you for getting that Goblin. Here is your reward.

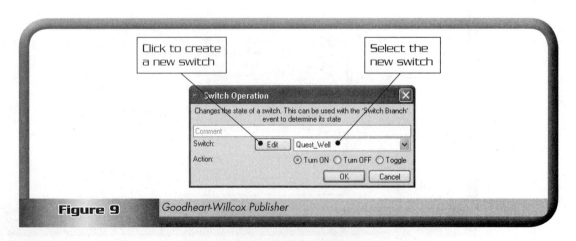

Figure 9 *Goodheart-Willcox Publisher*

87. Click the node below this new Message Box block, add double-click the **Change Money** command in the **Current Player/Party** area. The **Change Money** dialog box is displayed.

88. Click the **Amount of Money:** drop-down list, and click **Add** in the list, as shown in **Figure 10.** Enter 10 in the text box to the right of the drop-down list, and then click the **OK** button to close the dialog box.

89. In the **Actor Script** dialog box, add a Message Box block below the Change Money block that includes the message If you want more adventure, there are some treasures in the forest that is just past the well. Have a safe journey. This information will aid player navigation and allow the player to understand that the road past the well leads to the forest.

90. Click the "off" node of the Switch Branch block, and add a Message Box block that includes the message I think I left my treasure at the well, did you see it?.

91. Close the **Actor Script** dialog box, and close the **Actor: NPC** dialog box.

The last message helps redirect the player to the well to complete the quest even if the quest was not initially accepted. In this game, the player is continually directed to the well with each branch dialogue. The player could have accepted the quest and receive $10 on completion, or do the quest some other time for no money. Either way, the goblin will attack and need to be defeated, which helps the player gain skill.

Player Navigation

Remember the sign object that was placed by the well? Signs are a great way to give the player information about navigation and hazards in the game. You will now add information to the sign.

Zone

Zone

92. Add a zone named Zone_Nav01 that completely covers the sign object.

93. Select the trigger Action key pressed beside zone, and edit the script for the trigger.

94. Add a Message Box block that includes the message Beware of goblins! Forest to the east, an inn to the west, and unknown adventure awaits to the south. Now, when the player reads the sign, he or she will know where the roads will lead.

Extending the Game

You have the basic skills needed to create a simple, playable RPG. You can now complete additional maps for the game. The tasks below will extend the game beyond the front yard.

95. Enhance the front yard map with background music, including music for battle with the goblin, and other elements to increase player immersion.

96. Review the **Beginner's Tutorial** in the **Help** pull-down menu. Then, create a map for an inn located in the west direction (exit to the left) from the front yard.

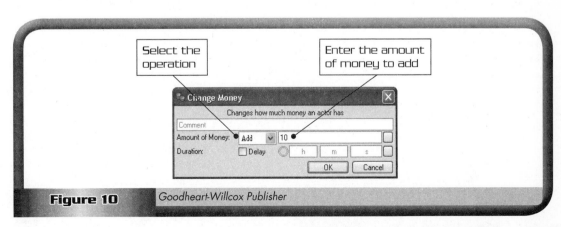

Figure 10   Goodheart-Willcox Publisher

97. Add a map to the east (exit to the right) for a forest. Be creative. Include trees, roads, and rivers to create an appropriate scene. Be aware to create a meaningful quest.

98. Create a map and an adventure to the south (exit to the bottom) of the front yard. Design a meaningful quest, and include appropriate thematic elements.

99. Test play the game, and debug any errors as needed.

100. Save your work.

Test Game

Feedback

Share your game with a classmate or friend to get feedback on how well the game functions and what elements were most enjoyed or most disliked. Make any changes you feel are necessary based on this feedback. Build a setup EXE file, and submit it for grading according to the directions provided by your instructor.

Review Questions

1. Why should the location of the cabin door in the Yard_Front map be in the same location left-to-right as the door in the Level 1 map?

   _____

   _____

2. What is teleporting in terms of gameplay?

   _____

   _____

3. Briefly describe why the cabin door cannot act as the teleporter in this game.

   _____

   _____

4. How is a programming switch used in this game?

   _____

   _____

5. Why does the dialog in this game continually direct the player to the well?

   _____

   _____

Chapter 4
Interface Composition

Objectives

After completing this chapter, you will be able to:
- Evaluate the HUD in existing video games.
- Design a basic HUD for a video game.
- Create a mockup of a HUD for a video game.
- Create a HUD for a video game.

sriwip/Shutterstock.com

Goodheart-Willcox Publisher; Picshve/Shutterstock.com

Goodheart-Willcox Publisher

Bellwork

Day	Date	Activity	Response
1		Complete the anticipation guide and the K and W columns of the KWL chart for this chapter.	
2		What does it mean to define the audience for a game?	
3		List four demographic data and the result for yourself.	
4		What evidence suggests that the designers for the original Xbox controller misunderstood the audience?	
5		List the three key items about the audience that the design must understand.	
6		Define *audience appeal*.	
7		List two types of audience-based testing.	
8		List five input devices used in video games.	
9		List three output devices used in video games.	
10		List the eight golden rules for human-computer interface design.	
11		How does increasing the clock speed on a processor improve performance?	

Day	Date	Activity	Response
12		The word *sans* means without. What characteristics make up a font in the sans serifs group?	
13		What trade-off is made when using a text box with a high alpha channel value to avoid gameplay interference?	
14		What are shell menus and shell screens?	
15		How does rollover help text work?	
16		How is the use of a cheat code unethical?	
17		Describe how your computer workspace at home differs from the recommendations for an ergonomic workstation in Figure 4-10. Does your home setup make you tired or sore?	
18		What is the purpose of "wings" on a game controller?	
19		Why do keyboard buttons require force to press while your smartphone text buttons do not?	
20		Complete the L column of the KWL chart and the After Reading column of the anticipation guide with what you learned from this chapter.	
21		Speculate how motion-capture controllers can cause injuries. List four injuries you think are most frequent.	

Anticipation Guide

Directions

Before reading the chapter, read each statement in the table below. In the column titled Before Reading, write the letter *T* if you agree with the statement or *F* if you disagree with the statement. After reading the chapter, reread each statement in the table below. In the column titled After Reading, write the letter *T* if you agree with the statement or *F* if you disagree with the statement. Be prepared to justify your answers in a class discussion.

Before Reading	Statement	After Reading
	A typical player profile helps designers understand the audience for a game.	
	Mental acuity is a measure of the intelligence of the player.	
	There are ten golden rules for human-computer interface design.	
	Input devices should be designed to conform to ergonomic use.	
	Including serifs on a font type will make them easier to read.	

KWL Chart

Directions

Before reading the chapter, fill in what you already know about the topic in the K column and what you want to learn in the W column. After reading the chapter, review what you know and wanted to learn about the topic. Reflect on what you have studied and completed in this chapter. Fill in what you learned in the L column. Be prepared to justify your answers in a class discussion.

Topic: Game Interface and Controls		
K What you already *know*	**W** What you *want* to learn	**L** What you *learned*

Activity 4-1

HUD Exploration

Objectives

Students will identify features of heads-up displays in existing games. Students will evaluate the importance, placement, and dominance of features in a heads-up display. Students will examine and explain how menus and other information storage are used in the design of a heads-up display.

Situation

The Really Cool Game Company will be developing a game that must store over 50 data types, such as player score, health points, magic points, weapon selection, ammo, and more, throughout the game. These data types will have to be displayed to the player at some point during gameplay. Since it is impossible to display all of these data types at once, the design of the heads-up display (HUD) for different scenes will be very important. Only the most important data can be displayed to the player at a given time, and the rest must be located in menus or displayed when the game is paused. Your job is to examine several different games and evaluate how the HUD is constructed.

How to Begin

1. Launch PowerPoint.
2. Create a title slide with the title **HUD Exploration** and a subtitle of your first and last name.
3. Save the presentation as *LastName_*HUD Exploration in your working folder.
4. Minimize PowerPoint.

Examining Data

5. Launch the Internet browser, and navigate to www.alfy.com or other free gaming site as directed by your instructor.
6. Locate four games that use a HUD to present game data, and play each one for no more than five minutes to familiarize yourself with the functions in the HUD. Do not select any games with inappropriate content.
7. Complete a HUD Evaluation Chart for each game to evaluate how well the game data are displayed.
8. List each game data feature used in the game or shown on the HUD. List all data features, including those displayed in menus, included on other pages, or omitted.
9. List where the game data feature is shown (HUD, drop-down menu, etc.).
10. Rank the importance of each data feature, with 10 being very important and 1 being not important at all.
11. Rank the dominance of each data feature, with 10 being large and dominant object, 1 being very small, and 0 being not shown at all.
12. Take a screen capture of each game by pressing the [Print Screen] key. Make sure the HUD is visible when the screen is captured.
13. Paste each screen capture into the HUD Exploration PowerPoint on a slide by itself.
14. Crop the screen capture as needed to best display the game.

15. Add the name of the game as a title on the slide, and add a text box to cite the source of the screen capture.

16. Use arrows and text boxes to identify the data displayed on the HUD.

Console Game HUD

17. Choose two of your favorite console games (Xbox 360, PS3, or Wii), and use the Internet to locate screen captures for each game that shows the HUD.

18. Complete a HUD Evaluation chart for each game.

19. Add the screen captures to the PowerPoint presentation. Include identification of HUD elements, the game name, and cite the source of the screen capture on each slide.

Handheld Game HUD

20. Using the Internet to locate screen captures for *Call of Duty: Black Ops* for the PS3.

21. Using the Internet to locate screen captures for *Call of Duty: Black Ops* for the Nintendo DS.

22. Complete a HUD Evaluation chart for each game.

23. Add the screen captures to the PowerPoint presentation. Include identification of HUD elements, the game name, and cite the source of the screen capture on each slide.

Higher-Order Thinking Strategy (HOTS) Activity 1

24. Add a new slide to the end of the PowerPoint presentation, and create a Venn diagram by drawing two overlapping ovals, as shown in **Figure 1.**

25. For each oval, set the fill color to no fill.

26. Add the title Call of Duty: Black Ops at the top of the slide.

27. Add text boxes to label each area of the Venn diagram, as shown in **Figure 1.**

28. Add text boxes below each label in the Venn diagram, and compare and contrast the HUD for the PS3 and Nintendo DS versions of *Call of Duty: Black Ops*.

29. Save your work.

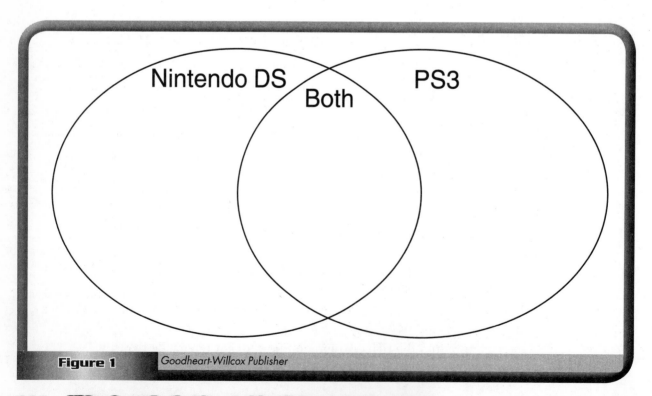

Figure 1 | *Goodheart-Willcox Publisher*

Name: _____

HOTS Activity 2

30. Choose one of the games for which you completed a HUD Evaluation chart.
31. In a blank Microsoft Word document, add a header of your name and class period.
32. Save the document as *LastName*_HUD Evaluation in your working folder.
33. Add the title HUD Evaluation for *GameName* at the top of the document. Format the title so it is centered, bold, and 20 point Times New Roman font.
34. Write an introduction paragraph describing the game, gameplay, and what data need to be accessed in the game.
35. In the second paragraph, describe the good elements of the HUD for this game.
36. In the third paragraph, describe the poor elements of the HUD for this game.
37. In the fourth paragraph, draw conclusions on how to improve the HUD for this game.
38. Save your work.

Demonstration

39. Present your PowerPoint slide show to the class. Briefly describe the HUD from each game pictured, the good and bad things about each HUD, and state any improvements to the HUD you feel are needed for better gameplay.
40. Submit all documents for grading.

HUD Evaluation Charts

Game Name			
Data Feature	HUD or Menu	Importance (1 to 10)	Dominance (1 to 10)

Game Name			
Data Feature	HUD or Menu	Importance (1 to 10)	Dominance (1 to 10)

Game Name			
Data Feature	HUD or Menu	Importance (1 to 10)	Dominance (1 to 10)

Name: _____

Game Name			
Data Feature	HUD or Menu	Importance (1 to 10)	Dominance (1 to 10)

Game Name			
Data Feature	HUD or Menu	Importance (1 to 10)	Dominance (1 to 10)

Game Name			
Data Feature	HUD or Menu	Importance (1 to 10)	Dominance (1 to 10)

Game Name			
Data Feature	HUD or Menu	Importance (1 to 10)	Dominance (1 to 10)

Name: _____

Game Name			
Data Feature	HUD or Menu	Importance (1 to 10)	Dominance (1 to 10)

Activity 4-2

HUD Development

Objectives

Students will use ergonomic principles to create game displays that convey meaningful information to the player, including scoring and asset control. Students will use game documents used to design representative frames for a game with a story.

Situation

The Really Cool Game Company has reviewed your RPG design documents from Chapter 3. The decision makers want to see how the interactive elements of your game will be delivered to the player. You need to create a presentation that will show a mock-up of how the heads-up display (HUD) will be integrated into the game. The game frames are not working frames, only display samples of how the game-interaction elements will be arranged in the HUD. Work with your team to design an appropriate HUD layout.

How to Begin

1. Working with the team formed in Activity 3-2, or other team as directed by your instructor, review the story documents from that activity.

2. Determine what information the player will need as he or she works through the tasks and story during gameplay.

3. In the HUD Planning Document, list each game feature that needs to be displayed to the player.

4. Rank the importance of each feature, and use that information to determine the dominance the feature should have on the screen. Remember, not all information needs to be displayed on the HUD. Some information should be displayed in a menu that the player can display when the game action is paused. Other information can be displayed on the title frame, ending frame, or a frame other than the game-level frame.

5. Use PowerPoint, Photoshop, or other appropriate software to create a representative game frame based on the environmental illustrations created in Activity 3-2. A representative scene is one that looks like it might be something from the game. It should include typical game elements, a background, and thematic elements.

6. Add the needed HUD elements to the representative game frame. Place the elements using ergonomic principles so that the HUD does not obscure the gameplay.

7. Create a title frame for the game.

8. Create an ending frame for the game.

9. Create any additional frames needed to display game data not shown in the HUD on the game frame.

10. Save the PowerPoint presentation (import frames as needed) as *TeamName*_Frames in your working folder.

11. Present the HUD design to the class, and explain the elements of the HUD and other frames.

12. Submit all work for grading.

Name: _____

HUD Planning Document

Game Feature	Displayed On (HUD or menu)	Frame Displayed (game, title, etc.)	Importance (1 to 10)	Dominance (1 to 10)

Activity 4-3

Interface Mockup

Objectives

Student will synthesize a mockup for a new game controller. Students will apply the six principles of interface ergonomics in the design of a controller. Students will explain how the features of a controller align to the principles of interface ergonomics and the golden rules of human computer interface design.

Situation

The Really Cool Game Company continues to be impressed with your skill, talent, and work ethic. A new client received funding to make video games more accessible to children with disabilities. The current design of the PlayStation and Xbox controllers has small buttons and other features that make it difficult for these children to use. The major issue with these current controllers is to properly activate the controls, a high degree of fine motor skills is needed. Your job will be to design a controller that requires less fine motor skills, but still has all of the features and functions of the standard controller.

How to Begin

1. Working with the team formed in Activity 3-2, or other team as directed by your instructor, choose a standard controller from a popular game system to redesign.

2. Research alternatives to using the standard control buttons. Keep in mind that the objective is to reduce the level of fine motor skills required to use the controller, such as reducing the amount of finger movement.

3. Create a physical mockup of a new controller using cardboard, foam, or any other resource available. Wiring, electronics, and other working parts are not required for a mockup.

4. Hold and test the device, and then make any changes needed to refine the shape, button placement, or other features.

5. Using a digital camera, take photographs of the mockup.

6. Create a PowerPoint presentation that shows how each of the six principles of interface ergonomics was integrated into the design and how it fits the target audience. Incorporate the digital photographs, and include lines and arrows to point out features.

7. Determine if this controller can be a better alternative for players without disabilities. Include a slide in the presentation explaining why or why not.

8. Present the slide show to the class, and demonstrate how the new controller device better meets the needs of children with disabilities.

9. Submit all materials for grading.

Activity 4-4

Custom HUD Composition

Objectives

Students will design a custom heads-up display (HUD). Students will evaluate the importance of gameplay elements and player information to display on the HUD. Students will create custom programming to allow the player to display game and navigational information.

Situation

The Really Cool Game Company has reviewed your work on the RPG game you have been creating. Beta testers felt that it was difficult to see all of the information needed to control weapons and understand their character's status. Knowing that you have the skills to design a better player-information system, the company has decided to train you on how to customize the HUD settings for the 001 Game Creator game engine software so you can implement a custom HUD and information system in your game.

How to Begin

1. Launch 001 Game Creator.
2. Create a new action/RPG game in your working folder named *LastName*_HUD.

Removing a Default HUD Element

3. In the bottom-left corner of the screen, click the **Interfaces** tab to display the HUD asset tree.
4. Click the HUD branch in the tree. The heads-up display overlay is displayed, as shown in **Figure 1.** This is what will appear on top of the game map during gameplay. You should recognize the red circle in the upper-left corner, which is the display of the player character's health. The rectangular bar in the center of the circle is a field holding the programming for the element HUD. Hover the cursor over the bar in the red circle, and HP is displayed as help text.
5. Right-click on the **HP** field in the red circle, and click **Delete** in the shortcut menu. This removes the default health element from the HUD.

Creating a New HUD

If the game were created with the HUD in its current state, the player would have little information on his or her character's health. You will create a new HUD that includes an element to display the character's health to the player. The new element will be of a different design than the default to better match the theme of the game.

6. Right-click on the HUD branch in the HUD asset tree, and click **New** in the shortcut menu. If a message appears asking to save the open interface, click the **Yes** button.
7. In the **Interface Properties** dialog box, click in the **Display Name:** text box, and enter Health_Bar_HUD, as shown in **Figure 2.**
8. Click the **OK** button to close the **Interface Properties** dialog box. The new HUD layout is added to the HUD asset tree, and a blank layout is displayed in the drawing area.

Click

Player character's health

Current HUD layout

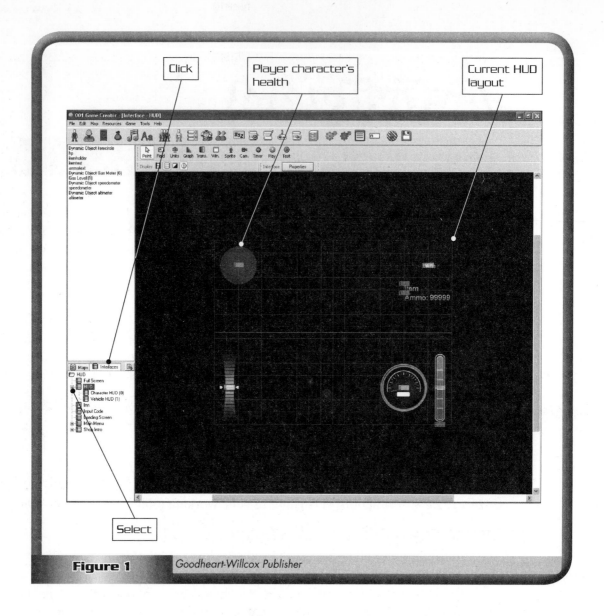

Figure 1

Enter the element name and scripting ID

Select

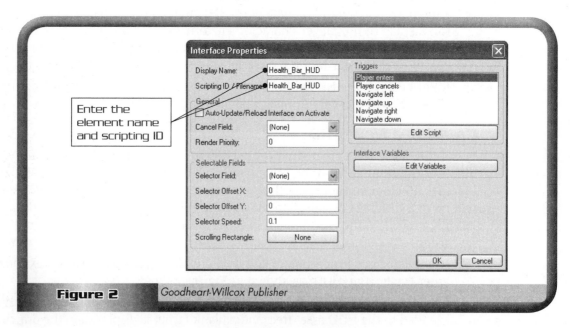

Figure 2

Text/Graphic Field

9. Click the **Text/Graphic Field** button on the toolbar.

10. Click at position (0,0,0) to place the field in that location. The coordinates are displayed on the toolbar as you move the mouse. When you click, the **Field** dialog box is displayed, as shown in **Figure 3.**

11. Click in the **Display Name:** text box, and enter HP. Enter HP in the **Scripting ID:** text box as well; dismiss the warning.

12. Click in the **Initial Text:** text box, and enter Health.

13. In the **Behavior** area, click the **Text Font:** drop-down list, and click **Health Font** in the list. This is a bolder font than the main font.

14. In the **Visual** area, click the **Normal** tab, click the left-hand **Color:** swatch, and select a red color in the **Color** dialog box. This sets the top of the text to red.

15. Click the right-hand **Color:** swatch, and select a yellow color. This sets the bottom of the text to yellow. A gradient blends the top and bottom colors.

16. Drag both **Opacity:** sliders to the middle. This changes each color to semitransparent.

17. Click the **OK** button to close the **Field** dialog box and create the HUD element.

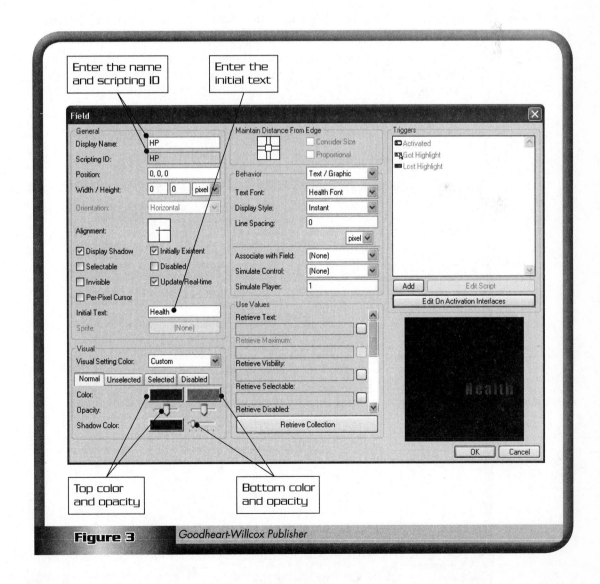

Figure 3   *Goodheart-Willcox Publisher*

Creating a Graphic for a HUD Element

A label has been created for the health element of the new HUD. Now, a graphic element needs to be created that will display to the player his or her character's changing health status.

Graph Field

18. Click the **Graph Field** button on the toolbar.

19. Click at position (0,16,0). The **Field** dialog box is displayed.

20. Enter HP_Bar in **Display Name:** and **Scripting ID:** text boxes.

21. Click in the left-hand **Width/Height:** text box, and enter 160. Click in the right-hand text box, enter 32. This value is in pixels. Each tile is 32 × 32, so these dimensions are five tiles (5 × 32 = 160) and one tile.

22. Click in the left-hand **Initial Value/Maximum:** text box, and enter 5. Click in the right-hand text box, and enter 10. This sets the starting value (initial) to a length of 5 and a maximum value of 10.

23. In the **Behavior** area, click the **Shape:** drop-down list, and click **Bar** in the list.

24. In the **Visual** area, change both color swatches to red, and drag both opacity sliders to about one-quarter from the left.

25. In the **Use Values** area, click the button to the right of the **Retrieve Value:** text box. The **Use Value** dialog box is displayed, as shown in **Figure 4.**

26. Expand the Actor branch, select the Health leaf, and click the **Select** button. This tells the game engine to look up the value of the actor's health.

27. In the **Health** dialog box that is displayed, select this and (main), and then click the **OK** button. This specifies the main character as the one from which to retrieve the health value.

28. Click the **OK** button to close the **Field** dialog box. The graphic display of health is added to the HUD, and it slightly overlaps the text Health because of the position initially selected.

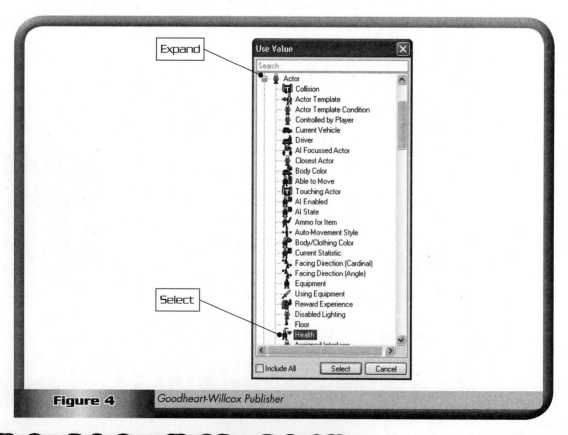

Figure 4   *Goodheart-Willcox Publisher*

Adding Experience Elements to the HUD

For consistency, it is important to have similar elements in the HUD be represented in a similar fashion. For this reason and to save time, copies will be made of the health interface elements and edited to create experience interface elements.

29. Right-click on the HP health text field, and click **Copy** in the shortcut menu.

30. Right-click below the HP_Bar health bar, and click **Paste** in the shortcut menu. The HP text field is copied to that location and renamed with a sequential number, such as HP 2.

31. Right-click on the copied field, and click **Edit** in the shortcut menu. The **Field** dialog box is displayed.

32. Change the display name and scripting ID to XP, the text color to a cool blue top with a grey bottom, and the initial text to Experience.

33. Click in the Position: text box, and enter 0,80,0. This sets the location of the insertion point for the text field.

34. Click the **OK** button to close the **Field** dialog box and update the text field.

35. Similarly, copy the HP_Bar health bar, and paste it below the XP experience text field.

36. Edit the copied bar, and change the display name and scripting ID to XP_Bar.

37. Change both color swatches to a cool blue.

38. Set the position to (0,96,0).

39. Change the retrieved value to Main Party/Game > Member > Experience, as shown in **Figure 5.** Select Hero as the member in the **Experience** dialog box.

40. Close the **Field** dialog box, and examine the HUD. It should appear similar to **Figure 6.**

41. Edit the XP_Bar experience bar.

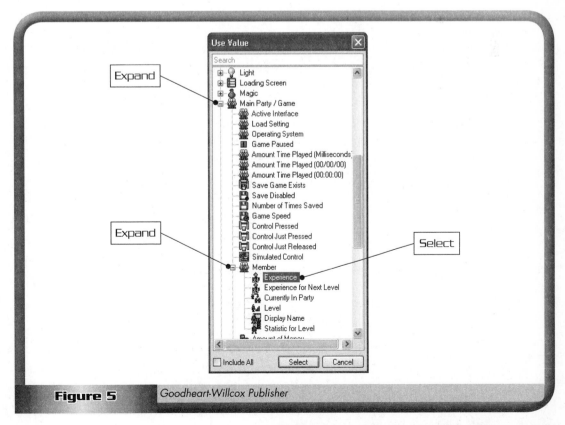

Figure 5 *Goodheart-Willcox Publisher*

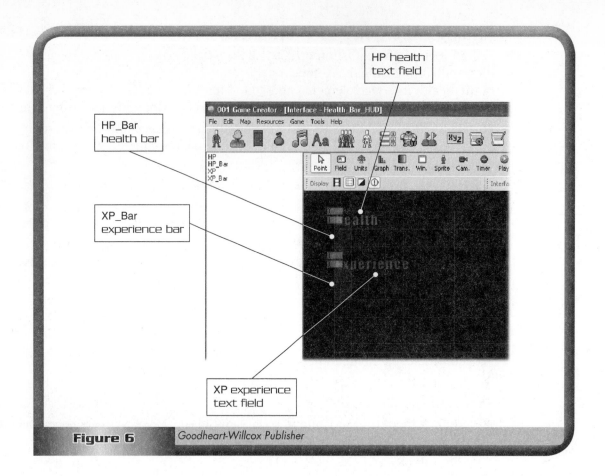

HP health
text field

HP_Bar
health bar

XP_Bar
experience bar

XP experience
text field

Figure 6   *Goodheart-Willcox Publisher*

42. Using what you have learned, program the **Retrieve Maximum:** entry to retrieve the experience points for the next level for the hero and player 1.

43. Close the **Field** dialog box, and examine how the HUD has improved.

Adding a Money Display

44. Copy the HP health text field, and edit it. Change the display name and scripting ID to Money, the top color to light green, the bottom color to yellow, the initial text to Money, and the position to (0,160,0).

45. Copy of the Money text field, and paste the copy below the Money text field. Since the money display is a numerical value, a text field is used instead of the bar graph that is used for health and experience.

46. Edit the copy, and change the display name and scripting ID to Money_Amount, the position to (0,185,90), the initial text to 1000, and the top color to yellow.

47. Click the button to the right of the **Retrieve Text:** text box. The **Use Value** dialog box is displayed.

48. Click in the search text box at the top of the **Use Value** dialog box, and enter money. This narrows the options displayed to find the items you are looking for easier and quicker.

49. Expand the Main Party/Game branch, and select the Amount of Money leaf, as shown in **Figure 7.** This will retrieve the amount of money the player has and display it as text. Click the **Select** button to close the **Use Value** dialog box.

50. Click the **OK** button to close the **Field** dialog box, and examine the HUD. There should be a row of health, experience, and money displays on the left-hand side of the HUD.

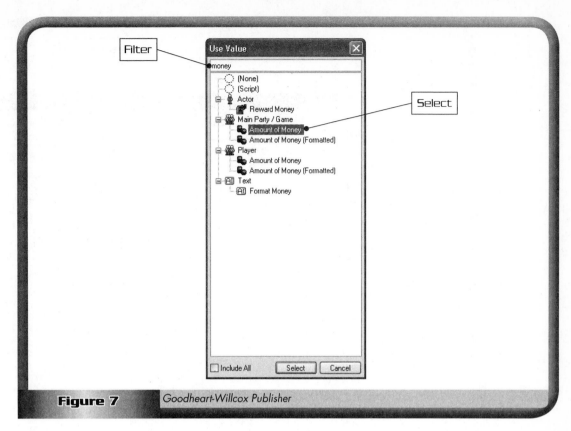

Figure 7   *Goodheart-Willcox Publisher*

User Interactivity

You have created a new, custom HUD. Now, programming needs to be added to give the player the option of showing or hiding the HUD. A toggle key will be added that displays or hides the HUD.

Controls

51. Click the **Controls** button on the main toolbar. The **Controls** dialog box is displayed, as shown in **Figure 8.**

52. Click the **Add Control** button at the top of the **Controls** dialog box. A blank entry is added to the bottom of the dialog box.

53. Click in the **Display Name:** text box for the blank entry, and enter Toggle_HUD. Enter this in the **Scripting ID:** text box as well.

54. Click the **Add** button in the **Player 1** area of the new entry. The **Input** dialog box is displayed.

55. In the Input dialog box, make sure **Key/Gamepad** is selected in the drop-down list, click in the text box to the right of the drop-down list, and enter H. This sets the control to the [H] key.

56. Click the **OK** button to close the **Input** dialog box.

57. Click the **OK** button to close the **Controls** dialog box.

Updating the HUD Information

58. Select the HUD branch in the HUD asset tree. If prompted, save the current interface.

Timer

Timer/Spawn

59. Click the **Timer/Spawn** button on the toolbar.

60. Click anywhere to place the timer; it will not be displayed during gameplay. The **Timer/Spawn** dialog box is displayed, as shown in **Figure 9.**

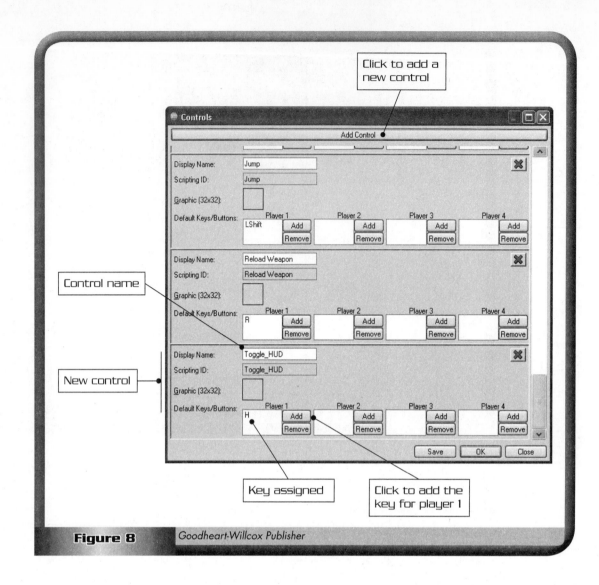

Click to add a new control

Control name

New control

Key assigned

Click to add the key for player 1

Figure 8   Goodheart-Willcox Publisher

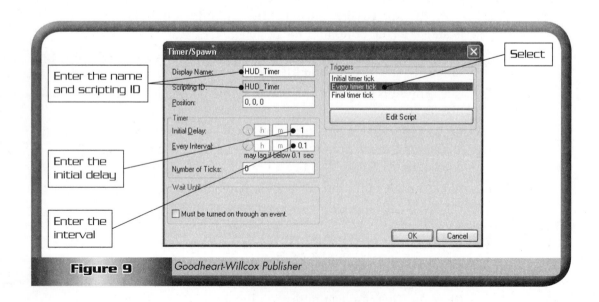

Enter the name and scripting ID

Select

Enter the initial delay

Enter the interval

Figure 9   Goodheart-Willcox Publisher

61. Enter HUD_Timer as the display name and scripting ID.

62. Click in the right-hand **Initial Delay:** text box, which is the number of seconds, and enter 1.

63. Click in the right-hand **Every Interval:** text box, which is the number of seconds, and enter 0.1.

64. In the **Triggers** area, select Every timer tick, and click the **Edit Script** button.

65. Double-click **Switch Branch** in the **Switches** area. The **Switch Branch** dialog box is displayed.

66. In the **Switch Branch** dialog box, click the **Edit** button. Add a switch named Health_HUD, and set it to be on. Refer to Activity 3-4 if you do not recall how to do this.

67. Select the Health_HUD as the switch in the **Switch Branch** dialog box, and click the **OK** button to close the dialog box.

68. In the **Spawn Script** dialog box, make sure the "on" node is active on the Switch Branch block, and then click the **Expand & Events** button.

69. Click the **Input Sets** option on the left. You may need to click the **Advanced** button to make this option available.

70. Double-click the **Wait for Control** option. The **Wait for Control** dialog box is displayed.

71. In the **Wait for Control** dialog box, select **Toggle HUD Control**, and click the **OK** button. This is the new control added earlier.

72. In the **Spawn Script** dialog box, click the **Expand & Events** button.

73. Click the **Interfaces** option on the left, and double-click the **Show/Hide Interface** option on the right. You may need to click the **Intermediate** button to display this option.

74. In the **Show/Hide Interface** dialog box, select **Health_Bar_HUD** in the **Interface:** list, as shown in **Figure 10.**

75. In the **Turn:** area, click the **On** radio button.

76. In the **Interaction:** area, click the **Overlay** radio button.

77. In the **Bring to Front:** area, click the **Yes** radio button.

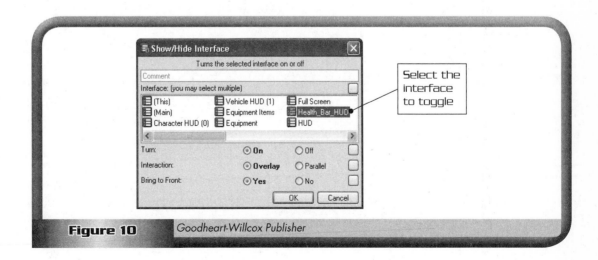

Figure 10   *Goodheart-Willcox Publisher*

78. Click the **OK** button to close the **Show/Hide Interface** dialog box.

79. In the **Spawn Script** dialog box, double-click **Switch Operation** in the **Switches** area.

80. In the **Switch Operation** dialog box, select **Health_HUD** in the drop-down list, click the **Turn Off** radio button, and click the **OK** button to close the dialog box.

81. Using skills you have learned, connect the bottom of the Switch Operation block to the top of the Switch Branch block.

82. Click the "off" node at the bottom of the Switch Branch block to activate it.

83. Using skills you have learned, program a Wait for Control block to look for the Toggle_HUD control, a Show/Hide Interface block to turn off the display of the Health_Bar_HUD interface, a Switch Operation block to turn on the Health_HUD switch, and connect this programming back to the Switch Branch block. Refer to **Figure 11.**

Test Game

84. Test play the game. Test toggling the new HUD on and off. This is the only thing that can be tested as no other game elements have been created.

85. Debug and fix any errors.

Tuning

In the game's current state, you cannot test if the HUD is correctly displaying player statistics. Challenges and rewards need to be added to the game to test if the HUD is working properly.

86. Using skills you have learned, program an enemy that will reduce the player character's health.

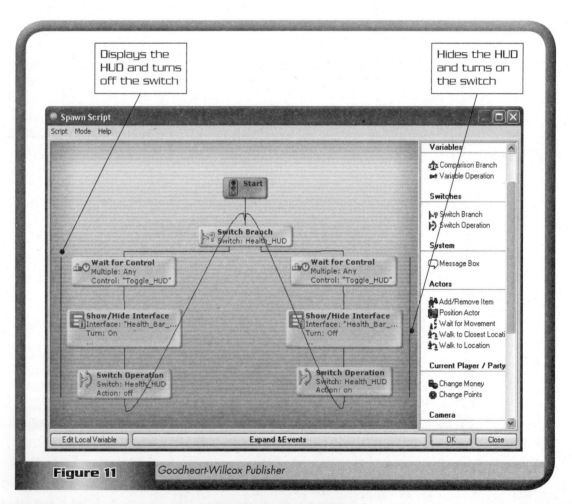

Figure 11   *Goodheart-Willcox Publisher*

87. Program the enemy to reward the player with 10 experience points and $10.

88. Program the player character with an attack that can easily defeat the enemy.

Test Game

89. Test play the game, and see how well the custom HUD provides information to the player.

Better Information

The HUD looks and functions great, but it could display more information to better aid the player. You will now add level-up information to the HUD and provide the player with more detailed health and experience information. This will allow the player to know what is required to level-up and the maximum values for health and experience, which will help the player pace the action and progress of the game. As the game progresses, a player will usually have greater maximum health and experience levels.

90. Select Health_Bar_HUD in the asset tree.

Text/Graphic Field

91. Create a new text field with the display name and scripting ID of HP#, the initial text of 100, and retrieve text from the main actor's health. The position and text colors are your choice.

92. Create a new text field with the display name and scripting ID of HP_Max, the initial text of 100, and retrieve text from the main actor's maximum health. Position and text colors are your choice.

93. Create a new text field with the initial text of ___ (three underscores).

Pointer

94. Click the **Point** button, and move the three new text fields into position over the health bar as shown in **Figure 12**. This allows the player to see a ratio of current health (top) over maximum health (bottom).

95. Similarly, create a ratio for the current experience points and the amount needed to level-up. Name the text fields XP# and XP_LevelUp. Refer to steps earlier in this activity if you do not recall how to retrieve experience points.

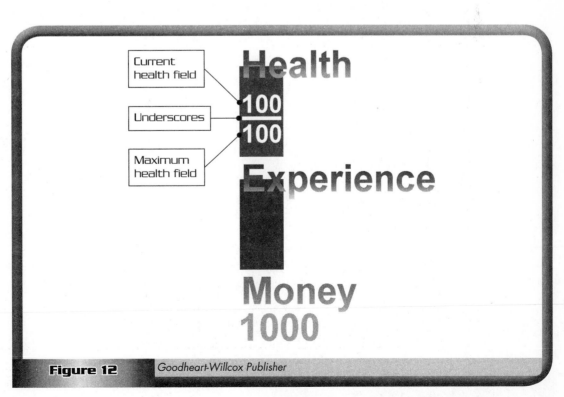

Figure 12   *Goodheart-Willcox Publisher*

Test Game

96. Test play the game, and debug the HUD if needed.

97. Save your work, build a setup EXE file, and submit it for grading according to the directions provided by your instructor.

Review Questions

1. How does this new HUD allow the player to see game action underneath?

_____

_____

2. Speculate why is it important to give the player the option of toggling the HUD on and off.

_____

_____

3. How does this new HUD improve gameplay immersion?

_____

_____

4. Why is it important to display the maximum health and experience values and the level-up requirement?

_____

_____

5. What other items would you include in the RPG custom HUD? Why?

_____

_____

Chapter 5
Immersion Composition

Objectives

After completing this chapter, you will be able to:

- Evaluate current video games to determine which competition model is used.
- Create a world map for use in a video game.
- Develop tile-based scenes for a video game.
- Construct a mod for an existing video game.

Goodheart-Willcox Publisher; images: Kristy Pargeter/Shutterstock.com, sellingpix/Shutterstock.com, roopert/Shutterstock.com, MarcelClemens/Shutterstock.com, martan/Shutterstock.com, 3drenderings/Shutterstock.com

Goodheart-Willcox Publisher; images: Andreas Meyer/Shutterstock.com, Algol/Shutterstock.com, Boris15/Shutterstock.com

Goodheart-Willcox Publisher; image: Ralf Juergen Kraft/Shutterstock.com, DarkGeometryStudios/Shutterstock.com

Bellwork

Day	Date	Activity	Response
1		Complete the anticipation guide and the K and W columns of the KWL chart for this chapter.	
2		Describe why anxiety for completing a task declines with age.	
3		What does it mean to escalate challenges for a game?	
4		Why is a sawtooth-challenge design preferred?	
5		What is challenge retracement, and why is it used in game design?	
6		How is token placement used as a navigational aid?	
7		Define *narrations*.	
8		Which is your favorite competition model? List three reasons why.	
9		Describe what intuitive physics would look like in a game world.	
10		Describe the three types of movement for a camera.	
11		What is out-of-scope action?	

Day	Date	Activity	Response
12		How do mods extend gameplay?	
13		Define *AI*. How is AI used to create a bot for a game?	
14		How is the use of a bot in an MMO game considered unethical?	
15		Summarize Moore's law.	
16		Why might players engage in a LAN party instead of playing at remote locations?	
17		List two ways the task of crossing a game map can be made more interesting to the player.	
18		How can a designer create a language-independent HUD?	
19		Define *back-office tasks.* Why should these tasks be automated for the player?	
20		What is the benefit to the designer of using a cookie-cutter design?	
21		Complete the L column of the KWL chart and the After Reading column of the anticipation guide with what you learned from this chapter.	
22		Speculate why games for children have increased in the difficulty of challenges versus similar games made 15 years ago.	

Anticipation Guide

Directions

Before reading the chapter, read each statement in the table below. In the column titled Before Reading, write the letter *T* if you agree with the statement or *F* if you disagree with the statement. After reading the chapter, reread each statement in the table below. In the column titled After Reading, write the letter *T* if you agree with the statement or *F* if you disagree with the statement. Be prepared to justify your answers in a class discussion.

Before Reading	Statement	After Reading
	Challenges should all increase in difficulty as the game progresses.	
	Team competitions are called multilateral competitions.	
	A type of camera movement in which the camera moves forward or backward, like walking in a first-person game, is called dolly movement.	
	Game mods have been developed into popular selling games.	
	Moore's law states that technology will eventually reach a point where it can augment human abilities.	

KWL Chart

Directions

Before reading the chapter, fill in what you already know about the topic in the K column and what you want to learn in the W column. After reading the chapter, review what you know and wanted to learn about the topic. Reflect on what you have studied and completed in this chapter. Fill in what you learned in the L column. Be prepared to justify your answers in a class discussion.

Topic: Game Competition		
K What you already *know*	**W** What you *want* to learn	**L** What you *learned*

Activity 5-1

Game Evaluation and Competition Models

Objectives

Students will determine the competition model used in a variety of current video games. Students will assess game attributes based on engagement and interest criteria.

Situation

Your team has been assigned to explore some of the most successful games available today. The point of this research is to discover the trends and techniques each uses to achieve engagement and maintain interest. Each game should be analyzed and data compiled for a presentation to the board of directors. Your result could help set the policy for future game production.

How to Begin

1. Form seven groups in the class, as directed by your instructor.
2. Each group will be assigned one competition model by your instructor. Refer to Figure 5-6 in the textbook and the associated text.
3. Using the Internet, personal experience, or other sources, research the assigned competition model. Identify at least four examples of current video game titles that are popular. The games may be for any game platform, console, or device.
4. Collaborate as a group to evaluate the games. Compare and contrast the games to discover what similarities exist between them.
5. Investigate game attributes used in each game to achieve the competition model.
6. Investigate game attributes used in each game to achieve engagement and interest.
7. Evaluate if the game is for a casual gamer or a core gamer. Describe why it is best suited for that type of game enthusiast.
8. Investigate the targeted customer base for each game to find the important demographics of the target market. Describe how the engagement and interest fit this market.
9. If possible, play each game for a few minutes to gain personal perspective on the features.
10. Form a group consensus on how successful each game is in achieving engagement and maintaining interest. Rank the games in order by how successful the game is at integrating engagement activities.
11. Create a five-minute PowerPoint presentation to summarize the information from your research.
12. Present the slide show to the class. Each member of the group must present a portion of the slide show.
13. Request questions, and respond appropriately to each question.

Activity 5-2

World Map Composition

Objectives

Students will develop an overview world map for use in creating individual game scenes. Students will create a player-interaction plan to detail the gameplay of the different world scenes. Students will outline implicit and explicit challenges for incorporation into gameplay design. Students will apply balancing elements to maintain player interest and player praise.

Situation

The Really Cool Game Company is very impressed with your ability to acquire new software skills and apply them to custom game design. They believe that you have what it takes to take the creative lead in designing a new game world for an RPG. Your job is to create a prototype map for a game world and to record all major gameplay interactions that will occur in the map sections. If your idea is approved, you and your team will be tasked with creating a proof of concept game for the game world.

How to Begin

1. Working with the team assigned by your instructor, brainstorm ideas for a game world.
2. Organize the ideas into scenes, towns, or areas of the game world. There must be at least five scenes that will exist in the game world.
3. In the World Overview Document, record the scene name, description and terrain, and major gameplay mode for each scene.
4. Using graph paper or a spreadsheet program such as Microsoft Excel, create a world map to show the location of each scene in the game world. An example done in Excel is shown in **Figure 1.**
5. Determine the pathways that the player should take to navigate the game world (linear, sandbox, branching, etc.) and the order in which a typical player would travel.
6. Construct pathways on the world map to achieve navigation and movement as needed.
7. Complete the Player Interaction Plan to detail the actions, challenges, and rewards for each scene. Include scenes from Starting through Ending.
8. Submit the World Overview Document, world map, and Player Interaction Plan for grading. Review with your instructor.

Name: _____

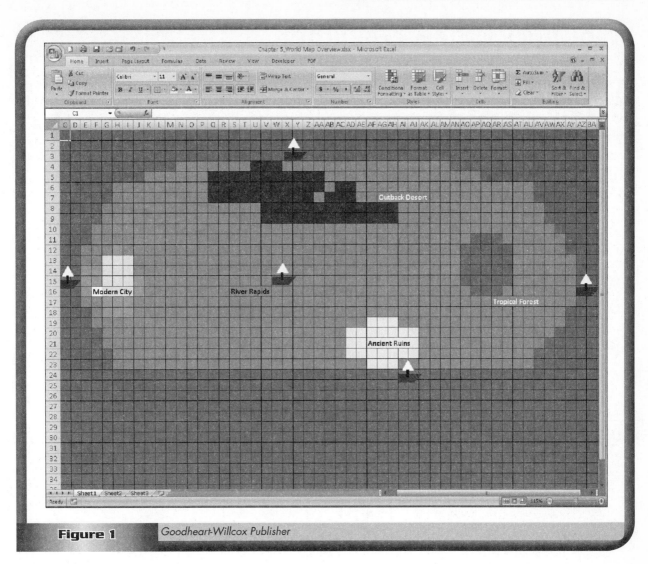

Figure 1 Goodheart-Willcox Publisher

World Overview Document

World Name:		
World Scene Name #1	**Brief Description of Scene and Terrain**	**Major Gameplay Mode or Activities**
World Scene Name #2	**Brief Description of Scene and Terrain**	**Major Gameplay Mode or Activities**
World Scene Name #3	**Brief Description of Scene and Terrain**	**Major Gameplay Mode or Activities**
World Scene Name #4	**Brief Description of Scene and Terrain**	**Major Gameplay Mode or Activities**
World Scene Name #5	**Brief Description of Scene and Terrain**	**Major Gameplay Mode or Activities**

Player Interaction Plan

Scene Name	Player Actions (Choose avatar, meet mentor, etc.)	Implicit Challenges (Build fire, mine coal, build housing, etc.)	Explicit Challenges (Disable circuit, pick lock, etc.)	Rewards (health points, experience points, items, praise, etc.)
Starting				
Ending				

Activity 5-3

Scene Navigation and World Creation

Objectives

Students will create tile-based scenes for a game world. Students will program scenes to provide navigation throughout the game world. Students will incorporate thematic elements to maintain continuity of design.

Situation

The Really Cool Game Company has approved your world design and given provisional approval to build the game world using 001 Game Creator. This task is not to build a *working* prototype, rather it is to build and link the game world. The player should be able to exit and enter each scene to match the world design documents created in the last activity. Each member of the team will work individually and be responsible for building a version of the game world. All designs will be reviewed, and the best interpretation of the game world will be selected. Today, you are the creator of worlds.

How to Begin

1. Launch 001 Game Creator.

2. In your working folder, begin a new action/RPG project named *LastName*_GameWorld.

3. Create a game map for each scene of the game world. You may include additional maps for paths, walkways, or transition scenes between main scenes.

4. Use appropriate tiles from the standard tile sets to create a map that matches your vision of the game world. Make notes for needed tiles that are not part of the standard tile sets.

Importing Tile Sets

Tile sets can be downloaded from many places on the Internet and imported into 001 Game Creator. A great resource for tile sets and sprites is the Engine001. com website. This is the publisher of 001 Game Creator. On this site are thousands of images that were contributed by users from all over the world.

5. Launch your Internet browser, and navigate to the www.engine001.com.

6. Locate the **Resources** option, and select **Tile Sets**. You will see a page similar to the one shown in **Figure 1.**

7. Use the search text box to conduct a keyword search, or click a category to limit the displayed results.

8. Click a tile set of your choice that will match the game world you are creating.

9. Download the file to your working folder, or move it to your working folder after it is downloaded.

10. In 001 Game Creator, click the **Manage Resources** in the **Resources** pull-down menu. The **Resources** dialog box is displayed.

11. Click the **Browse** button. A standard Windows open dialog box is displayed.

Name: _____

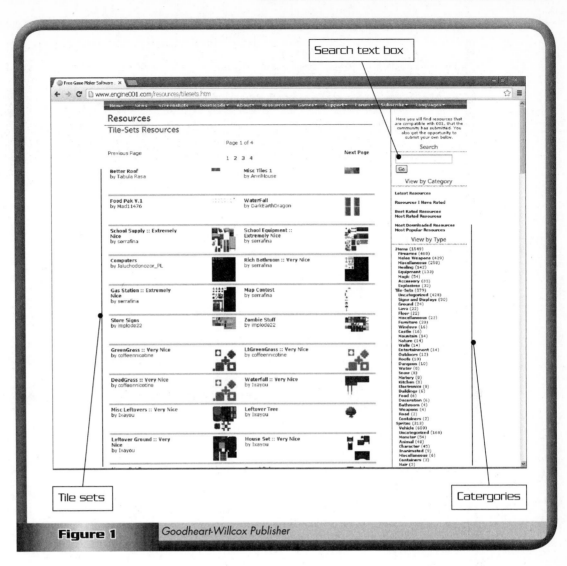

Tile sets

Catergories

Figure 1   *Goodheart-Willcox Publisher*

12. Navigate to your working folder, select the downloaded tile set file, and click the **Open** button. The tile set is listed in the **Resources** dialog box.

13. Verify the **Action** column is set to Import, as shown in **Figure 2.** Options for this setting are Import, Don't Import, and Overwrite. Overwriting is often helpful to reset a tile set back to the original state.

14. Click the **Go** button to add the tile set to the game.

15. When the **Action** column changes to Imported!, close the **Resources** dialog box.

16. Add tiles from the imported tile set to the game maps as appropriate.

Creating Tile Sets

In many cases, you may not be able to locate and download all of the tile sets needed for a game. In these cases, you must create them on your own. Base any tile sets you create on a 32 by 32 pixel setting. Using multiples of this standard size will make it much easier to import and use the graphics. Use graphic software such as Adobe Photoshop, Gimp, or other software to create the images. Once the tile set is created, import it as follows.

17. Click **Tile Sets** in the **Resources** pull-down menu. The **Tile Sets** dialog box is displayed, as shown in **Figure 3.**

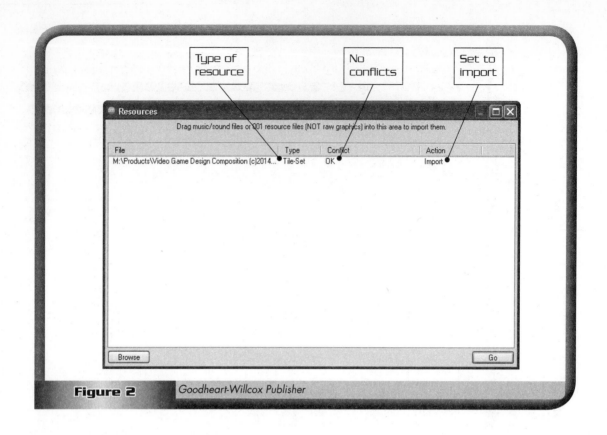

Type of resource

No conflicts

Set to import

Figure 2 Goodheart-Willcox Publisher

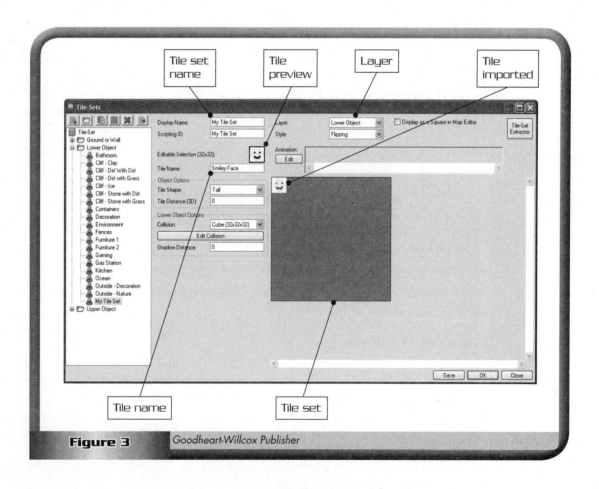

Tile set name

Tile preview

Layer

Tile imported

Tile name

Tile set

Figure 3 Goodheart-Willcox Publisher

Add Resource

18. Click the **Add Resource** button.

19. Click in the **Display Name:** text box, and enter a name for the tile set. This will be displayed as help text when the cursor is over the tile set in the library. The scripting ID should be the same as the display name.

20. In the large tile-set area of the dialog box, right-click in the location where the individual tile should appear, and click **Replace** in the shortcut menu. If the tile to be imported is greater than one tile, first select multiple tile areas. For example, when importing a 32 pixel by 64 pixel tile, select an area one tile by two tiles.

21. In the standard Windows open dialog box that is displayed, navigate to your working folder, select the image file for the tile, and click the **Open** button. The tile is added to the tile set, and the preview of the tile set is updated.

22. Click in the **Tile Name:** text box, and enter the name of the tile. This is the name of the specific tile, as opposed to the name of the tile set that was entered in the **Display Name:** text box.

23. Click the **Layer:** drop-down list, and in the list click the name of the layer on which the tiles in the tile set should be placed.

24. Set the options that appear below the **Tile Name:** text box as appropriate. The specific options displayed in this location depend on which layer is selected.

25. Continue selecting an open area in the tile set preview and adding new tiles as needed.

26. Click the **Save** button to save the tile set, then click the **Close** button to close the **Tile Sets** dialog box.

27. Add tiles from the custom tile set to the game maps as appropriate.

Finalizing the Build

28. Link all maps so the player can follow the story progression. The player must be able to access all maps.

29. Have each member of your team test play another team member's game.

30. Make changes to your game based on the feedback received from your team.

31. Save your work, build a setup EXE file, and submit it for grading according to the directions provided by your instructor.

Review Questions

1. Briefly describe how to import a downloaded tile set into 001 Game Creator.

_____

_____

2. When might you overwrite an existing tile set with an imported tile set?

_____

_____

3. What is the standard size a tile should be a multiple of to import into 001 Game Creator?

_____

4. Which menu item is selected after you right-click on the tile set preview area to insert a custom tile file?

_____

5. How many tiles must be selected in the tile set preview to import a tile file that is 96 pixels by 128 pixels?

_____

_____

Activity 5-4

Basic Mod Composition

Objectives

Students will add gameplay features through modding an existing game. Students will import and modify existing computer scripts. Students will program triggers and events.

Situation

The Really Cool Game Company has produced a new game called *Space Shooter*. It was created using 001 Game Creator using the same programming as an RPG game, but produced as a different genre. Based on feedback from the beta testing groups, the company wants some basic modifications incorporated to make the user experience better. Additionally, you will need to mod the game to input cheat codes for use by the quality assurance team. A *mod* is an alteration of an existing game.

How to Begin

1. Launch 001 Game Creator, or if it is already running, click **Open Game...** in the **File** pull-down menu.

2. In the **New/Open Game** dialog box, double-click on the Demo folder to open it.

3. Double-click on the Space Shooter game to open it.

4. Play the *Space Shooter* game to familiarize yourself with the controls and gameplay. Make a note of where the controls are located and how to implement the controls.

5. Close 001 Game Creator.

Test Game

Making a Copy of the Game

Before modifying the existing game, a copy should be made to modify. Creating a copy before making significant changes is a great way to undo any mistakes that cannot be recovered in the working copy. This is considered a best practice because a clean copy of the last stable build is always preserved so you can start over again from the stable version if needed.

6. Using Windows Explorer, open the My 001 Games folder. This is typically located in the user's My Documents folder on the local hard drive. Your instructor will provide specifics if the location is different.

7. Open the Demos folder in the My 001 Games folder. You should see subfolders, one of which is Space Shooter.

8. Right-click on the Space Shooter folder, and click **Copy** in the shortcut menu.

9. Right-click in an open part of the window, and click **Paste** in the shortcut menu. A new folder named Copy of Space Shooter is created, which is an exact copy of the contents of the Space Shooter folder.

10. Right-click on the Copy of Space Shooter folder, and click **Rename** in the shortcut menu. Name the folder *LastName*_Space Shooter, as shown in **Figure 1**.

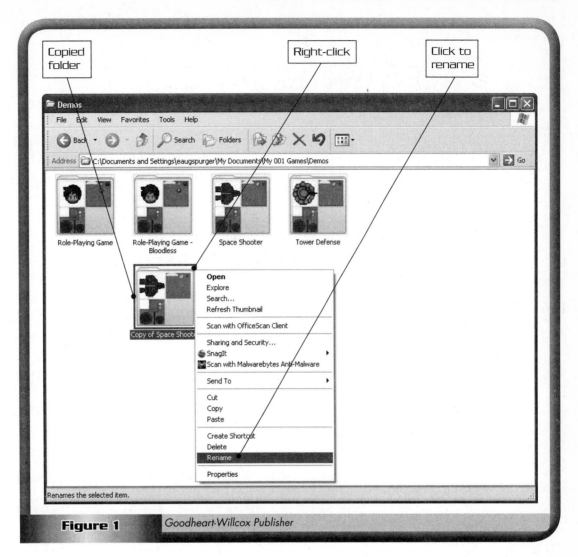

Figure 1   *Goodheart-Willcox Publisher*

11. Drag the renamed folder into your working folder where your other 001 Game Creator games are saved, and close Windows Explorer. The game copy is moved into your working folder.

12. Launch 001 Game Creator.

13. In the **New/Open Game** dialog box, open the *LastName_*Space Shooter game from your working folder.

14. Close the **Read Me** window if it is displayed.

15. Click the Level 1 map in the asset tree, and wait for all sprites and images to load. Notice there are no tiles displayed. This type of game does not use tile set layers as you have seen with the RPGs.

Modding the User Interface

The Really Cool Game Company beta testers had difficulty with the controls for the game. They felt using the left [Ctrl] key as the fire button was not intuitive, and they found they spent too much time focusing on the controls and not the gameplay. The testers found the game started too quickly for them to read the controls screen at the beginning. To address this report, the company wants the user interface to be changed so the space bar is the fire button, which the testers felt would be a more intuitive control.

Controls

16. Click the **Controls** button on the main toolbar. The **Controls** dialog box is displayed, as shown in **Figure 2.**

17. Click the **Add Control** button at the top of the **Controls** dialog box. A blank entry is added to the bottom of the dialog box.

18. Click in the **Display Name:** text box for the blank entry, and enter Fire. Enter this in the **Scripting ID:** text box as well.

19. Click the **Add** button in the **Player 1** area of the new entry. The **Input** dialog box is displayed.

20. In the **Input** dialog box, make sure **Key/Gamepad** is selected in the drop-down list, click in the text box to the right of the drop-down list, and press the space bar. The word Space is entered in the text box to indicate the control sets to the space bar.

21. Click the **OK** button to close the **Input** dialog box.

22. Click the **OK** button to close the **Controls** dialog box.

Input Triggers

23. Click the **Input Triggers** button on the main toolbar. The **Input Triggers** dialog box is displayed. This dialog box contains all of the input programming used in the game. Notice that there are folders for Cursor, Menu, and Regular Game.

24. Click the Regular Game folder, as shown in **Figure 3.** The controls in this folder are used during the play of the game.

25. Click the **Add Control Combination** button. The **Control Combination** dialog box is displayed, as shown in **Figure 4.**

26. Click the **Pressed** radio button, click in the text box next to the drop-down list, and press the space bar.

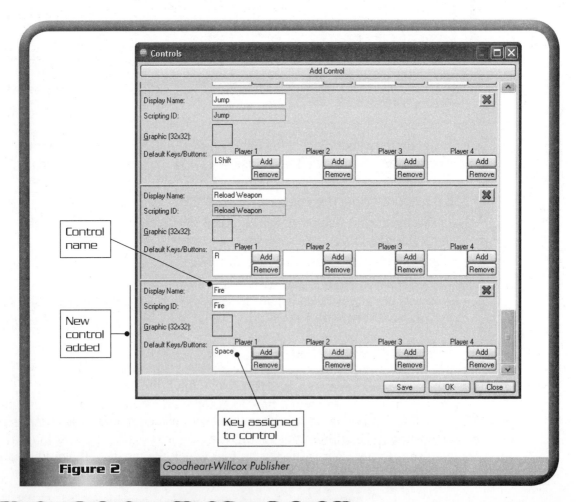

Figure 2   *Goodheart-Willcox Publisher*

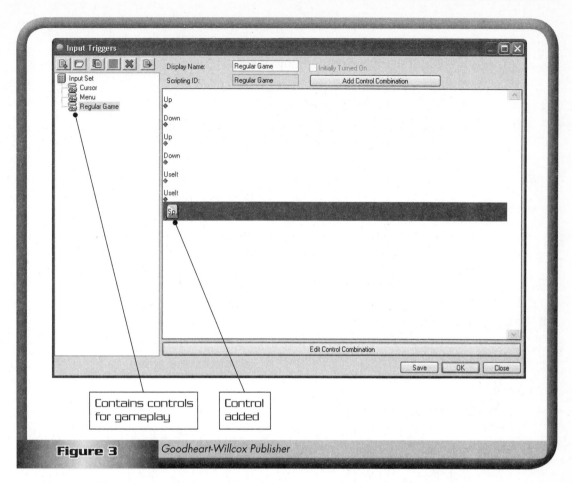

Figure 3 — Goodheart-Willcox Publisher

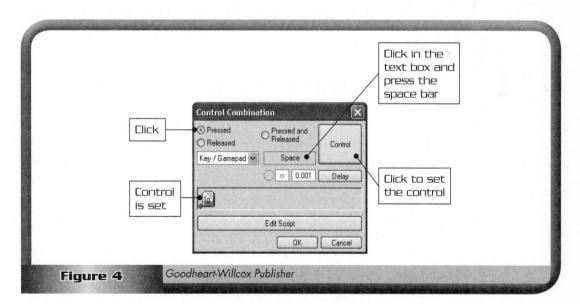

Figure 4 — Goodheart-Willcox Publisher

27. Click the **Control** button to set this control combination. A key icon with the label Sp appears in the space above the **Edit Script** button.

28. Click the **Edit Script** button. The **Input Script** dialog box is displayed.

29. Click the **Expand & Events** button, and use the search text box to locate the **Start/ Stop Using Equipment** command. Double-click on the command; the **Start/Stop Using Equipment** dialog box is displayed.

30. In the **Start/Stop Using Equipment** dialog box, click this, click Main, click Weapon, and click the **Start** radio button. Then click the **OK** button.

31. Close the **Input Script** dialog box.

32. Close the **Control Combination** dialog box.

33. Close the **Input Triggers** dialog box.

34. Similarly, add programming for a new control: **IF** the player releases the space bar, **THEN** stop the main actor from using the weapon.

35. Test play the game to see if the programming works. See how the user interface had improved with the new control?

Test Game

Modding Cheat Codes

To make games easier to test, a cheat code is often programmed so the game tester can try all features without having to constantly restart the game or level. You will now add some cheat codes for this game. Before you can program the keyboard to accept the cheat code input, the controls must be added.

36. Click the **Controls** button on the main toolbar. The **Controls** dialog box is displayed.

Controls

37. Using skills you have learned, add the controls shown in **Figure 5** for player 1.

38. Click the **OK** button to close the **Controls** dialog box and save the control assignments.

Modding Actor Templates

Programming for each cheat code must be added for the controls. This is done to the actor templates for the actors in the game. The actors are all configured with a parent-child relationship. In the parent-child relationship, the child object inherits any programming contained in the parent object. This structure saves time and programming because each child object does not have to include the same programming all child objects have in common. Instead, the parent object can be programmed, and all child objects of that parent will also have that programming.

Actor Templates

39. Click the **Actor Templates** button on the main toolbar. The **Actor Templates** dialog box is displayed.

40. Expand the Powerup branch in the tree, and select the Health Powerup leaf, as shown in **Figure 6.** In this case, Health Powerup is a child of the Powerup parent.

41. Click the **Edit Base Actor** button. The **Actor: Powerup** dialog box is displayed.

42. Double-click the first entry in the list in the **Triggers** area. A message is displayed indicating the trigger cannot be edited as it was programmed in the parent. All child objects of the Powerup parent inherit the first seven triggers, in this case, because they are programmed in the parent. Close the message.

Display Name	Interface Key
Health Cheat	[H]
Triple Gun Cheat	[G]
Missile Cheat	[M]

Figure 5   *Goodheart-Willcox Publisher*

Figure 6   Goodheart-Willcox Publisher

43. Click the Collided with actor ("Player Ship") trigger. This trigger is programmed only in this child object, as indicated by it not being grayed out in the list.

44. Click the **Edit Script** button. The **Actor Script** dialog box is displayed.

45. Right-click on the Change Health block, and click **Edit** in the shortcut menu. This programming block needs to be modified to: **IF** the player collides with the health power-up actor, **THEN** set the health to the maximum health.

46. In the **Change Health** dialog box, click **Set** in the **Health:** drop-down list.

47. Click the option button to the right of the **Health:** text box to display the **Use Value** dialog box.

48. In the **Use Value** dialog box, select the Actor > Maximum Health, and click the **Select** button.

49. In the **Maximum Health** dialog box that is displayed, click this and Main, then click the **OK** button.

50. Close the **Change Health** dialog box.

51. Close the **Actor Script** dialog box.

52. Close the **Actor: Powerup** dialog box.

53. Close the **Actor Templates** dialog box.

Test Game

54. Test play the game to see if the modification works when you collect the power-up object. The key for the cheat code will not work at this point because it has not been fully programmed.

Programming Pseudo Code

Pseudo code is similar to computer code, but is not actual code. *Pseudo code* breaks down game interactions into logical steps to describe the action, which is then written in a logic statement known as an **IF**...**THEN** statement. These logic statements can be later interpreted into the programming language or programming steps needed for the specific game engine. As you gain experience, future lessons will use pseudo code instead of step-by-step directions. Pseudo code is covered in detail in Chapter 12 of the textbook, but it is used throughout this software design guide.

The programming you just completed can be written in pseudo code using the basic programming operators of **IF**, **THEN**, **AND**, **OR**, and **ELSE**. The **IF** operator is sometimes reported as **WHEN**. Likewise the **THEN** operator is sometimes reported as **DO**. The **ELSE** operator can also be substituted with the **NOT** operator.

Input Triggers

55. Click the **Input Triggers** button on the main toolbar to open the **Input Triggers** dialog box.

56. In the Regular Game input set, create a control for: **IF** the player presses and releases the [H] key.

57. Edit the script as: **THEN** the main actor's health is increased by 1, as shown in **Figure 7**.

58. Close the **Input Triggers** dialog box.

Test Game

59. Test play the game to see if the health cheat code works. Each time the [H] key is pressed, the player character's health should increase by one up to the maximum.

Programming the First Weapon Cheat Code

See how easy it is to program the game using a pseudo code instruction? Now you will program the triple gun cheat code. The pseudo code for this cheat code is:

IF the player presses and releases the [G] key,

   THEN unequip and remove the current weapon item from the main actor

      AND equip and add the gun_triple (3-Way) item to the main actor.

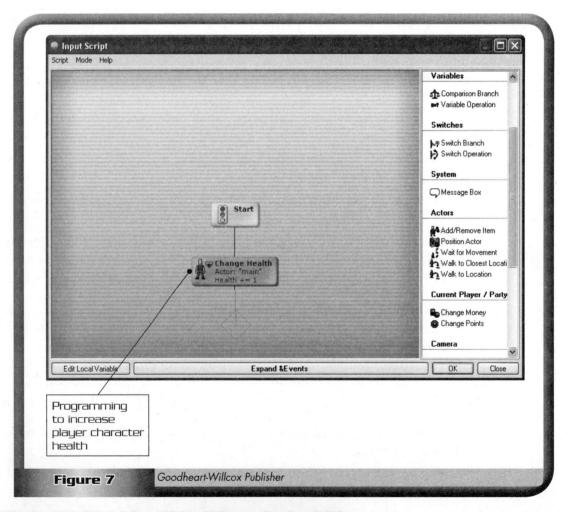

Figure 7   *Goodheart-Willcox Publisher*

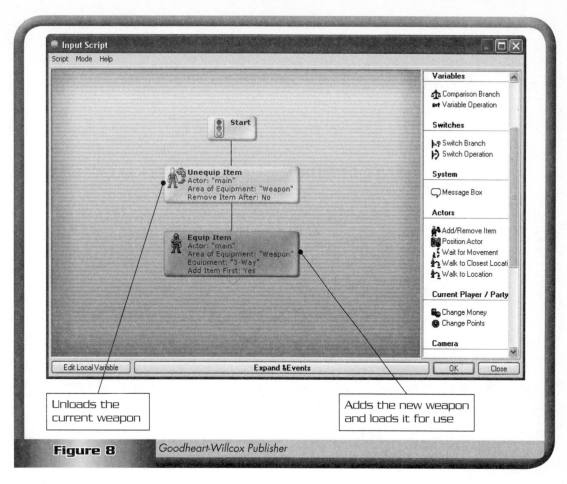

Unloads the current weapon

Adds the new weapon and loads it for use

Figure 8   Goodheart-Willcox Publisher

Follow these steps to program this pseudo code.

Input Triggers

60. Open the **Input Triggers** dialog box, and add a control to the Regular Game input set for the pressing and releasing of the [G] key.

61. Edit the script to add the actions for this control. Refer to **Figure 8.**

62. Add an Unequip Item programming block that removes the weapon from the main actor on this level. Do not remove the item from the actor's inventory.

63. Add an Equip Item programming block that adds the gun_triple (3-Way) weapon to the main actor on this level. Be sure to select the option to first add the item to the inventory.

64. Close the **Input Script** dialog box.

65. Close the **Control Combination** dialog box.

66. Close the **Input Triggers** dialog box.

Test Game

67. Test play the game. Check to see if the [G] key cheat code changes the weapon to the gun_triple (3-Way) weapon.

Programming the Second Weapon Cheat Code

Using the skills you learned, program the [M] cheat code from the pseudo code below. Refer to previous steps if you do not recall how to program something. This is the pseudo code:

IF the player presses and releases the [M] key,

> **THEN** unequip and remove the current weapon item for the main actor
>
> > **AND** equip and add the gun_missile (Big) item to the main actor.

Test Game

Save your work, and test play the game. Debug any errors.

Create three additional mods for this game. Examine the existing programming and gameplay to brainstorm ideas for these mods. Write pseudo code for each mod in the space below.

Mod #1

_____

_____

_____

Mod #2

_____

_____

_____

Mod #3

_____

_____

_____

Test Game

Test and debug any errors. Save your work, build a setup EXE file, and submit it for grading according to the directions provided by your instructor.

Review Questions

1. What is a mod?

_____

_____

2. Why is it considered a best practice to use a copy of a working game when making mods?

_____

_____

_____

3. Briefly describe how to make a copy of an existing game created with 001 Game Creator.

_____

_____

_____

4. How was the user experience enhanced by adding the space bar mod to the game?

_____

_____

5. Describe pseudo code.

_____

_____

_____

Chapter 6
Strategy Composition

Objectives

After completing this chapter, you will be able to:
- Evaluate the five key mechanics of a strategy game.
- Incorporate skill escalation in a game through modding.
- Develop original character dialog and gameplay.

What shall we buy, my liege?

75
45
500   1200

Goodheart-Willcox Publisher; images: Andreas Meyer/Shutterstock.com, 3drenderings/Shutterstock.com, Image Wizard/Shutterstock.com, martan/Shutterstock.com, Orla/Shutterstock.com, Algol/Shutterstock.com

Goodheart-Willcox Publisher; image: W7/Shutterstock.com

Goodheart-Willcox Publisher; images: Algol/Shutterstock.com, 3drenderings/Shutterstock.com

Bellwork

Day	Date	Activity	Response
1		Complete the anticipation guide and the K and W columns of the KWL chart for this chapter.	
2		What tactic would you take if your goal is to get an A in this class?	
3		Describe why an unbalanced strategy of defense and attack can lead to easily defeating an opponent.	
4		Define *resource management.*	
5		Describe how the game economy allows for player choices and decisions.	
6		Define *combined arms.*	
7		Describe how diversion is used in an overall maneuvering plan.	
8		Define *economy of force.*	
9		Describe why, in a multiplayer game, players transferring assets to other players can be considered cheating.	
10		List the five factors for establishing a sustainable community.	
11		Define *game flow.* Describe how elements of distraction are part of a game flow design.	

Day	Date	Activity	Response
12		How does a player act as an agent of change in a strategy game?	
13		Define *Easter egg* in terms of a video game. Why are Easter eggs a closely guarded secret?	
14		What is a tell?	
15		List four key areas in which computers provide benefits to strategy games.	
16		Why do game designers monitor metrics?	
17		In your strategy to become a green gamer, you installed CFL lightbulbs. What is the benefit to the environment, and what possible hazards exist with CFLs?	
18		What role do allies play in a resolution strategy model?	
19		Describe ways in which player immersion in strategy games has increased by bridging the gap between the real and virtual environments.	
20		Complete the L column of the KWL chart and the After Reading column of the anticipation guide with what you learned from this chapter.	
21		Speculate why players may be choosing archer groups more than cavalry groups in a battlefield strategy game. List four ways to balance the player selection of cavalry over archers.	

Anticipation Guide

Directions

Before reading the chapter, read each statement in the table below. In the column titled Before Reading, write the letter *T* if you agree with the statement or *F* if you disagree with the statement. After reading the chapter, reread each statement in the table below. In the column titled After Reading, write the letter *T* if you agree with the statement or *F* if you disagree with the statement. Be prepared to justify your answers in a class discussion.

Before Reading	Statement	After Reading
	A strategy is a plan for doing something, while tactics are the actions used to carry it out.	
	A combined-arms military strategy involves interlocking the arms of the soldiers to create a barrier.	
	When designing a game economy, the designer must create gains, drains, and complexity of mass.	
	Pattern recognition is a critical component of predicting the moves of an opponent.	
	A causal chain describes how a series of events lead to the final outcome.	

KWL Chart

Directions

Before reading the chapter, fill in what you already know about the topic in the K column and what you want to learn in the W column. After reading the chapter, review what you know and wanted to learn about the topic. Reflect on what you have studied and completed in this chapter. Fill in what you learned in the L column. Be prepared to justify your answers in a class discussion.

Topic: Strategy and Tactics		
K What you already *know*	W What you *want* to learn	L What you *learned*

Activity 6-1

Strategy Game Evaluation

Objectives

Students will evaluate the five key mechanics of a strategy game. Students will create tactics to implement a strategic plan through gameplay. Students will evaluate gameplay elements and recommend modifications to increase player engagement, interest, and balance. Students will synthesize solutions to improve a game. Students will successfully communicate findings, summarize evaluations, and suggest solutions in a public-speaking situation.

Situation

The Really Cool Game Company has a prototype for a strategy game called *Tower Defense* that it plans to release for the tablet app market. The company feels that you and your team have the skills to take a creative lead on this project. Your task is to complete a strategy analysis of the five key mechanics of strategy games and to assess how well each is implemented in the game. Your team will then prepare recommendations to increase the player engagement, interest, and balance.

How to Begin

1. Form teams as directed by your instructor.
2. Launch 001 Game Creator.
3. In the **New/Open Game** dialog box, double-click on the Demos folder, select the Tower Defense game, and click the **Open** button.
4. Close the read me window if it appears, and test play the game to familiarize yourself with the controls and features.

Test Game

Evaluating Game Features

5. As a team, review the Playability Testing, Continuity Testing, Functionality Testing, and Strategy Analysis documents on the following pages.
6. Discuss the Tower Defense game with your team, paying attention to the questions in the testing and analysis documents.
7. Individually, replay the game, and cite specific evidence from the game for each feature evaluated in the testing and analysis documents.
8. In a team discussion, compare the results of individual game testing.
9. Brainstorm suggestions for improving game features and correcting errors.

Documenting and Presenting

10. Form a group consensus and record that information on a set of team documents (paper or word processing document).

11. Create a 20 slide PechaKucha style presentation to summarize important findings. Include screen captures and animations when appropriate. Refer to Chapter 1 if you do not recall PechaKucha style.

12. Submit the testing and analysis documents and the slide show for grading.

13. Present the slide show to the class.

Playability Testing

Answer all of the following questions. Enter the questions and answers in a word processing document or on a separate sheet of paper.

1. Which competition model(s) is exploited?

2. What are the major implicit challenges in the gameplay?

3. What are the major explicit challenges in the gameplay?

4. Would story add to the game? Why or why not?

5. How is feedback achieved?

6. How is the game mentally stimulating?

7. Is the gameplay intuitive, or how can it be made more intuitive? What screens, messages, or demos are needed for the player to understand the gameplay?

8. Which player perspective does this game use?

9. Where is the game camera located?

10. Does the camera follow the player?

11. What action takes place out of scope?

12. What are some ways to display out-of-scope interactions to aid the player (statistics, minimaps, etc.)?

13. What customizing is offered to the player?

14. How does the player interact with the NPCs?

15. Are physical tasks within the range of the typical player? If not, how can these tasks be simplified?

16. What tasks are automated to allow the player to focus on core gameplay?

17. What other tasks should be automated to help the player focus on core gameplay?

18. How can gameplay be enhanced with online play for this game?

19. What additional technology, if any, would be needed to create the game for a mobile platform?

20. Is the player feedback based on a particular language or language independent? If based on a language, how can language independence be achieved?

21. Is the context of the game culturally sensitive for age or ethnicity? If not, what improvements would need to be made?

22. Does gameplay remain engaging? If not, how long into gameplay does player interest begin to fade?

23. What balancing elements could be implemented to maintain player interest?

24. What back office tasks are provided for the player?

25. What player tasks could be automated as back office commands?

26. How does the game vary the degree of challenge for different players?

27. How can additional degrees of challenge be added to the game?

28. Can the player select age or skill options?

29. What changes could improve the age or skill options?

30. How does the player receive rewards or praise during gameplay?

31. Is the player aware of the rewards as they occur? If not, how can they be more obvious to the player affecting immersion?

32. What additional rewards would you suggest?

33. List any points of frustration with operation or gameplay that you identified.

34. Are there any just barely fail events that are likely to occur? List any levels or enemies that are very difficult or impossible to defeat.

35. Can additional maps or levels be added as sellable downloadable content (DLC)? Describe how these levels would be different from existing maps.

Continuity Testing

Answer all of the following questions. Enter the questions and answers in a word processing document or on a separate sheet of paper.

1. Describe the setting (place, temporal).

2. Describe the basic theme of the gameplay.

3. List the major thematic elements.

   A. Map

   B. Characters

   C. Weapons

   D. HUD

   E. Gameplay

   F. Music and Sounds

4. Describe the mood of the scene.

5. How are changes between scenes consistent with the previous scene?

6. Suggest changes to items to better maintain consistency.

7. What improvements should be made to better match game assets to the setting, theme, and mood?

Functionality Testing

Answer all of the following questions. Enter the questions and answers in a word processing document or on a separate sheet of paper.

1. Describe the typical player for this game.

2. Describe any areas of player interaction that could be made more consistent.

3. How are frequent users able to use shortcuts, checkpoints, or restart gameplay?

4. How does the player understand what weapon or object has been selected?

5. What improvements would you suggest to provide feedback for asset selection?

6. Is dialogue or game information presented to yield closure and prepare player for the next course of action?

7. How does the player recognize when an error is made?

8. How are errors corrected or reversed?

9. Suggest how error correction can be made simpler.

10. Does the player feel in control of the outcome of the game?

11. Suggest how the player can be made to feel more in control of the outcome of the performance of NPCs or of the game.

12. On a scale of 1 to 10, with 10 the highest, evaluate the amount of short-term memory required to complete the level.

13. Suggest how the load on the player's short-term memory can be reduced.
14. Describe the user interface controls needed for screen navigation.
15. Describe the user interface controls needed for gameplay.
16. Are controls ergonomic for the typical player? Suggest improvements to the ergonomics of the user interface controls, button locations, and key combinations to aid the player.
17. Suggest improvements to the user interface technology to simplify actions for the player or for use on a mobile device.
18. Note any issues with button or text contrast or readability.
19. Describe the location of the HUD. Can this location be changed by the player?
20. What information is contained on the HUD?
21. Suggest improvements to the HUD to aid in information feedback and decreased distraction.
22. Suggest changes to the user interface system that would provide greater player feedback.

Strategy Analysis

Answer all of the following questions. Enter the questions and answers in a word processing document or on a separate sheet of paper.

Resource Management
1. How is resource management implemented?
2. How does resource allocation affect gameplay?
3. What strategic or tactical decisions need to be made to deal with limited resources?
4. How can game resources be exchanged, traded, or sold?
5. Suggest improvements for resource management and rank them in order of importance, with the most important listed first.

Dissimilar Assets
6. How are dissimilar assets implemented?
7. Describe how combined arms are required for victory.
8. Which aspects of combined arms are realistic and which are unrealistic?
9. Suggest aspects of the combined arms that need to be improved. Rank the suggestions.

Maneuvering
10. How is maneuvering implemented?
11. Describe how economy of force is required for victory.
12. Which aspects of the economy of force are realistic and which are unrealistic?
13. Suggest aspects of maneuvering that need to be improved.

Pacing
14. How is pacing implemented?
15. How is resource building used to pace the gameplay?
16. How is challenge escalation implemented?
17. How are items locked and unlocked to pace gameplay?
18. Identify areas of gameplay where pacing is too slow.

Name: _____

19. Identify areas of gameplay where pacing is too fast.

20. Suggest any changes to the pacing elements to better control the pacing. Rank the suggestions.

Economy

21. How is the game economy regulated?

22. How are provisioning factors (gains) achieved?

23. How are drains implemented in the economy?

24. Describe any infinite resources or unrealistic reloading times in the economy.

25. Suggest any changes to the game economy that would provide better decision making for the limited resources in the economy. Rank the suggestions.

Activity 6-2

Strategy Game Mod

Objectives

Students will modify existing gameplay to create skill escalation. Students will program randomization to enhance the replay value of a game. Students will program NPC movement to simulate artificial intelligence.

Situation

The Really Cool Game Company has sent word that all of your improvements and modifications are under consideration. While waiting for the final word on all of the enhancements you suggested, it wants you to begin by designing new levels to provide skill escalation and player-selected leveling. Your job is to design one map prototype that is less complex and one that is more complex. These maps will use the same programming framework and asset base as the current prototype. Later, the programmers will add items such as the ammo reloading objects and enemy return fire options suggested in the evaluation process.

How to Begin

1. Review the Evaluation Rubric on the last page of this activity.

2. Launch 001 Game Creator.

3. In the **New/Open Game** dialog box, open your working folder, and click the **New** button.

4. In the **New Game** dialog box, click the **Demos** tab, click **Tower Defense** in the list, enter *LastName_*Tower Defense Mod02 in the **Name of Project:** text box, and click the **OK** button. Close the read me window if it is displayed. This creates a copy of the Tower Defense game and locates it in your working folder.

5. Click **New Game...** in the **File** pull-down menu. The **New Game** dialog box is displayed.

6. In the **New Game** dialog box, click the **Demos** tab, click **Tower Defense** in the list, enter *LastName_*Tower Defense Mod01 in the **Name of Project:** text box, and click the **OK** button. Close the read me window if it is displayed. This creates a second copy of the Tower Defense game in your working folder.

7. The name of the currently open game is *LastName_*Tower Defense Mod01. Display the Level 1 map.

8. Using the same grass and dirt tiles as the original game, modify the path to include four additional intersections where a path choice can be made. Refer to the example in **Figure 1**. Do not change the existing paths, including the starting or ending points, and do not alter the existing zones.

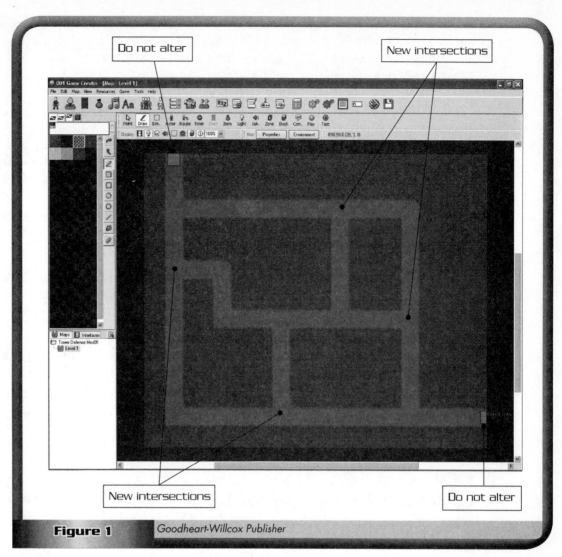

Figure 1   *Goodheart-Willcox Publisher*

9. Assume an NPC actor is currently in the starting zone (2,0,0) and can move only down and right, as seen from your perspective. On a sheet of graph paper, record each step the NPC would have to take to make it through a single pathway to get from start to finish. Each step is a single tile. Repeat this for both new pathways.

NPC Pathways

The first prototype mod will be the more complex version of the game. When a new NPC enemy is spawned, it must choose a pathway to make it from start to finish. Each step the NPC takes must be programmed and randomized so the NPCs travel different directions.

Zone

10. With the Level 1 map displayed, change to the **Zone** tool, and click the starting zone (2,0,0).

11. In the **Zone** dialog box, click the Collided with actor (Computer) trigger, and click the **Edit Script** button.

Before making any changes, it is important to understand the meaning of the current script. In the script, Actor (relate) is any actor that is the child of the parent actor. It is understood by the game engine as the specific actor that collided with the zone. The script follows this pseudo code:

IF Actor (relate) is not equal to the coin,

THEN create three random possible outcomes where the same one can occur consecutively

      AND program the specific movement path of the relative NPC that is spawned.

12. In the existing script, double-click Random Branch block to open the **Random Branch** dialog box. The Random Branch block randomizes the pathway for the script by providing a number of possible pathways.

13. Drag the slider to the third position. The label changes to read **Possibilities: 4**, and the block will have four possible random outcomes.

14. Click the **OK** button to close the **Random Branch** dialog box.

15. From the new, unassigned node on the Random Branch block, add a **Take Specific Movements** command. You will need to click the **Expand & Events** button to access this command.

16. In the **Take Specific Movements** dialog box, click this and (Relate).

17. Click the **Movement:** button. The **Movement** dialog box shown in **Figure 2** is displayed, which is used to create the steps the NPC will take.

18. Click the **Move and Face** button at the top of the **Movement** dialog box so it is on (depressed). This synchronizes the movement and facing of the NPC.

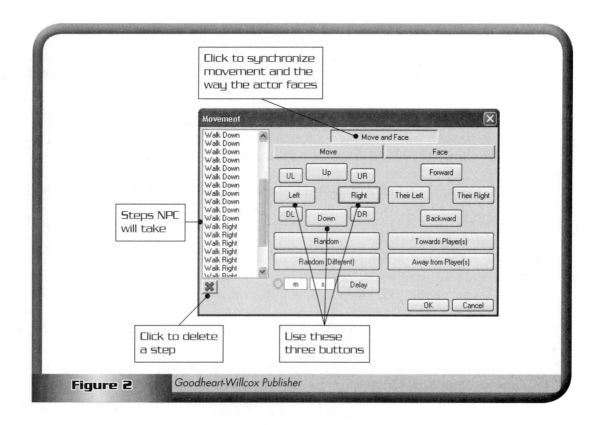

Figure 2   *Goodheart-Willcox Publisher*

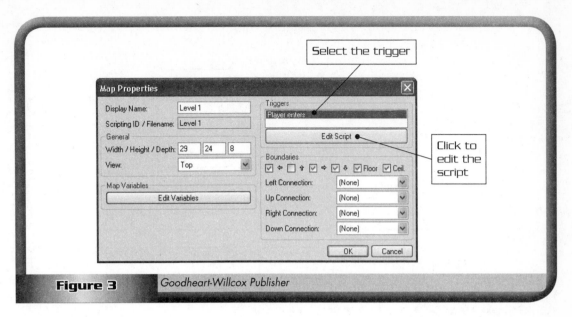

Select the trigger

Click to edit the script

Figure 3   *Goodheart-Willcox Publisher*

19. Using the path steps you recorded earlier, program path of the NPC using only the **Down**, **Right**, and **Left** buttons. As steps are added, they appear in the list on the left side of the dialog box. If you make a mistake, use the **Remove** button (**X**) at the bottom of the movement list to remove any unwanted move.

20. Close the **Movement** dialog box, the **Take Specific Movements** dialog box, the **Zone Script** dialog box, and the **Zone** dialog box.

21. Save the Level 1 map.

22. Test play the game.

23. Check that the NPCs stay on the new paths.

24. Using a similar procedure, map the other new pathway and program the NPC movement.

Test Game

Increasing Difficulty

Some beta testers suggested that advanced enemies appear too far into the game. In this section, you will modify the script for advanced enemies to randomly spawn on earlier levels.

25. Click the **Properties** button on the **Map** toolbar. The **Map Properties** dialog box is displayed, as shown in **Figure 3.**

26. Click the Player Enters trigger, and click the **Edit Script** button.

27. In the **Map Script** dialog box, double-click the Repeat Loop block. This opens the **Sub Script** dialog box.

The sub script displayed may look like a tangled mess of programming blocks and connecting threads. The script window can be zoomed using the mouse wheel, and it can be panned using the mouse wheel button. To better understand what you see in this window, focus on the first four layers of the script starting with the Repeat Loop block and continuing in the sub script. These layers can be expressed in pseudo code, as shown in **Figure 4.**

28. Double-click the Comparison Branch block for **IF** the Wave_Number variable is greater than 7. The Wave_Number variable stores the current wave number.

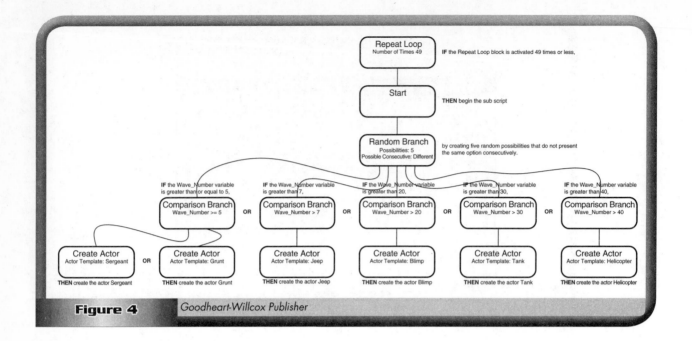

Repeat Loop
Number of Times 49

IF the Repeat Loop block is activated 49 times or less,

Start

THEN begin the sub script

Random Branch
Possibilities: 5
Possible Consecutive: Different

by creating five random possibilities that do not present the same option consecutively.

IF the Wave_Number variable is greater than or equal to 5,

Comparison Branch
Wave_Number >= 5

OR

Create Actor
Actor Template: Sergeant

OR

Create Actor
Actor Template: Grunt

THEN create the actor Sergeant

THEN create the actor Grunt

IF the Wave_Number variable is greater than 7,

Comparison Branch
Wave_Number > 7

OR

Create Actor
Actor Template: Jeep

THEN create the actor Jeep

IF the Wave_Number variable is greater than 20,

Comparison Branch
Wave_Number > 20

OR

Create Actor
Actor Template: Blimp

THEN create the actor Blimp

IF the Wave_Number variable is greater than 30,

Comparison Branch
Wave_Number > 30

OR

Create Actor
Actor Template: Tank

THEN create the actor Tank

IF the Wave_Number variable is greater than 40,

Comparison Branch
Wave_Number > 40

Create Actor
Actor Template: Helicopter

THEN create the actor Helicopter

Figure 4   *Goodheart-Willcox Publisher*

29. In the **Comparison Branch** dialog box, change the entry in the **Value:** text box from 7 to 4, and click the **OK** button. This makes the actor appear after the fourth wave instead of after the seventh wave.

30. Edit the script so the Blimp actor appears after the tenth wave.

31. Edit the script so the Tank actor appears after the fifteenth wave.

32. Edit the script so the Helicopter actor appears after the twentieth wave.

33. Test play the game, and check that the advanced enemies appear after the correct waves. The Grunt actor is a yellow vehicle, the Sergeant actor is a red vehicle, and the Jeep actor is a green vehicle.

Stronger Enemies

New actors can be quickly and easily added in 001 Game Creator. For this task, you will use the same enemy sprites, just change the color to indicate a different enemy with different characteristics. For the purpose of a prototype, it is not necessary to wait for new game art. Any object can be used as long as it allows for testing the feature and gameplay.

Actor Templates

34. Click the **Actor Templates** button on the main toolbar. The **Actor Templates** dialog box is displayed.

35. Click the Enemies branch in the tree. This is the parent of all enemy actors.

Add Resource

36. Click the **Add Resource** button at the top of the dialog box. This will add a child actor named Template to the Enemies parent. The new actor is automatically selected, and its properties displayed in the dialog box, as shown in **Figure 5.**

37. Click in the **Display Name:** text box, and enter to Sand Tank. Enter this as the scripting ID as well.

38. Click the **Edit Base Actor** button. The **Actor: Enemies [Actor Template]** dialog box is displayed.

39. In the **Sprite:** area, click the **Body:** button, and, in the **Pick Sprite** dialog box that is displayed, click the Tank sprite and the **OK** button.

40. The tank color is tan, by default. Click the color swatch next to the **Body:** button, and change the color to one of your choice.

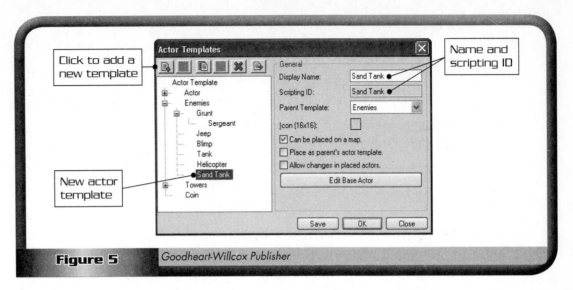

Click to add a new template

Name and scripting ID

New actor template

Figure 5 *Goodheart-Willcox Publisher*

41. Change the health points to 250.

42. Add a Killed/Destroyed trigger. This will be different from the one inherited from the parent, which is grayed out in the **Triggers** list. In the **Killed/Destroyed** dialog box, click the **OK** button. The **Actor Script** dialog box is displayed.

43. Program the script to add $50 to the player total.

44. Program the script to change the tint color (Change Tint/Opacity Color) for this actor with a delay of half a second.

45. Close the **Actor: Enemy [Actor Template]** dialog box. A warning appears indicating that AI is not set for the character. Click the **Continue** button to dismiss the warning. AI is not needed for this application.

46. Close the **Actor Templates** dialog box.

Properties

47. Click the **Map Properties** button, and in the **Map Properties** dialog box, edit the Player Enters trigger.

48. Double-click the Repeat Loop block to open the sub script.

49. Edit the Random Branch block to accept six possibilities.

50. Copy one of the Comparison Branch blocks below the Random Branch block, paste it in an open space, and connect it to the unassigned sixth node of the Random Branch block.

51. Edit the pasted Comparison Branch block, and enter 25 in the **Value:** text box.

52. Copy one of the Create Actor blocks, paste it below the Comparison Branch block that was just pasted, and connect it to the left node of that Comparison Branch block.

53. Connect the bottom node of the pasted Create Actor block to the top of the Variable Operation block to match the existing programming.

54. Edit the pasted Create Actor block, and change the actor to Sand Tank. Be sure to change the scripting ID as well.

55. Connect the right-hand node of the pasted Comparison Branch block to the top of the Random Branch block.

56. Close the **Sub Script** dialog box, the **Map Script** dialog box, and the **Map Properties** dialog box.

57. Test play the game, and check that the new actor appears after the twenty-fifth wave.

Test Game

More Enemies

58. Using the skills you have just learned, create four new, stronger enemies.

59. Program the game to add these new enemies after the thirtieth, thirty-fifth, and fortieth waves.

60. Edit the existing enemies and increase the health points of each to make each harder to defeat.

61. Test play the game, correct any bugs, and tune the game as needed.

Test Game

62. Have a classmate play your game, evaluate it, and suggest improvements.

63. Save your work, build a setup EXE file, and submit it for grading according to the directions provided by your instructor.

Create the Less Complex Prototype

The more complex mod has been created. The next task is to create a mod for less experienced players. This mod needs to be less complex to allow these players to build skill and to succeed in playing the game. Use the skills you have learned to complete this mod. You will need to extrapolate these skills to complete similar tasks in order to complete the mod.

64. Open the *LastName_*Tower Defense Mod02 file.

65. Design a single pathway that snakes and bends around the map many times without overlapping. See the example in **Figure 6.**

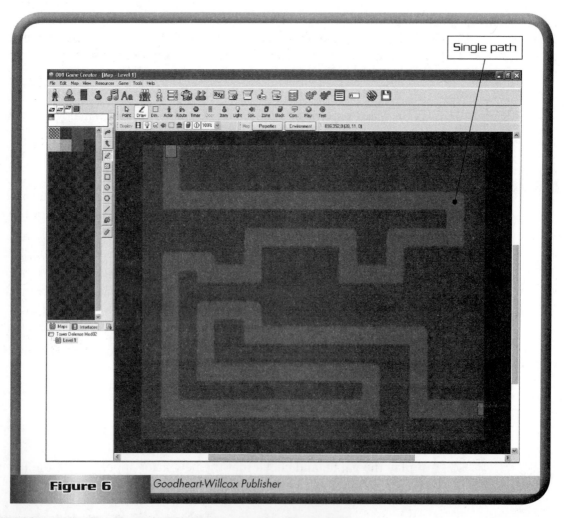

Figure 6   *Goodheart-Willcox Publisher*

66. Edit the programming for the existing NPCs so they follow the new path.

67. Adjust hit points and defense points of enemies to lower the difficulty.

Quality Control

Test Game

68. Test play the game, correct any bugs, and tune the game as needed.

69. Complete a Personal Evaluation rubric for your own game.

70. Have a classmate (a peer) complete the Peer Evaluation rubric for both skill levels of your game.

71. Save your work, build a setup EXE file, and submit it for grading according to the directions provided by your instructor.

Review Questions

1. What function does the Random Branch programming block serve?

_____

_____

2. Briefly describe how the path an NPC takes through the game is specified.

_____

_____

_____

_____

3. Briefly describe how the number of waves is tracked in the programming.

_____

_____

_____

_____

4. Other than adjusting the health points and defense points of the enemy, how can an enemy be made harder to defeat?

_____

_____

_____

_____

5. During gameplay, the [Esc] key pauses the game. What game action would you create to provide a pause-and-relax activity during gameplay?

_____

_____

_____

_____

Evaluation Rubric

Designer's Name:					

Personal Evaluation

Evaluation Item	Max Points	Not Present	Score	
			Mod 1	Mod 2
Four new intersections on the game map	10 points	Deduct five points for each missing intersection		
Sprites follow four random paths to the end	10 points	Deduct five points for each missing path		
Five new enemies (eleven total enemies)	15 points	Deduct five points for each missing enemy		
Strength of enemies adjusted to skill level of game	10 points	Deduct two points for each unmodified challenges		
Difficulty of gameplay escalates in waves	15 points	Deduct five points if waves do not add challenge		
Game is winnable	10 points	Deduct ten points if game is not winnable		
Winning requires selling assets to upgrade	20 points	Deduct ten points if sale is not required		
Game ending is a just barely win scenario	10 points	Deduct five points if final wave does not require player action		
Total				

Evaluator's Name:					

Peer Evaluation

Evaluation Item	Max Points	Not Present	Score	
			Mod 1	Mod 2
Four new intersections on the game map	10 points	Deduct five points for each missing intersection		
Sprites follow four random paths to the end	10 points	Deduct five points for each missing path		
Five new enemies (eleven total enemies)	15 points	Deduct five points for each missing enemy		
Strength of enemies adjusted to skill level of game	10 points	Deduct two points for each unmodified challenges		
Difficulty of gameplay escalates in waves	15 points	Deduct five points if waves do not add challenge		
Game is winnable	10 points	Deduct ten points if game is not winnable		
Winning requires selling assets to upgrade	20 points	Deduct ten points if sale is not required		
Game ending is a just barely win scenario	10 points	Deduct five points if final wave does not require player action		
Total				

Activity 6-3

Mastery Project

Objectives

Students will work in teams to create a playable game. Students will develop original character dialogue and gameplay.

Situation

The Really Cool Game Company has given your team a green light to build your game world prototype. Using the documents and designs your team created for the world design project in Activities 5-2 and 5-3, create the dialogue, interactions, and activities needed for each scene in the game.

How to Begin

1. Form teams as directed by your instructor.

2. Using the documents from Activities 5-2 and 5-3, develop the gameplay for the world you created.

3. Using 001 Game Creator, assemble the game maps into a single playable game.

4. Thoroughly test and debug the game.

5. Play the team's game, and evaluate it by completing the Designer Evaluation Rubric. This is a self-evaluation of the team's game design. Some items evaluate each scene, while others evaluate the entire game world as a whole. Each team member should complete a Designer Evaluation Rubric.

6. Have another team play and evaluate your team's game using the Peer Evaluation Rubric.

7. Play another team's game, and evaluate it by completing the Peer Evaluation Rubric. Each member of your team should complete a Peer Evaluation Rubric for the other team's game.

8. Save your work, build a setup EXE file, and submit it for grading according to the directions provided by your instructor.

Designer Evaluation Rubric				
Component	**Scale**			**Score**
Artistry	Poor visual design; used standard tile set only 0	Some items have appeal, while others do not 3	Great tile-based design elements 5	
Scene 1				
Scene 2				
Scene 3				
Scene 4				
Scene 5				

(Continued)

Component	Scale			Score
Thematic Elements	**Assets and scenes do not match** 0	**Some items match the theme** 3	**Assets and scenes match perfectly** 5	
Scene 1				
Scene 2				
Scene 3				
Scene 4				
Scene 5				
Navigation	**No links between scenes or trouble finding way around world** 5	**Mostly works, but player needs some help understanding where to go** 15	**Player knows where to go and how to get there; links between maps work and are in good locations** 30	
World				
Dialogue	**Does not work or is inappropriate** 5	**Is partially complete or has some continuity problems** 15	**Creates meaningful NPCs; adds to the player immersion** 30	
World				
Missions	**Aimless wandering around map; do not know what to do or actions do not make sense** 0	**Most interactions fit theme and are appropriate to the game** 3	**Interactions are exciting and challenging; all fit the theme and story** 5	
Scene 1				
Scene 2				
Scene 3				
Scene 4				
Scene 5				
Story	**Cannot follow the story** 5	**Understand the story, but some parts are confusing or missing** 20	**Great story!** 35	
World				
World Design	**Scenes seem disjointed or missing; missing sounds or other components** 5	**All scenes exist, but some seem out of place; missing some sounds or other components** 15	**All scenes present and all sounds are appropriate; each feels like part of the same game world** 30	
World				
Total score (add score from all areas, 200 points maximum)				

Name: _____

Peer Evaluation Rubric			
Component	**Scale**		**Score**
Artistry	Poor visual design; used standard tile set only 0	Some items have appeal, while others do not 3	Great tile-based design elements 5	
Scene 1			
Scene 2			
Scene 3			
Scene 4			
Scene 5			
Thematic Elements	Assets and scenes do not match 0	Some items match the theme 3	Assets and scenes match perfectly 5	
Scene 1			
Scene 2			
Scene 3			
Scene 4			
Scene 5			
Navigation	No links between scenes or trouble finding way around world 5	Mostly works, but player needs some help understanding where to go 15	Player knows where to go and how to get there; links between maps work and are in good locations 30	
World			
Dialogue	Does not work or is inappropriate 5	Is partially complete or has some continuity problems 15	Creates meaningful NPCs; adds to the player immersion 30	
World			
Missions	Aimless wandering around map; do not know what to do or actions do not make sense 0	Most interactions fit theme and are appropriate to the game 3	Interactions are exciting and challenging; all fit the theme and story 5	
Scene 1			
Scene 2			
Scene 3			
Scene 4			
Scene 5			

(Continued)

Component	Scale			Score
Story	Cannot follow the story 5	Understand the story, but some parts are confusing or missing 20	Great story! 35	
World				
World Design	Scenes seem disjointed or missing; missing sounds or other components 5	All scenes exist, but some seem out of place; missing some sounds or other components 15	All scenes present and all sounds are appropriate; each feels like part of the same game world 30	
World				
Total score (add score from all areas, 200 points maximum)				

Chapter 7
Puzzle Composition

Objectives

After completing this chapter, you will be able to:
- Develop game programming using qualifiers.
- Create escalation in a video game design by applying concepts from puzzle design.
- Program simulation elements in a video game.

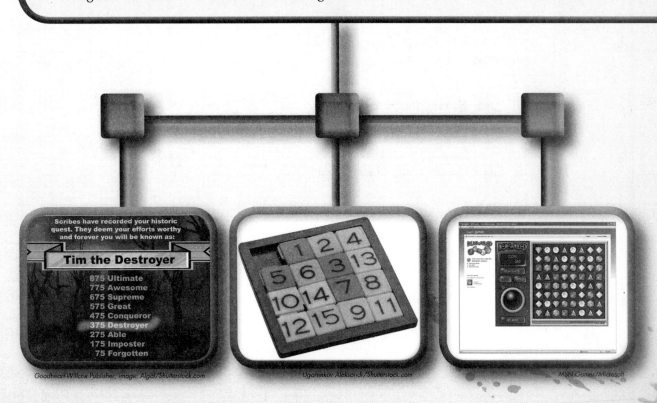

Goodheart-Willcox Publisher; Image: Algol/Shutterstock.com

Ugorenkov Aleksandr/Shutterstock.com

MSN Games/Microsoft

Bellwork

Day	Date	Activity	Response
1		Complete the anticipation guide and the K and W columns of the KWL chart for this chapter.	
2		Define *puzzles*.	
3		What are the four steps to help simplify a puzzle?	
4		What is the purpose of an editor in puzzle design?	
5		List the four major components of a puzzle.	
6		Describe how functional rules and playability attributes create the parts for a puzzle.	
7		List three elements of self-leveling.	
8		Describe how a metapuzzle design is used in a game.	
9		Define *aha moment*.	
10		Describe a linguistic puzzle.	
11		Describe how a logic-grid puzzle works.	

Day	Date	Activity	Response
12		Describe the essential tricky part of a recursive puzzle.	
13		Define *circular logic*. What happens when a computer attempts to solve circular logic?	
14		List six types of mechanical puzzles.	
15		What is the essential tricky part of a transport puzzle?	
16		How can word puzzles be used in education?	
17		List the seven benefits of a computerized puzzle.	
18		Examine Figure 7-5. Explain the chart in terms of challenge and ability if a player is in the frustration zone.	
19		Examine Figure 7-3. In what theme category would you place this puzzle? Cite specific evidence in your explanation.	
20		Complete the L column of the KWL chart and the After Reading column of the anticipation guide with what you learned from this chapter.	
21		Speculate why players would be ending an online game before completing the final metapuzzle. List four ways to reveal covert clues that would direct players to find the missing pieces.	

Name: _____

Date: _____

Class: _____

Anticipation Guide

Directions

Before reading the chapter, read each statement in the table below. In the column titled Before Reading, write the letter *T* if you agree with the statement or *F* if you disagree with the statement. After reading the chapter, reread each statement in the table below. In the column titled After Reading, write the letter *T* if you agree with the statement or *F* if you disagree with the statement. Be prepared to justify your answers in a class discussion.

Before Reading	Statement	After Reading
	Puzzle elements are found in games in almost every genre.	
	Rules for puzzles require defining the map, parts, moves, and victory condition.	
	A player will get bored if the challenge exceeds his or her ability.	
	Covert hints are directly communicated to the player.	
	Computers allow puzzles to contain moves impossible to duplicate in the real world.	

KWL Chart

Directions

Before reading the chapter, fill in what you already know about the topic in the K column and what you want to learn in the W column. After reading the chapter, review what you know and wanted to learn about the topic. Reflect on what you have studied and completed in this chapter. Fill in what you learned in the L column. Be prepared to justify your answers in a class discussion.

Topic: Puzzles		
K What you already *know*	**W** What you *want* to learn	**L** What you *learned*

Activity 7-1

Transport Puzzle Composition

Objectives

Students will use varied software applications to build games and game assets. Students will develop game programming using qualifiers. Students will apply puzzle design concepts in video games.

Situation

The Really Cool Game Company believes you have demonstrated great skill in acquiring knowledge and skills. It believes you are ready to work on a new project using different software. The project involves several mini-puzzles that will be bundled together in a new app for casual gamers. These simple puzzles will allow you to practice the new software while creating new content. The first puzzle is a classic transport puzzle, like the one shown on Figure 7-14 of the textbook. Your task is to design the tutorial level of the game. Later levels will increase in size and use custom images to add difficulty.

The software you will be using is Multimedia Fusion 2 (MMF2). If you have never used either MMF2 or The Games Factory 2 (TGF2) software, complete the Getting Started activity provided by your instructor before beginning this activity. You need a basic knowledge of either MMF2 or TGF2 to start this activity.

How to Begin

New

1. Launch MMF2.
2. Click the **New** button on the **Main** toolbar.
3. In the **Workspace** window, right-click on the Application 1 branch, select **Rename** from the shortcut menu, and enter Slide_Puzzle.
4. Right-click on the Frame 1 branch, select **Rename** from the shortcut menu, and enter Puzzle 1.
5. In the **Window** tab of the **Properties** window for the application (not the frame), change the Size property to 300 wide × 350 tall. You may need to float or resize the **Properties** window to access the property. When you enter the second dimension, a message appears asking if you want to resize all frames to match the application size, as shown in **Figure 1.** Click the **Yes** button.
6. Click **Save As** in the **File** pull-down menu, and save the game build as *LastName*_Puzzle_Transport in your working folder.

Game Map

The frame editor is where the game map is designed in Multimedia Fusion 2. The map does not have to be a tile based, as it did in 001 Game Creator. However, for this game, a tiled game map makes the most sense in organizing the objects. MMF2 uses a grid system to create the tiled area for the map.

7. In the storyboard editor, double-click the thumbnail of the Puzzle 1 frame to open the frame editor.

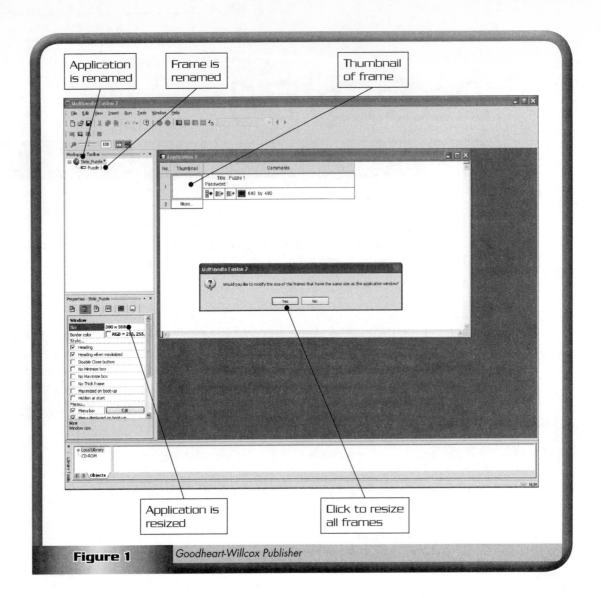

Application is renamed

Frame is renamed

Thumbnail of frame

Application is resized

Click to resize all frames

Figure 1   Goodheart-Willcox Publisher

Grid Setup

8. Click the **Grid Setup** button on the **Frame Editor Toolbar**. The **Grid Setup** dialog box is displayed, as shown in **Figure 2**.

9. Enter 50 in the **Width** and **Height** text boxes. This sets the size of the grid in pixels.

10. Check the **Snap to** and **Show grid** check boxes, and click the **OK** button.

Game Tiles

11. Click **New Object** in the **Insert** pull-down menu.

12. In the **Create New Object** dialog box, click All Objects on the left, and double-click Active on the right.

13. Click anywhere on the frame to place the new active object, which has a default image of a blue diamond.

14. With the active object selected, click the **Size/Position** tab of the **Properties** window, and enter 100 in the **Width** and **Height** text boxes.

15. Enter 0 in the **X** text box in the **Position** area, and enter 50 in the **Y** text box.

16. Click the **About** tab in the **Properties** window, and enter Tile 1 in the **Name:** text box.

17. Double-click on the blue diamond to open the image editor, as shown in **Figure 3**.

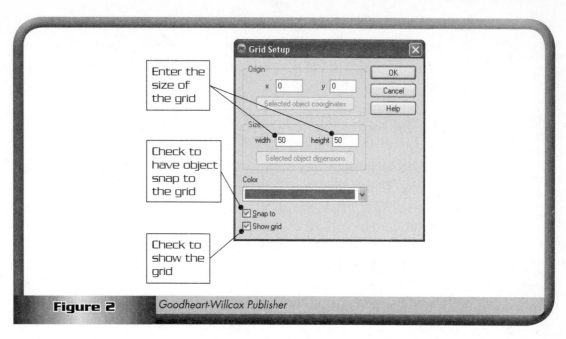

Enter the size of the grid

Check to have object snap to the grid

Check to show the grid

Figure 2   Goodheart-Willcox Publisher

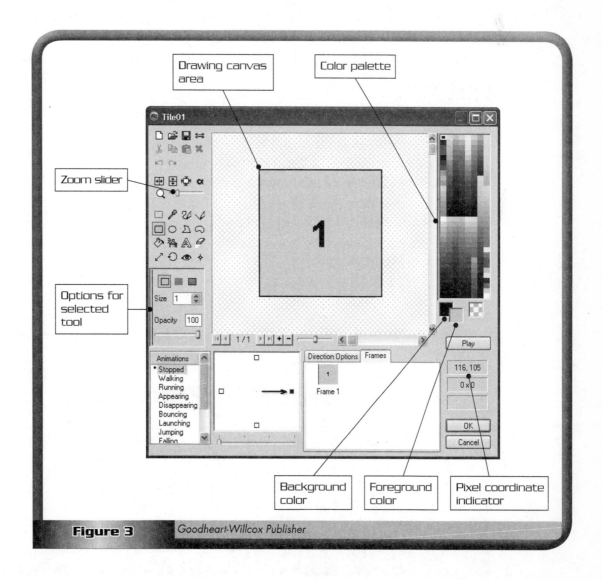

Drawing canvas area

Color palette

Zoom slider

Options for selected tool

Background color

Foreground color

Pixel coordinate indicator

Figure 3   Goodheart-Willcox Publisher

Clear

18. Click the **Clear** button to erase the default image.

19. Use the slider in the middle of the tools to increase the magnification.

20. Change the foreground color swatch to black by left-clicking on the black color swatch in the palette.

Text tool

21. Click the **Text tool** button.

22. Click the **Font** button that appears below the **Text tool** button, and change the font settings to Arial, bold, and 22 points.

23. Click in the top-left corner of the drawing canvas. The **Text** dialog box is displayed.

24. Enter 1. The number 1 is placed on the drawing canvas.

25. With the **Text** dialog box open, drag the 1 to the visual center of the drawing canvas, and then close the **Text** dialog box. It is important to make changes to the position of the text before closing the dialog box.

Rectangle

26. Click the **Rectangle** button, and click the left-hand button that appears below it, which creates only an outline.

27. Draw the rectangle by clicking at (0,0) and dragging to (100,100). The pixel coordinate indicator below the **Play** button displays the cursor location.

28. Change the foreground swatch color to a light color of your choice.

Fill tool

29. Click the **Fill tool** button, and click anywhere in the transparent area of the drawing canvas to fill it with color. The transparent area is indicated by the checkerboard of white and gray squares.

30. Click the **OK** button to close the image editor and update the object's image.

Qualifiers

In 001 Game Creator, objects are classified as good, neutral, or bad or as a parent or child. MMF2 offers a similar ability to classify objects using qualifiers. A *qualifier* assigns a classification to the object.

31. Select the Tile 1 object, if it is not already selected.

32. Click the **Events** tab in the **Properties** window.

33. Click the **Qualifier(s)** property, and then click the **Edit** button that is displayed. The **Object Qualifiers** dialog box is displayed.

34. Click the **Add** button. The **Add a Qualifier to an Object** dialog box is displayed, as shown in **Figure 4**.

Figure 4   *Goodheart-Willcox Publisher*

35. Click the Good qualifier, click the **OK** button to close the **Add a Qualifier to an Object** dialog box, and click the **OK** button to close the **Object Qualifiers** dialog box. The qualifier is applied to the Tile 1 object.

Cloning Tiles

The game requires a total of nine tiles for the player to manipulate on the game map. You might think the easiest way to do this would be to copy one tile and paste it eight times. However, when copying and pasting an object in MMF2, the new object is associated as a child of the original. The copy has the same look and programming as the original. This is called an *instance* of the original. Any changes to the copy or parent are applied to *all* instances. To create a copy in MMF2 that is different from the original parent object, a *clone* must be created. Cloning an object creates a new parent object that is not associated with the original. Any changes to the clone are not applied to the original.

36. Right-click on the Tile 1 object, and click **Clone Object** in the shortcut menu. The **Clone Object** dialog box is displayed, as shown in **Figure 5.**

37. Enter 3 in the **Rows** and **Columns** text boxes, and click the **OK** button. An array of nine objects is created. Each clone is also automatically sequentially named as Tile 2, Tile 3, etc., which is one reason to be thoughtful in naming objects.

38. Double-click on the tile named Tile 2 to open the image editor.

Color picker

39. Click the **Color picker** button, and click on the fill color in the drawing canvas area. This sets the foreground color to that color.

Fill tool

40. Click the **Fill tool** button, and click inside the 1 in the drawing canvas area. This effectively removes the 1 from the image.

41. Change the foreground color back to black, add the text 2 to the middle of the canvas, and close the image editor to update the image.

42. Repeat this process to number the tiles 1 through 8. If you wish, use different background colors similar to what is shown in textbook Figure 7-14.

Empty Space

There needs to be an empty space in the game board so the player can shift the tiles around. The game only contains eight tiles, but there are currently nine. The Tile 9 object will simulate the empty space.

43. Click the Tile 9 object to select it.

44. In the **About** tab of the **Properties** window, change the name to Blank Space.

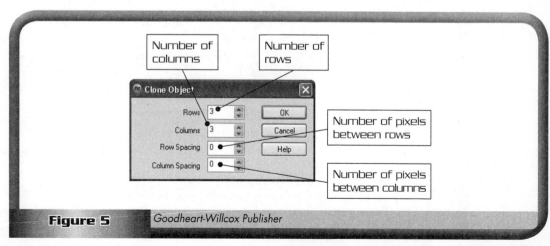

Figure 5 *Goodheart-Willcox Publisher*

45. In the **Events** tab of the **Properties** window, edit the **Qualifier(s)** property and delete the Good qualifier.

46. Double-click the Tile 9 object to display the image editor.

47. Change the background color and the text to gray (or other light color), and close the image editor. The game should look like a blank space is located in the lower-right corner, as shown in **Figure 6**.

Marker Object

A marker object will be used to assist in moving the tiles and the blank space. The marker will be created when the player clicks a tile, and then used as a reference point for movement of the tile and blank space. The marker will not be visible to the player.

48. Insert a new active object outside of the game frame area (on the gray area).

49. Name the object Click Marker.

50. Set the size of the Click Marker object to 30×30. The specific size of this object is not important. It can be larger or smaller if you choose.

51. Open the Click Marker object in the image editor, clear the image, and fill it with a color not used as a background color for the tiles or blank space. The image will be visible for testing, but will not be visible to the player when all programming is added.

52. Close the image editor.

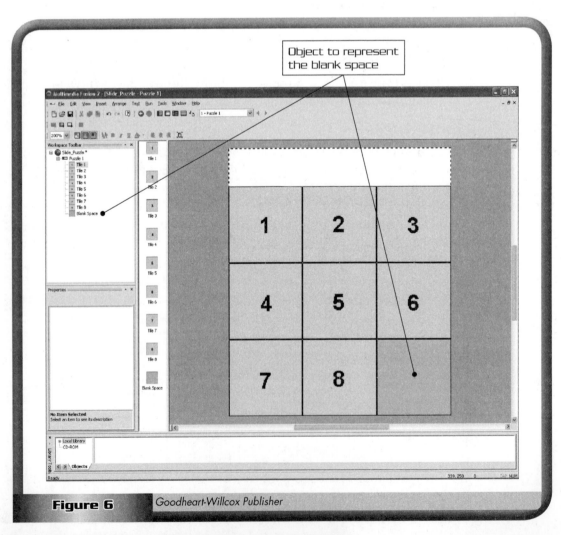

Figure 6   *Goodheart-Willcox Publisher*

Programming the User Interface

The game is ultimately going to be programmed by another team for use with a touch-screen device. For your task, this can be simulated on the computer for testing and design by using the mouse inputs. The first part of the pseudo code for this control is:

IF the player left-clicks a Group.Good object,

THEN create a Click Marker object in the same location as the Group.Good object.

In MMF2, the condition side of the event is the **IF** side of the logic statement. Imagine the word "if" where the line numbers are in the event editor, and you should be able to see how the programming in the event editor matches the pseudo code perfectly.

Event Editor

53. Click the **Event Editor** button on the **Navigate Toolbar** to open the event editor.

54. Click New condition on the first line. The **New Condition** dialog box is displayed.

55. Right-click on the keyboard/mouse icon, and click **The mouse** > **User clicks on an object** in the shortcut menu as shown in **Figure 7.** The **User Clicks on an Object** dialog box is displayed.

56. Click the **Left button** and **Single click** radio buttons, and then click the **OK** button. A different **User Clicks on an Object** dialog box is displayed.

57. Click the Group.Good object, which looks like an apple, and click the **OK** button. The condition is created, as shown in **Figure 8.**

58. Locate the **Create New Object** column in the actions programming section of the event editor. Hover the cursor over each column heading to see the name of the column.

59. Right-click in the cell where the **Create New Object** column and the **Line 1** row intersect, and click **Create object** in the shortcut menu.

60. In the **Create Object** dialog box, click the Click Marker object, and click the **OK** button. A different **Create Object** dialog box is displayed, and the frame editor is temporarily displayed.

61. Click the **Relative to:** radio button. The **Choose an Object** dialog box is displayed.

62. Click the Group.Good object, and click the **OK** button.

63. In the **Create Object** dialog box, enter 0 in the **X** and **Y** text boxes, then click the **OK** button. The event editor is redisplayed.

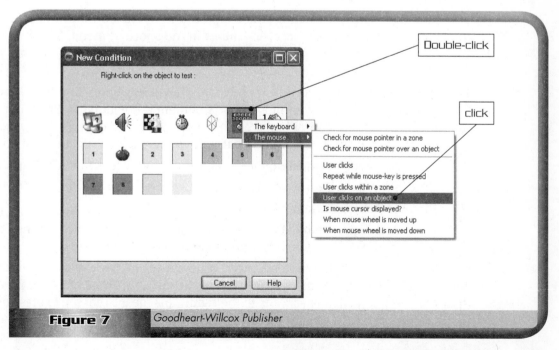

Figure 7 *Goodheart-Willcox Publisher*

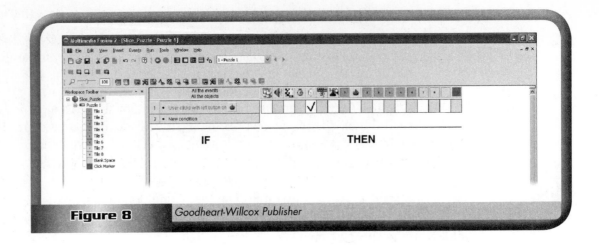

Figure 8   *Goodheart-Willcox Publisher*

The first line of programming is now complete. In this programming, relative coordinates were used. Relative coordinates are different from the absolute or actual coordinates as the XY coordinates will use an absolute value equal to the exact coordinate points entered. Relative coordinates are defined from the current location of a specified object. The specified object is a reference point in the game. To best associate relative coordinates with programming pseudo code, a relative coordinate specification can be "where this object is" or "where this object was before."

The next programming checks for the location of the tile the user clicked in relation to the blank space. This is done is several steps, the first one checking to see if the blank space is to the right of the clicked tile. This pseudo code is:

> **IF** the Click Marker object overlaps the Group.Good object
>> **AND** the blank space is 100 pixels to the right of the Click Marker object
>> **AND** the blank space is in the same row as the Click Marker object

64. Click New condition on line 2. The **New Condition** dialog box is displayed.

65. Right-click on the Click Marker object, and click **Collisions** > **Overlapping another object** in the shortcut menu.

66. In the **Test a Collision** dialog box that is displayed, click the Group.Good object, and click the **OK** button.

67. To add an **AND** statement to the condition, right-click on the condition in line 2 (not the line number), and click **Insert** in the shortcut menu. The **New Condition** dialog box is displayed, which is where you start constructing the first **AND** statement of the pseudo code.

68. Right-click on the Blank Space object, and click **Position** > **Compare X position to a value** from the shortcut menu. The **Compare X Position to a Value** dialog box is displayed, as shown in **Figure 9.** This dialog box is known as the *expression editor,* and the name shown in the title bar will change depending on what you are doing.

69. Click the **Choose comparison method:** drop-down list, and click **Equal** in the list.

70. Click in the **Enter expression to compare with:** text box, and delete the zero.

71. Click the **Retrieve data from an object** button.

72. In the **New Expression** dialog box that is displayed, right-click on the Click Marker object, and click **Position** > **X Coordinate** in the shortcut menu.

The expression in the expression editor now reads X("Click Marker"). This is the way MMF2 states "the X coordinate of the Click Marker object." Remember, the pseudo code states to check if the blank space is to the right. This means that the expression still needs some work. Click at the end of the expression in the expression editor, and enter +100.

Name: _____

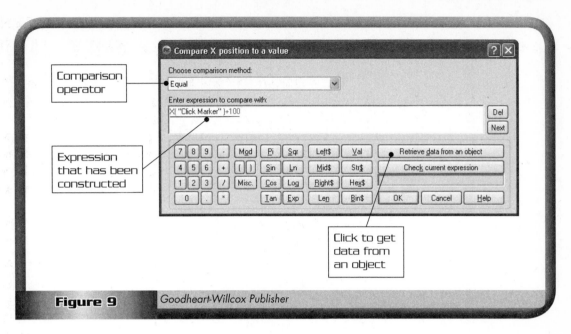

| Comparison operator |
| Expression that has been constructed |

Click to get data from an object

Figure 9   *Goodheart-Willcox Publisher*

The expression now means MMF2 will check to see if the X position of the Blank Space object is 100 pixels to the right of the Click Marker object, which has been created on the location of the tile the user clicks. The expression should match **Figure 9.**

73. Click the **OK** button to close the expression editor and return to the event editor. Line 2 now contains two conditions.

74. Insert another condition on line 2. This will be for the third line of pseudo code, as shown in **Figure 10.**

75. In the **New Condition** dialog box, right-click on the Blank Space object, and click **Position** > **Compare Y position to a value** in the shortcut menu.

76. In the expression editor, construct an expression that checks for the position equal to the Y position of the Click Marker object. In this case, the "same row" would have the same Y value as the Click Marker object. The "same column" would have the same X value as the Click Marker object.

Additional Directions

In the game, the player has limited moves available. A tile can be moved left, right, up, or down and always only to the open space. Below are the steps needed to efficiently allow for the movements. To save time, you will copy, paste, and edit the existing conditions.

77. Right-click on the line number for line 2, and click **Copy** in the shortcut menu. The entire contents of line 2 will be highlighted in black if you have done this correctly.

78. Right-click on the line number for line 3, and click **Paste** in the shortcut menu.

79. Paste in line 4 and then line 5. There should be five lines, numbered 1 through 5, and lines 2 through 4 contain the same conditions.

80. Double-click the text of the condition on line 3 that states X position of *(Blank Space object icon)* = X("*(Click Marker object icon)*")+100. The expression editor is displayed. Do not double-click the icons, as doing so will not display the expression editor.

81. Edit the expression by changing +100 to −100. This will check if the X position of the Blank Space object is 100 pixels to the left of the current object.

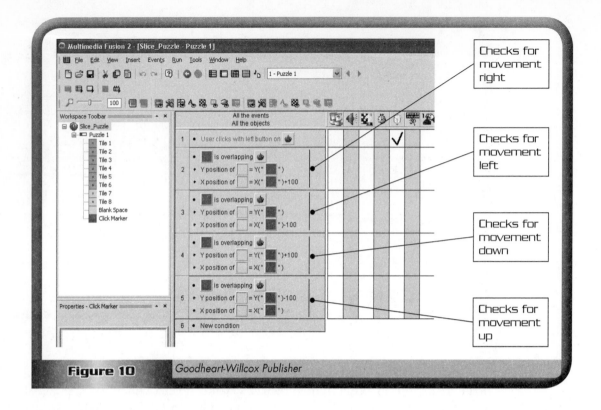

Figure 10

Goodheart-Willcox Publisher

82. Click the **OK** button to close the expression editor. Line 3 should match **Figure 10**.

83. Edit the "X condition" on line 4, and edit the expression by deleting +100. The expression should be X("Click Marker"). Line 4 will check for downward movement, and tiles in the same column have the same X value.

84. Edit the "Y condition" on line 4, and add +100 to the expression. The expression should be Y("Click Marker")+100. This checks for downward movement. Remember, in MMF2, the +Y direction is down. Line 4 should match **Figure 10**.

85. Edit both conditions on line 5 to match this pseudo code:

> **IF** the Click Marker object is overlapping a Group.Good object
> > **AND** the Blank Space object is 100 pixels above the Click Marker object
> > **AND** the Blank Space object is in the same column as the Click Marker object

Moving the Tiles

An event in MMF2 consists of a condition (**IF**) and an action or event (**THEN**). Events are programmed by adding actions to the objects shown in the table in the event editor. Looking at the event editor, it is set up like a table, with rows, columns, and cells. The conditions appear as rows, and the objects appear as columns. The cells where the condition rows and object columns intersect are where event programming is added. Event programming is represented by a check mark.

First, the game needs to detect a valid game move. A valid game move is clicking a game tile that is next to the Blank Space object. Clicking a tile that is not next to the empty space is an illegal move. Additionally, when the player makes a valid game move, the Click Marker object needs to be placed in the location where the player clicked. The programming for this has already been completed. Next, the clicked tile needs to be moved to the blank space. Finally, the Blank Space object needs to be moved over the Click Marker object and the Click Marker object deleted.

Name: _____

The pseudo code needed to move to the right is:

> **IF** the player left-clicks a Group.Good object
>> **AND** the Blank Space object is 100 pixels to the right of the Click Marker object
>> **AND** the Blank Space object is in the same row as the Click Marker object,
> **THEN** move the Group.Good object to the location of the Blank Space object
>> **AND** move the Blank Space object to the location of the Click Marker object
>> **AND** delete the Click Marker object.

86. Right-click in the cell where the **Group.Good** column and the **Line 2** row intersect, and click **Position** > **Select position** in the shortcut menu. The **Select Position** dialog box is displayed, and the frame editor is temporarily displayed, as shown in **Figure 11.**

87. Click the **Relative to:** radio button. The **Choose an Object** dialog box is displayed.

88. Click the Blank Space object, and click the **OK** button.

89. In the **Create Object** dialog box, enter 0 in the **X** and **Y** text boxes, then click the **OK** button. The event editor is redisplayed.

90. Hover the cursor over the check mark in line 2. The programming appears in a pop-up window, which states Set position at (0,0) from *Blank Space icon.* This means the Group.Good object will be placed in the same location as the Blank Space object.

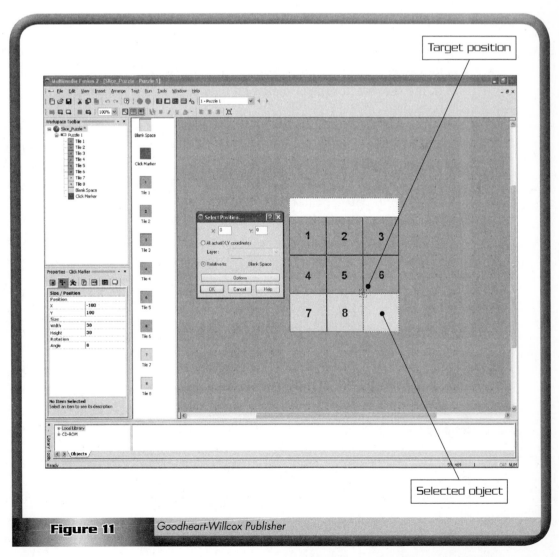

Figure 11 *Goodheart-Willcox Publisher*

91. Drag this check mark to the cell directly below in the **Line 3** row. This copies the programming. MMF2 allows the designer to quickly copy code using this drag-and-drop method.

92. Similarly, copy programming into the **Group.Good** column for the **Line 4** and **Line 5** rows.

Moving the Space

Programming has been created to record the position of the tile the player clicks and to move the clicked tile into the blank space. Next, the blank space needs to be moved to where the clicked tile was. This is the pseudo code:

IF the Group.Good object is overlapping the Blank Space object,
THEN move the Blank Space object to the location of the Click Marker object
AND delete the Click Marker object to reset the gameplay for another player turn.

93. Click New condition on line 6.

94. In the **New Condition** dialog box, right-click on the **Group.Good** icon, and click **Collisions > Overlapping another object** in the shortcut menu. The **Test a Collision** dialog box is displayed, as shown in **Figure 12.**

95. Click the Blank Space object, and click the **OK** button to close the **Test a Collision** dialog box. Note: if you edit this condition later, the dialog box will appear different than what is shown at this time.

96. Right-click in the cell where the **Blank Space** column intersects with the **Line 6** row, and click **Position > Select position...** in the shortcut menu. The **Select Position** dialog box is displayed, and the frame editor is temporarily displayed.

97. In the **Select Position** dialog box, click the **Relative to:** radio button.

98. In the **Choose an Object** dialog box, click the Click Marker object, and click the **OK** button.

99. In the **Select Position** dialog box, enter 0 in the **X** and **Y** text boxes, and click the **OK** button. This specifies to move the object directly on top of the Click Marker object.

100. In the event editor, right-click in the cell where the **Click Marker** column intersects the **Line 6** row, and click **Destroy** in the shortcut menu. This cleans up the game frame so the player can take another turn.

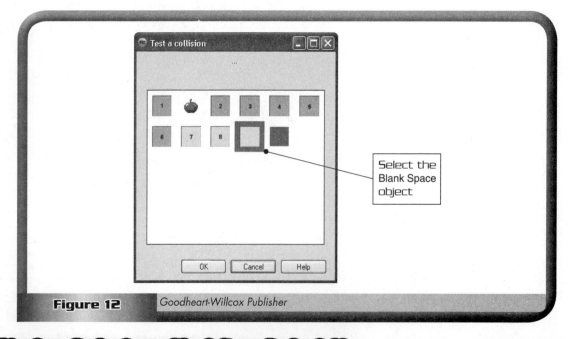

Figure 12   *Goodheart-Willcox Publisher*

Video Game Design Composition Software Design Guide

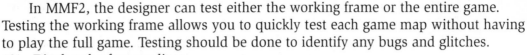
Testing

In MMF2, the designer can test either the working frame or the entire game. Testing the working frame allows you to quickly test each game map without having to play the full game. Testing should be done to identify any bugs and glitches.

Frame Editor

101. Display the frame editor.

102. Move the game tiles to produce a random pattern with the blank space in the center. Make sure the edges of the objects align.

Run Frame

103. Click the **Run Frame** button on the **Run** toolbar. The game appears in a new window.

104. Click the numbered tiles of the game to see if they will move correctly. Note any bugs. Be sure to test for diagonal movement. See if you can solve the puzzle.

105. Close the game window when done testing.

Bug Repair

You should have noticed a Level A bug. If the player clicks a tile that is diagonal to the blank space, the marker appears, but the tile and blank space do not switch places. This also occurs if the player clicks a tile that is not adjacent to the blank space. While it is correct that the tile should not move, the marker is not deleted and the game freezes. This is a Level A bug because it prevents gameplay. Refer to Figure 1-14 in the textbook. It must be fixed.

Event Editor

106. Display the event editor.

107. Add a new condition, and in the **New Condition** dialog box, right-click on the timer icon, and click every in the shortcut menu. The **Every** dialog box is displayed, as shown in **Figure 13.**

108. Enter 0 in the **Hour(s)**, **Minute(s)**, and **Second(s)** text boxes.

109. Enter 1 in the **1/100** text box. This means the event will occur every .01 seconds.

110. Click the **OK** button to close the **Every** dialog box.

111. Right-click in the cell where the **Marker Counter** column intersects the **Line 7** row, and click **Destroy** in the shortcut menu.

Run Frame

112. Test play the frame. Make sure the bug is fixed. You should be able to fully solve the puzzle now.

GUI Design and Player Feedback

Hopefully, you were able to solve the puzzle. However, there was little feedback and no reward for achieving the victory condition. Controls and feedback information will be inserted in the space above the game pieces at the top of the game map, as shown in **Figure 13.**

Frame Editor

113. Display the frame editor.

114. Click the **Show Grid** and **Snap to Grid** buttons to turn off the grid and snap. The buttons are highlighted blue when on.

Show Grid

115. Insert a new button object. The button object is located in the **Interface** group in the **Create New Object** dialog box.

116. Double-click the inserted button to edit the text displayed on the button.

Snap to Grid

117. Enter Reset in the **Enter New Button Text** dialog box, and click the **OK** button.

118. Using the **Properties** window, change the position of the button to (230,10).

119. Change the **Name** property for the button to Reset.

120. Insert a new static text object, and place it next to the **Reset** button.

121. Double-click the static text object to edit the text, and enter Score. The static text object is located in the **All Objects** group in the **Create New Object** dialog box.

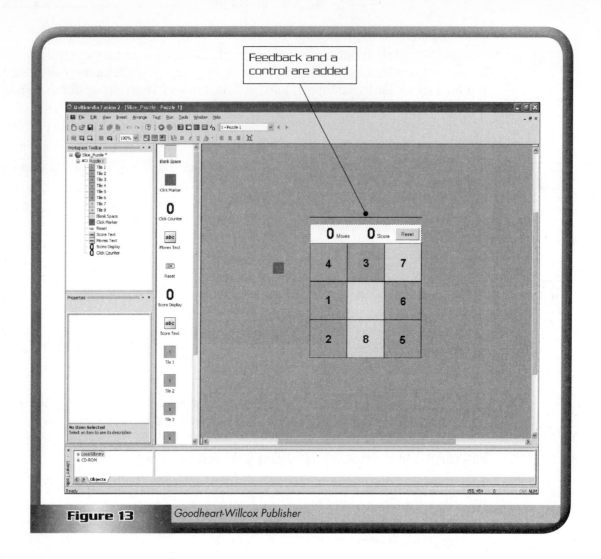

Feedback and a control are added

Figure 13   *Goodheart-Willcox Publisher*

122. Use the sizing handles to resize the static text box so it is only a bit larger than the word.

123. In the **Settings** tab of the **Properties** window, uncheck the **Border** check box. By default, static text has a border around the object.

124. Set the position of the static text to (180,15).

125. Change the **Name** property to Score Text.

126. Insert a new static text object, enter Moves, place it at (70,15), remove the border, resize the object, and change its name to Moves Text.

127. Insert a new score object. The score object is located in the **Games** group in the **Create New Object** dialog box.

128. Set the position of the score object to (175,40), its size to 20 × 30, and its name as Score Display.

129. Insert a new counter object. The counter object is located in the **Data** group in the **Create New Object** dialog box.

130. Set the position of the counter object to (65,40), its size to 20 × 30, and its name to Click Counter.

Scoring and Counting

One part of the feedback provided to the player will be how many times the player clicks a tile, either a valid move or an invalid move. The other part of the feedback will be a score. Each time the player clicks, points will be subtracted from the score. The victory condition will be achieving the high score.

First, you will add a comment to the programming. Comments are a very important part of programming. They inform others, as well as the programmer, what is happening in the code. Do not overlook adding comments. It is very easy to get caught up in adding lines of code and to forget to add comments. Even if you think what you are doing at the moment is clear and can be understood by anyone, somebody else may not feel that way, and you may not feel that way a few weeks later when you look at the code again.

Event Editor

131. Display the event editor.

132. Right-click on the line number for line 8, and click **Insert > A comment** the shortcut menu. The **Edit Text** dialog box is displayed, as shown in **Figure 14.**

133. Enter Scoring and Counting Programming in the text box, and click the **OK** button. The comment is added on line 8. Now anybody looking at the code knows that the programming following the comment is for scoring and counting.

134. Create a new condition on line 9, and program this pseudo code:

> **IF** the **Reset** button is clicked,
> > **THEN** restart the current frame.

135. Create a new condition on line 10, and program the following pseudo code. To change the player 1 score, right-click in the **Player 1** column, click **Score > Subtract from score** in the shortcut menu, and enter 1 in the expression editor.

> **IF** the user left-clicks on a Group.Good object,
> **THEN** subtract 1 from the player 1 score
> > **AND** add 1 to the click counter.

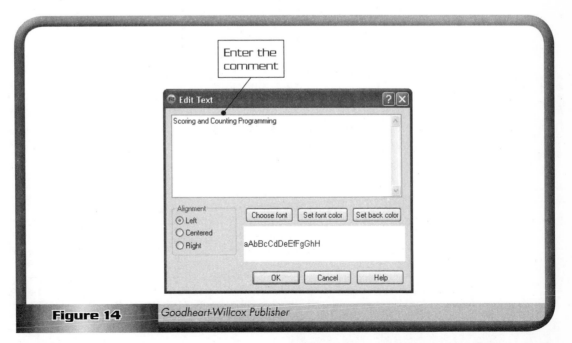

136. Save your work, and test play the frame. Check the score, counter, and **Reset** button functions. Note any bugs.

Run Frame

Enter the comment

Figure 14   *Goodheart-Willcox Publisher*

Debugging the Feedback Information

You should have noticed that pressing the **Reset** button will reset the tiles but does not reset the counter and score. You should also have noticed that the score does not change.

137. Create a new condition on line 11, and program this pseudo code:

> **IF** at the start of the frame,
> **THEN** set the player 1 score to 500
> > **AND** set the click counter to 0.

138. Save your work, test play the frame, and debug if needed.

Run Frame

Winner Page Formatting

The victory condition is achieving the high score. There should be a way to display the player's score so it can be compared to the scores of other players. This will be achieved with a high-score page, which will also serve as a reward for the player.

Storyboard Editor

139. Display the storyboard editor, and click the 2 on the second line to add a second frame to the game.

140. Change the name of the new frame to Winner.

141. Double-click on the thumbnail image for the Winner frame, which is currently blank, to open the frame in the frame editor.

142. Insert a new formatted text object, and resize the text box to the width of the frame.

143. Enter the text Winner!, and use the tools on the **Frame Editor Toolbar** to center the text, make the font bold, and set the font size to 22 points.

144. Add to the frame the buttons shown in **Figure 15.**

145. Insert a new high score object.

146. Set the position to (10,100) and the size to 280 × 250.

147. Move the Winner! text so it is vertically centered in the space above the high score object.

148. Select the Winner frame in the project tree. The properties for the frame are displayed in the **Properties** window.

149. In the **Settings** tab of the **Properties** window, change for the **Background** property to the color R0, G255, B0. Choose a different color to match the color theme of your tiles, if you wish.

Flags

The game has a winner frame, but there currently is no way to display it to the player. The Puzzle 1 frame must contain programming to test for the condition when all pieces of the puzzle are in the correct locations, and then to display the Winner frame to the player. To do this, you will be using *flags*, which are switches.

Button Text	Button Name	Position	Size
Quit	Quit Button	0,50	64 × 32
Next Puzzle	Next Button	110,50	82 × 32
Replay	Replay Button	235,50	64 × 32

Figure 15   *Goodheart-Willcox Publisher*

Video Game Design Composition Software Design Guide

Flags can be on or off. The steps below detail how to set the flag for each puzzle piece to on. When the flags on all pieces are switched on, the puzzle is solved.

Event Editor

150. Display the event editor for the Puzzle 1 frame. To do this, select the frame in the project tree, and click the **Event Editor** button.

151. On line 12, add a comment that states Victory Condition Programming.

152. On line 13, add a new condition to check the Tile 1 object's position compared to an X value equal to 0.

153. On line 13, add a second condition to check the Tile 1 object's position compared to an Y value equal to 50. The two conditions check to see if the Tile 1 object has the XY coordinates of the winning position for the tile.

154. On new lines, create the conditions needed to test the position for the rest of the game pieces, as shown in **Figure 16.** You can copy, paste, and edit programming to save time. To change the object, double-click on the object icon in the condition statement. To change the value in the expression, double-click on the condition statement.

155. Right-click in the cell where the **Tile 1** column intersects the **Line 13** row, and click **Flags** > **Set On** in the shortcut menu. The expression editor is displayed.

156. Enter 1 as the expression, and close the expression editor. This value is the number of the flag on the object.

157. Similarly, turn on a flag that matches the object number, such as flag 2 for Tile 2 and so on, when the object is in the correct position. Refer to **Figure 17.** Remember to copy, paste, and edit programming to save time.

The programming you just added sets a flag if the tile is in the correct position. However, the game still needs to check to see if all flags are on. If so, the player has solved the puzzle. The Winner frame can be displayed and the high score shown.

158. Add a new condition on line 21.

159. In the **New Condition** dialog box, right-click on the Tile 1 object, and click **Alterable Values** > **Flags** > **Is flag on?** in the shortcut menu. The expression editor is displayed.

160. Enter 1 in the expression editor, and click the **OK** button.

161. In the same condition insert additional conditions to test if the flag on each tile is on. There will be a total of eight conditions, one for each tile.

Object	Coordinates
Tile 1	0,50
Tile 2	100,50
Tile 3	200,50
Tile 4	0,150
Tile 5	100,150
Tile 6	200,150
Tile 7	0,250
Tile 8	100,250

Figure 16   *Goodheart-Willcox Publisher*

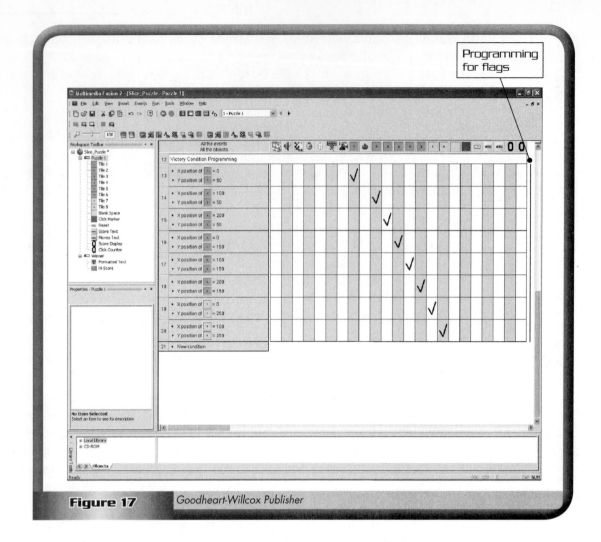

Figure 17   *Goodheart-Willcox Publisher*

162. Right-click in the cell where the **Storyboard Controls** column intersects the **Line 22** row, and click Jump to the Winner frame. The **Choose a Storyboard Frame** dialog box is displayed, as shown in **Figure 18.**

163. Click the Winner frame, and click the **OK** button.

Run Application

164. Save your work, and test play the game by clicking the **Run Application** button. Note any bugs.

Bug Repair

You may have noticed a level B bug. The flag for each tile is turned on the first time the tile is in the correct position. If the tile is moved out of position, the flag is still on. A player could just move around the screen and trip all flags without getting the correct solution to the puzzle. To fix this issue, the game will reset all flags to off each time the player clicks. The pseudo code for this for the first object is:

> **IF** the user left clicks,
>> **THEN** set internal flag 1 for the Tile 1 object to off.

165. Locate the line of programming with the condition User clicks with left button.

166. Right-click where this line intersects the **Tile 1** column, and click **Flags** > **Set off** in the shortcut menu.

167. In the expression editor, enter 1, and click the **OK** button to close the expression editor.

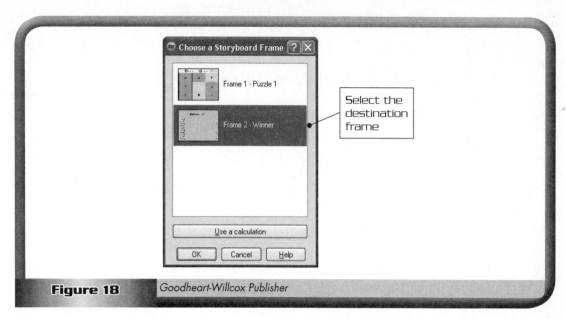

Figure 18   *Goodheart-Willcox Publisher*

168. Program objects Tile 2 through Tile 8 to turn off the correct internal flag every time the player clicks. Remember to copy, paste, and edit programming to save time.

Frame Editor

169. Display the frame editor, and organize the game map tiles so you can easily achieve victory.

170. Test play the game. Check that the tiles must be in their correct locations for the Winner page to display.

Run Application

Loser

By setting the score to count down from 500 for each click, a player can only take 500 moves before exhausting the available score. Not every player will be able to solve the puzzle in less than 500 moves. There should be a way to let the player know he or she did not succeed at the puzzle.

171. Display the storyboard editor, copy the Winner frame, and paste it as frame 3. To paste in the storyboard editor, do not right-click on the line number for the next line, rather right-click on the line number for the last existing frame. The frame will be pasted above the current last frame.

Storyboard Editor

172. Rename the new frame as Loser.

173. Open the Loser frame in the frame editor.

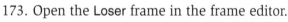
Frame Editor

174. Delete the high score object.

175. Edit the formatted text to read Please Try Again.

176. Insert a new button object, and change the display text to **Retry**.

177. In the event editor for the Loser frame, program this pseudo code: **IF** the player clicks the **Retry** button, **THEN** display the Puzzle 1 frame.

178. Display the event editor for the Puzzle 1 frame.

179. Add a new condition at the end of the programming script, and program this pseudo code: **IF** the player 1 score is zero, **THEN** jump to Loser frame.

Run Application

180. Save your work, test play the game, and debug it as needed.

Building the Application

MMF2 can export in many formats to support play on an iPhone, Android, and more. Add-ons to allow for exporting in these formats are available for purchase from the developer at www.clickteam.com. By default, a game built in MMF2 can be saved as an executable file for play on a PC without purchasing any add-ons.

181. Click **Build** > **Application** in the **File** pull-down menu. A standard Windows save dialog box is displayed.

182. Name the file *LastName_*Transport Puzzle, navigate to your working folder, and click the **Save** button.

183. Playing the executable version of the game by double-clicking on the EXE file in your working folder.

184. If the game is bug free, submit the game for grading as directed by your instructor.

Review Questions

1. In which module is the game map designed in MMF2?

   _____

   _____

2. Briefly describe how to change the image associated with an inserted object.

   _____

   _____

   _____

   _____

3. In MMF2, what is used to assign a classification to an object?

   _____

   _____

4. What is created if the copy of an object does not have properties associated with the parent object?

   _____

   _____

5. What is the purpose of the event editor in MMF2?

   _____

   _____

   _____

   _____

Activity 7-2

Mechanical Puzzle Composition

Objectives

Students will design a puzzle game using sensor objects. Students will apply puzzle design elements to create escalation. Students will program randomizing object attributes.

Situation

The Really Cool Game Company believes you are ready for more skills in puzzle design. It has a concept for a mechanical puzzle in which the player removes matching objects with a goal of having only one object remaining. Your task is to complete the proof of concept game build using two configurations for the sensor. Each configuration of the game will be tested by different audiences to see which is preferred and best understood.

How to Begin

New

1. Launch MMF2, and start a new game build.

2. Rename the application as Block Out.

3. Change the size of the application window to 320 × 576.

4. Rename the first frame as Level 1.

Frame Editor

5. Display the frame editor for Level 1, and change the grid setup so that the grids are 32 × 32. Also activate snap and show the grid.

6. Save your work as *LastName*_BlockOut.

Grid Setup

Puzzle Parts

7. Insert a new active object anywhere on the frame.

8. Rename the active object as Block.

9. Set the position of the Block object to (64,224).

Clear

10. Double-click the Block object to open the image editor.

11. Clear the default image from the canvas.

12. Fill the canvas with red.

13. Draw a black border around the edge of the canvas that is one pixel thick.

Fill tool

14. Click the **Hot Spot** button, and then click the center **Quick Move** button. This moves the origin of the object from the default location of the top-left corner to the center of the object, as shown in **Figure 1**.

Rectangle

15. In the **Frames** tab below the drawing canvas, right-click on Frame 1, and click **Copy** in the shortcut menu.

16. Right-click in a blank space of the **Frames** tab, and click **Paste** in the shortcut menu. A new frame is added to the animation.

View Hot Spot

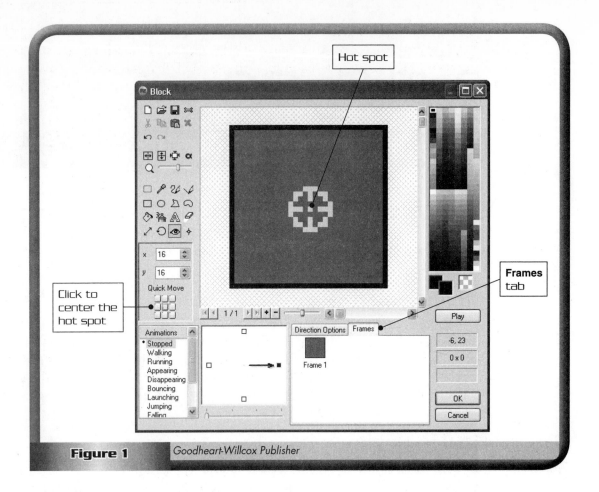

Figure 1 *Goodheart-Willcox Publisher*

17. Paste two more copies. There should be four frames named Frame 1, Frame 2, Frame 3, and Frame 4.

18. Click Frame 2 in the **Frames** tab. This makes it the current frame shown in the canvas area.

19. Change the background color to yellow.

20. Change the background color of Frame 3 to green.

21. Change the background color of Frame 4 to blue.

22. Close the image editor.

23. Right-click on the Block object, and click **Duplicate** in the shortcut menu. The **Duplicate Object** dialog box is displayed. *Duplicates* are copies that are identical to the original, including programming. Recall that *clones* are instances that do not inherit any properties from the original.

24. Enter 6 in the **Rows:** and **Columns:** text boxes, then click the **OK** button to create the duplicates. There are now 36 objects. Notice that each is named Block, and only one is shown in the list of objects to the left of the game frame area.

25. Insert a new active object, and place outside of the frame. The frame is represented by the white area, and outside the frame is the gray area.

26. Name the new object Sensor.

27. Change the size to 5 × 5.

28. Edit the image so the object is a black square.

Random Color Blocks

The game requires blocks in one of four different colors. To be efficient in constructing the game, you have created one block that has the four colors built in as frames in an animation. During gameplay, the movement directions of the block objects will be used to show different colors. The block objects will not move, so the player will see this as changing from one color of block to another color. This method allows for more efficient programming than if multiple active objects were created, one for each color of block.

29. Open any of the Block objects in the image editor. Remember, these objects are duplicates, so changes made to one are applied to all of them.

30. In the **Frames** tab, right-click on the frame with the yellow background, and click **Cut** in the shortcut menu. Click the **Yes** button in the warning that appears. You are removing the frame from the current animation set and direction, which is named Stopped and facing right. The animation set direction is indicated by the position indicator to the left of the frame, as shown in **Figure 2.**

31. Click the block at the top of the position indicator to set the direction for the Stopped animation to up. There are currently no frames in the animation set for the Stopped animation when the object is facing up.

32. In the **Frames** tab, right-click in the blank area, and click **Paste** in the shortcut menu. The animation frame with the yellow background is added to the animation set for the Stopped animation when the object is facing up.

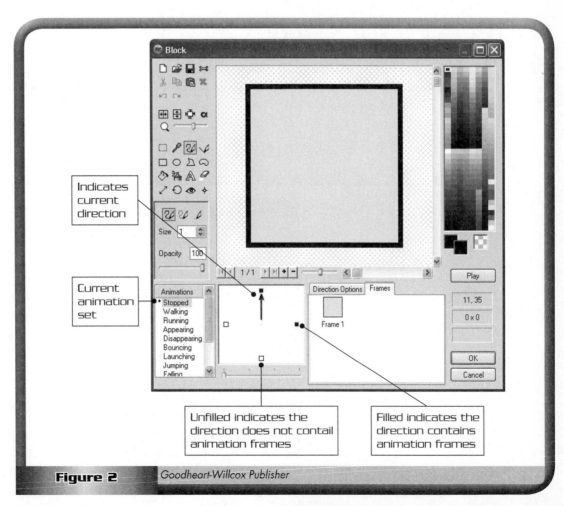

Figure 2   Goodheart-Willcox Publisher

33. Cut the frame with the green background from the right-facing Stopped animation, and paste it in the left-facing Stopped animation.

34. Cut the frame with the blue background from the right-facing Stopped animation, and paste it in the downward-facing Stopped animation. Each of the four direction now has a single animation frame, each with a different colored background.

35. Close the image editor.

Run Frame

36. Test play the frame. Make sure all Block objects are generated as red.

Programming Random Distribution of Blocks

At the beginning of the game, there needs to be a random distribution of colored blocks. This will be achieved by displaying different facing directions of the Stopped animation for each Block object duplicate.

Event Editor

37. Display the event editor.

38. On line 1, add a new condition for **IF** at the start of the frame. This is done by right-clicking on the **Storyboard Controls** icon in the **New Condition** dialog box, and clicking **Start of frame** in the shortcut menu.

39. Right-click in the cell in the **Block** column, and click **Direction > Set direction...** in the shortcut menu. The **Select Direction** dialog box is displayed, as shown in **Figure 3.**

40. Click the blocks at the **8**, **16**, and **24** positions. Arrows are displayed pointing to those directions, along with the default arrow at the **0** position. The game engine will randomly select the direction from any of these four directions.

41. Click the **OK** button to close the **Select Direction** dialog box.

42. On line 2, create the programming needed for this pseudo code:

> **IF** the player presses the space bar,
> **THEN** randomly set the block direction to up, down, left, or right.

Run Frame

43. Run the frame. Make sure the Block objects are randomly colored at the beginning of the game, and check that the colors are randomly changed when the space bar is pressed.

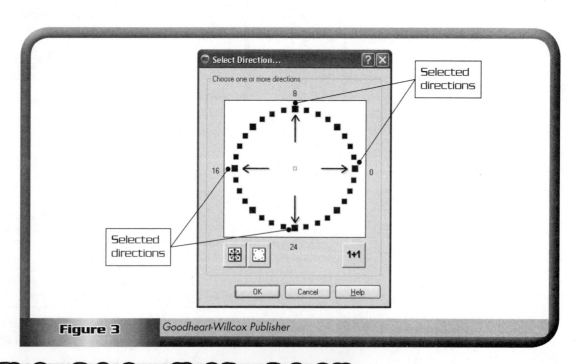

Figure 3   *Goodheart-Willcox Publisher*

Setting Sensor Objects

The rules for this game specify that any block touching the one the player clicks and the same color as the one the player clicks will be removed. The sensor object will be used to test if the blocks next to the clicked block meet the criteria to be removed.

44. On line 3, add a comment stating Sensor Placement and Block Removal.

45. On line 4, create the programming for this pseudo code:

    IF the user left-clicks on a Block object

46. Right-click in the cell where the **Line 4** row and **Create New Objects** column intersect, and click **Create Object** in the shortcut menu. The **Create Object** dialog box is displayed.

    The **IF** side of the logic statement is **IF the user left-clicks on a Block object**. You are now constructing the **THEN** side of the logic statement, which is expressed with this pseudo code:

    THEN create a Sensor object that is 32 pixels to the right of the Block object.

47. In the **Create Object** dialog box, click the Sensor object, and click the **OK** button. The frame editor is temporarily displayed, and a different **Create Object** dialog box is displayed, as shown in **Figure 4.**

48. In the **Create Object** dialog box, click the **Relative to:** radio button. The **Choose an Object** dialog box is displayed.

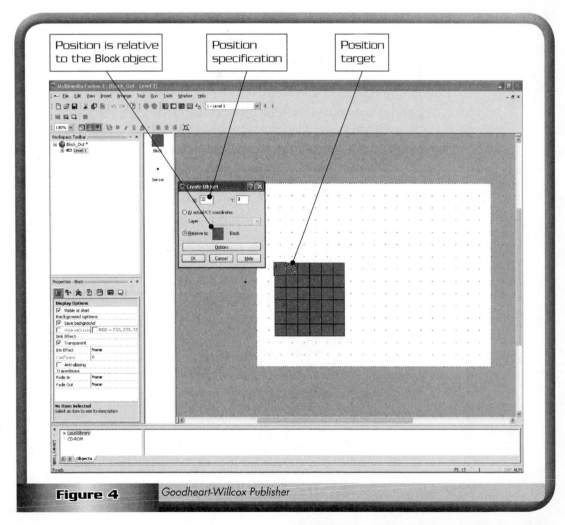

Figure 4   *Goodheart-Willcox Publisher*

49. In the **Choose an Object** dialog box, click the Block object, and click the **OK** button. The **Create Object** dialog box is redisplayed.

50. In the **X:** text box, enter 32. This specifies the sensor will be created 32 pixels to the right of the Block object.

51. Click the **OK** button to close the **Create Object** dialog box. The event editor is redisplayed.

52. Right-click on the check mark in line 4, and click **Create Object** in the shortcut menu. This allows adding more actions to this event. Add programming for this pseudo code, as shown in **Figure 5:**

> **AND** create a Sensor object that is 32 pixels to the left of the Block object
> **AND** create a Sensor object that is 32 pixels above the Block object
> **AND** create a Sensor object that is 32 pixels below the Block object

53. Test play the frame. See if a sensor appears in the exact center of the surrounding blocks when a block is clicked.

Run Frame

54. If the placement of the sensor is not correct, edit the image for the Sensor object, and move the hot spot to the center of the object.

Detecting Matching Colors

The sensors are used to detect if the blocks surrounding the clicked block are the same color. However, the game engine cannot "see" the color of the surrounding blocks objects. Instead, the programming must detect the current animation direction of each block. A counter object will be used for this. The pseudo code for this is:

> **IF** the player left-clicks a Block object,
> **THEN** set the counter to the animation direction of the Block object that was clicked.

Frame Editor

55. In the frame editor, add a new counter object named Direction Counter at (32,32).

56. In the event editor, right-click in the cell where the **Line 4** row and the **Direction Counter** column intersect, and click **Set Counter** in the shortcut menu. The expression editor is displayed.

Event Editor

57. Click the **Retrieve data from an object** button.

58. In the **New Expression** dialog box, right-click on the Block object, and click **Animation > Current direction value** in the shortcut menu.

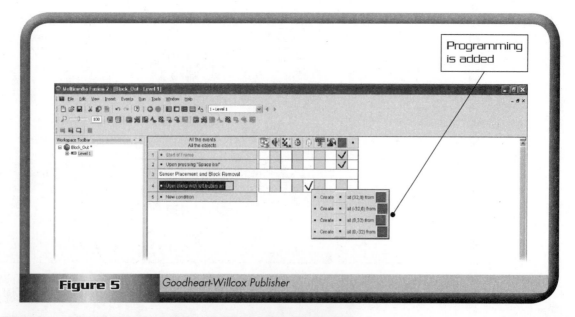

Figure 5 *Goodheart-Willcox Publisher*

59. The expression in the expression editor is Dir("Block"). Click the **OK** button to close the expression editor.

Run Frame

60. Test play the frame. Click each block. The counter should display the direction value of the clicked block, which corresponds to the color of the block: right, or red, is 0; up, or yellow, is 8; left, or green, is 16; and down, or blue, is 24. The sensor objects should be visible, as shown in **Figure 6.**

Collision Detection

Now the game can place a Sensor object in the correct place and detect the color of the block the player clicked. Next, this pseudo code needs to be programmed:

    IF the Sensor object is overlapping the Block object

        AND the Block object is facing the same direction as indicated by the Direction Counter object,

    THEN destroy the Sensor object and the Block object that overlap.

Event Editor

61. In the event editor, add a new condition on line 5. In the **New Condition** dialog box, right-click on the Sensor object, and click **Collision > Overlapping another object** in the shortcut menu.

62. In the **Test a Collision** dialog box that is displayed, click the Block object, and click the **OK** button.

63. Right-click on the condition for line 5, and click **Insert** in the pull-down menu.

64. In the **New Condition** dialog box, right-click on the Block object, and click **Direction > Compare direction of "Block"** in the shortcut menu.

1+1

65. In the **Compare Direction of "Block"** dialog box that is displayed, click on the **Calculate Direction** button. The expression editor is displayed.

Calculate Direction

66. In the expression editor, click the **Retrieve data from an object** button.

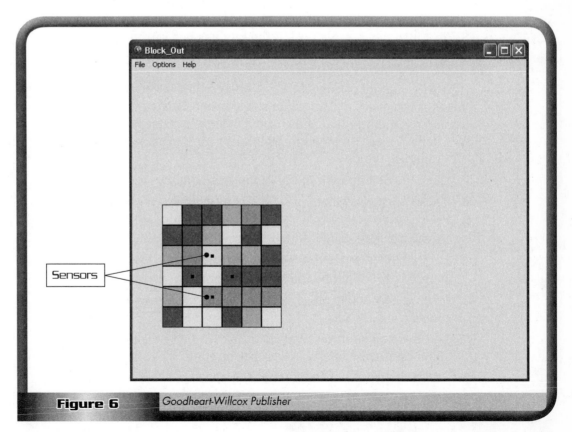

Figure 6   *Goodheart-Willcox Publisher*

67. In the **New Expression** dialog box that is displayed, right-click on the Direction Counter object, and click **Current Value** in the shortcut menu.

68. The expression in the expression editor is value("Direction Counter"). Click the **OK** button to close the expression editor.

69. On line 5, right-click in the **Block** column, and click **Destroy** in the shortcut menu.

70. On line 5, right-click in the **Sensor** column, and click **Destroy** in the shortcut menu.

Run Frame

71. Test play the frame. Click a block that has blocks of the same color touching it. Check to make sure the touching blocks are destroyed along with the sensors, but that the clicked block is *not* destroyed. Also check the functionality if a block is clicked that has no blocks of the same color touching it. Press the space bar to check if the remaining blocks are randomly recolored.

Bug Repair

Currently, sensor objects are destroyed only when they overlap blocks of the same color as the clicked block. Not only is this an ugly display, but it is also a bug because it allows the player to cheat. Since the sensors remain active if they are not deleted, the player can keep pressing the space bar until the colors of the blocks below the sensors are displayed in the same color as the clicked block. When this happens, those blocks are automatically deleted even though the player has not clicked another block. This pseudo code will correct the bug:

> **IF** always,
> **THEN** destroy the Sensor object.

Can you think of another way to program the game to correct the bug?

72. In the event editor, add a new condition on line 6.

Event Editor

73. In the **New Condition** dialog box, right-click on the Special icon, and click **Always** in the shortcut menu.

74. On line 6, right-click in the **Sensor** column, and click **Destroy** in the shortcut menu.

Run Frame

75. Test play the frame. Check if the bug has been fixed.

Aesthetic Improvements

This is a proof of concept game build, but it is very bland. For example, when a block is removed, a plain white space is left. Use the steps below to create a more pleasing background that is displayed when blocks are removed.

76. Click the Level 1 branch in the project tree to display its properties in the **Properties** window.

77. Click the **Settings** tab in the **Properties** window.

78. Click the color swatch in the **Background color** property.

79. Click a color swatch to select a color that will complement the display colors of the blocks. Make note of the RGB color values.

80. Display the frame editor, and move the Direction Counter object outside of the game frame so it will not be visible during gameplay.

81. Insert a new active object outside of the game frame, name it Filler Block, and set the size to 32 × 32.

82. Edit the image for the Filler Block object so it has a black border filled with the same color used for the screen background.

83. Set the hot spot to the center of the image.

Event Editor

Run Frame

84. Display the event editor, and add this pseudo code to line 5:

    THEN create a Filler Block object at (0,0) relative to the Block object.

85. Test play the frame. Make sure the filler block is added to each space created when a colored block is removed. It should appear as if the background color is showing, as shown in **Figure 7.**

GUI

The graphical user interface needs input and navigation buttons that will work with a handheld touch screen. Using an interface input such as pressing the space bar will not work on a handheld device.

86. In the frame editor, insert three button objects.

Frame Editor

87. Name the three buttons: **Replay**, **Shuffle**, **Quit**. Change the **Text** property to match the button name.

88. In the event editor, right-click on the condition line 2, and click **Replace** in the shortcut menu.

Event Editor

89. Program this pseudo code: **IF** the **Shuffle** button is clicked.

90. On line 7, add the comment: GUI Control Buttons.

91. On line 8, add this pseudo code as the condition: **IF** the **Replay** button is clicked.

92. On line 8, right-click in the **Storyboard Controls** column, and click **Restart the current frame** in the shortcut menu.

93. On line 9, add this pseudo code as the condition: **IF** the **Quit** button is clicked.

94. On line 9, right-click in the **Storyboard Controls** column, and click **End the application** in the shortcut menu.

95. Drag line 2 so it is part of the GUI Control Buttons group.

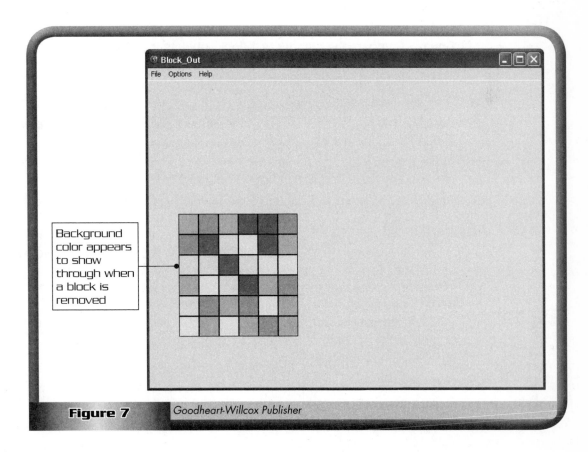

Figure 7   *Goodheart-Willcox Publisher*

Game Scoring

So far you have created a video game puzzle. It has rules, a game environment, and a victory condition. It also needs some additional gameplay attributes to increase player involvement and interaction. Currently, pressing the **Shuffle** button will allow the player the opportunity to win the game each time with a good strategy. Adding in a point reduction each time will add challenge. Adding in a high score table will reward the player for obtaining the most efficient solution.

Frame Editor

96. In the frame editor, add a new score object.

97. Set the position of the Score object to (200,60) and its size to 32 × 50.

Event Editor

98. Display the event editor, and edit the existing programming on line 1 (start of frame) to include this pseudo code: **AND** set the player 1 score to 500. Do this by right-clicking in the **Player 1** column, clicking **Score** > **Set Score** in the shortcut menu, and entering 500 in the expression editor.

99. On line 9 (**Shuffle** button clicked), edit the existing programming to include the following pseudo code: **THEN** the points for player 1 are reduced by 10. Do not enter a negative number, as the command is to subtract the specified number from the score.

Run Frame

100. Test play the frame. Check that the **Shuffle**, **Replay**, and **Quit** buttons function correctly. Also check that the score is reduced each time the **Shuffle** button is clicked.

Victory Condition

Storyboard Editor

101. Add a winner page.

102. Insert a high score object on the winner page. The victory condition is achieving the highest score.

Frame Editor

103. Display the event editor for the Level 1 frame, and add a comment on line 10 stating Victory Condition.

104. Add a new condition on line 11.

Event Editor

105. In the **New Condition** dialog box, right-click on the Block object, and click **Pick or Count** > **Compare the number of "Block" objects in a zone** in the shortcut menu. The **Zone Setup** dialog box is displayed, and the frame editor is temporarily displayed, as shown in **Figure 8.**

106. Drag the sizing handles on the zone so the zone covers all blocks in the play area.

107. Click the **OK** button to close the **Zone Setup** dialog box. The event editor is redisplayed, and the expression editor is displayed.

108. In the expression editor, select the **Equal** comparison method, and enter 1. If the player completes the puzzle (wins), only one block is remaining.

109. On line 11, program this pseudo code for the event: **THEN** jump to the Winner frame.

Puzzle Mod

One of the features beta testers are examining is the interface and how feedback is provided to the player so he or she can understand the gameplay. The creative director wants to have a game that displays a sensor as the player moves to better demonstrate the interface of the game.

Storyboard Editor

110. In the storyboard editor, make a copy of the Level 1 frame, and paste it below the existing Level 1 frame.

111. Rename the pasted frame as Level 2.

Frame Editor

112. Open the frame editor for Level 2.

113. Insert a new active object anywhere on the frame.

114. Name the active object Visible Sensor, set its size as 96 × 96, and set its position to (128,320).

Name: _____

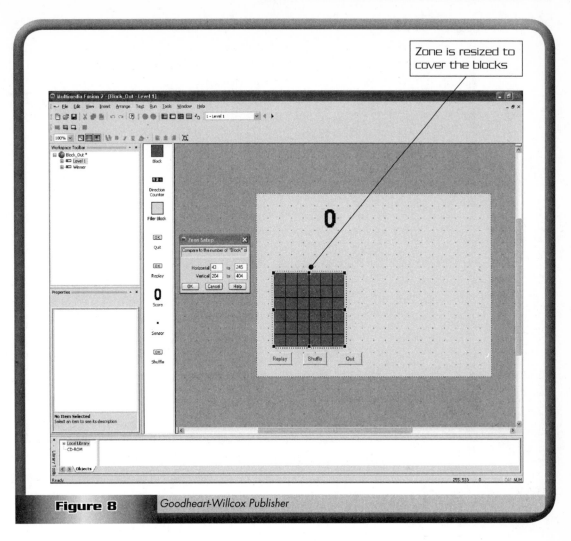

Zone is resized to cover the blocks

Figure 8   *Goodheart-Willcox Publisher*

Clear

Rectangle

Fill tool

View Hot Spot

Event Editor

115. Open the Visible Sensor object in the image editor.
116. Clear the default image.
117. Select a medium gray color in the color palette.
118. Click the **Rectangle** button, and click the outline only option.
119. Move the cursor over the canvas until it is at (32,0), click, and drag to (64,96). This draws an open rectangle down the center of the canvas.
120. Draw another open rectangle from (0,32) to (96,64).
121. Click the **Fill Tool** button, and fill the boxes to form a plus sign or crosshairs, as shown in **Figure 9**.
122. Set the hot spot to the center of the image.
123. Close the image editor.
124. Open the event editor for the Level 2 frame.
125. Edit the appropriate existing line of programming to match this pseudo code:

    IF always,
    THEN destroy the Sensor object
        AND set the visibility of the Visible Sensor object to a semitransparent value of 30.

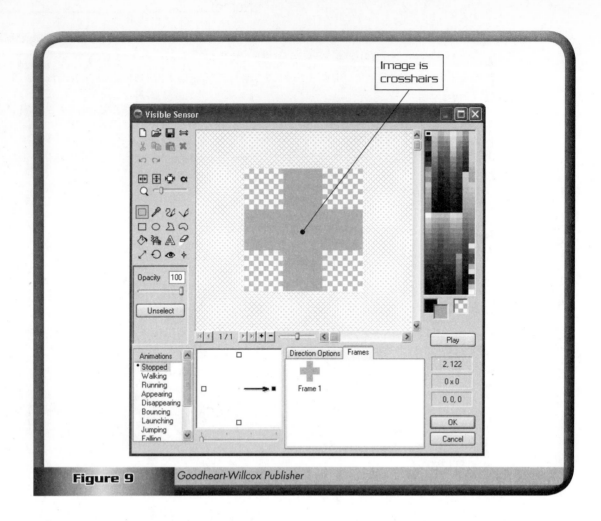

Image is crosshairs

Figure 9　Goodheart-Willcox Publisher

Moving the Visible Sensor

Programming is needed to allow the Visible Sensor object to be moved around the game map by the player. The idea is to move the Visible Sensor object to the midpoint of whichever block the cursor is touching. The pseudo code for this is:

> **IF** the cursor is over a Block object
>> **AND** the X coordinate of the cursor is 16 pixels greater than the X coordinate of the Visible Sensor object,
>
> **THEN** set the X coordinate of the Visible Sensor object to 32 pixels relative to itself.

Event Editor

126. Display the event editor for the Level 2 frame.

127. On line 12, add a comment that states Visible Sensor Movement.

128. Add a new condition on line 13.

129. In the **New Condition** dialog box, right-click on the mouse/keyboard icon, and click **The mouse > Check for mouse pointer over an object** in the shortcut menu.

130. In the new dialog box that is displayed, click the Block object, and click the **OK** button to close the dialog box.

131. The condition on line 13 is: **IF** the cursor is over a Block object. Right-click on this condition, and click **Insert** in the shortcut menu to begin the **AND** section of the programming.

132. In the **New Condition** dialog box, right-click on the **Special** icon, and click **Compare two general values** in the shortcut menu.

133. In the expression editor, click in the top text box, and erase the zero.

134. With the cursor still in the top text box, click the **Retrieve data from an object** button.

135. In the **New Expression** dialog box, right-click on the mouse/keyboard icon, and click **Current X position of the mouse** in the shortcut menu. The expression in the expression editor is XMouse.

136. Click the comparison method drop-down list between the top and bottom text boxes, and click **Greater** in the list.

137. Click in the bottom text box, and erase the zero.

138. With the cursor still in the bottom text box, click the **Retrieve data from an object** button.

139. In the **New Expression** dialog box, right-click on the Visible Sensor object, and click **Position > X coordinate** in the shortcut menu.

140. The expression in the bottom text box in the expression editor is X("Visible Sensor"). Add +16 to the end of this expression. This adds 16 pixels to the relative position of the Visible Sensor object.

141. Close the expression editor.

142. On line 13, right-click in the **Visible Sensor** column, and click **Position > Set X coordinate** in the shortcut menu. The expression editor is displayed.

143. In the expression editor, erase the zero, and click the **Retrieve data from an object** button.

144. In the **New Expression** dialog box, right-click on the Visible Sensor object, and click **Position > X coordinate** in the shortcut menu.

145. Add +32 to the expression so it reads X("Visible Sensor")+32.

146. Close the expression editor.

147. Copy line 13, and paste three copies as lines 14, 15, and 16.

148. Edit the programming of each line as shown in **Figure 10.** Make sure to change the comparison from greater to less than (lower) as needed.

149. Test play the Level 2 frame. Check for proper movement of the Visible Sensor object.

150. Debug if needed.

151. Save your work, and submit it for grading according to the directions from your instructor.

Run Frame

Line	Condition	Action
14	YMouse > Y("Visible Sensor")+16	Set Y position to Y("Visible Sensor")+32
15	XMouse < X("Visible Sensor")–16	Set X position to X("Visible Sensor")–32
16	YMouse < Y("Visible Sensor")–16	Set Y position to Y("Visible Sensor")–32

Figure 10   *Goodheart-Willcox Publisher*

Review Questions

1. How is the image of an object centered on the object's position?

   _____

   _____

2. Describe how a duplicate differs from a clone.

   _____

   _____

   _____

3. Describe how a single animation set can have more than one animation.

   _____

   _____

   _____

4. How is a random distribution of blocks created for this game build?

   _____

   _____

   _____

5. Describe how sensors are used in this game build.

   _____

   _____

   _____

Activity 7-3

Sand Simulation Game

Objectives

Students will design simulation elements and program them into a playable game. Students will program gravity, stacking, and persistence.

Situation

The Really Cool Game Company sees promise in you as a superstar employee. You have quickly grasped the principles of game design and are able to develop game concepts and build quality prototypes. The next puzzle in the series is a gravity/particle puzzle. The team has received a concept for a series of puzzle elements that will be built into a game featuring gameplay through Egyptian ruins. The company needs to see if a proof of concept game can be made to the requirements specified by the technical director. These requirements focus on minimizing the load for the small processor used in a handheld device, such as a smartphone or tablet. Pay special attention to these requirements as you build this game.

Sands of Time is a series of puzzles using grains of sand as the primary element of gameplay. Players will position bricks and bags of sand to guide the sand into the desired location. The location may be a cup, scale, balance beam, or other object that is integrated into the story line. Each puzzle will force players to test their intellectual capabilities to advance through the obstacle within the pyramids.

How to Begin

1. Launch MMF2, and start a new game build.
2. Name the application Sand Puzzle Concept.
3. Set the application window size to 320 × 576.
4. Rename the default frame to Level 1.
5. Save your work as *LastName_*Sand Puzzle.

Assets

Frame Editor

6. Display the frame editor.
7. Set the grid size to 32 × 34. Show the grid and turn on the snap.
8. Create the prototype assets shown in **Figure 1.** These will be replaced by other designers with better game art once the proof of concept has been approved and scheduled for full production.
9. Copy the **Block** object nine times, and align them in a column to the far left and right sides of the frame, as shown in **Figure 2.**

Type	Name	Size	Position	Content	Color
Button	Reset	64,32	130,10	**Reset**	—
Button	Draw Line	80,32	10,48	**Draw Line**	—
Button	Start Sand	80,32	120,48	**Start Sand**	—
Button	Move Blocks	80,32	230,48	**Move Blocks**	—
Counter	Sand Counter	12,18	180,100	—	—
Active	Sandbag	32,32	145,105	Square	Fill of light brown
Active	Block	32,32	16,186	Square; hot spot in the center	Fill of gray
Active	Goal	32,5	261,361	Thin rectangle	Fill of yellow
Active	Emitter	32,32	145,105	Default	Default
Backdrop	Cup	32,32	261,368	Square; black line on the left, right, and bottom only (top open); Set the **Obstacle Type** property to Obstacle	
Backdrop	Ground	320,32	0,400	Rectangle; set the **Obstacle Type** property to Obstacle	Fill of dark brown
Counter	Goal Counter	12,18	300,420	—	—
Active	Draw Dot	15,15	−100,200	Circle; hot spot in the center	Transparent background with a black-filled circle centered in the frame
Active	Sand	1,1	−20,20	Square; hot spot in the bottom center	Fill of light brown
Formatted text*	Rules	256,140	32,435	Drag blocks into position to guide falling sand into the cup. Click the **Start Sand** button when blocks are in place. Catch 1000 grains of sand to move to the next level.	

Figure 1   *Goodheart-Willcox Publisher*

*To add content to formatted text, double-click the object on the game frame, and enter the text. Use the buttons on the **Frame Editor Toolbar** to format the text as 12 point Arial. Click off the object to complete editing the text.

Programming

Event Editor

The technical director has laid out the basic programming for the GUI. In the event editor, program the following pseudo code to match the specifications provided by the technical director.

10. On line 1, program **IF** at the start of the frame, **THEN** set the Sandbag counter to 5000 **AND** make the goal invisible.

11. On line 2, program **IF** the sand collides with the goal, **THEN** add 1 to the goal counter.

Name: _____

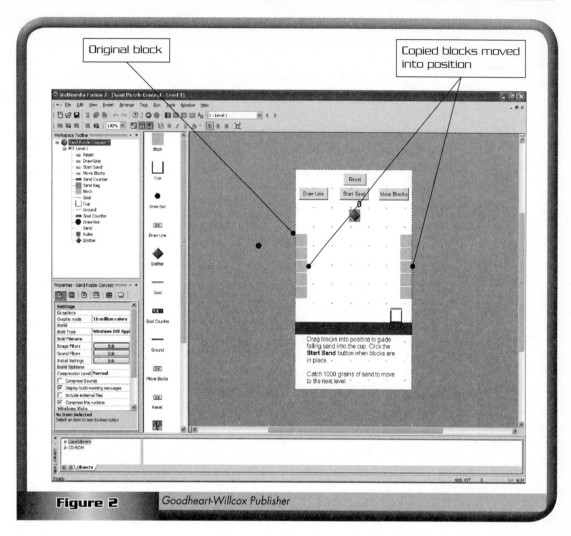

Original block

Copied blocks moved into position

Figure 2   *Goodheart-Willcox Publisher*

12. On line 3, program **IF** the **Reset** button is clicked, **THEN** restart the current frame.

13. On line 4, program **IF** the **Start Sand** button is clicked.

14. On line 5, program **IF** the **Move Blocks** button is clicked.

15. On line 6, program **IF** the **Draw Line** button is clicked.

16. Save your work. The actions for lines 4, 5, and 6 will be programmed later.

Subroutine Groups

This program requires transition between different gameplay modes on the same game map when the player clicks the GUI buttons. When in a certain mode, a group of events must be activated and all other groups of events deactivated to avoid serious errors. A subroutine will be used to allow the player to click the **Start Sand** button when all the blocks and drawings are in place. The sand should not begin to fall at the beginning of the frame.

17. Right-click on the number for line 7, and click **Insert > A group of events** in the shortcut menu. The **Group Events** dialog box is displayed.

18. Click in the **Title of the group** text box, add enter Sand Falling. Also, uncheck the **Activate when frame starts** check box, and click the **OK** button to close the dialog box. A label, similar to a comment, is added as a line in the event editor. Line 8 is indented to show it is part of the Sand Movement subroutine group. Line 9 is not indented and is not part of the subroutine.

19. On line 8, program the following pseudo code. Remember, positive Y in MMF2 is downward, so this will move the sand down as if gravity is affecting it.

> **IF** always,
> **THEN** set the Y coordinate of the Sand object to +1 relative to itself.
> > **AND** create a Sand object at (0,16) relative to the Emitter object

20. Notice that line 9 is indented once line 8 contains programming, as shown in **Figure 3.** On the now indented line 9, program this pseudo code for the condition: **IF** the Sand Counter is greater than 0.

21. Right-click on the condition for line 9, and click **Insert** in the shortcut menu to add an **AND** statement to the line.

22. In the **New Condition** dialog box, right-click on the Sand object, and click **Pick or Count** > **Compare number of "Sand" objects** in the shortcut menu. The expression editor is displayed.

23. Set the expression to less (lower) than 260, and close the expression editor.

24. On line 9, program this pseudo code for the event: **THEN** subtract 1 from the Sand Counter object. Remember, the entered value is subtracted, so do not enter –1.

This programming makes sure that there is still sand in the sandbag (Sand Counter) and also limits the number of sand particles that can be moving at any one time. If there are a large number of active objects, gameplay will lag as the processor is loaded with calculations. Since this game is for a handheld device, low load on the processor is one of the requirements. Later you will add programming to convert Sand objects into backdrop objects when they reach the goal to further reduce the load on the processor.

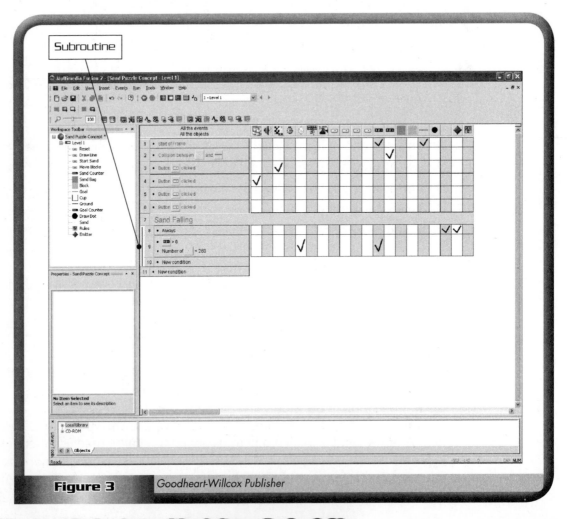

Figure 3 *Goodheart-Willcox Publisher*

Next, you will program the Sand object to have the same X coordinate as the Sandbag object. To add some variety to this location, a programming method named **Random** will be added. This is a built-in method to create randomness in an expression. Methods are discussed in more detail in Chapter 12.

25. Right-click in the cell where the **Emitter** column intersects the **Line 9** row, and click **Position** > **Set X coordinate** in the shortcut menu.

26. In the expression editor, delete the zero, and click the **Retrieve data from an object** button.

27. In the **New Expression** dialog box, right-click on the Sandbag object, and click **Position** > **X coordinate** in the shortcut menu.

28. Edit the expression box so it reads X("Sandbag")+Random(32). The number in parentheses is the range of pixels by which the computer can vary the location.

29. Close the expression editor.

Simulating Gravity

Basic gravity has been simulated with programming to move the sand down one pixel at a time. Now programming must be added to form the sand into piles. Refer to **Figure 4.** The first line of this programming will move the sand one pixel to the right when it contacts an obstacle.

30. Add a new condition on line 10, which is indented and part of the subroutine. In the **New Condition** dialog box, right-click on the Sand object, and click **Collisions** > **Overlapping a backdrop** in the shortcut menu.

31. Right-click in the cell where the **Sand** column intersects the **Line 10** row, and click **Position** > **Set X coordinate** in the shortcut menu.

32. In the expression editor, construct an expression to move one pixel to the right of the Sand object.

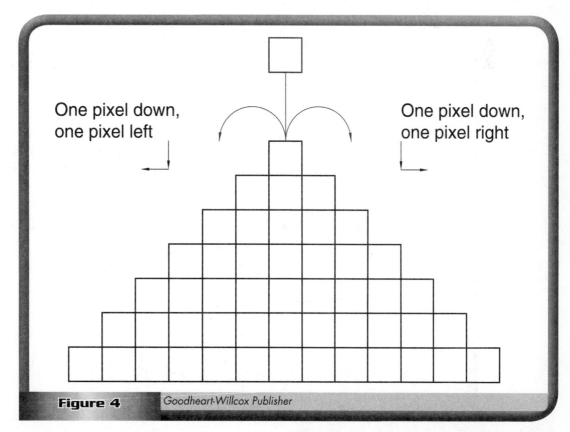

Figure 4   *Goodheart-Willcox Publisher*

33. On line 10, add another action to set the internal flag #1 to "on" for the Sand object. Review Activity 7-1 if you do not recall how to program flags. Note: a cell in the table (the check mark) can contain more than one action.

34. On line 11, which is part of the subroutine, program this pseudo code:

IF the Sand object is overlapping a backdrop
　　AND the internal flag #1 is on,
THEN move the Sand object two pixels to the left relative to its current position.

This movement is one pixel to the left of the Sand object's original position. This way, the sand has had the opportunity to fall one pixel to the right or one pixel to the left when downward motion is stopped. The flag is used to determine if the sand has moved to the right.

35. On line 11, add programming to the Sand object to set internal flag #1 to "off" and internal flag #2 to "on."

36. On line 12, which is part of the subroutine, program this pseudo code:

IF the Sand object is overlapping a backdrop
　　AND internal flag #2 is on,
THEN move the Sand object one pixel to the right relative to its current position
　　AND move the Sand object one pixel up relative to its current position.

This moves the sand particle back to the exact point where it was before it collided with the backdrop. Basically, this means if the sand cannot move left or right, then it will be placed where it started. This, in part, creates the piles of sand.

Activating the Sand

When the player clicks the **Start Sand** button, the sand will start falling from the sandbag. Before the sand falling can be tested, this button needs to be programmed to activate the sand falling. Line 4 contains the condition for **IF** the **Start Sand** button is clicked.

37. Right-click in the cell where the **Special Conditions** column and the **Line 4** row intersect, and click **Group of events** > **Activate** in the shortcut menu. The **Activate** dialog box is displayed, as shown in **Figure 5**.

38. Click the Sand Falling subroutine, and click the **OK** button. Now, when the button is clicked, all actions contained within the subroutine will be activated.

Run Frame

39. Save your work, and test play the frame. Check that sand is generated from the sandbag.

Blitting

Blitting is the process of converting a game object into part of the background image. Blit stands for bit block transfer. To reduce the load on the processor, any sand particle that is stopped can be converted from an active object to a stationary object,

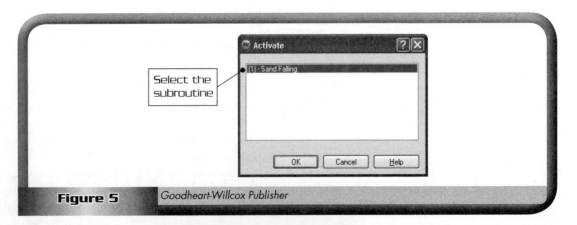

Select the subroutine

Figure 5 *Goodheart-Willcox Publisher*

known as a backdrop object in MMF2, that in essences is part of the background image. Once blitted into the background image, the game engine will not need to track these sand particles. The converted objects will also serve as obstacles to stop the path of other falling sand particles.

The sand particles are not the only objects that can be blitted. The blocks will be programmed so the player can move them left and right before starting the sand. Once the sand starts to fall, the blocks will be stationary and, as such, can be blitted.

40. Right-click in the cell where the **Sand** column and the **Line 12** row intersect, and click **Animation > Paste image into background** in the shortcut menu. The **Paste Image into Background** dialog box is displayed, as shown in **Figure 6.**

41. Click the **Obstacle** radio button, and click the **OK** button. This blits the object and makes it an obstacle for active objects whenever it cannot move left, right, or down; in other words, when it has stopped falling.

42. Right-click in the same cell, and click **Destroy** in the shortcut menu. Once the Sand object has been blitted, the original active object can be destroyed so the computer stops tracking it.

43. Test play the frame to see if the sand forms a nice pile on the Ground object.

44. On line 13, which is part of the subroutine, add a new condition.

Run Frame

45. In the **New Condition** dialog box, right-click on the **Special** icon, and click **Group of events > On group activation** from the shortcut menu.

46. Right-click in the cell where the **Block** column intersects the **Line 13** row, and click **Animation > Paste image into background** in the shortcut menu.

47. In the **Paste Image into Background** dialog box, click the **Obstacle** radio button, and click the **OK** button. This blits the Block objects and makes them obstacles for active objects. The Sand objects are active objects until blitted.

Block Movement

The game concept calls for the player to be able to move the blocks to direct the sand toward the goal. Each block will only be allowed to move left and right (X coordinates) for this proof of concept. Once the player starts the sand falling, the blocks cannot be moved. You have already added that part of the programming. Now you need to add the programming to allow for the movement of the blocks.

48. On line 15, which is not part of the subroutine, create a new group of events named Block Movement that is active when the frame starts. This will allow the player to move the blocks before the sand falls.

49. On line 16, which is part of the new subroutine, program this pseudo code: **IF** the player left-clicks the Block object, **THEN** set internal flag #1 for the Block object to on.

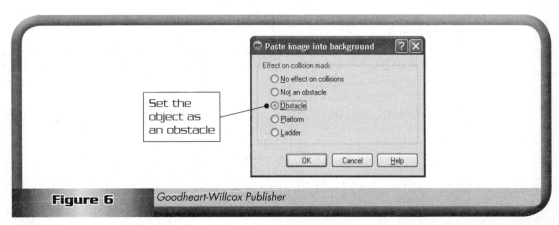

Set the object as an obstacle

Figure 6   *Goodheart-Willcox Publisher*

50. On line 17, which is part of the new subroutine, program this pseudo code: **IF** flag #1 is on for the clicked Block object, **THEN** set the position of the Block object to the X coordinate of the current mouse position.

NOT Operator

The Block object has been programmed to follow the X coordinate of the mouse, but there is no way to get it to stop following the mouse. To make that happen, a **NOT** operator will need to be added to the pseudo code. This pseudo code is:

      IF the left mouse button is **NOT** pressed,
      THEN set internal flag #1 for the Block object to off.

51. In line 18, which is part of the Block Movement subroutine, add a new condition.

52. In the **New Condition** dialog box, right-click on the keyboard/mouse icon, and click **The mouse > Repeat while mouse-key is pressed** in the shortcut menu. The **Repeat while Mouse-Key Is Depressed** dialog box is displayed.

53. Click the **Left** radio button, and click the **OK** button.

54. This condition is the opposite of the condition needed. To create a **NOT** operator, right-click on the condition in line 18, and click **Negate** in the shortcut menu. A red X appears in front of the condition, as shown in **Figure 7.** This makes the statement opposite of what is stated in the condition and action. In this case, the statement now means **IF** the left mouse button is **NOT** pressed.

55. Right-click in the cell where the **Block** column intersects the **Line 18** row, add an action to set internal flag #1 to off. When the flag is off, the block will no longer follow the mouse.

Run Frame

56. Save your work, and test play the frame. Try moving the blocks, and then start the sand to see if you can make it fall into the cup. You may notice that you can move the blocks after the sand is falling. This will be fixed later when you program the remaining control buttons.

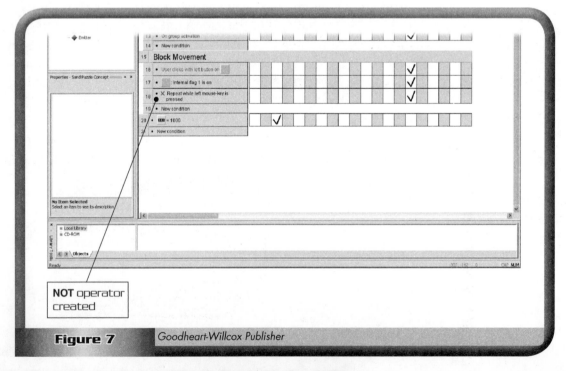

NOT operator created

Figure 7   *Goodheart-Willcox Publisher*

Drawing Gameplay Mode

A basic drawing mode will be included in some of the levels of the sand puzzles. You will now add the programming needed to allow the player to draw lines.

57. On line 20, which is not part of any subroutine, create a new group of events named Drawing that is not active at the start of the frame.

58. On line 21, which is part of the Drawing subroutine, add a condition to repeat while the left mouse button is pressed.

59. Right-click in the cell where the **Create New Objects** column intersects with the **Line 21** row, and click **Create object** in the shortcut menu.

60. Create a Draw Dot object at the actual coordinates of (–25,100). The specific coordinates do not matter. The point is to create a dot somewhere to be used as a paintbrush for the line the player is drawing.

61. Right-click in the cell where the **Draw Dot** column intersects the **Line 21** row, and click **Position** > **X coordinate** in the shortcut menu.

62. In the expression editor, delete the zero, and click the **Retrieve data from an object** button.

63. In the **New Expression** dialog box, right-click on the keyboard/mouse icon, and click **Current X position of the mouse** in the shortcut menu.

64. Close the expression editor.

65. Add the programming to complete this pseudo code:

> **IF** the left mouse button is pressed,
> **THEN** set the X coordinate of the Draw Dot object to the current X coordinate of the mouse
> > **AND** set the Y coordinate of the Draw Dot object to the current Y coordinate of the mouse.

66. Add a new line to the Drawing subroutine to blit the Draw Dot object by programming this pseudo code: **IF** always, **THEN** paste the Draw Dot object into the background as an obstacle.

Changing Modes

The buttons you added to the interface control the different gameplay modes. These need to be programmed to function properly. Currently, the **Start Sand** button only has the function of activating the Sand Falling subroutine. This button will also need to deactivate, or turn off, all other gameplay modes to avoid errors. The other buttons also need to be programmed.

67. Right-click in the cell where the **Special Conditions** column intersects the **Line 4** row (**Start Sand** button), and click **Group of events** > **Deactivate** in the shortcut menu. The **Deactivate** dialog box is displayed, as shown in **Figure 8**.

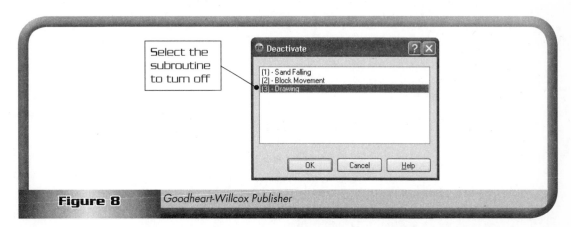

Figure 8   *Goodheart-Willcox Publisher*

68. Click the Drawing group, and click the **OK** button.

69. Similarly, program the **Start Sand** button to deactivate the Block Movement group as well. In addition to the blitting, deactivating this group will help reduce the processor load because the game engine will not process this code while the sand is falling.

70. Program this pseudo code:

> **IF** the **Move Blocks** button is clicked,
> **THEN** activate the Block Movement group
>> **AND** deactivate the Drawing group.

71. Program this pseudo code:

> **IF** the Draw Line button is clicked,
> **THEN** activate the Drawing group
>> **AND** deactivate the Block Movement group.

72. Test play the frame. Try switching between drawing lines and moving blocks. Check that the blocks cannot be moved or lines drawn once the sand is started.

Tuning

The game needs to have feedback to the player for the victory condition. Also, the emitter is currently visible, which is not aesthetically pleasing. The emitter should be invisible to the player.

73. Add a Winner frame to the game.

74. Add text to the Winner frame to indicate the player has won.

75. Add **Replay** and **Quit** buttons to the frame.

76. In the event editor for the Winner frame, program the **Replay** button to jump to the Level 1 frame.

77. Program the **Quit** button to end the application.

78. In the event editor for the Level 1 frame, program this pseudo code:

> **IF** the Goal Counter value equals 1000,
> **THEN** display the Winner frame.

79. On line 1, add the programming necessary to make the emitter invisible at the start of the frame.

80. Test play the application. Note any bugs, and debug as needed.

81. Compile an EXE file, and submit the game for grading according to the directions provided by your instructor.

Run Frame

Storyboard Editor

Frame Editor

Event Editor

Run Application

Review Questions

1. How is a subroutine created in MMF2?

   _____

   _____

2. Briefly describe how gravity is simulated in this game build.

   _____

   _____

   _____

   _____

3. What is blitting?

   _____

   _____

   _____

   _____

4. Describe how to create a statement with a **NOT** operator in MMF2.

   _____

   _____

   _____

   _____

5. Briefly explain how the drawing mode functions in this game build.

   _____

   _____

   _____

   _____

6. Speculate how other gameplay modes or other puzzles using falling sand could be developed. Complete the Brainstorming Document on the next page.

   _____

   _____

   _____

   _____

	Sort (✔, +, or ✕)	Idea (record all ideas without evaluating them)	Comments and Possible Uses
1			
2			
3			
4			
5			
6			
7			
8			
9			
10			
11			
12			
13			
14			
15			

Chapter 8
Sound FX Composition

Objectives

After completing this chapter, you will be able to:
- Classify sounds for video games.
- Record sounds for video games.
- Incorporate sounds into a video game.
- Explain the project flow and areas of specialization in video game design.
- Assess the quality of personal work and the work of others.

Alexey Fursov/Shutterstock.com

MAFord/Shutterstock.com

riekephotos/Shutterstock.com

Name: _____

Date: _____

Class: _____

Bellwork

Day	Date	Activity	Response
1		Complete the anticipation guide and the K and W columns of the KWL chart for this chapter.	
2		Define *sound FX*.	
3		Compare and contrast sampling and composing.	
4		What is sound context?	
5		What is the standard PCM format for recorded sounds for an Apple computer?	
6		Describe the difference between sounds optimized for a theater and the same sounds optimized for a smartphone.	
7		What does *mixing in-the-box* mean?	
8		How can you demonstrate environmentally conscious behavior when purchasing a video game from a retail store?	
9		Describe how being off-task in the computer lab is unethical behavior.	
10		List two software applications that can be used to create a database for your personal sound library.	
11		How does a workflow identifier help the project meet the deadline?	

Day	Date	Activity	Response
12		How can looping help reduce the file size needed for a sound?	
13		List two sounds you would record in the field recording and two sounds you would record in the studio.	
14		What is the process of changing an analog sound to a digital sound?	
15		Why is a sound meter an important piece of field-recording equipment?	
16		How does a shock mount help improve sound quality?	
17		How should a sound engineer decide which editing software to use?	
18		How is a chorus effect different from a reverb effect?	
19		What type of earplugs should you wear when working with loud sound or music?	
20		Complete the L column of the KWL chart and the After Reading column of the anticipation guide with what you learned from this chapter.	
21		Speculate as to the purpose of the unusual wall shown in Figure 8-1. What do you believe is the purpose of the bumpy wall?	

Name: _____

Date: _____

Class: _____

Anticipation Guide

Directions

Before reading the chapter, read each statement in the table below. In the column titled Before Reading, write the letter *T* if you agree with the statement or *F* if you disagree with the statement. After reading the chapter, reread each statement in the table below. In the column titled After Reading, write the letter *T* if you agree with the statement or *F* if you disagree with the statement. Be prepared to justify your answers in a class discussion.

Before Reading	Statement	After Reading
	Sound engineers match the sound with the action cue in the game.	
	Sounds should be preloaded to prevent lag during gameplay.	
	Sounds for game consoles use CD-quality sounds that meet the Blue Book standard.	
	Stereo recording should be done with a pair of identical microphones to maintain quality.	
	An echo effect takes a single sound and adds layers of the same sound to create echo.	

KWL Chart

Directions

Before reading the chapter, fill in what you already know about the topic in the K column and what you want to learn in the W column. After reading the chapter, review what you know and wanted to learn about the topic. Reflect on what you have studied and completed in this chapter. Fill in what you learned in the L column. Be prepared to justify your answers in a class discussion.

Topic: Sound Effects		
K What you already *know*	**W** What you *want* to learn	**L** What you *learned*

Activity 8-1

Sound Library

Objectives

Students will match sound assets to required applications in a video game. Students will classify sounds and apply a naming convention to sound files for quick reference. Students will create a database to store sound assets.

Situation

The Really Cool Game Company had been looking to hire a freelance sound engineer for a new game prototype, but instead of outsourcing the work, it believes you have the knowledge and skills to do the job. Since the game is in the prototype stage, the sound assets do not have to be a perfect match to the game action. This is a perfect opportunity for you to get some experience and show the bosses you are a real go-getter. Make sure you do the highest-quality job possible with the resources provided.

How to Begin

1. Within your working folder, create a subfolder named Sound Library. Your instructor may provide a different location to create this folder.

2. Review the cue sheet on the next page to see the sounds the game needs. All sounds should be sampled at 44.1 Hz or better.

3. Use the Internet to research royalty free sound effects or similar search topic. All sounds located for this activity must be labeled as freely distributed and royalty free. If you use copyrighted sounds, you are stealing, and the Really Cool Game Company will have to pay fines, penalties, and fees.

4. Locate and download an appropriate sound file to match each requirement on the cue sheet.

5. Rename each sound file using the naming convention represented in Asset ID on the cue sheet.

6. Create nested subfolders inside the Sound Library folder as needed to help organize the sound library by grouping similar items. Organizing a system of subfolders can make it easier and more efficient to find sounds in a large sound library.

7. Record the specifications for each sound effects file on the sound asset specification sheet that follows the cue sheet. Each asset should not exceed the maximum listed on the cue sheet.

Cue Sheet

ID	Asset ID	Cue	Description	Loop	Length Max (sec.)	File Max (mb)	Bit Rate Min.	Stereo
101	GUI_Button-click	**Start** button clicked	Button click	N	1	0.1	8	N
201	AMBIENT_City_Level1_Scene1	Window opens	Urban background noise	Y	3	0.5	16	Y
202	CHILDREN_Doorbell-ring	Children at door	Doorbell rings	N	1	0.1	8	N
203	VEHICLE_Car_Garage	Car at garage door	Garage door opening	N	3	0.5	16	Y
204	ENVIRONMENT_Earthquake_Distant	End of dialogue; start next scene	Earthquake in the distance	N	7	1	16	Y
205	VEHICLE_Airplane_Propeller-flyby	Propeller-driven airplane flies by	Propeller sound fading	N	3	0.6	16	Y
206	VEHICLE_Airplane_Jet-flyby	Jet airplane flies by	Jet sound fading	N	2	0.5	16	Y
207	ENVIRONMENT_Earthquake_Hit-City	Begin quake animation	Items in a room rattling	N	9	1.2	16	Y
208	ELECTRIC_Sparks	Spark effect initiated	Electrical arcing (sparks jumping)	N	2	0.5	16	Y
209	ELECTRIC_Wire-buzz	After earthquake	Buzzing or humming of electrical device	Y	3	0.5	16	Y
210	TOOLS_Jackhammer	Jackhammer animation initiated	Jackhammer on concrete or rocks	Y	2	0.5	16	Y
301	ENVIRONMENT_Beach_Waves-gentle	Scene 3 starts	Waves gently lapping a shoreline	Y	9	1	16	Y
302	ENVIRONMENT_Beach_Waves-large	Blend in scene 3 variation	Large wave crashing on a shoreline	N	4	1	16	Y
401	ENVIRONMENT_Jungle_Background	Scene 4 starts	Jungle background noise	Y	9	1	16	Y
402	ANIMALS_Bat_Group-chatter	Player character enters cave	Chirps and chatter of bats with echo	Y	2	0.5	16	Y
501	DOORS_Handle-rattle	Player character touches a handle	Doorknob rattling (locked)	N	2	0.3	16	Y
502	DOORS_Handle-turn	Player character turns a handle	Doorknob turning (unlocked)	N	2	0.3	16	Y
503	DOORS_Wooden_Creak-Open	Door opens	Door creaking on hinges	N	2	0.5	16	Y
504	DOORS_Wooden_Creak-Close	Door closes	Door creaking on hinges, then latches	N	2	0.5	16	Y
505	DOORS_Screen_Open	Player character exits rear door	Banging of a storm door on door frame	N	2	0.5	16	Y
601	MILITARY_Army_March-large	Army enters	Synchronized boots on pavement (marching)	Y	9	1	16	Y
602	DOORS_Jail_Slam-close	Door closing animation initiated	Heavy metal door closes with echo	N	2	0.3	16	Y
701	ACTOR_Firebreath_Fireburst	Fire breathing animation initiated	Man breathes fire	N	2	0.5	16	Y
702	ANIMALS_Camel_Grunt	Player character mounts a camel	Camel bleating or grunting	N	2	0.5	16	Y
703	WEAPON_Sword_Hit_Sword-Steel	Player character's sword hits an enemy's sword	Metal drawn across metal	N	3	0.5	16	Y
704	WEAPON_Sword_Draw_Sheath-metal	Player character draws sword from sheath	Metal drawn across wood or leather	N	3	0.5	16	Y
705	WEAPON_Knife_Throwing_Hit-Wood	Player character throws a knife; knife hits a wooden object	Object contacting wood and vibrating	N	3	0.5	16	Y
706	WEAPON_Sword_Hit_Armor-plate	Player character's sword hits enemy armor	Metal hitting a metal can	N	3	0.5	16	Y
707	FIGHT_Punch_Hit-body	Player character punches soft object or NPC	Fist hitting a punching bag	N	2	0.5	16	Y
708	CROWD_Cheer	Player character achieves task	Crowd cheers	N	3	0.5	16	Y
709	CROWD_Boo	Player character fails at task	Crowd boos	N	3	0.5	16	Y
710	CROWD_Laugh	Falling animation concludes	Crowd laughs	N	3	0.5	16	Y
711	CROWD_Applause	Player character enters	Crowd applause	N	3	0.5	16	Y
801	ANIMALS_Bear_Roar	Bear NPC enters	Bear roaring	N	2	0.5	16	Y
802	ANIMALS_Bear_Breath-whine	Bear NPC waiting to enter	Bear breathing and whining	N	3	0.5	16	Y
803	ANIMALS_Bobcat_Howl	Bobcat NPC enters	Bobcat howl	N	3	0.5	16	Y
804	ANIMALS_Kitten_Yelp	Kitten NPC picked up	Kitten cries	N	2	0.5	16	Y
805	ANIMALS_Cougar_Howl	Cougar NPC enters	Cougar howl	N	3	0.5	16	Y
806	ANIMALS_Dog_Bark-angry	Player character walking at gait	Dog barks aggressively	N	3	0.5	16	Y
807	ANIMALS_Dog_Snarl	Player character moves atop a wall with a dog below	Dog snarls	N	3	0.5	16	Y
809	ANIMALS_Dog_Whine-injured	Dog NPC receives damage	Dog whines	N	3	0.5	16	Y
901	ACTIONS_Jump_Boing	**Jump** button is pressed	Spring vibrating	N	1	0.2	16	N

Sound Assets Specification

ID #	Asset ID	Length (sec.)	File (mb)	Quality (kHz)	Bit Rate	Loop Y/N	File Type
101	GUI_Button-click						
201	AMBIENT_City_Level1_Scene1						
202	CHILDREN_Doorbell-ring						
203	VEHICLE_Car_Garage						
204	ENVIRONMENT_Earthquake_Distant						
205	VEHICLE_Airplane_Propeller-flyby						
206	VEHICLE_Airplane_Jet-flyby						
207	ENVIRONMENT_Earthquake_Hit-City						
208	ELECTRIC_Sparks						
209	ELECTRIC_Wire-buzz						
210	TOOLS_Jackhammer						
301	ENVIRONMENT_Beach_Waves-gentle						
302	ENVIRONMENT_Beach_Waves-large						
401	ENVIRONMENT_Jungle_Background						
402	ANIMALS_Bat_Group-chatter						
501	DOORS_Handle-rattle						
502	DOORS_Handle-turn						
503	DOORS_Wooden_Creak-Open						
504	DOORS_Wooden_Creak-Close						
505	DOORS_Screen_Open						
601	MILITARY_Army_March-large						
602	DOORS_Jail_Slam-close						
701	ACTOR_Firebreath_Fireburst						
702	ANIMALS_Camel_Grunt						
703	WEAPON_Sword_Hit_Sword-Steel						
704	WEAPON_Sword_Draw_Sheath-metal						
705	WEAPON_Knife_Throwing_Hit-Wood						
706	WEAPON_Sword_Hit_Armor-plate						
707	FIGHT_Punch_Hit-body						
708	CROWD_Cheer						
709	CROWD_Boo						
710	CROWD_Laugh						
711	CROWD_Applause						
801	ANIMALS_Bear_Roar						
802	ANIMALS_Bear_Breath-whine						
803	ANIMALS_Bobcat_Howl						
804	ANIMALS_Kitten_Yelp						
805	ANIMALS_Cougar_Howl						
806	ANIMALS_Dog_Bark-angry						
807	ANIMALS_Dog_Snarl						
809	ANIMALS_Dog_Whine-injured						
901	ACTIONS_Jump_Boing						

Activity 8-2

Field Recording and Foley Effects

Objectives

Students will record sounds for use in video games. Students will use sound recording equipment to capture digital sound.

Situation

The Really Cool Game Company needs to create some similar sounds for a game project. A local Foley effects artist has listed some suggestions to help you get started. These ideas will guide you in building your knowledge of similar sounds used in digital recordings.

A *Foley effect* is sound in a live theater or film production that is similar to a real-life sound, but simulated using props. These similar sounds replace real-life sounds in movies or video games. The term Foley effect originates from Jack Foley, who pioneered the modern techniques for creating similar sounds.

A microphone is required for this activity. Also make sure the freeware Audacity has been installed before beginning this activity. Audacity is freeware software that is available for most operating systems. It can be used to record and edit sounds.

How to Begin

1. Sign out a microphone, and plug it into your computer workstation.
2. Launch Audacity. If using a microphone, skip to step 14. Otherwise, continue as follows.

Recording with a Handheld Device or Digital Audio Recorder

3. Launch the sound-recording app on your smartphone, tablet, or other handheld device, or use a digital audio recorder.
4. Press the record button.
5. Say testing, testing, 1, 2, 3, and press the stop button.
6. Record a second sample of you saying ahhhh, only changing the volume of your voice throughout the recording and keeping the pitch and frequency the same.
7. Record a third sample of you saying hello, my name is *your name.*
8. Connect the handheld device or digital audio recorder to your computer workstation using a data transfer cable.
9. Upload the three sound files to your working folder on the computer.
10. Switch to Audacity.
11. Select **Import** > **Audio...** from the **File** pull-down menu.
12. In the standard Windows open dialog box that is displayed, browse to hello sound file, select it, and click the **Open** button.
13. Skip to the Sound Editing in Audacity section.

Audacity Recording

Record

Stop

14. Switch to Audacity.

15. Click the **Input Device** drop-down list, as shown in **Figure 1.**

16. In the drop-down list, click the location where the microphone is plugged in. If the microphone supports stereo input, select that option.

17. Click the **Record** button.

18. Speak testing, testing 1, 2, 3 into the microphone.

19. Click the **Stop** button.

20. Click **New** in the **File** pull-down menu. A second session of Audacity is launched in a new window.

21. In the second session, record a sample of you saying ahhhh, only changing the volume of your voice throughout the recording and keeping the pitch and frequency the same.

22. Click **New** in the **File** pull-down menu. A third session of Audacity is launched in a new window. There should now be three sessions of Audacity open. Each one will contain a separate recording.

23. In the third session, record a sample of you saying hello, my name is *your name.*

Sound Editing in Audacity

The recording or sound file loaded into Audacity is displayed as a waveform of the sound, as shown in **Figure 2.** The *waveform* in Audacity is a graph showing the change in volume for the sound. Notice the peaks and valleys in the waveform. These correspond to the volume levels in the recorded sound. Also the waveform most likely has a *head* (beginning) and a *tail* (ending) that are basically flat. This means there is no sound in those parts of the waveform. With the hello waveform displayed in Audacity, continue as follows.

Play

24. Click the **Play** button to hear the sample. Watch the progress bar move across the waveform as the sound is played. Try to match what you see in the waveform to what you hear in the sound. Also, pay attention to the volume meters at the top of the screen.

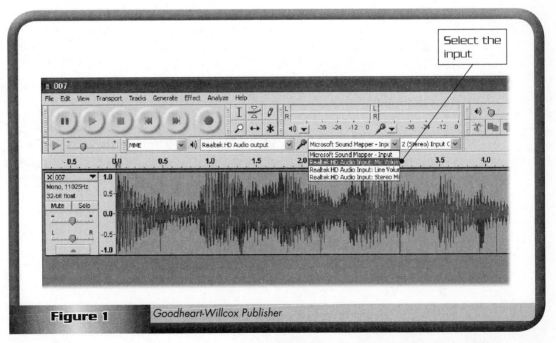

Select the input

Figure 1   *Goodheart-Willcox Publisher*

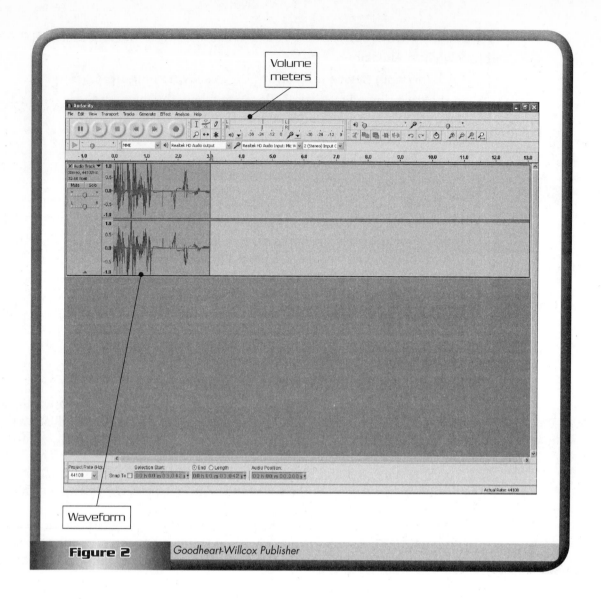

Volume meters

Waveform

Figure 2   *Goodheart-Willcox Publisher*

25. Click **Reverse** in the **Effect** pull-down menu. The reverse effect mirrors the sound. In other words, the end of the sound becomes the beginning, and the beginning of the sound becomes the end. This can be seen in the waveform, which is now the reverse of what it was before.

26. Play the sample. Your words are backward. This effect may be used to create the sound effect for dialogue spoken by a space creature.

27. Click **Undo Reverse** in the **Edit** pull-down menu to return to the previous waveform.

28. Click and hold at the beginning of the waveform, drag to the end of the head, and release to highlight the first part of the waveform that represents the time span containing no sound. The time span is highlighted in dark gray, as shown in **Figure 3**.

29. Press the [Delete] key on the keyboard to remove the head.

30. Similarly, remove the tail.

31. Highlight portion of the remaining waveform that is just your name, and click the **Play** button.

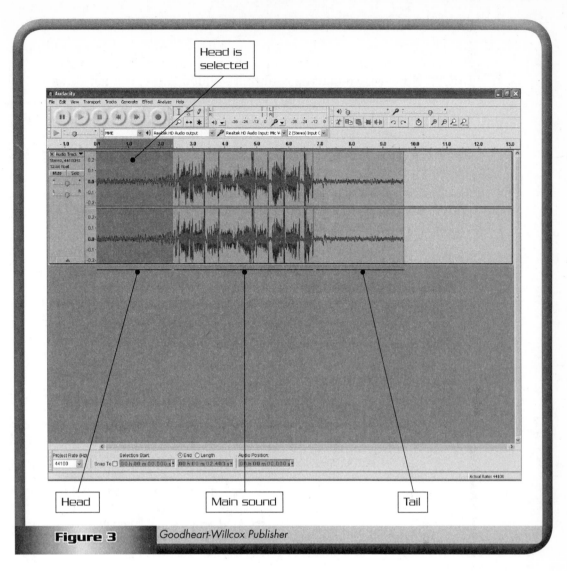

Head is
selected

Head

Main sound

Tail

Figure 3 *Goodheart-Willcox Publisher*

Trim

Play

Copy

Paste

32. Refine the selection by dragging the edges of the highlighted area left or right until your name is completely included in the selection.

33. Click the **Trim** button to remove all of the waveform that is not highlighted. This should be everything except your name.

34. Play the sound.

35. Highlight the portion of the waveform that is the sound for just the first letter of your name.

36. Click the **Copy** button to copy that portion of the waveform.

37. Click at time position 0.0 to place the insertion point at that location.

38. Click the **Paste** button.

39. Move the insertion point to time position 0.0, and click the **Paste** button.

40. Play the sample. It now sounds like you have said the first letter of your name three times before speaking the rest of your name.

Exporting

The **Save** command in Audacity creates an Audacity project file (AUP). This type of file can be opened in Audacity, and you can continue to work on the project. However, to use the sound in a video game, it must be saved in a format that the game engine can understand. In order to do this in Audacity, the **Export** command is used.

41. Click **Export...** in the **File** pull-down menu.

42. In the standard Windows save dialog box that is displayed, browse to the Sound Library subfolder in your working folder.

43. Click in the **File name:** text box, and enter Speech Stumble.

44. Click the **File type:** drop-down list, and click **WAV (Microsoft) signed 16 bit PCM** in the list.

45. Click the **Save** button. The file is exported in the selected format.

Creating Foley Sounds

46. Record the sounds shown in **Figure 4.** Use the examples provided to create the similar sounds, or be inventive in other ways to create the similar sounds.

47. Edit each sound to remove head and tail.

48. Save each sound in your Sound Library folder using the file name specified.

Foley Sound	Creation Process	File Name
Bone break	Break pencil, carrot, or stick.	Break.wav
Strong wind	Blow into the top an empty can or water bottle. For variation, jiggle the can a bit while blowing. To get a swirling wind, leave some liquid in the can and swirl the liquid while blowing across the can.	Wind.wav
Cracking ice	Crinkle a plastic wrapper. Using a bag full of peanuts, for example, gives a nice variation to the sound.	Ice-crack.wav
Slap	Pop a ruler against a table.	Slap.wav
Punch	Hold a sheet of paper on the short ends so that the middle of the page sags down. Quickly snap the page tight to remove the sag. The larger the paper, the lower pitch of the sound.	Punch.wav
Rain on a roof	Place your hands on a table or desk so the tips of your fingers (not your fingernails) are touching the surface. Quickly and randomly tap your fingertips on the table.	Rain-roof.wav
Kick or punch without making impact	Quickly swing a ruler past the microphone.	Kick.wav

Figure 4   *Goodheart-Willcox Publisher*

Video Game Design Composition Software Design Guide

Review Questions

1. What is a Foley effect?

   _____

   _____

   _____

   _____

2. Briefly describe the process of loading a sound recording from a handheld device into the software Audacity.

   _____

   _____

   _____

   _____

3. In terms of the software Audacity, what is a waveform?

   _____

   _____

   _____

   _____

4. In terms of the waveform for an audio recording, what are a head and a tail?

   _____

   _____

   _____

   _____

5. Briefly describe how to save a sound in WAV format in Audacity.

   _____

   _____

   _____

   _____

Activity 8-3

Sound Programming

Objectives

Students will program sounds to play in a video game. Students will select appropriate sounds for game interactions.

Situation

The Really Cool Game Company liked the work you did programming the puzzle games in Chapter 7. It would like sounds added to the puzzle games that you created. Use sounds from your sound library folder or create new sounds as needed.

How to Begin

1. Review the sound asset specifications sheet in Activity 8-1.
2. Check the file type of asset 101.
3. If asset 101 is not a WAV file, open the sound file in Audacity.
4. Export the sound file as a WAV file.
5. Similarly, check assets 301 and 708, and convert them to WAV files if needed.
6. Close Audacity.

Adding Sound to Multimedia Fusion 2

Sound samples to be played in MMF2 can be saved in many formats, including WAV, OGG, AIFF, MOD, and MIDI file types. MIDI files are played as music in MMF2, while the other files types are played as samples. This is important to remember when programming game sounds.

7. Launch MMF2.
8. Open the transport puzzle created in Activity 7-1. Save it as *LastName*_Puzzle_Transport_Sounds in your working folder.
9. Display the event editor for the Puzzle 1 frame.

Event Editor

10. For line 1, which is the condition **IF the player clicks on a Group.Good object**, right-click in the **Sound** column and click **Samples** > **Play Sample** in the shortcut menu. The **Play Sample** dialog box is displayed, as shown in **Figure 1.**
11. Click the **Browse** button next to the **From a file** label.
12. In the standard Windows open dialog box that is displayed, browse to the Sound Library subfolder in your working folder, select the GUI_Button-click file, and click the **Open** button.
13. Click the **OK** button to close the **Play Sample** dialog box.

Run Application

14. Test play the game. Check that the sound is played each time you click a tile.

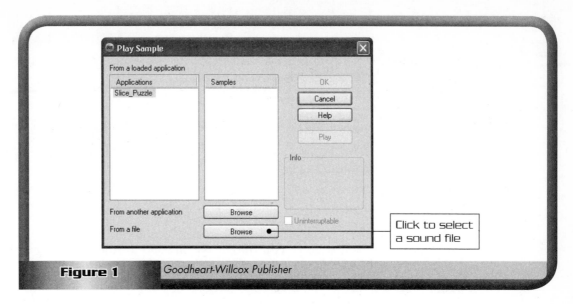

Figure 1 | *Goodheart-Willcox Publisher*

Adding Ambient Sound

Event Editor

15. Display the event editor for the Winner page.

16. Add a new condition, and program this pseudo code:

    IF at the start of the frame,
    THEN play the sound CROWD_Cheer.wav.

17. Right-click in **Sound** column for the programming line you just added, and click **Samples** > **Play and Loop Sample** from the shortcut menu. By adding a second sound, the two sounds are layered and played at the same time when the condition is met, as shown in **Figure 2**.

18. In the **Play and Loop Sample** dialog box, which is the same as the **Play Sample** dialog box, browse for the ENVIRONMENT_Beach_Waves-gentle sound file. The expression editor is displayed.

19. In the expression editor, enter 0, and click the **OK** button. The value entered in the expression editor is the number of times the sound file will be played, or looped. Entering 0 means the sound will loop continuously without stopping.

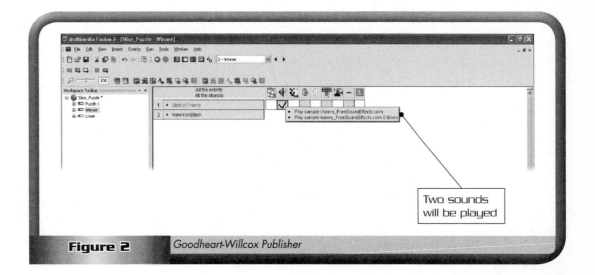

Figure 2 | *Goodheart-Willcox Publisher*

Run Application

20. Save your work, and test play the game. Check that the two sounds play at the same time, that the cheers sound plays once, and that the waves sound loops. Debug as needed.

21. Compile an EXE file, and submit the game for grading according to the directions provided by your instructor.

Audio Design

22. Open the block out game created in Activity 7-2. Save it as *LastName*_BlockOut _Sounds in your working folder.

23. Review the programming for each level of the game.

24. On a separate sheet of paper, write pseudo code for sounds you feel the game needs.

25. Using the cue sheet from Activity 8-1 as a model, create a cue sheet for the sounds you want to add to the game.

26. Record the needed sounds, edit the files as needed in Audacity, and save the sounds as WAV files in your **Sound Library** folder.

27. Add programming to the block out game to add the sounds.

28. Save your work, and test play the game. Debug as needed.

Run Application

29. Compile an EXE file, and submit the game for grading according to the directions provided by your instructor.

Review Questions

1. How is a WAV file added (played) in the event editor in MMF2?

2. How is a MIDI file added (played) in the event editor in MMF2?

3. Interpret this pseudo code: **IF** a tile moves, **THEN** play once the music file for a sliding sound.

4. When a sound file is played continuously, what is that action called?

5. What happens if two sound files are specified to be played in the same cell (check mark) in the event editor in MMF2?

Activity 8-4

Frog Crossing Prototype

Objectives

Students will build a playable video game using placeholders for final game assets. Students will explain the project flow and areas of specialization for game design. Students will program sound samples and music in a playable video game. Students will be able to program using the **OR** and **NOT** operators.

Situation

The Really Cool Game Company is developing a series of games for handheld devices and tablets that can be used for fundraiser events in schools. The first game of the series is based on the classic arcade game *Frogger.* The game must be designed so it can be quickly and easily customized with mascots and characters from the schools. The prototype version will be made for play on the computer. Later, a different team will port the game to tablet and smartphone apps.

This activity builds on the skills you have learned in previous activities. If you do not recall how to complete a task, review previous game builds to see how it is done. All of the remaining activities in this software design guide are based on a foundation of skills learned in previous game builds.

How to Begin

1. Launch MMF2, and start a new game build.
2. Rename Frame 1 to Level 1.
3. Set the size for Level 1 to 640 wide by 480 high.
4. Save as *LastName*_Frog Crossing in your working folder.

Placeholder Assets

This version of the game will be created using placeholder assets. A *placeholder asset* is an object that can be programmed with finalized actions, but that displays basic or generic art that will be replaced with final art once the art department delivers it. The artwork for the placeholder assets is shown in **Figure 1.**

Frame Editor

Grid Setup

5. Display the frame editor for Level 1.
6. Set the grid to 32 × 32, and turn on the snap and grid.
7. Create the placeholder assets described in **Figure 2.** Use **Figure 1** as a visual reference if needed. All hotspots should be left in the default location.
8. Right-click on the River object and choose **Order > To Back** from the shortcut menu. This moves the object to the bottom of the stack of objects, similar to adjusting the order of objects in PowerPoint.
9. Copy the Destroyer object, and paste it at location (832,0). The Destroyer objects will be used to delete objects when they have moved completely out of the scope.
10. Copy the Goal object, and paste it at (160,32), (288,32), (416,32), and (544,32).
11. Copy the Block object, and paste it at (−32,32), (224,32), (352,32), (480,32), and (608,32).

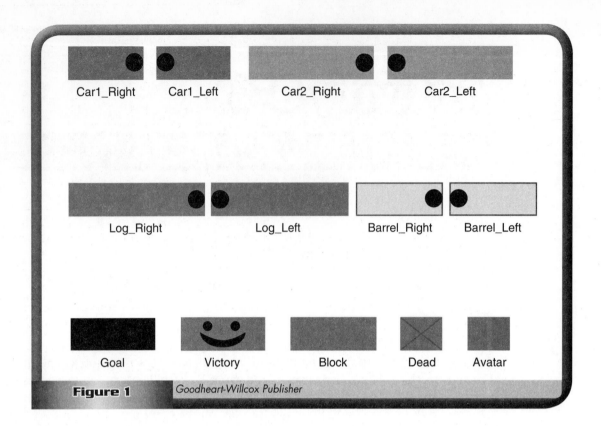

Car1_Right   Car1_Left   Car2_Right   Car2_Left

Log_Right   Log_Left   Barrel_Right   Barrel_Left

Goal   Victory   Block   Dead   Avatar

Figure 1   *Goodheart-Willcox Publisher*

12. Open the Road object in the image editor.

13. Set the foreground color to white.

Rectangle

14. Click the **Rectangle** button, and click the middle button that appears below it, which creates only a fill with no outline. Draw a rectangle from (0,30) to (12,32). This creates a white block in the lower-left corner of the image.

15. Close the image editor.

16. Right-click on the Road object, and click **Create** > **Quick Backdrop Object** from the shortcut menu.

17. Click anywhere on the game map to place the quick backdrop object. A *backdrop object* is not an active object, and does not appear in the event editor. However, a backdrop object can be included in the programming for an action, such as **IF** the object collides with a backdrop object.

18. Set the position to (0,256) and the size to 640 × 192. A six-lane highway is created at the bottom of the screen. Notice how the four car objects fall between the white lines of the road.

19. Delete the original Road object.

20. Copy and paste additional cars, logs, and barrel to create a game map similar to that shown in **Figure 3.** It is very important that all objects in a given row are of the same type, but exact locations are not important.

21. Space car objects so the player has a path to get to the river when these objects are not moving. The exact path is not important as long as the player character can get to the river without touching a car.

22. Set the log and barrel objects to create a path for the player to jump from one to another to one of the goals when these objects are not moving. The exact path is not important as long as the player character can get to a goal without touching the river.

Object Type	Object Name	Size	Position	Attributes
Active	Avatar	32 × 32	288,448	Magenta fill
Active	Dead	32 × 32	−50,−50	Green fill; red lines to form an X
Active	Car1_Right	64 × 31	64,416	Red fill; black-filled circle on the right; member of the Bad group
Active	Car1_Left	64 × 31	32,352	Red fill; black-filled circle on the left; member of the Bad group
Active	Car2_Right	128 × 31	384,384	Orange fill; black-filled circle on the right; member of the Bad group
Active	Car2_Left	128 × 31	192,288	Orange fill; black-filled circle on the left; member of the Bad group
Active	Log_Right	96 × 32	0,128	Brown fill with a blue* outline; black-filled circle on right; member of the Good group
Active	Log_Left	96 × 32	320,160	Brown fill with a blue* outline; black-filled circle on left; member of the Good group
Active	Barrel_Right	64 × 32	288,64	Yellow fill with a blue* outline; black-filled circle on the right; member of the Good group
Active	Barrel_Left	64 × 32	128,192	Yellow fill with a blue* outline; black-filled circle on the left; member of the Good group
Active	Goal	64 × 32	32,32	Black fill
Active	Block	64 × 32	96,32	Green fill; member of the Bad group
Active	Victory	64 × 32	100,−100	Green fill with a black smiley face; member of the Bad group
Active	Destroyer	32 × 478	−224,0	Gray fill
Active	River	640 × 160	0,64	Blue* fill
Backdrop	Road	32 × 32	−64,256	Gray fill
Lives	Lives	—	0,0	—
Score	Score	—	635,25	—
Counter	Randomize	—	315,25	—

*Use the same blue for the river and outlines. The purpose of the outline is to simulate a gap between the objects, while the edges of the objects will, in reality, be perfectly aligned to allow the player character to jump from one object to the next.

Figure 2   *Goodheart-Willcox Publisher*

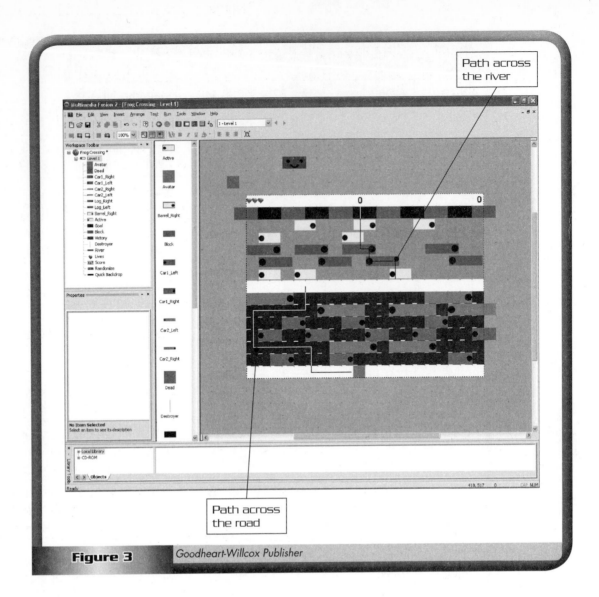

Path across the river

Path across the road

Figure 3
Goodheart-Willcox Publisher

Player Avatar Movement

The prototype game will use the arrow keys on the keyboard to move the player avatar. The team that later ports the game to tablet and smartphones will adjust the user interface to allow gameplay using a touch screen.

23. Display the event editor for Level 1.

Event Editor

24. On line 1, insert a comment that states Player Movement.

25. On line 2, add a new condition. In the **New Condition** dialog box, right-click on the mouse/keyboard icon, and click **The keyboard** > **Upon pressing a key** in the shortcut menu.

26. When prompted, press the up arrow key. This sets the condition as: **IF** the player presses the up arrow key.

27. Right-click in the cell where the **Avatar** column intersects the **Line 2** row, and click **Position** > **Set Y Coordinate...** in the shortcut menu.

28. In the expression editor, click the **Retrieve data from an object** button.

29. In the **New Expression** dialog box, right-click on the Avatar object, and click **Position** > **Y Coordinate** in the shortcut menu.

30. In the expression editor, change the expression to Y("Avatar")–32. Remember, in MMF2, the up direction is negative Y.

31. Close the expression editor.

The programming to move the avatar up one grid space is now created. Refer to **Figure 4.** Recall, the grid is set to 32 pixels × 32 pixels. The pseudo code for this is:

IF the player presses the up arrow key,

THEN set the Y coordinate of the avatar to –32 pixels relative to its current position.

32. On line 3, program this pseudo code:

IF the player presses the down arrow key,

THEN set the Y coordinate of the avatar to +32 pixels relative to its current position.

33. On line 4, program this pseudo code:

IF the player presses the right-hand arrow key,

THEN set the X coordinate of the avatar to +32 pixels relative to its current position.

34. On line 5, program this pseudo code:

IF the player presses the left-hand arrow key,

THEN set the X coordinate of the avatar –32 pixels relative to its current position.

Run Frame

35. Save your work, and test play the frame. Check to see that you can move the avatar using the arrow keys. Try moving the avatar off the edges of the screen.

Movement Bugs

You may have noticed that the avatar cannot be seen when it is in the same location as some objects, such as the river, cars, logs, or the goal. This is because the Avatar object is below the other objects in the stack of objects. This needs to be fixed. Also, the avatar can be moved out of the scope on all edges of the screen. Programming needs to be added to prevent this error. For now, you will only correct the error of moving off the bottom of the screen. The left, right, and top edges will be handled differently later in the build.

Frame Editor

36. Display the frame editor, right-click on the Avatar object, and click **Order > To Front** in the shortcut menu. This moves the Avatar object to the top of the stack when it is part of a stack of objects. If you add other objects later, you may need to repeat this.

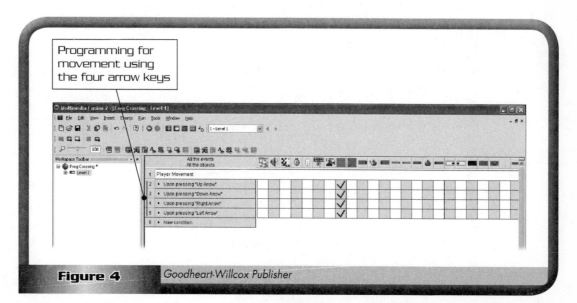

Programming for movement using the four arrow keys

Figure 4   *Goodheart-Willcox Publisher*

Event Editor

37. Display the event editor.

38. On line 6, add a new condition. In the **New Condition** dialog box, right-click on the Avatar object, and click **Position > Compare Y position to a value** in the shortcut menu.

39. In the expression editor, create an expression for greater than 448. Close the expression editor.

40. Right-click in the cell where the **Avatar** column intersects the **Line 6** row, and program this pseudo code: **THEN** set Y position to 448. Refer to **Figure 5.**

Run Frame

41. Save your work, and test play the frame. Check to see that the avatar cannot move off the bottom edge of the screen.

The lowest point the Avatar object should be able to reach is Y = 448. The screen is 480 pixels tall, and the Avatar object is 32 pixels tall. Thus, 480 – 32 = 448. If the object goes lower than Y = 448, it will be outside the scope to the bottom of the frame. If this occurs, the programming resets the object's position to Y = 448.

Road Obstacles

The Avatar object can now be moved all around the screen. However, the obstacles do not act as obstacles. The Avatar object can move over the top of the cars without any penalty.

42. On line 7, insert a comment that states Obstacles.

43. On line 8, program this pseudo code:

> **IF** the Avatar object collides with a Group.Bad object,
> **THEN** subtract one life from player 1
> > **AND** set the position of the Avatar object to the starting point (288,448).

44. On line 9, program the following pseudo code. Refer to Activity 7-3 if you do not recall how to use the **NOT** operator.

> **IF** the Avatar object is overlapping the River object,
> > **AND NOT** overlapping a Group.Good object,
> **THEN** subtract one life from player 1
> > **AND** set the position of the Avatar object to the starting point (288,448).

Run Frame

45. Save your work, and test play the frame. Check that the Avatar object can be moved to the goal. Debug as needed.

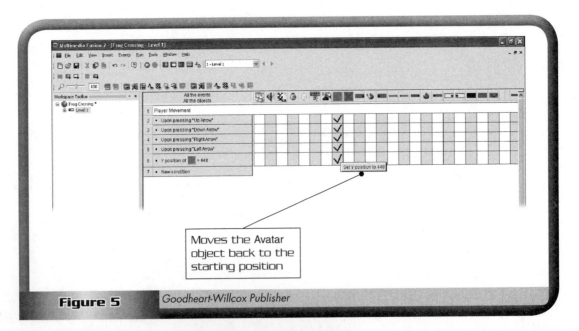

Moves the Avatar object back to the starting position

Figure 5   *Goodheart-Willcox Publisher*

Reaching the Goal

The goal of the game is to fill all of the Goal object "slots" with Avatar objects. Currently, when the Avatar object reaches the Goal object, nothing happens, and the player can continue to move the Avatar object around the screen. Now, you will add programming to change the Avatar object to the Victory object when the player moves the Avatar object into a Goal object slot. Also, the next Avatar object for the player to move will be created at the starting location.

46. On line 10, insert a comment that states Goal, as shown in **Figure 6**.

47. On line 11, program this pseudo code:

> **IF** the Avatar object collides with a Goal object,
> **THEN** create a Victory object at (0,0) relative to the Goal object
> > **AND** destroy the Goal object
> > **AND** set the position of the Avatar object to the starting point (288,448).

Run Frame

48. Save your work, and test play the frame. Check to see if the Victory object appears when the Avatar object is moved into a Goal object slot. Not any bugs.

Debugging

Did you notice a bug? When you move the Avatar object into a Goal object slot, a life is removed. This occurs because the Victory object spawns before the Avatar is moved to the starting position. Since the Victory object is a member of the Bad group, the programming on line 8 is activated. Fixing this is easy.

Frame Editor

49. Display the frame editor, select any of the Goal objects, and change it to be a member of the Good group. The Avatar object can land on a Group.Good group object.

50. Right-click on a Goal object, and click **Order > To Front** in the shortcut menu. This is so the Group.Good object will be on top of the newly spawned Victory object, which allows the Avatar object to land on it. Also, change the order of the Avatar object so it is at the top of the stack. It must always be the top object to be visible at all times.

Run Frame

51. Save your work, and test play the frame. Make sure the Victory object blocks the Avatar object. Check colliding the Avatar object with a Block object. Debug if needed.

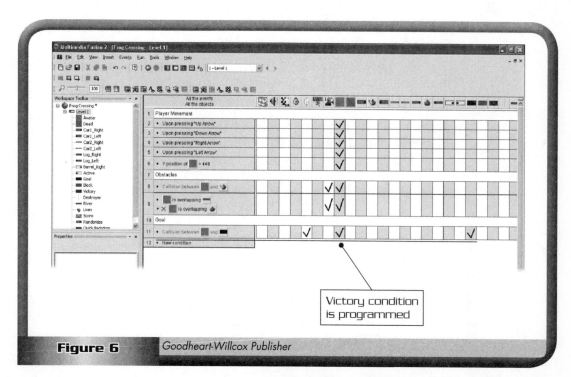

Figure 6 *Goodheart-Willcox Publisher*

Victory condition is programmed

Victory Condition

Pause-and-relax activities are important to include in gameplay. When setting a victory condition, often a slight delay in gameplay is added so the player can realize the victory, assess the situation, and prepare for the next game tasks. This delay can be created using a countdown timer. When the timer is finished, the game can shift to the next level or the winner page. The pseudo code that will be used for the timer is:

IF all of the Goal objects have been destroyed,
THEN start the countdown timer.
IF the countdown timer has ended,
THEN display the next game frame.

Frame Editor

52. In the frame editor, insert a new Date & Time object outside the playable frame. In the **Clock/Date Object** dialog box that is displayed, click the **Create a Clock object** button. This object will be used as the countdown timer.

53. In the **Properties** window for the Date & Time object, click the **Settings** tab.

54. Change the **Type of clock** property to **Digital**.

55. Change the **Face** property to the hours, minutes, and seconds format (**01:27:18**).

56. Change the **Mode** property to **Count down**.

57. In the **Count down setup** property, click the **Edit** button. The **Count Down Initial Value Setup** dialog box is displayed, as shown in **Figure 7**.

58. Enter 0, 0, and 3 in the text boxes. This sets the initial value to three seconds.

59. Display the event editor.

Event Editor

60. On line 12, insert a comment that states Victory Condition.

61. On line 13, add a new condition. In the **New Condition** dialog box, right-click on the Goal object, and click **Pick or count > Have all "Goal" been destroyed** in the shortcut menu.

62. On line 13, right-click in the **Date & Time** column, and click **Count down > Start count down** in the shortcut menu.

63. On line 14, add a new condition. In the **New Condition** dialog box, right-click on the Date & Time object, and click **Compare to countdown** in the shortcut menu. The **Compare to Count Down** dialog box is displayed, as shown in **Figure 8**.

64. In the **Compare to Count Down** dialog box, enter 0 in the **Hour(s)**, **Minute(s)**, and **Second(s)** text boxes and 1 in the **1/100** text box.

65. Click the **Less** radio button in the **How to Compare:** area. The timer counts down in increments of 1/100th of a second, so less than 1/100th of a second is zero.

66. Close the **Compare to Count Down** dialog box.

67. Right-click in the cell where the **Storyboard** column intersects with the **Line 14** row, and click **Next frame** in the shortcut menu. Later, you will add more frames to the game.

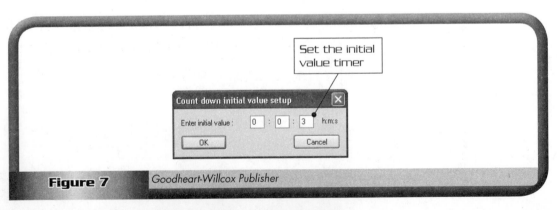

Figure 7   *Goodheart-Willcox Publisher*

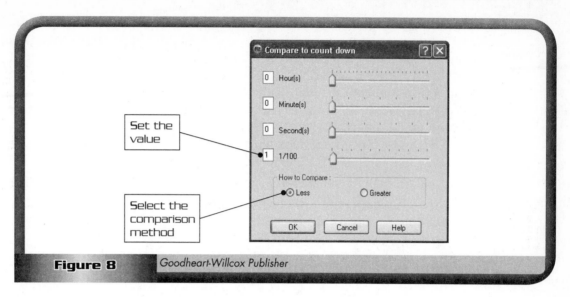

Figure 8   *Goodheart-Willcox Publisher*

Moving Obstacles

Currently, the game is pretty easy to navigate as the cars, logs, and barrels are static. These assets need to be programmed for movement. Path movement will be used. First, program the movement for the car objects.

Frame Editor

68. Display the frame editor. Click **Zoom > 50%** in the **View** pull-down menu. This will allow you to see more of the area outside of the game scope.

69. Select the Car1_Right object located at (64,416).

70. Click the **Movement** tab in the **Properties** window.

71. Set the **Movement Type** property to **Path**.

72. In the **Edit Movement** property, click the **Edit** button. The **Path Movement Setup** dialog box is displayed, as shown in **Figure 9**.

New Line

73. Click the **New Line** button. A straight rubber band line is attached to the hotspot of the selected object.

74. Move the cursor straight right to (1380,416), and click to place the end node of the path. Use the coordinate indicator at the bottom of the screen to check the location of the cursor. The X coordinate does not have to be exact; however, the Y coordinate *must* be exactly 416. If the Y coordinate is off by even one pixel, the line will not be perfectly horizontal.

75. Drag a selection box around the node attached to the hot spot of the object to select the node.

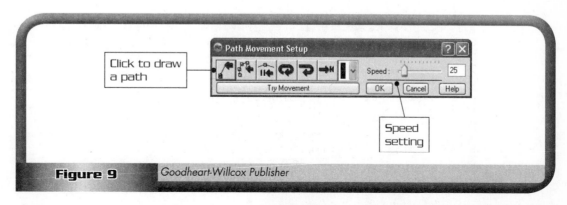

Figure 9   *Goodheart-Willcox Publisher*

Be very careful not to move the first node. If the node is moved by even one pixel, it must be moved back to (64,416). When the first node is selected, the node and the path line flash white. The first node on the path contains the settings for the entire path. The path must be at least 1000 pixels long in the X direction and *cannot* vary in the Y direction. Only one car of each type will need to have a path. Since these were copies, all the copies will inherit the change made on any other.

76. Click in the **Speed:** text box in the **Path Movement Setup** dialog box, and enter 25, as shown in **Figure 9**. Click the **OK** button to close the dialog box.

77. Program path movement and speed for the car objects as shown in **Figure 10.**

78. Save your work, and test play the frame. Check that the movement and speed are working. Debug as needed. This programming is for movement only. The cars will be programmed later to respawn.

Run Frame

Moving Helper Objects

While the cars are obstacles, the logs and barrels are helper objects. The programming to have these objects function as helper objects has already been created. Now, to add challenge to the game, these objects need to be programmed to move. Instead of path movement, a different method will be used to move these objects. The pseudo code is:

> **IF** every 0.05 seconds,
> **THEN** move the right-facing logs and barrels one pixel to the right relative to their current positions
> **AND** move the left-facing logs and barrels one pixel to the left relative to their current positions

79. Display the event editor, and on line 15, insert a comment that states Log and Barrel Movement.

Event Editor

80. On line 16, add a new condition. In the **New Condition** dialog box, right-click on the **Timer** icon (not the Date & Time object), and click **Every** in the shortcut menu. The **Every** dialog box is displayed, as shown in **Figure 11.**

81. Enter 0 in the **Hour(s)**, **Minute(s)**, and **Second(s)** text boxes and 5 in the **1/100** text box. This specifies every 5/100 seconds or 0.05 seconds.

82. Close the **Every** dialog box.

83. Right-click in the cell where the **Log-Right** column intersects the **Line 16** row, and click **Position > Set X Coordinate...** in the shortcut menu.

84. In the expression editor, click the **Retrieve data from an object** button.

85. In the **New Expression** dialog box, right-click on the Log_Right object, and click **Position > X coordinate** in the shortcut menu.

86. In the expression editor, modify the expression to read X("Log-Right")+3.

Object	Object Location	End Node	Speed
Car1_Left	(32,352)	(–1500,352)	35
Car2_Right	(384,384)	(1380,384)	10
Car2_Left	(192,288)	(–1500,288)	15
Figure 10	*Goodheart-Willcox Publisher*		

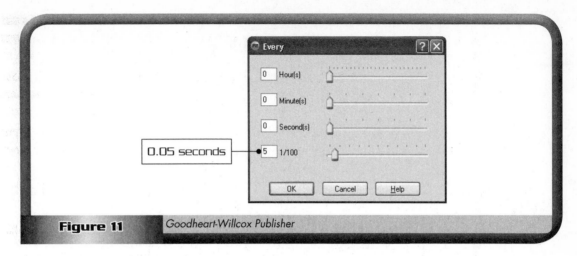

Figure 11   *Goodheart-Willcox Publisher*

87. Close the expression editor.

88. Similarly, on line 16, program this pseudo code:

> **AND** set the position of the Barrel_Right object three pixels to the right relative to its current position
>
> **AND** set the position of the Log_Left object one pixels to the left relative to its current position
>
> **AND** set the position of the Barrel_Left object one pixel to the left relative to its current position

Run Frame

89. Save your work, and test play the frame. Check if the logs and barrels are moving in the correct directions. The longer objects (logs) should move slightly faster than the shorter objects (barrels).

Wrapping Movement of the Helper Objects

The helper objects on river are moving to add challenge, but the game quickly runs out of helper objects. For purposes of testing, these objects can be respawned on the opposite side of the screen when they exit the scope. This motion is called *wrap*. The pseudo code is:

> **IF** a Group.Good object leaves the play area to the right or left,
>
> **THEN** wrap the movement of the object to the opposite side of the play area.

This type of movement will be used only for testing. The final movement for the game will be refined later.

90. On line 17, add a new condition. In the **New Condition** dialog box, right-click on the Group.Good icon, and click **Position > Test position of "Group.Good"** in the shortcut menu. The **Test Position** dialog box is displayed, as shown in **Figure 12.**

91. Click the arrow pointing to the left and the arrow pointing to the right. Hovering the cursor over these arrows displays the help text Leaves in the right? and Leaves in the left?.

92. Close the **Test Position** dialog box.

93. Right-click in the cell where the **Group.Good** column intersects the **Line 17** row, and click **Movement > Wrap Around Play Area** in the shortcut movement.

Run Frame

94. Save your work, and test play the frame.

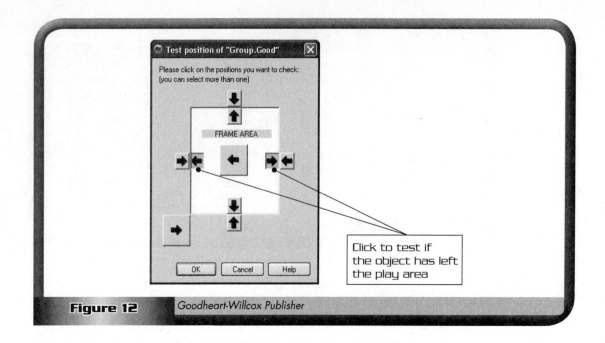

Click to test if
the object has left
the play area

Figure 12   *Goodheart-Willcox Publisher*

Riding the Logs and Barrels

The Avatar object is programmed to allow the player to jump onto a helper object, but there is no way for the Avatar object to automatically move with these objects. The pseudo code to allow this is:

> **IF** every 5/100ths of a second
> > **AND** the Avatar object is overlapping a log or barrel
> > **AND** the log or barrel is moving,
> **THEN** set the position of the Avatar object to move the same speed and direction
> > as the log or barrel.

Since all of the logs and barrels in the Good group, there needs to be an indicator as to which ones move right and which ones move left. This can be done using flags. For this game build, setting the internal flag to on will indicate the Group.Good object is moving to the right.

95. On line 18, program this pseudo code:

> **IF** at the start of the frame,
> **THEN** set internal flag #1 for the Log_Right to on
> > **AND** set internal flag #1 for the Barrel_Right to on.

96. Click the line number for line 18, drag up to the top of the list, and drop. It becomes line 1, and all other lines are renumbered. It is a best practice to have all events for "start of frame" or "always" placed at the beginning of the script or the subroutine.

97. On line 19, add a new condition for this pseudo code:

> **IF** every 5/100th of a second
> > **AND** the Avatar object is overlapping a Group.Good object
> > **AND** internal flag #1 for the Group.Good object is on
> **THEN** set the position of the Avatar object three pixels to the right of its current position.

98. On line 20, program this pseudo code to check if the Avatar object is riding a left moving log or barrel:

> **IF** every 5/100th of a second
> > **AND** the Avatar object is overlapping a Group.Good object
> > **AND** the Group.Good internal flag 1 is off
> **THEN** set the position of the Avatar object one pixel to the left of its current position.

99. Save your work, and test play the frame. Check that the Avatar object moves in the same direction and at the same speed as the logs and barrels when on a helper object. See if you can ride the logs and barrels to reach the goals.

Run Frame

Bug Repair Using the OR operator

You may have noticed a bug. If the Avatar object rides a helper object off of the screen, it is stuck and cannot come back into the scope. If the Avatar object travels out of the scope to the right or left, one life should be subtracted from player 1 and the Avatar object should be returned to its starting location. An **OR** operator is used in this programming. The pseudo code is:

> **IF** the X coordinate of the Avatar object is less than 0
> > **OR** the X coordinate of the Avatar object is greater than 640
>
> **THEN** subtract one life from player 1
> > **AND** set the position of the Avatar object to the starting point.

100. On line 21, add a new condition. In the **New Condition** dialog box, right-click on the Avatar object, and click **Position > Compare X position to a value** in the shortcut menu.

101. In the expression editor, enter 0, select the Lower comparison method, and close the editor.

102. Right-click on the condition in line 21, and click **OR operator (logical)** in the shortcut menu.

103. Right-click on **OR (logical)** in line 21, and click **Insert** in the shortcut menu. Program this pseudo code: **IF** the X coordinate of the Avatar object is greater than 640.

104. On line 21, program the **THEN** side of the pseudo code shown above. Refer to **Figure 13.**

105. Save your work, and test play the frame.

Run Frame

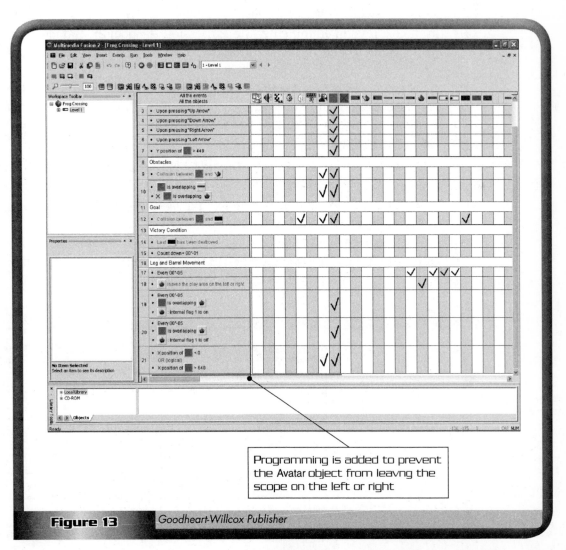

Programming is added to prevent the Avatar object from leavng the scope on the left or right

Figure 13   *Goodheart-Willcox Publisher*

Spawning Cars

Currently, the cars quickly exit the scope and leave the road empty. No challenge crossing the road there! New cars need to be spawned to randomly replace the cars that exit the scope. Additionally, to reduce the load on the game engine, cars must be destroyed once they leave the scope.

The type of car that is spawned and its placement will be randomized to add to the entertainment and replay value of the game. The Randomize counter object will be set to randomly choose 0 or 1 every 0.75 seconds. This random value will determine the type and placement of a newly spawned car. The pseudo code for one car is:

> **IF** the Randomize counter object is equal to 0,
> **THEN** create a Car1_Right object just outside the scope and in the same row as the original CAR1_Right object.

106. On line 22, insert a comment that states Spawning Cars.

107. On line 23, program this pseudo code:

> **IF** a Group.Bad object collides with the Destroyer object,
> **THEN** destroy the Group.Bad object.

108. On line 24, add a new condition. In the **New Condition** dialog box, right-click on the **Timer** icon (not the Date & Timer object), and click **Every** in the shortcut menu.

109. In the **Every** dialog box, enter 0 in the **Hour(s)**, **Minute(s)**, and **Second(s)** text boxes and 75 in the **1/100** text box.

110. Right-click in the cell where the **Randomize** column intersects the **Line 24** row, and click **Set Counter** in the shortcut menu.

111. In the expression editor, enter the expression Random(2), and close the expression editor. Refer to **Figure 14.** Entering the value 2 specifies to randomly choose from the first two positive integer values. Those two values are 0 and 1.

112. On line 25, add a new condition. In the **New Condition** dialog box, right-click on the Randomize counter object, and click **Compare the counter to a value...** in the shortcut menu. The expression editor is displayed.

113. Select the **Equal** operator, enter 0, and close the expression editor.

114. Right-click in the cell where the **Create Object** column intersects the **Line 25** row, and click **Create object** in the shortcut menu.

115. In the **Create Object** dialog box, select the Car1_Right object, and click the **OK** button. The frame editor is temporarily displayed.

116. In the **Create Object** dialog box, click the **At actual X,Y coordinates** radio button, enter −70 in the **X:** text box, enter 416 in the **Y:** text box, and click the **OK** button.

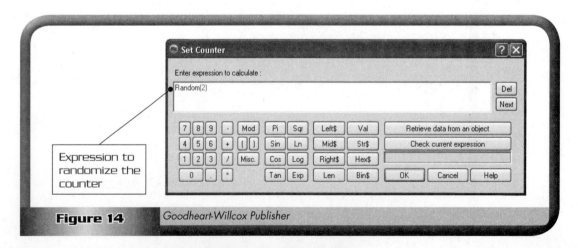

Figure 14   *Goodheart-Willcox Publisher*

117. Similarly, add this pseudo code to line 25: **AND** create a Car1_Left object at (750,352).

118. Save your work, and test play the frame. Check for any errors with spawning of the cars. The "car2" objects have not yet been programmed to spawn, so only the "car1" objects will spawn at this point.

Run Frame

Spawning Error

The "car1" objects spawn in the correct location, but groups of objects are formed, not individual objects. This is because the Randomize counter does not change for two seconds, but the script is processed every 1/30th of a second. New car objects are continuously created while the counter is equal to zero. The fix for this bug is to add programming to change the counter. The pseudo code is:

 IF the Randomize counter is equal to 0,
 THEN set the Randomize counter to 9.

When the condition is true, the counter is immediately set to 9. This stops the cars from stacking up. The number 9 is not significant. Any number that the expression Random(2) will not evaluate to could be used.

119. On line 25, right-click in the **Randomize** column, and click **Set Counter** in the shortcut menu.

120. In the expression editor, enter **9**, and close the expression editor.

121. Test play the frame. Note any errors.

Run Frame

More Cars

The player now has some challenge on the road. Since the "car1" objects respawn, the player cannot simply wait for the road to be clear before moving to the edge of the river. Now, the "car2" objects must be set to respawn as well.

A new counter will be used to regulate the spawning of "car2" objects. Pay attention to the Y coordinate values of the existing "car2" objects. New items must be spawned outside the scope, but at the same Y coordinate of the original objects. The X coordinate must be far enough outside the scope so the cars drive into the scope without flashing, but not so far away that the cars collide with the Destroyer objects.

122. In the frame editor, insert a new counter named Randomize_Car2. Place the counter outside of the scope.

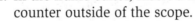
Frame Editor

Event Editor

123. In the event editor, program this pseudo code on line 26:

 IF every 2.5 seconds,
 THEN set Randomize_Car2 counter to choose a random number of 0 or 1.

124. Program this pseudo code on line 27:

 IF the Randomize_Car2 counter equals 0,
 THEN create a Car2_Right object at (–100,384)
   AND create a Car2_Left object at (700,288)
   AND set the Randomize_Car2 counter to 9.

125. Program this pseudo code on line 28:

 IF the Randomize counter equals 1,
 THEN create a Car1_Left object at (750,256)
   AND set the Randomize counter to 9.

126. Program this pseudo code on line 29:

 IF the Randomize_Car2 counter equals 1,
 THEN create a Car2_Right object at (–100,320)
   AND set the Randomize counter to 9.

127. Save your work, and test play the frame. Debug as needed.

Run Frame

Error Prevention

When the player crashes the Avatar object into a car or the river, it may not be apparent the Avatar object was destroyed and the player presses the up arrow key. Since the Avatar object is moved to the starting position, the player may accidentally move the Avatar object into traffic and destroy the newly spawned object. To resolve this, a pause-and-relax activity should be programmed to allow the player to understand the Avatar object has been reset to the starting position.

128. In the frame editor, open the Dead object in the image editor.

Frame Editor

129. Click the **Frames** tab at the bottom of the image editor.

130. Right-click on Frame 1, and click **Zoom** in the shortcut menu. The **Insert Resized Frames** dialog box is displayed, as shown in **Figure 15.**

131. Enter 1 in the **Final width** and **Final height** text boxes.

132. Enter 15 in the **Number of frames** text box, and click the **OK** button. Fifteen frames are automatically created in the animation, each smaller in size than the previous frame. This process is called keyframing, which is discussed in detail in Chapter 11.

133. Click the **Direction Options** tab.

134. Enter 20 in the **Speed** text box.

135. Click the **Play** button to see the animation. Close the animation preview.

136. Close the image editor.

Event Editor

137. Display the event editor, and add a new condition on line 30.

138. In the **New Condition** dialog box, right-click on the Dead object, and click **Animation > Which animation of "Dead" is Playing?** in the shortcut menu.

139. In the dialog box, click the Stopped animation set, and click the **OK** button, as shown in **Figure 16.** There is only one animation set on the Dead object, so there is only one displayed in this dialog box.

140. Complete the action on line 28 by programming this pseudo code: **THEN** set the Avatar object to position (288,448). This will freeze the Avatar object in place until the Dead animation has finished playing. The player will no longer accidentally jump into traffic and will have a brief pause before starting again.

141. Add programming to destroy the avatar when all the Goal objects are destroyed. This prevents the Avatar object from moving if the timer is running during the victory condition programming and also visible at the starting point while the time runs.

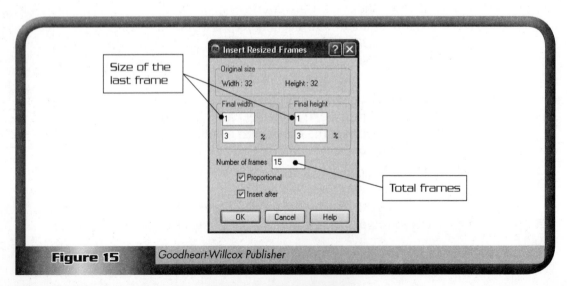

Figure 15   *Goodheart-Willcox Publisher*

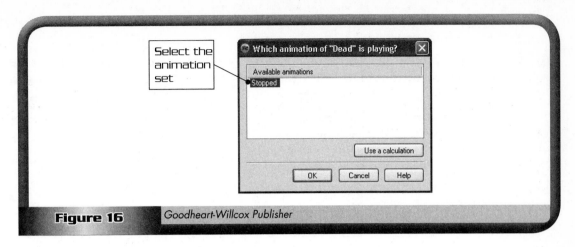

Figure 16 *Goodheart-Willcox Publisher*

142. Click on the number for line 30 (animation stopped), drag it upward, and drop it under line 10. It is good practice to keep related lines of programming together. This line belongs under the Obstacles comment.

143. Save your work, and test play the frame. See if this new pause-and-relax activity helps with gameplay. Debug as needed.

Run Frame

Sound Engineering

The gameplay is complete for the proof of concept build. Elements of refinement such as sound and art will make the gameplay even better. For now, the focus is on adding sound elements. Art enhancements will take place in Chapter 9. Using your personal sound library and any new sounds you wish to add to the library, program the following sounds to occur in Level 1. Be sure to use a sample or music as appropriate.

144. Program this pseudo code: **IF** at the start of the frame, **THEN** loop the AMBIENT_City_Level1_Scene1 sound.

145. Program this pseudo code: **IF** the player presses any arrow key, **THEN** play once the ACTION_Jump_Boing sound.

146. Program this pseudo code: **IF** the Avatar object is destroyed by a car, **THEN** play a squishing sound.

147. Program this pseudo code: **IF** the Avatar object is destroyed by falling in the river, **THEN** play a splashing sound **AND** stop playing any other sounds.

148. Program this pseudo code: **IF** the Avatar object collides with the goal, **THEN** play the Crowd_Applause sound **AND** stop playing all other sounds.

149. Program this pseudo code: **IF** the player achieves victory, **THEN** play the Crowd_Cheer sound **AND** stop playing all other sounds.

150. Program this pseudo code: **IF** the Avatar is destroyed by moving off of sides of the game map, **THEN** play a squishing sound.

151. Program this pseudo code: **IF** the Avatar tries to exit the game from the bottom, **THEN** play an error sound.

152. Program this pseudo code:

> **IF** the **Avatar** object is overlapping a Group.Good object
> > **AND** the ENVIRONMENT_Beach_Waves-gentle sound sample is not playing,
> **THEN** stop playing the City sound sample
> > **AND** loop the ENVIRONMENT_Beach_Waves-gentle sound.

153. Investigate all other game interactions, and program an appropriate sound to play.

154. Save your work, and test play the frame. Test the sounds to make sure they match the interactions. Debug as needed.

Run Frame

155. Compile an EXE file, and submit the game for grading according to the directions provided by your instructor.

Review Questions

1. Describe a backdrop object.

_____

_____

_____

_____

2. If a screen is 780 pixels wide and an object is 13 pixels wide, what X value would be used to reset the object's position to prevent it from moving off of the screen to the right? Assume the hotspot is in the default location of the upper-left corner. Show your work.

_____

_____

3. Describe an appropriate sound that could be used to warn the player if a bicycle was randomly programmed to travel in the safe area between the road and the river.

_____

_____

_____

_____

4. What is *wrap* in video game?

_____

_____

_____

_____

5. What are the possible values for the expression Random(5)?

_____

_____

Name: _____

Date: _____

Class: _____

Activity 8-5

Game Review

Objectives

Students will effectively evaluate the quality of their work through reflection and analysis. Students will effectively evaluate the quality of the work of others. Students will identify positive aspects of the playability and functionality of a software design project. Students will provide constructive criticism to peers and suggest possible solutions to problems.

Situation

The client has asked for an evaluation report on the playability and functionality of the game built in Activity 8-4. Each member of the design team needs to evaluate the product and suggest reasons why each item achieves or fails to achieve the objective. An assigned quality assurance (QA) evaluator will also review the game on behalf of the client. The QA evaluator will note any issues, errors, or bugs in your game. Be accurate and complete in evaluations.

Design Reasoning—Personal Evaluation

Completed by:							
Item	0	2	4	6	8	10	Score
Concept How well the idea is developed.	No main idea.					Clear throughout.	
Aesthetics Look, layout, colors, and animations.	Poor graphics and color.					Awesome graphics and theme-based colors; objects fit the game.	
Sound Effects Playing of sounds, volume, background sounds, etc.	No sound; too loud or not related to the game.					Sound added to game experience.	
Functionality Does everything work?	Unfinished; could not play; major errors.					Plays perfectly; no bugs, glitches, or errors.	
Replay Desire to play the game again.	Game too easy or uninteresting.					Cannot wait to play it again!	
						Total Score (higher is better)	
ESRB Rating:		Why:					

Reflection and Improvements: Reflect on your work, explain your score for each item, and list improvements needed for your game. Attach additional sheets of paper if needed or complete this using word processor software. Give this evaluation sheet to a classmate for him or her to complete the peer evaluation.

_____

_____

_____

_____

_____

_____

_____

_____

_____

_____

_____

Quality Assurance—Peer Evaluation

Completed by:

Item	0	2	4	6	8	10	Score
Concept How well the idea is developed.	No main idea.					Clear throughout.	
Aesthetics Look, layout, colors, and animations.	Poor graphics and color.					Awesome graphics and theme-based colors; objects fit the game.	
Sound Effects Playing of sounds, volume, background sounds, etc.	No sound; too loud or not related to the game.					Sound added to game experience.	
Functionality Does everything work?	Unfinished; could not play; major errors.					Plays perfectly; no bugs, glitches, or errors.	
Replay Desire to play the game again.	Game too easy or uninteresting.					Cannot wait to play it again!	
						Total Score (higher is better)	
ESRB Rating:		Why:					

Name: _____

Comments and Constructive Criticism: Explain the score for each item. Explain what you liked about the item and how it should be improved. Be detailed and complete. Cite specific examples from the game. Attach additional sheets of paper if needed or complete this using word processor software. Be honest and provide constructive criticism.

Items not fully documented and cited may reduce the total score for the QA evaluator. Being unprofessional or lowering a score on a personal issue unrelated to the game design *will* reduce the total score for the QA evaluator.

_____

_____

_____

_____

_____

_____

_____

_____

_____

_____

_____

Chapter 9
Art Composition

Objectives

After completing this chapter, you will be able to:
- Describe various color models.
- Create basic vector-based artwork.
- Explain how the human brain interprets images from contextual clues.
- Apply various artistic techniques to create the perception of depth in artwork.
- Integrate original artwork into a video game build.

Shamleen/Shutterstock.com

Linda Bucklin/Shutterstock.com

Pixel Europe/Shutterstock.com

Bellwork

Day	Date	Activity	Response
1		Complete the anticipation guide and the K and W columns of the KWL chart for this chapter.	
2		What is an art movement?	
3		Describe how art is used to depict culture.	
4		Describe the presentation of a video game.	
5		How does digital artwork differ from other types of artwork?	
6		How are primitives used to create complex objects?	
7		How is an implied line created?	
8		Define *gamut*.	
9		Compare and contrast additive color and subtractive color.	
10		Describe how length, frequency, and amplitude affect the color of light.	
11		What role does value play in a monochromatic image?	

Day	Date	Activity	Response
12		What is chiaroscuro?	
13		What are two benefits to using sleep or shutdown energy-monitoring software?	
14		Describe the three components of value on a 3D object.	
15		Define *spatial*.	
16		Describe how emphasis is commonly used in a video game.	
17		What are texture fills?	
18		How can the rule of thirds apply to an image?	
19		Describe how proportion is used to create depth in a 3D video game.	
20		Complete the L column of the KWL chart and the After Reading column of the anticipation guide with what you learned from this chapter.	
21		Speculate why an entire image would turn red when a digital artist applied a red fill to a small section of the image.	

Name: _____

Date: _____

Class: _____

Anticipation Guide

Directions

Before reading the chapter, read each statement in the table below. In the column titled Before Reading, write the letter *T* if you agree with the statement or *F* if you disagree with the statement. After reading the chapter, reread each statement in the table below. In the column titled After Reading, write the letter *T* if you agree with the statement or *F* if you disagree with the statement. Be prepared to justify your answers in a class discussion.

Before Reading	Statement	After Reading
	Historical periods of art include expressionism, surrealism, and pop art.	
	Art can be presented so it can only be seen from far overhead.	
	Implied lines are not solid lines.	
	The color model used for televisions and computer monitors is CMYK.	
	Diffuse color is the highlight color caused by the light source.	

KWL Chart

Directions

Before reading the chapter, fill in what you already know about the topic in the K column and what you want to learn in the W column. After reading the chapter, review what you know and wanted to learn about the topic. Reflect on what you have studied and completed in this chapter. Fill in what you learned in the L column. Be prepared to justify your answers in a class discussion.

Topic: Digital Art		
K What you already *know*	**W** What you *want* to learn	**L** What you *learned*

Activity 9-1

Additive Color Model

Objectives

Students will construct color using the RGB color model to a 32-bit depth. Students will convert colors using the HSL/HSB color model. Students will synthesize shapes by assembling 2D primitives to create objects. Students will save work in compressed and uncompressed file formats. Students will explain the application of different image file formats and their limitations.

Situation

The Really Cool Game Company is cross-training employees in each game design specialty as part of its management training program. Each employee needs to be trained on the basic art and design needed in game production. You must familiarize yourself with each type of art project so you can understand the work needed and to properly schedule and manage game art production.

How to Begin

1. Launch Microsoft PowerPoint.

2. Delete any existing text boxes to create a blank slide.

Oval

3. Click the **Shapes** button on the **Illustrations** panel of the **Insert** tab in the ribbon. Click the **Oval** button in the drop-down menu. Notice that the cursor changes to crosshairs (+), which indicates you can draw on the page.

4. Click and drag to draw. Create an oval that is wider than it is tall.

5. Click the **Shape Outline** button on the **Shape Styles** panel of the **Format** tab in the ribbon. Select a red or gray color swatch in the drop-down menu.

6. With the oval still selected, click the **Shape Fill** button, and click **More Fill Colors...** in the drop-down menu. The **Colors** dialog box is displayed in which you can edit the color, as shown in **Figure 1**. This dialog box will remain open for most of the rest of this activity.

7. Click the **Custom** tab.

8. Click the **Color model:** drop-down list, and click **RGB** in the list. This sets the color model.

9. Click in the **Red:** text box, and enter **100**. Notice how the sample color swatch in the bottom-right corner of the dialog box has changed.

10. Click in the **Green:** text box, and enter **200**.

11. Click in the **Blue:** text box, and enter **50**. The new color should be a bright green.

HSL Conversion

HSL stands for hue, saturation, and luminescence. Hue is the pigment color. Saturation is how dark or rich the color is. Luminescence is how much light is shining on the color. Think of saturation as like having a glass of water and an ink dropper.

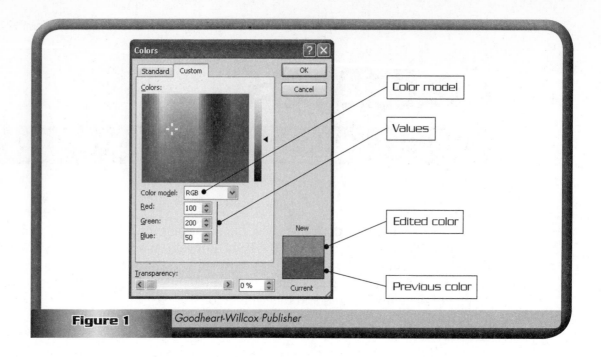

Figure 1   Goodheart-Willcox Publisher

Imagine 255 drops of ink in the dropper. If you put one drop of red ink in the glass, the water is very light red because most of the color is diluted by the water. The ink solution has low ink saturation. If you put another 50 drops of red ink in the water, the ink solution is redder than before. When you get up to 250 drops, the water is almost unable to hold more ink and is almost the same color as the ink in the dropper. When you get to 255 drops, the water is the same color as the ink that was in the dropper. This level of color is high ink saturation.

12. Click the **Color model:** drop-down list, and click **HSL** in the list. Notice the text boxes have changed, but the color has not changed. HSL is simply a different way to define a color.

13. Click in the **Lum:** text box, and enter 0. Notice how the color has changed. If the luminescence value is 0, the effect is as if no light is shining on the color. It is like the lights are turned off, and everything is as in the dark.

14. Change the color model to RGB. The red, green, and blue values are all 0, which is pure black.

15. Change the color model to HSL.

16. Change the luminescence value to 255, and notice how the color has changed. The highest luminescence value is 255, which is like shining many lights on the color. All you can see is white light.

17. Change the color model to RGB. The red, green, and blue values are at the maximum of 255, which is pure white.

18. Change the color model to HSL, and change the luminescence value to 100. Notice the color has changed to a darker green than the original R200, G10, B50 color.

19. Click and hold the up arrow to the right of the **Sat:** text box, as shown in **Figure 2**. As the saturation increases, the crosshairs in the color matrix moves upward as the color changes. The top of the color matrix is full saturation (255).

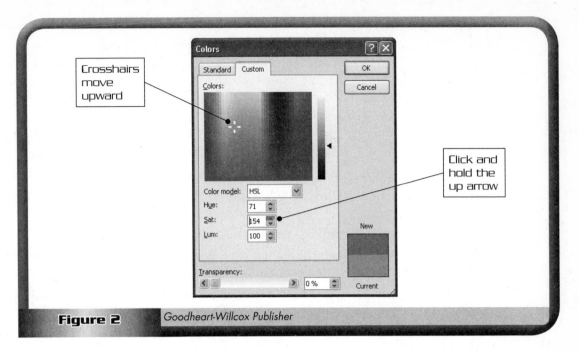

Figure 2   *Goodheart-Willcox Publisher*

20. Click and hold the down arrow to the right of the **Sat:** text box. The crosshairs move downward. The bottom of the matrix is no saturation (0). Set the saturation value to 0.

21. Change the color model to RGB. All the values are 100, which is a dark gray. This is because a saturation of 0 makes the color gray.

Did you notice the value of the gray is the same as the luminescence value? Similarly, a luminescence value of 200 and a saturation value of 0 is equivalent to R200, G200, B200, which is a light gray. This is because the saturation value of 0 means black. The luminescence value is how light the color is. Since the base color is black, luminescence determines if the color will be black (R0, G0, B0), white (R255, G255, B255), or somewhere in-between. Whenever the red, green, and blue values are equal, the color will be either white, black, or a shade of gray.

RGB Mixing

Using the RGB color model in PowerPoint, over 16 million different colors can be created. Each of the colors can have a value from 0 to 255, which is 256 values. Cubing this value, since there are three color components, provides the total number of possible colors ($256 \times 256 \times 256 = 16,777,216$). By adding the colors red, green and blue in different amounts, different colors are created. This is just like the paint store mixing paint. Take a little red, add some blue, and the result is purple. Since the colors are added, the RGB color model is called an *additive color model.*

22. Set the RGB values to 100, if not already set to that. This is a dark gray that will be used as a base for changing the color.

23. Change the red value to 200. In other words, "add" 100 red to the color. Notice how the new color is a brick red.

24. Change the green value to 0. In other words, "add" –100 green to the color. Notice how the new color is a purple-red. This is because the color now only contains red and blue, no green.

25. Change the blue value to 200. In other words, "add" 100 blue to the color. The new color is now a bright purple because the red and blue values are equal.

Alpha Channel

The *alpha channel* is used to control transparency. When transparency is added to the RGB color definition, the color model is called RGBA. When used in a color definition, the alpha channel value typically is specified as a value from 0 to 255. In PowerPoint, the alpha channel specification is a percentage.

26. Set the color to R200, G0, B200, if not already set to those values.

27. Change the transparency value to 50%. This can be done by entering **50** in the **Transparency:** text box or dragging the slider until that value is displayed.

28. Click the **OK** button to apply the fill color to the oval.

Oval

29. Draw a second oval over the top of the existing oval. Make the new oval taller than it is wide.

30. Fill the new oval with the color R0, G200, B0.

31. Right-click on the new oval, and click **Send to Back** > **Send to Back** in the shortcut menu. This moves the new oval behind the first oval, as shown in **Figure 3.**

Because the first oval has an alpha value of 50%, part of the second oval is visible through the first oval. The colors where the two ovals overlap are blended. Effectively, the overlapping area has a color of R200, G200, B200. That is why the overlapping section turns gray.

The alpha channel is not just for mixing colors. The alpha channel can also be used to outline an image and drop, or remove, the background. This is the most common use of the alpha channel. For example, sprites for video games often have the main image outlined with a path that is set in the alpha channel, as shown in **Figure 4.** In gameplay, the background of the sprite is dropped out so the player sees only the main image of the sprite.

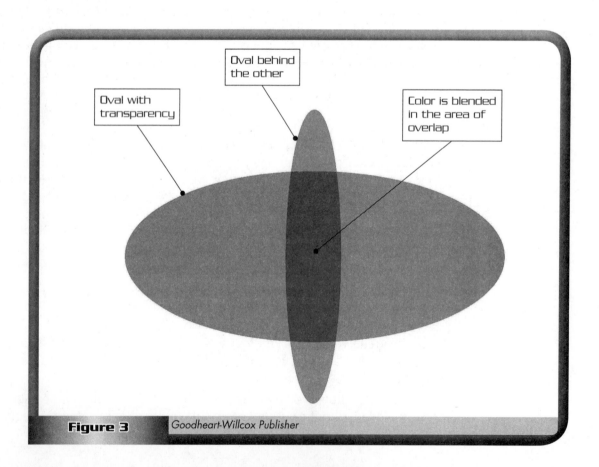

Oval with transparency

Oval behind the other

Color is blended in the area of overlap

Figure 3   *Goodheart-Willcox Publisher*

Sprite background
is visible

Sprite is outlined with
a path in alpha channel

Figure 4   *Algol, Unholy Vault Designs/Shutterstock.com*

Review Questions

1. What are the channels used in the RGB color model? What are the channels used
   in the HSL color model?

   _____

   _____

   _____

2. What does the alpha channel control?

   _____

   _____

   _____

3. In the RGB color model, what are the settings for pure black? In the HSL color
   model, what are the settings for pure white?

   _____

   _____

   _____

4. What is the saturation value of red if it is fully saturated?

   _____

5. If the computer makes an image transparent by removing pixels from the top image to let pixels of the bottom image show through, an image that is 10% transparent has 10% of its pixels removed. Apply this principle to complete the table below.

Image Size in Pixels	Total number of Pixels	Transparency %	Number of pixels removed	Total pixels remaining in original
50 × 50		10%	250	
400 × 600		25%		
480 × 720			138,240	
600 × 800				120,000

Activity 9-2

Vector Art Composition

Objectives

Students will explain the role and importance of primitives in game art. Students will describe layering and compositing of shapes. Students will perform basic computer drawing functions to create vector art and primitives.

Situation

The Really Cool Game Company uses vector-art primitives for game art in many prototype games and in concept art. Creating these computer drawings requires little artistic skill. Any team member should be able to draw this type of art. Many software programs have primitive shapes that can be assembled for basic art. Learning how to create primitives in one program will help you understand how to perform similar actions in any vector-drawing software.

The art department needs to create concept art for a children's game that will be used to teach math skills. The proposed characters for this game include a father, mother, son, dog, cat, pig, shark, and space creature. The characters will be part of the question-and-answer system for the game. Your job is to create these characters using only primitive shapes. Before you get started with the art, read the handout provided by your instructor, which provides a basic overview of artwork.

How to Begin

1. Launch PowerPoint 2010.
2. Delete any existing text boxes to create a blank slide.
3. Save the file as *LastName*_Vector in your working folder.

Face Primitive

Shapes

Oval

In PowerPoint, drawing primitives are located in the **Illustrations** panel on the **Insert** tab of the ribbon. Click the **Shapes** button to display a drop-down menu that contains buttons for drawing primitives, as shown in **Figure 1**.

4. In the **Shapes** drop-down menu, click the **Oval** button.
5. Draw an oval of any size on the slide. With the oval selected, the **Format** tab is available in the ribbon.
6. Click **Format** tab.
7. In the **Size Panel** of the **Format** tab, enter 5 in the **Shape Height** and **Shape Width** text boxes. This makes the oval 5″ high by 5″ wide, which is a circle.

8. Fill the oval with the color R255, G255, B150. This is the skin tone of the character. You may change the skin tone to suit your preference.

9. Make the shape outline color black.

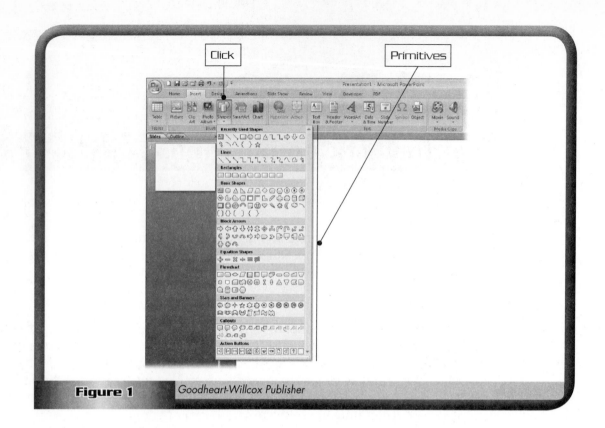

Figure 1   Goodheart-Willcox Publisher

Ears Primitives

Oval

10. Draw a 2.0″ × 0.7″ oval.

11. Fill the oval with the skin tone color, and outline the oval with black.

12. Right-click on the small oval, and click **Send to Back** > **Send to Back** in the shortcut menu. **Send Backward** moves the object to the very bottom of the stack, while **Send to Back** > **Send Backward** moves the primitive down in the stack of objects by one.

13. Copy and paste the ear.

14. Send the new small oval to the back of the stack.

15. Place ears on the side of the face so the face overlaps them by about half, as shown in **Figure 2**.

Eyes Primitives

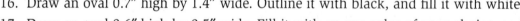

Oval

You will now create an eye from three oval primitives. One oval will be the white, one will be the iris, and one will be the pupil. After grouping the three ovals, the group will be copied to create a second eye.

16. Draw an oval 0.7″ high by 1.4″ wide. Outline it with black, and fill it with white.

17. Draw an oval 0.6″ high by 0.5″ wide. Fill it with an eye color of your choice, and set the outline to no color.

18. Draw an oval 0.15″ high by 0.15″ wide. Fill it with black, and set the outline to black.

19. Hold down the [Shift] key, and click each part of the eye. This selects all three ovals.

20. Click the **Align** button on the **Arrange** panel of the **Format** tab in the ribbon, and click **Align Center** in the drop-down menu. Click the button again, and click **Align Middle** in the drop-down menu. This centers all three objects both vertically and horizontally.

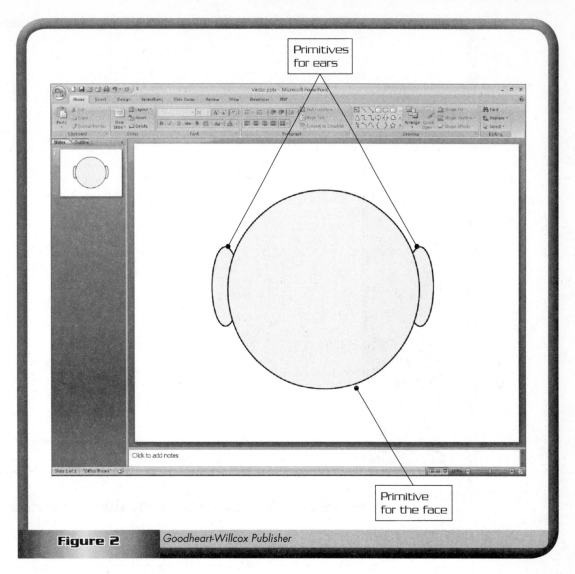

Primitives
for ears

Primitive
for the face

Figure 2   *Goodheart-Willcox Publisher*

21. Click the **Group** button on the **Arrange** panel of the **Format** tab in the ribbon, and click **Group** in the drop-down menu. This makes all selected primitives act as a single object.

22. Copy and paste the eye group. Move the two eyes into a good location on the face, similar to **Figure 3**.

Nose Primitive

Isoceles Triangle

The basic nose shape is formed with four primitives. It will be easier to build this facial feature in the blank area of the slide and not on the face. Once created, it can be moved into place on the face.

23. Click the **Shapes** button on the **Illustrations** panel of the **Insert** tab of the ribbon, and click the **Isosceles Triangle** button in the drop-down menu.

24. Draw a triangle, and set its size to 1.7″ high by 0.6″ wide.

25. Fill the triangle with the same color used to fill the face and ears, and set the outline to no color.

Oval

26. Create an oval, and set its size to 0.4″ high by 0.5″ wide. This is one nostril for the nose.

27. Place the oval so its center is at one of the bottom corners of the triangle. The location does not need to be exact.

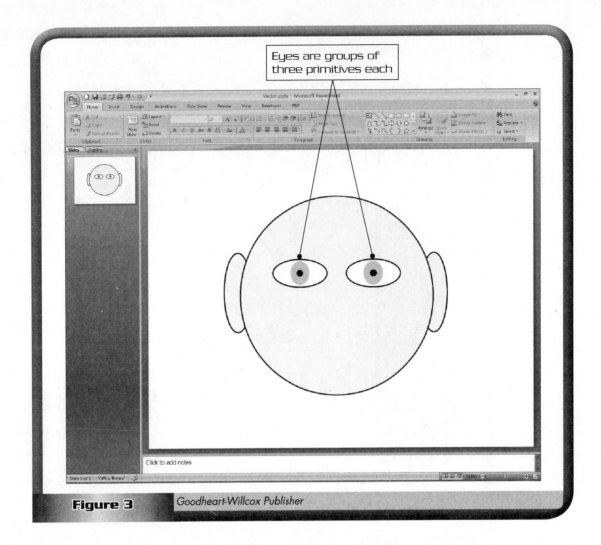

Figure 3   *Goodheart-Willcox Publisher*

28. Fill the oval with the skin tone color, and set the outline to no color.

29. Copy and paste the nostril oval, and place it on the opposite bottom corner of the triangle. Notice how primitives can be overlapped to construct a different shape. This is a common procedure.

30. Create an oval, set its size to 0.5″ high by 0.3″ wide, fill it with the skin tone color, and set the outline to no color. This is the tip of the nose.

31. Place the tip of the nose between the nostrils. If needed, use the arrow keys to nudge the shape into position. Hold the [Shift] key down while pressing an arrow key to move the shape one pixel at a time.

32. Select all of the primitives composing the nose and group them.

33. Copy and paste the nose group.

34. Increase the size of the pasted nose by 0.2″ in each direction. This larger nose will be used as a shadow, as shown in **Figure 4.** Without this contrast, the nose could not be seen as it would be the same color as the face.

35. Change the fill color of the larger nose to R255, G200, B100. This is a slightly darker version of the skin tone color. If your character has a different skin tone, create a slightly darker version of that color.

36. Change the object order so the lighter nose group is above the darker nose group.

37. Move the darker nose group onto the face in the proper location.

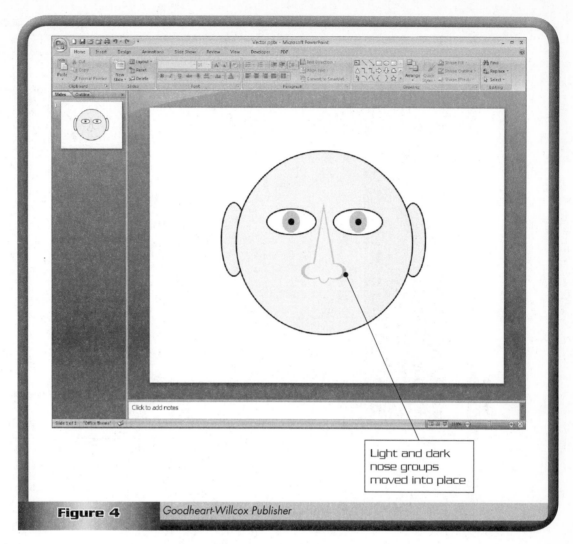

Figure 4   *Goodheart-Willcox Publisher*

Light and dark nose groups moved into place

38. Move the lighter nose group on top of the darker nose group. Use the arrow keys to nudge the nose groups to assure that a slight amount of the darker nose borders the lighter.

Eye Lids Primitives

Primitives can be altered to form new shapes. Each eyelid will be created from a single primitive. The primitive will then be modified to create the final eyelid.

Moon

Rotate

39. Draw a moon shape, and set its size to 0.6″ high by 1.4″ wide.

40. Click the **Rotate** button on the **Arrange** panel in the **Format** tab of the ribbon, and click **Rotate Right 90°** in the drop-down menu. The points of the crescent face downward, and the rounded part of the crescent is on top.

41. Click the yellow diamond on the selected crescent shape, and drag down until it stops moving, as shown in **Figure 5.** This changes the thickness of the crescent shape. The thickness determines how open the eye is. For a sleepy eye, use the maximum thickness. For a surprised eye, use a thin crescent.

42. Change the fill color to the skin tone, and set the outline color to black.

43. Move the eyelid over the eye.

44. Copy and paste the eyelid and place it over the other eye.

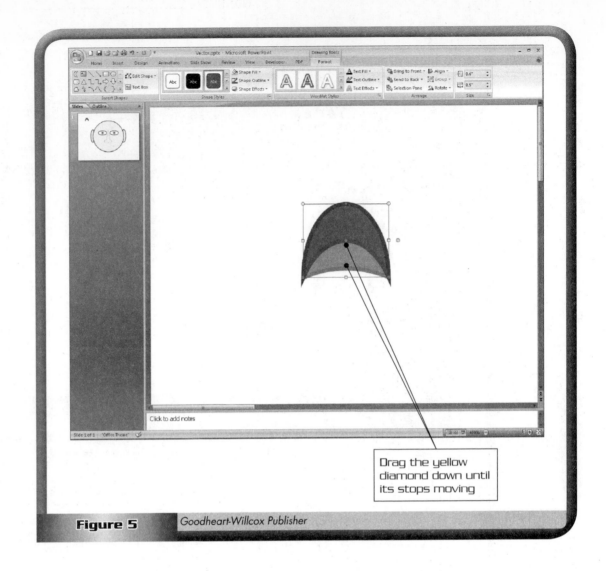

Drag the yellow diamond down until its stops moving

Figure 5 Goodheart-Willcox Publisher

Eyebrows Primitives

Moon

45. Create a crescent primitive, and set its size to 1.2″ high by 0.25″ wide.
46. Fill the shape with black or other hair color, and set the outline to black.
47. Rotate the primitive 90 degrees to the right.
48. Place the primitive above an eyelid.
49. Copy and paste the eyebrow primitive, and place it over the other eye.

Mouth Primitive

Moon

Rotate

50. Create a crescent primitive, and set its size to 2.5″ high by 0.2″ wide.
51. Set the fill and outline colors to dark red or other lip color.
52. Rotate the primitive 90 degrees to the left.
53. Place the mouth on the face centered under the nose.

Hair Primitives

Cloud

Hair can sometimes be a bit tricky to create. In this case, a cloud primitive will be used to create slightly curly hair. Multiple circle primitives of different sizes can be stacked to create very curly hair. Straight hair can be created by stacking oval and rectangle primitives.

54. Create a cloud primitive, and set its size to 0.7″ high by 1.7″ wide.

55. Fill the primitive with the same hair color used for the eyebrows, and set the outline color to black.

56. Make four copies of the primitive

57. Place the five primitives on top of the head from ear to ear. Rotate each primitive as needed to follow the contour of the head, as shown in **Figure 6.** Drag the green handle on a selected primitive to free rotate it.

58. Add a text box at the top of the slide (**Insert** > **Text** > **Text Box**), and enter the name Steve. This is the son character, and you may use a name of your own choosing.

Dad

For concept art, the dad will be very similar to the son character. The differences will be some features to provide contextual clues to age and authority.

59. Right-click on the mini slide in the sorter on the left of the screen, and click **Copy** in the shortcut menu.

60. Right-click below the mini slide, and click **Paste** in the shortcut menu. A copy of the slide is added to the presentation and is the current slide.

61. Click in the text box on the slide, and change the name to Sam. This is the father character, and you may use a name of your own choosing.

62. Edit the thickness of the eyelids so the eyes are open wider than the son character's.

63. Rotate the mouth to create a bit of a frown.

64. Remove hair primitives to create a bald spot on top of the head. Refer to **Figure 7.**

Figure 6   *Goodheart-Willcox Publisher*

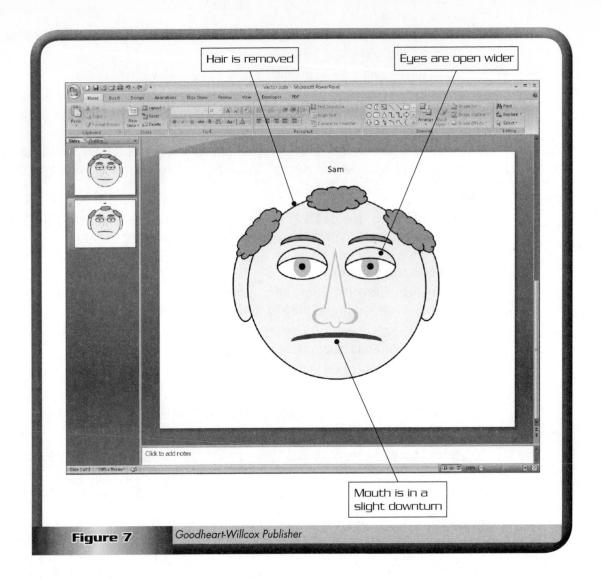

Hair is removed

Eyes are open wider

Mouth is in a slight downturn

Figure 7   *Goodheart-Willcox Publisher*

Mom

65. Copy the first slide, and paste it at the bottom of the mini slide sorter list.

66. Click in the text box on the slide, and change the name to Shirley. This is the mother character, and you may use a name of your own choosing.

67. Copy and paste the hair primitives add more hair. For example, you may wish to cover the ears or place hair below the ears for long hair.

68. Change the fill color of the hair primitives to a color of your choice. You may wish to vary the color of the fill between primitives to create a stylized effect, as shown in **Figure 8.** Using the HSL color model is a good way to create variations in the same color family.

69. Change the curve of the eyelids.

More Characters

The lead artist has some simple drawings for the other characters that need to be created. Included is a drawing and a list of primitives to help you complete each task. Add a new slide for each character by right-clicking at the bottom of the list of mini slides and selecting **New Slide** in the shortcut menu.

70. Create a pig character using the information shown in **Figure 9.** Select height and width settings to create a character of your own design. Shapes may need to be rotated and layered to complete the design. Name the character.

Name: _____

Hair is added and the fill color varied

Figure 8 *Goodheart-Willcox Publisher*

Feature	Primitives	Fill Color	Outline	Quantity
Face	Oval	Pink	Black	1
Ear, right	Isosceles triangle	Pink	Black	1
Ear, right	Isosceles triangle	Black	Black	1
Ear, left	Isosceles triangle	Pink	Black	1
Ear, left	Trapezoid	Pink	Black	1
Ear, left	Trapezoid	Black	Black	1
Eye	Oval	Black	Black	2
Eye	Oval	White	Black	2
Snout	Oval	Pink	Black	1
Nostril	Oval	Black	None	2
Mouth	Crescent	Red	Black	1

Figure 9 *Goodheart-Willcox Publisher*

71. Create a shark character using the information shown in **Figure 10.** Select height and width settings to create a character of your own design. Shapes may need to be rotated and layered to complete the design. Name the character.

72. Create a cat character using the information shown in **Figure 11.** Select height and width settings to create a character of your own design. Shapes may need to be rotated and layered to complete the design. Name the character.

73. Create a dog character using the information shown in **Figure 12.** Select height and width settings to create a character of your own design. Shapes may need to be rotated and layered to complete the design. Name the character.

74. Save your work, and submit it for grading.

Feature	Primitives	Fill Color	Outline	Quantity
Face	Oval	Gray	None	1
Mouth	Oval	Red gradient	Red	1
Tooth	Isosceles triangle	White	Black	Several
Gill	Crescent	Black	None	4–6
Eye	Oval	White	Black	2
Eye	Oval	Black	Black	2
Fin	Isosceles triangle	Gray	Black	1
Body	Trapezoid	Gray	Black	1
Tail	Crescent	Gray	Black	1

Figure 10   *Goodheart-Willcox Publisher*

Feature	Primitives	Fill Color	Outline	Quantity
Face	Oval	Gray	Black	1
Ear	Isosceles triangle	Gray	Black	2
Ear	Isosceles triangle	Black	Black	2
Eye	Oval	White	Black	2
Eye	Oval	Black	Black	2
Muzzle, sides	Oval	White	None	2
Muzzle, top	Oval	White	None	1
Nose	Oval	Red	None	1

Figure 11   *Goodheart-Willcox Publisher*

Feature	Primitives	Fill Color	Outline	Quantity
Face	Oval	Brown	Black	1
Ear	Oval	Black	Black	2
Eye	Oval	White	Black	2
Eye	Oval	Black	Black	2
Muzzle	Oval	Light Brown	None	2
Muzzle	Oval	Gray	None	2
Nose	Trapezoid	Black	None	1
Tongue	Oval	Red	None	1

Figure 12 Goodheart-Willcox Publisher

Review Questions

1. Describe the purpose of reordering the stack of objects.

_____

_____

_____

_____

2. What happens to primitives if they are grouped?

_____

_____

_____

_____

3. For the human characters, why were two nose groups used?

_____

_____

_____

_____

4. Compare and contrast the visual elements that created the cat, pig, and dog.

_____

_____

_____

_____

5. Speculate why the shark character included a body. Cite specific evidence to support your speculation.

_____

_____

_____

_____

Activity 9-3

Contrast Composition

Objectives

Students will apply contrast in digital designs. Students will correct contrast errors and explain how the human brain interprets images from contextual clues. Students will create illusion using contrast.

Situation

The Really Cool Game Company is training new game artists in the art of illusion and depth perception. One of the most powerful means of creating illusion of depth and shadow is the application of contrast. In this training, you will build the simple objects to demonstrate your mastery of contrast.

How to Begin

1. Launch Microsoft PowerPoint 2010.

2. Click the **Layout** button on the **Slides** panel in the **Home** tab of the ribbon, and click **Blank** in the drop-down menu.

New Slide

3. Click the **New Slide** button on the **Slides** panel in the **Home** tab of the ribbon to add a new slide. Add slides until there is a total of five slides.

4. Save the presentation as *LastName_*Contrast Effects in your working folder.

Implied Line Contrast

In this effect, contrast will be used to create a rectangular tunnel effect. Implied lines will be used to help create the effect.

5. Click the first slide in the mini slide sorter to make it current.

Rectangle

6. Click the **Shapes** button on the **Illustrations** panel of the **Insert** tab on the ribbon, and click the **Rectangle** shape button in the drop-down menu.

7. Create a rectangle of any size.

8. Change the size of the rectangle to 2″ × 2″.

9. Change the fill color to black, and the outline to no color.

10. Copy and paste to create a second rectangle.

11. Move the new square to the bottom-right corner of the original square. As you create more squares, each should be located at this same point.

12. Change the size of the new rectangle 1.8″ × 1.8″.

13. Change the fill color to the color swatch labeled **Black, Text 1, 15% lighter**, as shown in **Figure 1**. The name of each color swatch is displayed as help text when the cursor is hovered over it. The new rectangle is slightly lighter in color than the original.

14. Continue copying and editing rectangles as specified in **Figure 2**. Each square is slightly smaller and lighter than the one below it. The effect should look like a tunnel with a bright light at the far end. It could also be seen as a pyramid rising out of the screen.

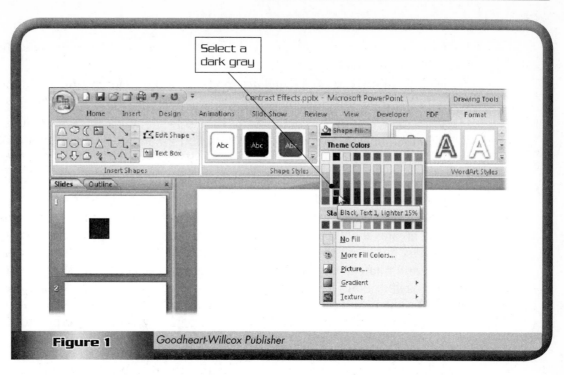

Figure 1 *Goodheart-Willcox Publisher*

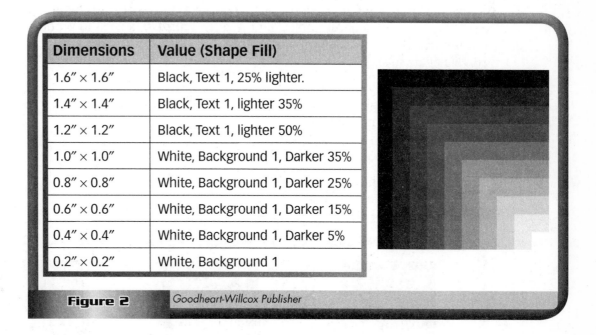

Dimensions	Value (Shape Fill)
1.6″ × 1.6″	Black, Text 1, 25% lighter.
1.4″ × 1.4″	Black, Text 1, lighter 35%
1.2″ × 1.2″	Black, Text 1, lighter 50%
1.0″ × 1.0″	White, Background 1, Darker 35%
0.8″ × 0.8″	White, Background 1, Darker 25%
0.6″ × 0.6″	White, Background 1, Darker 15%
0.4″ × 0.4″	White, Background 1, Darker 5%
0.2″ × 0.2″	White, Background 1

Figure 2 *Goodheart-Willcox Publisher*

15. Drag a selection box around all rectangles, and group them.

16. Copy and paste the group.

17. Move the copy near the top-left corner of the slide.

18. Move the original group near the top-center of the slide, and ungroup the rectangles.

19. With the ungrouped rectangles selected, click the **Align** button on the **Arrange** panel in the **Format** tab of the ribbon, and click **Align Center** in the drop-down menu.

20. Group the rectangles, copy the group, paste it, and move the copy near the top-right corner of the slide.

21. Ungroup the new copy, and click **Align Middle** in the **Align** drop-down menu.

22. Group this set of rectangles, copy the group, paste it, and move the copy near the center of the slide.

23. Change the size of the copied group to 0.8″ × 0.8″. Notice how the implied lines between the corners of the rectangles are more apparent.

24. With the group in the center of the slide selected, click the **Rotate** button on the **Arrange** panel in the **Format** tab of the ribbon, and click **More Rotation Options...** in the drop-down menu.

25. In the dialog box that is displayed, enter 45 in the **Rotation:** text box, and close the dialog box. The group is rotated 45 degrees, as shown in **Figure 3.**

Notice how the change in color value has created three different tunnels. Each example creates the illusion of 3D. An optical illusion of implied lines is created in all the objects, but is most dominant in the object in the middle of the slide that has been reduced and rotated. The implied lines created by the corners of the rectangles look brighter as your brain tries to fill in the line. The corners of each square are, in fact, not any brighter than the rest of the square. By rotating the object 45 degrees, the brain makes an easier implied line as the lines are perfectly vertical and horizontal.

Relative Contrast

When seeing changes in value, the brain attempts to interpret what is seen based on what it believes to be true. It often makes assumptions that are not valid. The concept of trompe l'oeil is a good example of this. In the next example, the contrast in value relative to adjacent objects, or *relative contrast,* is used to produce an optical illusion related to the color value of an object.

26. Navigate to slide 2.

27. Draw a rectangle that is 1″ × 1″.

Rectangle

28. Fill the rectangle with the color labeled **White, Background 1, Darker 35%**, and set the outline to no color.

29. Copy and paste the rectangle. Move one rectangle to the top-right corner of the slide and the other to the top-left corner.

30. Draw a rectangle that is 3″ × 3″.

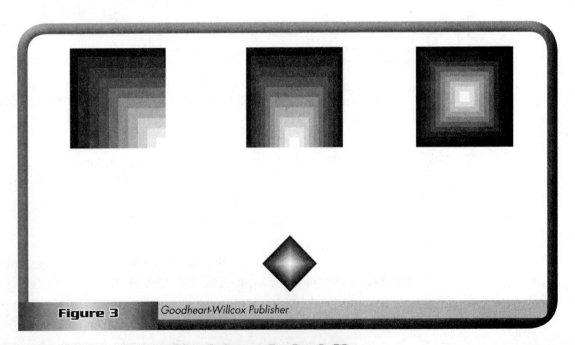

Figure 3 *Goodheart-Willcox Publisher*

31. Fill the new rectangle with the color labeled **Black, Text 1, Lighter 35%**, and set the outline to no color.

32. Copy and paste the rectangle, and place it to the right of the original.

33. Change the fill color of the new rectangle to **White, Background 1, Darker 25%.**

34. Select both large rectangles, and send them to the back of the object stack.

35. Drag one of the small rectangles to the middle of the dark large square.

36. Drag the other small rectangle to the light large square.

Notice how contrast has changed the perception of each of the small squares. One looks darker than the other, as shown in **Figure 4.** However, the color of neither is changed. The brain is fooled into seeing a different color value based on the adjacent color.

Depth Contrast

37. Navigate to slide 3.

Rectangle

Parallelogram

38. Create a rectangle that is 0.5″ high by 5.5″ wide.

39. Set the fill color to **White, Background 1, Darker 50%** and the outline to no color.

40. Create a parallelogram primitive, and set its size to 0.5″ high by 6.0″ wide.

41. Set the fill color to **White, Background 1, Darker 25%** and the outline to no color.

42. Place the parallelogram on top of the rectangle so the bottom left edge of the parallelogram is aligned with the top left of the rectangle, as shown in **Figure 5.**

43. The yellow diamond at the top of the parallelogram is used to adjust the angle of the sides. Click the yellow diamond, and drag it until the bottom-right corner of the parallelogram aligns with the top-right corner of the rectangle.

44. Draw a selection box around both primitives, and group them.

45. Copy the group and paste it three times.

46. Align the groups to form stairs.

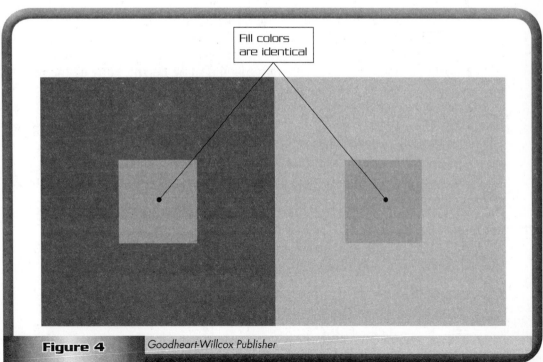

Fill colors are identical

Figure 4 *Goodheart-Willcox Publisher*

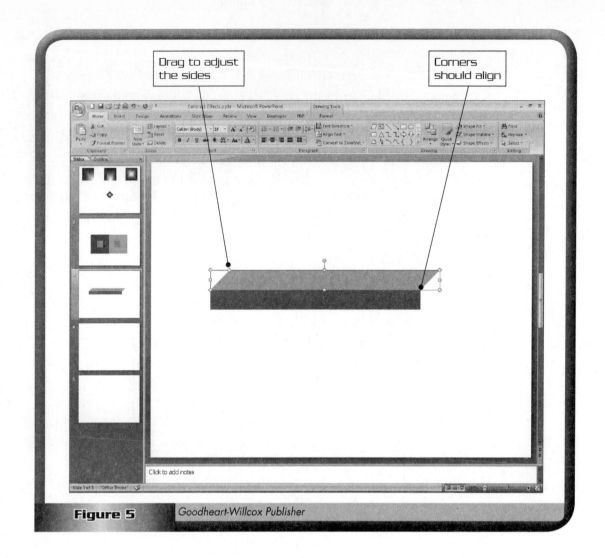

Drag to adjust the sides

Corners should align

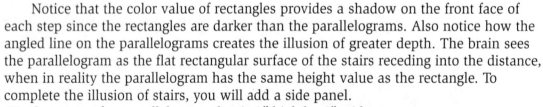

Figure 5

Goodheart-Willcox Publisher

Notice that the color value of rectangles provides a shadow on the front face of each step since the rectangles are darker than the parallelograms. Also notice how the angled line on the parallelograms creates the illusion of greater depth. The brain sees the parallelogram as the flat rectangular surface of the stairs receding into the distance, when in reality the parallelogram has the same height value as the rectangle. To complete the illusion of stairs, you will add a side panel.

Parallelogram

Rotate

47. Create another parallelogram that is 2″ high by 4″ wide.

48. Rotate the shape by first flipping it horizontally and then rotating it 90 degrees to the right.

49. Send the parallelogram to the back of the object stack.

50. Set the fill color to **White, Background 1, Darker 35%** and the outline to no color.

51. Move the parallelogram so its top-right corner aligns with the top right-corner of the top step, as shown in **Figure 6.**

52. Notice how the bottom edge of the parallelogram does not match the horizontal surfaces of the stairs. To correct the perspective, drag the yellow diamond until the edges match the horizontal surfaces.

Relative Line Contrast

53. Navigate to slide 4.

Rectangle

54. Create a rectangle that is 0.5″ high by 6″ wide.

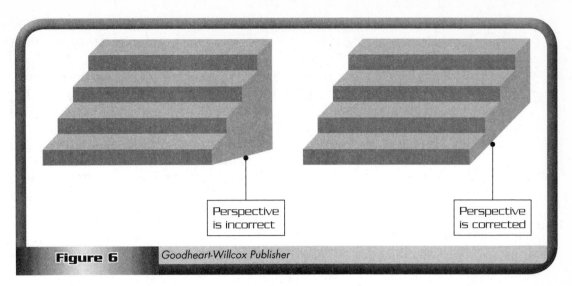

Figure 6 *Goodheart-Willcox Publisher*

55. Set the fill color to black and the outline to no color.

56. Copy and paste the rectangle, and move the copy so it is directly above the first rectangle with no space in-between. The left and right edges of the rectangles should align.

57. Change the fill color of the copied rectangle to yellow.

58. Group the two rectangles, and then make five copies so there is a total of six black and six yellow rectangles.

59. Move all of the groups so there is a single stack of rectangles with no space in-between. The left and right edges of all rectangles should align.

60. Create a rectangle that is 0.5″ high by 1.5″ wide.

Rectangle

61. Set the fill color to **White, Background 1, Darker 50%** and the outline to no color.

62. Copy and paste this rectangle 11 times.

63. Arrange these copies into two stacks as shown in **Figure 7.** Notice how one stack is over the black rectangles and the other stack is over the yellow rectangles.

Figure 7 *Goodheart-Willcox Publisher*

Notice how the gray rectangles that are over black appear lighter in color value than the gray rectangles that are over the yellow rectangles. However, all of the gray rectangles have the same color value. This is an optical illusion. The brain is fooled into thinking there is a color difference due to the contrast between adjacent colors. This is more apparent if the yellow rectangles are change to no fill. The higher contrast between gray and white makes the color value of the gray rectangles look even darker.

Rhythm Contrast

In most of the pervious examples, the contrast with the surrounding colors influenced the perceived color. The next example demonstrates how one color can seem to absorb the surrounding color.

64. Navigate to slide 5.

Oval

65. Create an oval that is 0.4″ × 0.4″. Place it in the middle of the slide.

66. Set the fill color to red and the outline to no color.

Block Arc

67. Create a block arc that is 1.2″ × 1.2″.

68. Set the fill color to **White, Background 1, Darker 50%** and the outline to no color.

69. Rotate the block arc 90 degrees to the right, and move it so the red oval is bisected by one leg of the block arc, as shown in **Figure 8.**

70. Drag the yellow diamond on the inside curve, not the one on the outside curve, straight up until the thickness of the arc matches the diameter of the oval.

Be very careful to move the diamond straight up. If moved left or right, the block arc will change in arc length and thickness. If needed, undo the action, and start over. The purpose of this is to create an arc with a thickness equal to the diameter of its center, which is also the diameter of the red circle. It may be easier to scale up the objects, edit the thickness, and then reset the size of the objects.

71. Delete the red oval.

72. Copy and paste the block arc.

73. Rotate the copied block arc by flipping it horizontally.

74. Move the copy to make a complete circle with the two block arc primitives.

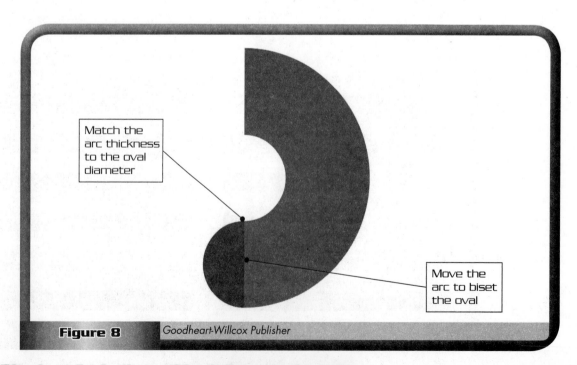

Match the arc thickness to the oval diameter

Move the arc to biset the oval

Figure 8 *Goodheart-Willcox Publisher*

75. Create a rectangle that is 3″ × 3″.

76. Set the fill color to **White, Background 1, Darker 35%** and the outline to no color.

77. Copy and paste to create an identical rectangle.

78. Change the fill color of the copy to **Black, Text 1, Lighter 35%**.

79. Move both rectangles to the back of the object stack.

80. Align the rectangles so they are next to each other and at the midpoint of the block arc circle, as shown in **Figure 9.**

81. Select one of the block arc primitives, and use the down arrow key to move the primitive until the end of the arc is in the center of the other block arc. Notice how each half of the circle takes on the color of the opposite rectangle. When the concept of *rhythm contrast* is applied, the brain tries to interpret the rhythm of the image and completes the arcs with an implied circular cap.

82. Save your work, and submit it for grading.

Review Questions

1. Describe implied lines.

   _____

   _____

   _____

   _____

2. What is relative contrast?

   _____

   _____

   _____

   _____

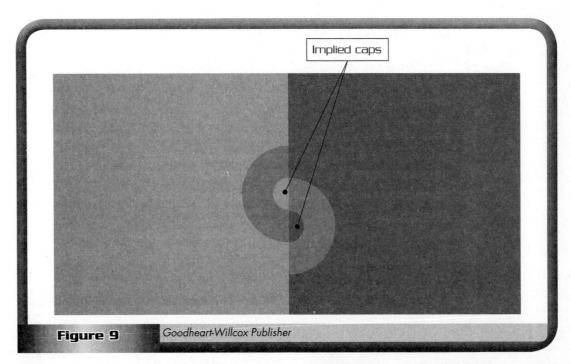

Implied caps

Figure 9   *Goodheart-Willcox Publisher*

3. Describe how two flat primitives can be used to simulate depth in stairs.

_____

_____

_____

_____

4. Why does a gray square appear darker when it is on top of a yellow square than when it is on top of a black square?

_____

_____

_____

_____

5. Describe the concept of rhythm contrast.

_____

_____

_____

_____

Activity 9-4

Value Composition

Objectives

Students will apply chiaroscuro, specular color, diffuse color, and ambient color to objects to create the perception of depth. Students will create the illusion of a 3D sphere in a 2D environment. Students will use color value to create optical illusions.

Situation

The Really Cool Game Company is creating art for a 2D game. However, the art needs to appear as if it is 3D. Based on your study of the elements of art, the company feels that you have the background and knowledge to complete this task. It needs to see if you have the skills to go with that knowledge. Using basic software, you must create 2D objects that appear to be 3D.

How to Begin

1. Launch Microsoft PowerPoint 2010.

2. Click the **Layout** button on the **Slides** panel in the **Home** tab of the ribbon, and click **Blank** in the drop-down menu.

3. Save the presentation as *LastName*_Value-Effects in your working folder.

4. Draw an oval that is 2.5″ × 2.5″.

Oval

5. Set the fill color to **White, Background 1, Darker 50%** and the outline to no color.

6. Copy the oval and paste it three times.

7. Arrange the four ovals so three are in a row at the top and fourth is at the bottom, as shown in **Figure 1.**

8. Add four text boxes to the slide, and label the ovals in the top row Flat, Gradient, and Volumetric, and label the oval in the bottom row Spatial.

Text Box

Gradient

A gradient is adjacent colors that fade into each other instead of being divided by a sharp line. A gradient will be applied to the second oval to give the basic appearance of volume. A gradient stop sets the color and location for one of the colors being blended. By changing the gradient stop location, the designer sets the location where the gradient color will stop blending and be solid.

9. Select the oval labeled Gradient.

10. Click the **Shape Fill** button on the **Shape Styles** panel of the **Format** tab in the ribbon, and click **Gradient > More Gradients...** in the drop-down menu.

11. Drag the dialog box that is displayed to the side so you can see changes to the primitive as settings are changed.

12. Click **Fill** on the left side of the dialog box, and click the **Gradient fill** radio button on the right side of the dialog box. Notice how the gradient is applied to the primitive.

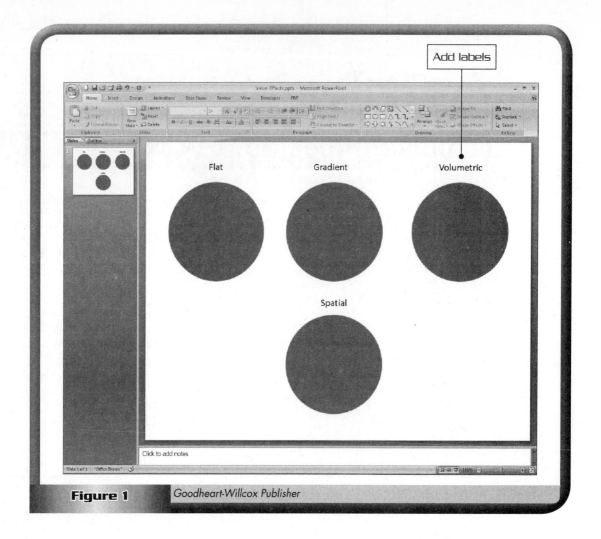

Figure 1
Goodheart-Willcox Publisher

13. Click the **Direction:** button, and click the **Linear Up** button in the drop-down menu. Notice how the gradient has changed.

14. Click on the left-hand gradient stop (stop 1).

15. Click the **Color:** button, and select black.

16. Click in the **Position:** text box, and enter 15. Notice how the bottom of the gradient increases in the amount of black.

17. Click the middle gradient stop (stop 2).

18. Click the **Remove** gradient stop button. Now instead of three gradient stops, there are only two stops.

19. Select the right-hand stop (now stop 2), click in the **Brightness:** text box, and enter–15% (earlier versions of PowerPoint do not have this option). This setting is the same as setting the color to **White, Background 1, Darker 15%**.

20. Close the dialog box. Notice how the primitive appears to have some depth, as shown in **Figure 2**.

Volumetric Object

A volumetric object is a three-dimensional object. It has volume. A volumetric object can be simulated in 2D with chiaroscuro. Value will range from a bright highlight to shadow.

21. Select the oval labeled Volumetric.

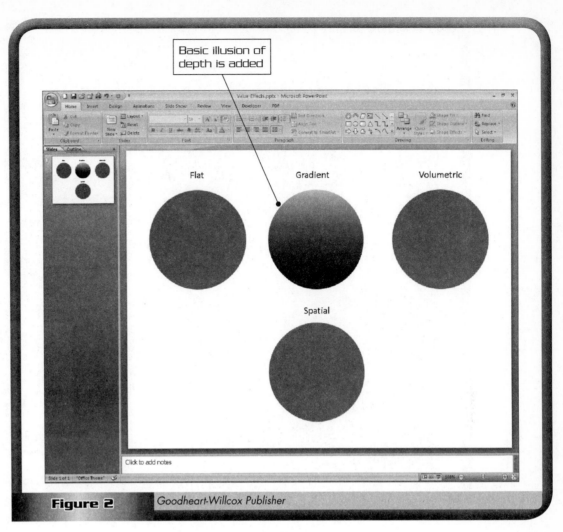

Figure 2   *Goodheart-Willcox Publisher*

 22. Click the **Shape Fill** button on the **Shape Styles** panel of the **Format** tab in the ribbon, and click **Gradient > More Gradients...** in the drop-down menu.

23. Select gradient and set the type to linear and the direction to linear up.

24. Set the left-hand gradient stop (stop 1) to black and its position to 15%. This will be ambient color of the volumetric sphere, which is the color of the sphere in shadow.

25. Set the center gradient stop (stop 2) to medium gray and its position to 65%. This will be the diffuse color of the volumetric sphere, which is the main color for the object.

26. Set the right-hand gradient stop (stop 3) to white and its position to 95%. This will be the specular color of the volumetric sphere, which is the highlight on the object.

27. Close the dialog box. This effect provides more depth than the gradient oval, but to see the effect better, the background color needs to be changed to provide contrast between the white specular highlight and the background.

Rectangle
28. Create a rectangle that covers the entire slide, change its fill color to medium blue or other medium color, and move the rectangle to the back of the object stack.

 29. Rotate the volumetric oval so that the specular highlight is at the top-right. This simulates directional lighting that looks more realistic than top-down lighting, as shown in **Figure 3**.

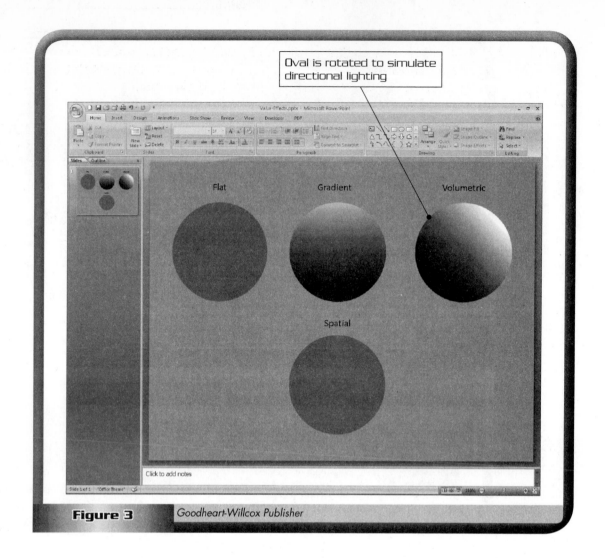

Oval is rotated to simulate directional lighting

Figure 3   *Goodheart-Willcox Publisher*

Spatial Object

Spatial objects have volume, but also include lighting and other features that help the viewer determine where these objects are located in the space. Shadow is one of the features that helps provide contextual clues to the volume and spatial position of an object. Backlighting is used to help separate the object from the background. Backlighting is discussed in more detail in Chapter 10.

30. Select the oval labeled Spatial.

31. Click the **Shape Fill** button on the **Shape Styles** panel of the **Format** tab in the ribbon, and click **Gradient > More Gradients…** in the drop-down menu.

32. Select gradient and set the type to radial and the direction to the top-right corner. This will place a specular highlight in the same location as for the volumetric oval.

33. Click the **Add** gradient stop button so there are four gradient stops.

34. Select the right-hand gradient stop (stop 4), set the color to white, and its position to 85%. This will be the specular highlight.

35. Select the next gradient stop (stop 3), set the color to medium gray, and its position to 70%. This will be the diffuse color, and the specular color is blended into it.

36. Select the next gradient stop (stop 2), set the color to black, and its position to 45%. This will be the ambient color.

37. Select the next gradient stop (stop 1), set the color to a dark gray, and its position to 0%. This will be the backlighting. Backlighting typically produces a white edge in areas of shadow, but in this 2D application, the dark gray serves the same purpose of separating the object from the background.

38. Close the dialog box.

The final component in creating the spatial object in 2D is to add a ground shadow, as shown in **Figure 4.** This provides a contextual clue for the viewer to determine where object is located in space. A separate primitive will be used for the ground shadow.

39. Create an oval shape that is 0.6″ high by 2.3″ wide.

Oval

40. Change the fill color to a darker shade of the background color. This will simulate a shadow by adding value to the background color.

41. Move the ground shadow below the spatial object, and move it below the spatial object in the object stack.

The greater the space separating the spatial object from the ground shadow, the farther the spatial object appears to be above a surface. If the space is removed, the spatial object appears to be resting on a surface. The ground shadow provides the contextual clue as to where the spatial object is located in three-dimensional space. Be sure the location of the ground shadow is consistent with the direction of the lighting creating the highlight.

Skill Application

42. Add a new blank slide.

43. Using only one rectangle primitive and two trapezoid primitives, create the illusion of a square prism or box shape. Apply value to each primitive to simulate lighting and depth.

44. Add another blank slide. Use shadow to create the illusion of a box at rest on a table.

45. Add another blank slide. Use shadow and the animation features of PowerPoint to create the illusion of a box falling.

46. Save your work, and submit it for grading.

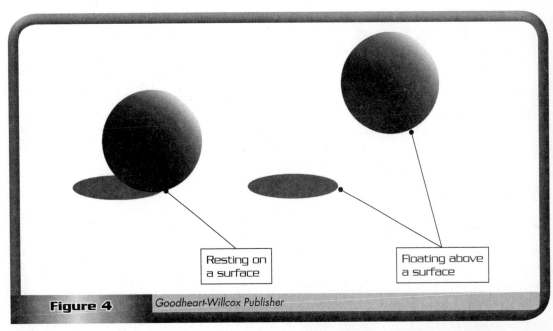

Resting on a surface

Floating above a surface

Figure 4   *Goodheart-Willcox Publisher*

Review Questions

1. What is a volumetric object?

   _____

   _____

2. Which directional lighting is more realistic, top-down or from an angle? Support your answer with at least two details.

   _____

   _____

   _____

   _____

3. How does a volumetric object differ from a spatial object?

   _____

   _____

   _____

   _____

4. List two features that provide contextual clues to the viewer as to the location of a spatial object in three dimensions.

   _____

   _____

   _____

   _____

5. What is the purpose of a ground shadow?

   _____

   _____

Activity 9-5

Art Integration

Objectives

Students will create static game art for 2D games by applying knowledge of primitives. Students will integrate custom art into a playable game. Students will apply the elements of art and principles of design to game art creation.

Situation

The Really Cool Game Company has reviewed the *Frog Crossing* prototype game created in Chapter 8. You have been given a green light to add concept game art to the game. You will also need to refine the programming.

How to Begin

1. Launch a PowerPoint.

2. Click the **Layout** button on the **Slides** panel in the **Home** tab of the ribbon, and click **Blank** in the drop-down menu.

Page Setup

3. Click the **Page Setup** button on the **Page Setup** panel of the **Design** tab in the ribbon. In the Page Setup dialog box, change the slide to 2″ wide by 2″ high. The art will be considerably smaller in the actual game, but this provides a drawing canvas that is proportional to the size of the art in the game and easily reduced.

4. Save the presentation as *LastName_*Frog Art in your working folder.

5. Create the primitives shown in **Figure 1.** Each primitive has a green fill and no outline.

6. Group the primitives for the hind leg.

7. Make one copy of the leg group.

8. Flip the copy horizontally to make the other hind leg.

9. Position each hind leg so that the toes touch the bottom and side edges of the slide.

10. Move the body so that the top touches the top edge of the slide and is centered between the hind legs.

11. Create the primitives shown in **Figure 2.**

12. Group the primitives, copy and paste, and flip the copy to create the other front leg.

13. Add two red-filled ovals for eyes.

Contrast

To assure visibility of the frog even in the areas of green grass, an outline needs to be added. Since the image is constructed from primitives instead of a single line filled with color, the outline feature in PowerPoint cannot be used.

14. Group the entire frog.

15. Copy and paste the frog.

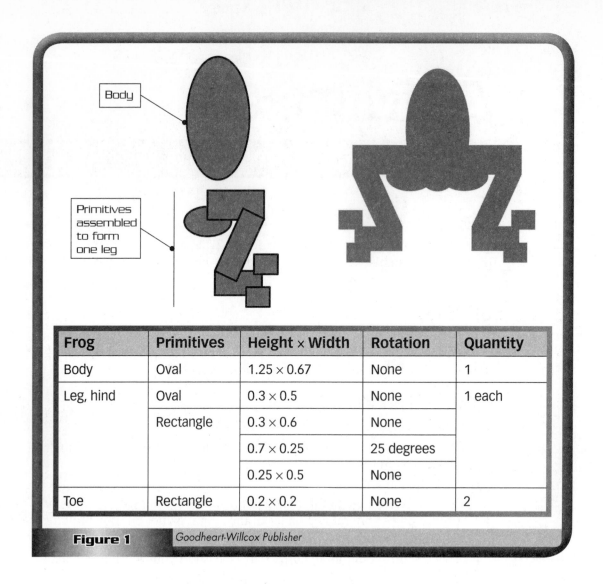

Frog	Primitives	Height × Width	Rotation	Quantity
Body	Oval	1.25 × 0.67	None	1
Leg, hind	Oval	0.3 × 0.5	None	1 each
	Rectangle	0.3 × 0.6	None	
		0.7 × 0.25	25 degrees	
		0.25 × 0.5	None	
Toe	Rectangle	0.2 × 0.2	None	2

Figure 1   *Goodheart-Willcox Publisher*

16. Change the size of the copy to 2.1″ × 2.1″.

17. Change the fill to black, and set the outline to no color.

18. Send the black object to the back of the object stack, and position so it creates an outline for the frog, as shown in **Figure 3.** The shadow will extend beyond the edges of the slide.

19. Create a 2″ × 2″ rectangle, fill it with white, and place it behind the frog. This will be used to set the transparency with the alpha channel.

Variety

Adding some variety to the coloring of the frog will give it a more realistic look. Add some spots to the frog use small ovals filled with darker and lighter green. Do not use white. This should be more like a camouflage pattern like the one seen in nature to make the frog harder for predators to see. As you work, change the zoom setting to 20%. This will simulate the size and appearance of the frog in the game to give you an idea of how the art will look during gameplay.

Name: _____

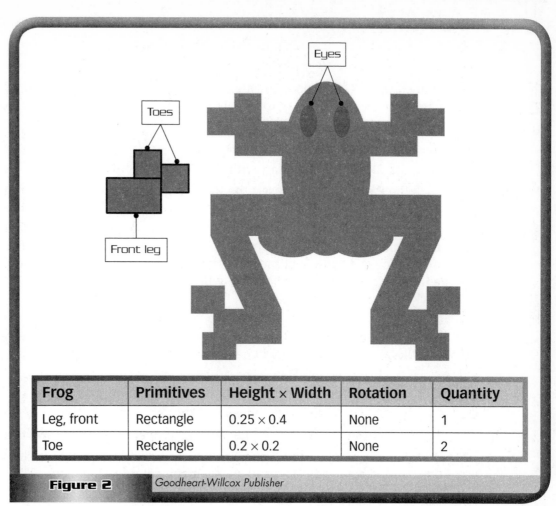

Frog	Primitives	Height × Width	Rotation	Quantity
Leg, front	Rectangle	0.25 × 0.4	None	1
Toe	Rectangle	0.2 × 0.2	None	2

Figure 2   *Goodheart-Willcox Publisher*

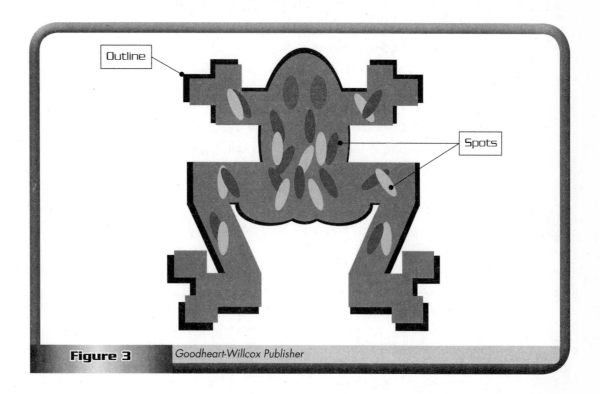

Figure 3   *Goodheart-Willcox Publisher*

Transferring Artwork into the Game

20. Group all objects, including the background rectangle.

21. Copy the group.

22. Launch MMF2, and open the *Frog Crossing* game from Chapter 8. Save it as *LastName_*Frog Crossing w Art in your working folder.

23. Display the frame editor for Level 1.

Frame Editor

24. Open the Avatar object in the image editor.

25. Click the **Clear** button to start with a transparent canvas.

Clear

26. Click the **Paste** button to insert the frog image copied from PowerPoint. In the message that appears asking if you want to resize the canvas, click the **Yes** button.

Paste

Notice how the black outline in the image has disappeared, and the white background is visible. By default in MMF2, the color black is used to define the alpha channel, which is why the outline has disappeared. For this image, white should be set as the transparency masking color that defines the alpha channel.

27. Click the **Transparency** button.

28. Click on any part of the frog image that is white. This changes the color used to define the alpha channel from black to white. The black outline is now visible, and the white background will be transparent during gameplay.

Transparency

29. Close the image editor. Notice the Avatar object is much larger. This is because the canvas was resized in the image editor.

30. Change the size of the Avatar object to 32 × 32.

31. Select Level 1 in the asset tree to display its properties in the **Properties** window.

32. On the **Settings** tab of the **Properties** window, click the color swatch for the **Background color** property, and click a green color in the palette. This changes the background color of the frame from white to green.

Run Frame

33. Test play the frame. Check if the frog avatar has enough contrast. If not, change the green used for the frame background, or change the frog's colors in PowerPoint and reinsert the image for the Avatar object.

Directional Movement

34. Open the Avatar object in the image editor. Notice the image is not as clear as it was before. This is because the software interpolated pixels when the object was resized.

35. On the **Frames** tab, copy Frame 1 in the Stopped animation set.

36. Click the box at the top of the direction panel to change to the Up animation, and paste Frame 1, as shown in **Figure 4**.

37. Change to the Right animation.

38. Click the **Rotate** button.

Rotate

39. In the options that are displayed, click the **90->** button to face the frog to the right, as shown in **Figure 4**.

40. Change to the Down animation, paste Frame 1, and rotate the frame so the frog faces downward.

41. Change to the Left animation, paste Frame 1, and rotate the frame so the frog faces to the left.

42. Close the image editor.

Run Frame

43. Save your work, and test play the frame. Notice that the frog does not change directions. This is because you have not yet programmed the directions to change.

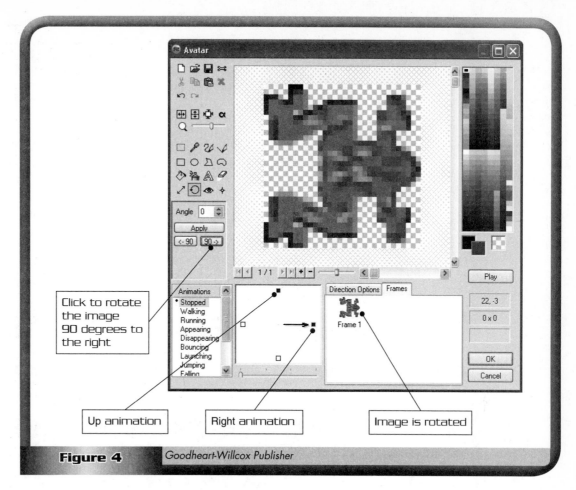

Click to rotate the image 90 degrees to the right

Up animation

Right animation

Image is rotated

Figure 4   *Goodheart-Willcox Publisher*

Programming Directional Movement

The animation direction for the frog must be changed to match the direction the player is moving the character. The first step is to set the correct animation direction when Level 1 begins. The pseudo code is:

IF at the start of the frame,
THEN display the Up animation.

44. Display the event editor for Level 1.

45. On line 1 (start of frame), right-click in the **Avatar** column, and click **Animation** > **Change** > **Direction of animation...** in the shortcut menu.

46. In the dialog box that is displayed, click block where the existing arrow is pointing (0 position) to remove the arrow, and click the block at the 8 position (up) to add an arrow, as shown in **Figure 5.** This specifies to set the Up animation. Close the dialog box.

47. Similarly, add an action to lines 3 through 6 to change the direction of animation to match the movement.

48. Save your work, and test play the frame. Wow! Gameplay is really messed up. This is because the hotspot needs to be in the same location on each animation frame.

49. Display the frame editor, and open the Avatar object in the image editor.

50. Click the **View Hot Spot** button.

51. Change the hotspot for all direction animations to (0,0), as shown in **Figure 6.**

Frame Editor

Run Frame

Frame Editor

View Hot Spot

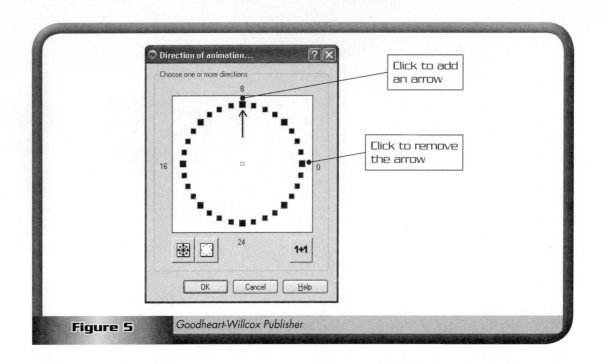

Click to add an arrow

Click to remove the arrow

Figure 5   *Goodheart-Willcox Publisher*

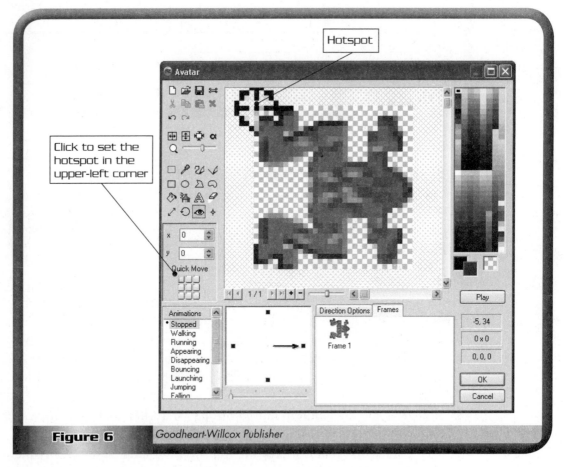

Hotspot

Click to set the hotspot in the upper-left corner

Figure 6   *Goodheart-Willcox Publisher*

52. Close the image editor.

Run Frame

53. Save your work, and test play the frame. Check that the Avatar object faces the direction of movement. Debug if needed.

Logs

The Avatar object now has concept art applied to it, and the animations correctly match the movement. The other objects need art as well. A wooden texture will be applied to the image for the log objects.

54. Open a blank PowerPoint presentation, save it as *LastName*_Log Art in your working folder, and set the slide size to 6″ wide by 2″″ tall.

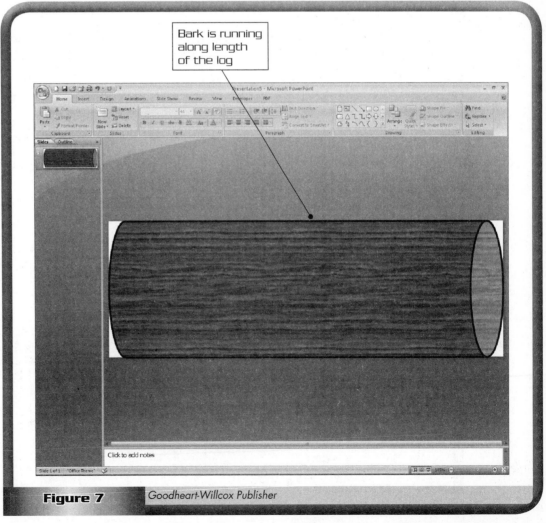

Can

55. Create a can primitive that is 5.9″ high by 1.9″ wide, and center it on the slide.

56. Rotate the primitive 90 degrees to the right.

57. Change the outline color to black.

58. Click the **Shape Fill** button on the **Shape Styles** panel in the **Format** tab of the ribbon, and click **Texture > Medium wood** in the drop-down menu. A wood texture is applied to the image, but the bark lines are not running in the correct direction.

59. Click the **Shape Fill** button on the **Shape Styles** panel in the **Format** tab of the ribbon, and click **Texture > More textures…** in the drop-down menu.

60. In the dialog box that is displayed, click **Fill** on the left, and uncheck the **Rotate with shape** check box on the right. Close the dialog box. The texture is now correctly applied, as shown in **Figure 7**.

61. Create a rectangle that is 2″ high by 6″ wide, fill it with white, align it to the edges of the slide, and send it to the back of the object stack.

Figure 7 *Goodheart-Willcox Publisher*

62. Group the rectangle and can primitives, and copy the group.

63. Switch to the *Frog Crossing* game in MMF2.

64. Display the frame editor, and open any left-facing log in the image editor.

65. Clear the existing image, and paste the log image copied from PowerPoint. Resize the canvas.

Transparency

66. Change the transparency mask color to white.

67. Set the hotspot to (0,0).

View Hot Spot

68. Close the image editor, and change the size of the object to 96 × 32.

69. Open any right-facing log in image editor, clear the canvas, paste the image from PowerPoint, and rotate the image 180 degrees.

Transparency

70. Change the transparency mask color to white.

71. Set the hotspot to (0,0).

72. Close the image editor, and change the size of the object to 96 × 32.

Barrels

73. Open a blank PowerPoint presentation, save it as *LastName*_Barrel Art in your working folder, and set the slide size to 4″ wide by 2″ high.

74. Using trapezoids, rectangles, ovals, and other primitives along with appropriate fills, create a barrel similar to the one shown in **Figure 8.** The final size should be 3.9″ × 1.9″ and centered on the slide.

75. Add a white rectangle as a background.

76. Group the barrel, and copy it.

77. In MMF2, update the left- and right-facing barrel objects with the barrel artwork. Be sure to set the alpha channel and hotspot as needed. Set the size of the barrel objects to 64 × 32.

Cars

78. Open a blank PowerPoint presentation, save it as *LastName*_Car Art in your working folder, and set the slide size to 4″ wide by 2″ high.

79. Using various primitives, fills, and other art techniques, create a car similar to the one shown in **Figure 9.** The final size should be 3.9″ × 1.9″ and centered on the slide.

Figure 8 Goodheart-Willcox Publisher

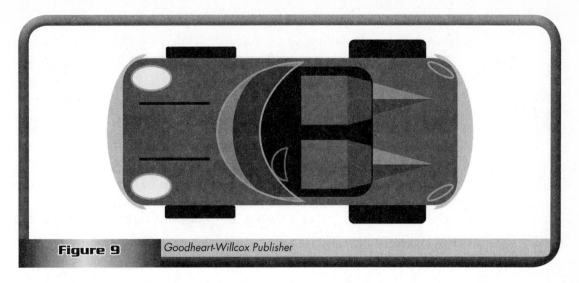

Figure 9   *Goodheart-Willcox Publisher*

80. Add a white rectangle as a background.

81. Group the car, and copy it.

82. In MMF2, update the left-facing "car1" objects with the car artwork. Be sure to set the alpha channel and hotspot as needed. Set the size of the car objects to 64 × 31.

83. In PowerPoint, change the color of the car, and face it to the right.

84. In MMF2, update the right-facing "car1" objects with the car artwork. Be sure to set the alpha channel and hotspot as needed. Set the size of the car objects to 64 × 31.

Tractor-Trailers

85. Open a blank PowerPoint presentation, save it as *LastName*_Truck Art in your working folder, and set the slide size to 8″ wide by 2″ high.

86. Using various primitives, fills, and other art techniques, create a tractor-trailer semi similar to the one shown in **Figure 10.** The final size should be 7.9″ × 1.9″ and centered on the slide.

87. Add a white rectangle as a background.

88. Group the truck, and copy it.

89. In MMF2, update the left-facing "car2" objects with the car artwork. Be sure to set the alpha channel and hotspot as needed. Set the size of the car objects to 128 × 31.

Figure 10   *Goodheart-Willcox Publisher*

90. In PowerPoint, change the color of the truck, and face it to the right.

91. In MMF2, update the right-facing "car2" objects with the car artwork. Be sure to set the alpha channel and hotspot as needed. Set the size of the car objects to 128 × 31.

92. Save your work, and test play the frame. Check that the artwork is correct. Debug the object images if needed.

Run Frame

Custom Lives Artwork

Currently, the Lives object displays the remaining lives as hearts. This is clear to almost all players. However, adding a custom image to the Lives object to tailor it to the game is a nice finishing touch.

93. Open the Frog Art PowerPoint file, and save it as *LastName_*Frog Lives Art in your working folder.

94. Group the frog and background, if not already grouped, and set its size to 0.3″ × 0.3″.

95. Copy the frog and background.

96. In MMF2, open the Lives object in the image editor.

97. Clear the default image, and paste in the frog image. Be sure to set the alpha channel as needed.

98. Close the image editor to update the Lives object to the new artwork.

Car Selection

Right now, the cars and trucks in the game are always the same. It would improve the player's immersion if some new cars randomly appear. This can be done using different animation directions.

99. Open the Car1_Right object in the image editor.

100. Copy Frame 1, and close the image editor.

101. Open the Car1_Left object in the image editor.

102. Paste the copied frame into the Left animation.

View Hot Spot

103. Flip the image to face left, and reset the hotspot to the upper-left corner.

104. Copy the flipped frame, and paste it into the Up and Down animations. Now there is a left-facing car in the Right animation and a different color of left-facing car in the Left, Up, and Down animations.

105. Repeat this process to add the frame in the Right animation for the Car1_Left object to the Left animation of the Car1_Right object. Make sure you flip it and reset the hotspot.

106. Display the event editor.

Event Editor

107. On line 26, hover the cursor over the **Create Object** column to see the programming. Notice that this action creates a Car1_Left object and a Car1_Right object.

108. Right-click in the cell where the **Car1_Right** column intersects the **Line 26** row, and click **Direction > Set direction...** in the shortcut menu. Set the direction to up, down, left, or right, as shown in **Figure 11.**

109. Copy this programming into the **Car1_Left** column on line 26.

110. Similarly, program the "car2" objects to randomly change colors.

Run Frame

111. Save your work, and test play the frame to see if the cars are spawned in different colors. There will be mostly one color as the three of the four choices are the same.

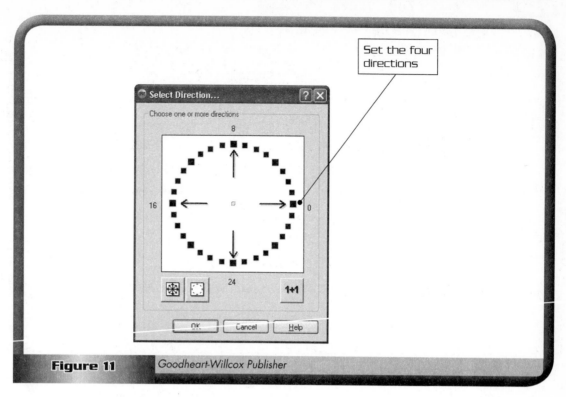

Set the four directions

Figure 11   *Goodheart-Willcox Publisher*

Difficulty Setting

A way to help make the game easier is to eliminate some cars. With the new random selection programming in place, this is a very easy task.

Frame Editor

Run Frame

112. Open the Car1_Left object in image editor.

113. Delete Frame 1 from the Down animation, and close the image editor.

114. Save your work, and test play the frame. You should see more holes in the rows of cars as 25% of the time the car will be a blank.

Skill Application

115. Create additional game art images for vehicles and items floating in the river. Be creative, and apply your artistic skills.

116. Change the "car1" objects so the game engine will randomly display one of three different cars or a blank.

117. Change the "car2" objects so the game engine will randomly display one of three different trucks or a blank.

118. Change both "barrel" objects so the game engine will randomly display one of three different floating barrel pieces or a blank.

119. Change both "log" objects so the game engine will randomly display one of three different floating branches or a blank.

120. Save your work, and test play the frame. Debug as needed.

121. Compile an EXE file, and submit the game for grading according to the directions provided by your instructor.

Review Questions

1. Why is the PowerPoint canvas for the frog art set to the size it was?

   _____

   _____

   _____

   _____

2. Describe the basic procedure for transferring artwork created in PowerPoint into MMF2.

   _____

   _____

   _____

   _____

3. Why was it important not to use white as part of the main image color in the artwork created in this activity?

   _____

   _____

   _____

   _____

4. After the artwork has been inserted into MMF2 and the object reset to its original size, what happens to the artwork when it is opened in the image editor?

   _____

   _____

   _____

   _____

5. Describe how four different appearances can be given to one object.

   _____

   _____

   _____

6. Complete the probability table to produce the correct number of cars and blank spaces.

Total Objects	Cars	Blanks	Probability of a Blank Fraction	Probability of a Blank Percentage
4	3	1	1/4	25%
6		1		
10				20%
14			2/7	

Chapter 10
Three-Dimensional Art Composition

Objectives

After completing this chapter, you will be able to:
- Create objects in 3D space.
- Program a two-player game in which the players have mutually exclusive goals.
- Apply materials to a 3D object.
- Create complex 3D models.
- Construct triangle lighting for a 3D scene.

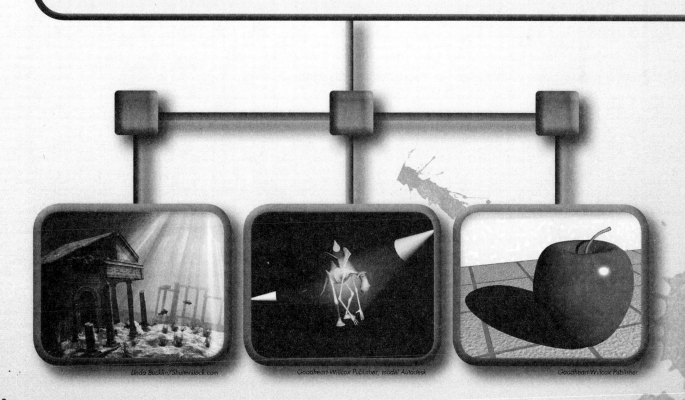

Linda Bucklin/Shutterstock.com   Goodheart-Willcox Publisher, model Autodesk   Goodheart-Willcox Publisher

Bellwork

Day	Date	Activity	Response
1		Complete the anticipation guide and the K and W columns of the KWL chart for this chapter.	
2		How is 3D art different from 2D art?	
3		Define *color palette*.	
4		Evaluate each of the seven game art careers presented at the beginning of this chapter. Which do you feel you would do best? Explain why.	
5		What is a mesh?	
6		Explain how to create triangle lighting.	
7		What does the energy or value setting of a light alter?	
8		In 3D modeling, what is a material?	
9		Describe opacity in terms of transparency.	
10		What is the relationship between analogous colors?	
11		What is a texture map?	

Day	Date	Activity	Response
12		Analyze isosurfacing and bump mapping benefits and disadvantages. Why would isosurfacing be used instead of bump mapping? List one application where isosurfacing is a better choice than bump mapping.	
13		Explain how data are stored in a raster image.	
14		Compare and contrast lossy and lossless compression algorithms. List the benefits of using lossy over lossless compression.	
15		How are data stored in a vector image?	
16		Why would an image need to be rasterized?	
17		Define *plagiarism*.	
18		Describe ownership of material in terms of a work-for-hire contract.	
18		Explain two agreements that you may be required to sign as part of a contract and the purpose of each.	
20		Compare and contrast case law and statutory law.	
21		Complete the L column of the KWL chart and the After Reading column of the anticipation guide with what you learned from this chapter.	
22		Speculate why many games require downloadable content (DLC) and registration before play can begin. Describe how a gamer like yourself feels about this practice.	

Name: _____

Date: _____

Class: _____

Anticipation Guide

Directions

Before reading the chapter, read each statement in the table below. In the column titled Before Reading, write the letter *T* if you agree with the statement or *F* if you disagree with the statement. After reading the chapter, reread each statement in the table below. In the column titled After Reading, write the letter *T* if you agree with the statement or *F* if you disagree with the statement. Be prepared to justify your answers in a class discussion.

Before Reading	Statement	After Reading
	Meshes are errors in digital artwork.	
	A 3D scene should use triangle lighting with a key light, fill light, and backlight.	
	A 3D object can have a picture applied to the diffuse color.	
	You can resell artwork you create for your employer.	
	Game programs include antipiracy measures, such as a software key code.	

KWL Chart

Directions

Before reading the chapter, fill in what you already know about the topic in the K column and what you want to learn in the W column. After reading the chapter, review what you know and wanted to learn about the topic. Reflect on what you have studied and completed in this chapter. Fill in what you learned in the L column. Be prepared to justify your answers in a class discussion.

Topic: Three-Dimensional Art		
K What you already *know*	**W** What you *want* to learn	**L** What you *learned*

Activity 10-1

Simulated 3D Models

Objectives

Students will describe the components of a 3D model. Students will create and manipulate objects in 3D space. Students will join 3D objects to create complex models. Students will apply textures to 3D models and render images.

Situation

The Really Cool Game Company has many games that require 3D assets. There are many different software applications that can be used to create 3D models. The lead artist has decided to give you some basic training in the principles of 3D art to help you develop your skills. Your first step is to simulate a 3D environment. Creating this simulated environment will help you understand working in 3D. The skills and understanding you gain in this activity can be transferred to working in true 3D environments.

How to Begin

1. Launch a PowerPoint 2010.

2. Click the **Layout** button on the **Slides** panel in the **Home** tab of the ribbon, and click **Blank** in the drop-down menu.

3. Save the presentation as *LastName*_3D Simulation in your working folder.

Spheres

Oval

In Activity 9-4, a basic oval primitive was shaded to create the illusion of 3D. PowerPoint has other ways to simulate a 3D sphere. The resulting object is a representation of a 3D object, because it does not have volume and does not occupy space with three dimensions.

4. On slide 1, create an oval that is 2″ × 2″.

5. Click the **Shape Effects** button on the **Shape Styles** panel of the **Format** tab in the ribbon, and click **3D Rotation > 3D Rotation Options...** in the shortcut menu. The **Format Shape** dialog box is displayed.

6. Move the **Format Shape** dialog box so the oval is visible. The changes made in the dialog box will be applied in real time to the oval.

7. Click **3D Format** on the left side of the dialog box, and click the **Top:** button in the **Bevel** area to display a drop-down menu.

8. Click each of the preset options in the drop-down menu, and watch how the oval primitive changes to provide the illusion of depth. The dark and light areas on the primitive are changed to provide the illusion.

9. Click the **Circle** option. The oval appears to have a slightly rounded edge.

10. Click in the **Width:** text box next to the **Top:** button, and enter 72.

11. Click in the **Height:** text box next to the **Top:** button, and enter 72. Notice how this creates the illusion of 3D depth, as shown in **Figure 1.** A specular highlight can be seen along with a shadow and backlighting.

12. Click **3D Rotation** on the left of the dialog box.

13. Click in the **Y:** text box in the **Rotation** area, and 180. This flips the oval to show its back. The 3D effect is not visible because it was only applied to the top.

14. Click in the **Y:** text box in the **Rotation** area, and 90. The oval clearly shows the 3D effect is applied only to the top, which simulates a half sphere.

15. Click **3D Format** on the left side of the dialog box.

16. Click in the **Height:** text box next to the **Bottom:** button, and enter 72. This extrudes the oval downward into a simulated cylinder. Remember, you are looking at the side of the oval primitive, so the cylinder appears like a rectangle in this view.

17. Click in the **Width:** text box next to the **Bottom:** button, and enter 72. This makes the bottom curve like the top to form a full simulated sphere. The backlighting is more apparent now as well.

18. Change the rotation back to Y = 0.

19. Click **Shadow** on the left side of the dialog box. Click the **Presets:** button, and click **Perspective Diagonal Lower Left** in the drop-down menu. This creates a virtual light sources above and to the right of the sphere that casts a shadow below and to the left of the sphere. The shadow provides a spatial reference for the sphere.

20. Click in the **Distance:** text box, and enter 72 or drag the slider to the right. This moves the shadow, which simulates changing the distance the sphere is from the imaginary surface on which the shadow is cast, as shown in **Figure 2.**

21. Click **3D Rotation** on the left side of the dialog box, and click the up arrow next to the **X:** text box in the **Rotation** area. Notice how the light and shadow change as the simulated sphere rotates. The dark band visible as the object is rotated is the original oval.

22. Click **Line Color** on the left of the dialog box, and click the **No line** radio button. The dark band disappears from the simulated sphere.

23. Click **Fill** on the left of the dialog box. Click the **Color:** button, and click a red color swatch in the drop-down palette. This applies a different diffuse color to the simulated sphere.

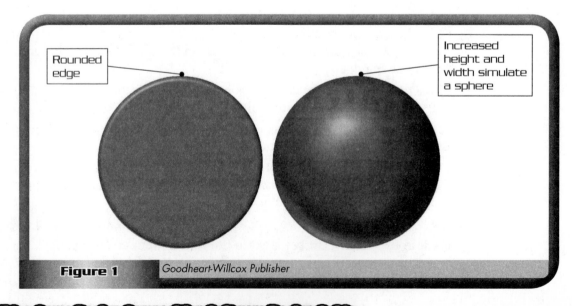

Rounded edge

Increased height and width simulate a sphere

Figure 1   *Goodheart-Willcox Publisher*

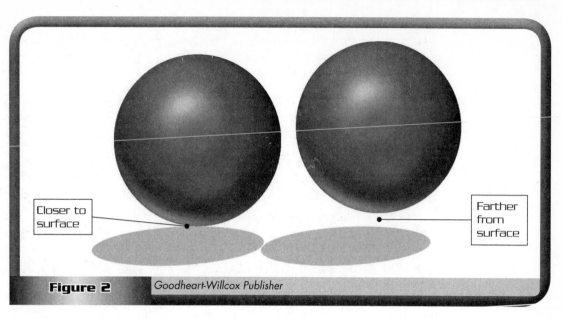

Closer to surface

Farther from surface

Figure 2   *Goodheart-Willcox Publisher*

24. Remove the shadow, and close the dialog box.

25. Copy the object, and paste it 11 times for a total of 12 simulated spheres.

26. Arrange the objects in three rows and four columns.

Rectangle

27. Create a rectangle that covers the entire slide, fill it with blue, and send it to the back of the object stack. This will serve as a background for the simulated 3D environment.

28. Copy the slide, and paste it twice so there are three identical slides.

29. Make slide 1 active, select the first simulated sphere, and open the **Format Shapes** dialog box using the dialog box launcher on the **Shape Styles** panel.

30. Click **3D Format** on the left of the dialog box, and click the **Material:** button. This material setting controls the transparency and reflectivity of the object.

31. Apply a different material to each of the simulated spheres on slide 1, as shown in **Figure 3.** Notice how the specular highlight changes with each material.

Text Box

32. Add a text box under each simulated sphere, and label the material setting used.

Lighting

Proper lighting is very important in creating a realistic 3D model. Changing the position and intensity of the illumination source will alter the specular highlight and shadows. As you go through this next section, pay attention to the change in the appearance of the object as the lighting changes.

33. Make slide 2 active, select the first simulated sphere, and open the **Format Shapes** dialog box using the dialog box launcher on the **Shape Styles** panel.

34. Click **3D Format** on the left of the dialog box, and click the **Lighting:** button.

35. Between slides 2 and 3, assign each lighting setting to a different sphere. Notice how the object changes when each color setting is applied. Most of settings produce subtle differences, but a couple produce dramatic differences.

Text Box

36. Add a text box below each sphere labeling the lighting used.

37. On slide 3, apply three-point lighting to the nine remaining spheres using the settings shown in **Figure 4.** Notice how the specular and ambient colors move as the lighting changes.

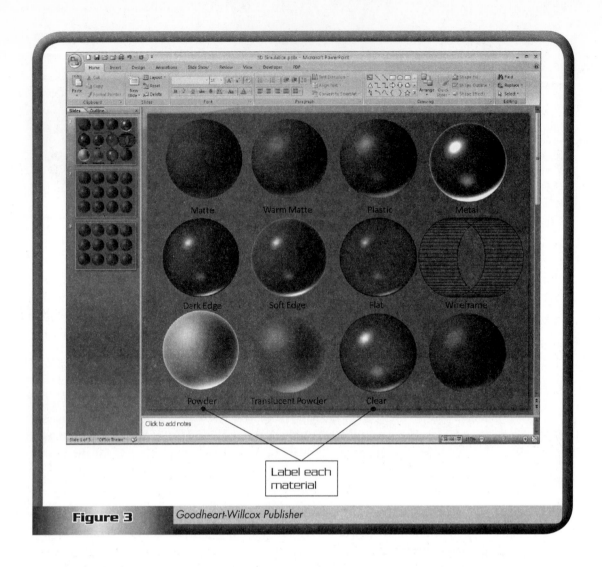

Label each material

Figure 3 Goodheart-Willcox Publisher

Sphere	Lighting	Angle
Slide 3, sphere 4	Three point	0
Slide 3, sphere 5	Three point	30
Slide 3, sphere 6	Three point	60
Slide 3, sphere 7	Three point	90
Slide 3, sphere 8	Three point	120
Slide 3, sphere 9	Three point	150
Slide 3, sphere 10	Three point	180
Slide 3, sphere 11	Three point	210
Slide 3, sphere 12	Three point	240

Figure 4 Goodheart-Willcox Publisher

Diffuse Color Texture Mapping

The diffuse color is the main color you see when looking at an object. A texture map is an image or pattern applied to a component of a material definition. Therefore, a diffuse color texture map is an image or pattern applied to the diffuse color component of a material definition.

Oval

38. Add a new blank slide as slide 4.

39. Create an oval that is 2″ × 2″, and remove the outline color.

40. Using clipart, find a round image of a basketball, and place it on the slide.

Clip Art

41. Crop the basketball image tightly to the basketball image leaving no space between the ball and the edge of image. The better job you do cropping the better the effect. You may need to use the **Size and Position** dialog box, which is accessed by clicking the dialog box launcher on the **Size** panel in the **Format** tab of the ribbon, as shown in **Figure 5**.

Crop

42. Right-click on the cropped basketball image, and click **Save as Picture…** in the shortcut menu.

43. Save the picture as Basketball Texture.jpg in your working folder.

44. Delete the basketball image on the slide.

Shape Fill

45. Select the oval, click the **Shape Fill** button on the **Shape Styles** panel in the **Format** tab of the ribbon, and click **Picture…** in the drop-down menu.

46. In the standard Windows open dialog box, navigate to your working folder, and open the Basketball Texture image file. The image is applied to the shape as a fill, or diffuse color texture map. The image will be wrapped around the object when the object is turned into a simulated sphere.

47. Using the 3D effects, enter 72 for the height and width for both top and bottom of a bevel to create a simulated sphere.

48. Rotate the object to see how well the basketball texture map looks on the simulated sphere. If you see color banding in the middle of the object, make sure the outline color is removed. If it is, the banding is the background color of the basketball image. Cropping the image closer should correct this. It may be necessary to clip part of the basketball to completely remove the banding.

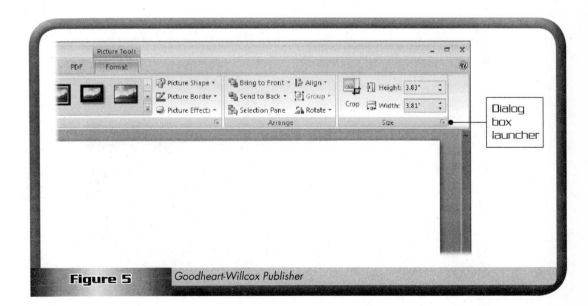

Figure 5   *Goodheart-Willcox Publisher*

Extruding Shapes

Extruding is a basic skill in creating 3D objects. Basic 2D polygonal primitives can be *extruded,* or given height, to create 3D objects. As you saw earlier when creating the back of the simulated sphere, PowerPoint can simulate extruded objects.

Rectangle

49. Add a new blank slide.

50. On slide 5, create a rectangle that is 1″ × 1″, and remove the outline color.

51. With the rectangle selected, enter your first and last names. The type will automatically appear in the rectangle as you enter it.

52. Open the **Format Shapes** dialog box, and click **3D Format** on the left of the dialog box.

53. Click in the **Depth:** text box, and enter 72.

PowerPoint measures in points, which is a unit of measure common in the publishing industry. Since there are 72 points per inch, this means you have extruded the rectangle one inch. The rectangle primitive is 1″ × 1″, so when extruded one inch, the object becomes a simulated cube.

54. Rotate the object to see the depth. Notice how your name stays attached to the front face of the simulated cube, as shown in **Figure 6.**

55. Change the depth color to yellow.

56. Change the fill color to yellow.

57. Apply three-point lighting, and then rotate the object to see how pixel shading is applied to the simulated cube as it is rotated.

58. Create the simulated extruded objects described in **Figure 7.** Rotate each object to show more than one face of the object.

Coins

Clip Art

59. Add a new blank slide.

60. Use clipart to locate images of the face of a penny and a nickel. You may need to locate images marked for free distribution on the Internet.

61. Add these images to slide 6.

Crop

62. Crop each image so that the image edge is the exact edge of the coin, and save each image in your working folder. Once saved, delete the images from the slide.

Extrusion is visible when the object is rotated

Figure 6   *Goodheart-Willcox Publisher*

Shape	Height × Width	Depth	Fill Color	Line Color	Depth Color	Top Bevel	Bottom Bevel
Oval	1″ × 1″	144	None	Gray	Automatic	—	—
Octagon	1″ × 1″	30	Red	Gray	Black	50W × 72H	—
Smiley Face	1″ × 1″	15	Yellow	Black	Yellow	36W × 36H	—
Moon	2.5″ × 0.8″	0	Yellow	None	Yellow	30W × 15H	30W × 15H

Figure 7   *Goodheart-Willcox Publisher*

Oval

63. Create an oval that is 1.5″ × 1.5″.

64. Set the shape fill to the penny image.

65. Set the outline color to R180, G100, G50.

66. Open the **Format Shapes** dialog box, and click **3D Format** on the left of the dialog box.

67. Set the depth to 11, and the depth color to the same color as the outline.

68. Rotate the object to show the depth. Notice that the image is in reverse on the back of the simulated extrusion.

69. Similarly, create a nickel that is 1.75″ × 1.75″.

Ship Mesh

So far, you have created simulated 3D primitives from 2D primitives. Now, you will create a simulated 2D mesh from multiple 2D primitives.

70. Add a new blank slide.

Rectangle

71. Create a rectangle that is 4″ high by 1″ wide.

72. Copy and paste that rectangle. Move the copy so the rectangles are exactly side by side, as shown in **Figure 8.**

73. Create an isosceles triangle at the top to make the bow of the ship.

Isoceles Triangle

74. Group the objects, and move the group to the left-hand side.

75. Copy and paste the group. Place the copy to the right of the original.

76. Create a 0.3″ × 0.3″ oval in the middle of the bottom side of the left-hand isosceles triangle.

77. With the oval selected, open the **Format Shapes** dialog box, and click **3D Format** on the left of the dialog box.

78. Change the depth to 400, and close the dialog box.

79. Change the fill and outline colors for the oval to black.

Shape Fill

80. Select the right-hand group. Change the fill to an oak texture.

81. Change the outline color of this group to light gray.

82. Change the outline color of the left-hand group to a light gray and the fill to no color.

83. With the left-hand group selected, open the **Format Shapes** dialog box, and click **3D Format** on the left of the dialog box.

84. Change the depth to 72. Leave the dialog box open.

85. Bring the right-hand group to the front of the object stack, and move it to cover the left-hand group.

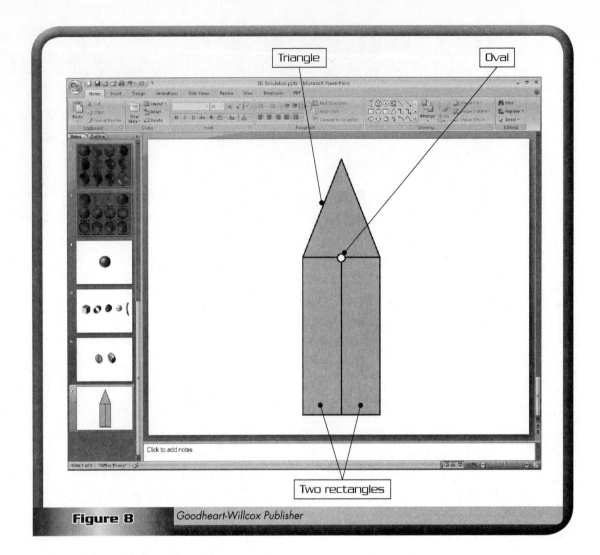

Triangle | Oval

Two rectangles

Figure 8 *Goodheart-Willcox Publisher*

86. Select and group all objects to form a simulated mesh.

87. Click **3D Rotation** on the left of the dialog box. In the **Rotation** area on the right, enter 125 in the **X:** text box, 25 in the **Y:** text box, and 110 in the **Z:** text box. These values will stand the ship upright, as shown in **Figure 9.**

88. Using clipart, locate sailors, a captain, and a ship's steering wheel (helm). Insert these images, and arrange them inside the ship.

89. Create a right triangle or isosceles triangle as a sail for the ship. Position it in front of the mast. Use a gradient fill to give it the illusion of being billowed by the wind. Rotate the triangle with a 3D effect to match the perspective of the ship.

Skill Application

90. Add a new blank slide as slide 5.

91. Create a green-filled rectangle with no outline to be the background of the slide.

92. Create two moon primitives, one overlapping the other, with different thicknesses to form a bowl, as shown in **Figure 10.** Apply an appropriate texture fill to make the bowl look like it is made of wood, stone, or fabric.

93. Using your new skills, create primitives to fill the bowl with fruit. Apply colors, textures, and 3D effects as needed to realistically simulate 3D objects.

94. Save your work, and submit it for grading.

Right Triangle

Isoceles Triangle

Rectangle

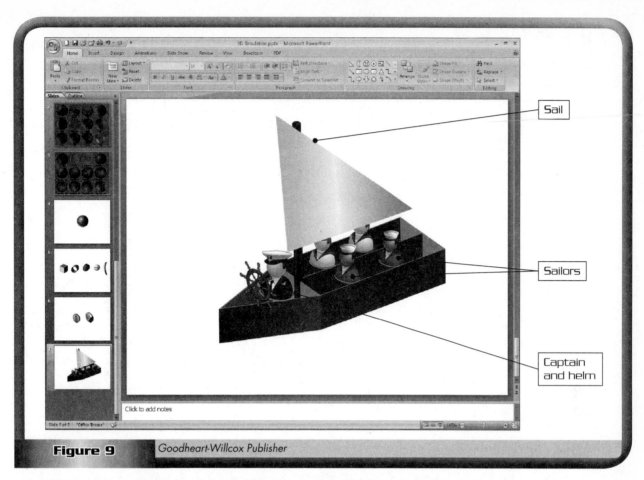

Figure 9   *Goodheart-Willcox Publisher*

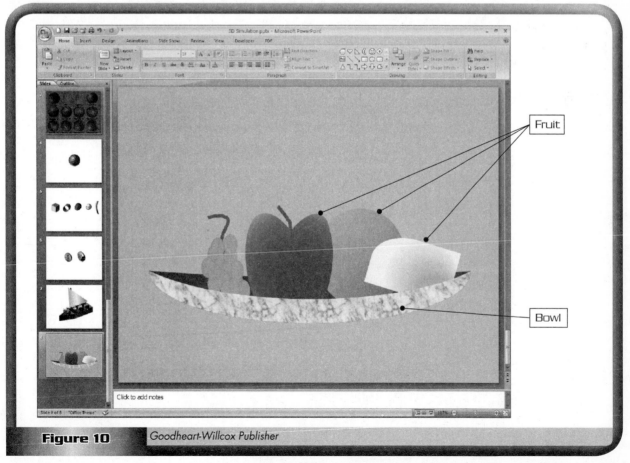

Figure 10   *Goodheart-Willcox Publisher*

Review Questions

1. Why are the 3D objects created in PowerPoint simulations of 3D, not actually 3D objects?

   _____

   _____

   _____

   _____

2. What happens if the position and intensity of the illumination source are changed?

   _____

   _____

   _____

   _____

3. Describe a diffuse color texture map.

   _____

   _____

   _____

   _____

4. What does it mean to extrude a 2D primitive?

   _____

   _____

   _____

   _____

5. What is the poly count of the ship? Assume the sides of the ship do not have tops and bottoms. Do not count the mast, sail, sailors, captain, or helm. Explain your answer.

   _____

   _____

   _____

   _____

   _____

   _____

   _____

   _____

   _____

   _____

   _____

   _____

Name: _____

Date: _____

Class: _____

Activity 10-2

Integrating Simulated 3D Assets

Objectives

Students will create and modify a two-player game in which players have mutually exclusive goals. Students will add simulated 3D art to a 2D game. Students will edit existing programming and controls. Students will explain level creation and difficulty settings.

Situation

The Really Cool Game Company is experimenting with a multiplayer game that will be ported to play on various mobile device platforms. This game will have many levels that increase in difficulty and have different themes. Due to processor limitations on mobile devices, the game will use simulated 3D objects in a 2D environment instead of an actual 3D environment. You are in charge of creating the PC and online prototype that will later be built for play on different sized tablets. The user interface for the computer will use keyboard controls. When ported for mobile devices, the user interface will use the touch screen.

How to Begin

1. Launch MMF2, and start a new game build.
2. In the **Workspace** window, rename the application to Ricochet.
3. In the **Window** tab of the **Properties** window, change the size of the application to 800 × 600. When prompted to resize all frames, click the **Yes** button.
4. Save the game as *LastName*_Ricochet in your working folder.

Controls for Two Players

5. Click the **Runtime Options** tab in the **Properties** window for the application.
6. In the **Players...** area of the tab, click the **Edit** button for the **Default Controls** property, as shown in **Figure 1**. The **Player Controls** dialog box is displayed.
7. Click the X in the cell where the **Player 2** column and **Keyboard** row intersect. The **Keyboard Setup** dialog box is displayed, as shown in **Figure 2**.
8. Click the **Up** button, and press the [A] key on the keyboard.
9. Click the **Down** button, and press the [Z] key on the keyboard. Player 2 will use the [A] and [Z] keys to move the paddle up and down during gameplay. Player 1 will use the default controls of the up and down arrows.
10. Close the **Keyboard Setup** and **Player Controls** dialog boxes.

Making Frames

11. Rename the first frame as Title Page.
12. In the storyboard, click the **2** on the second line to add a second frame.
13. Rename this frame as Level 1.

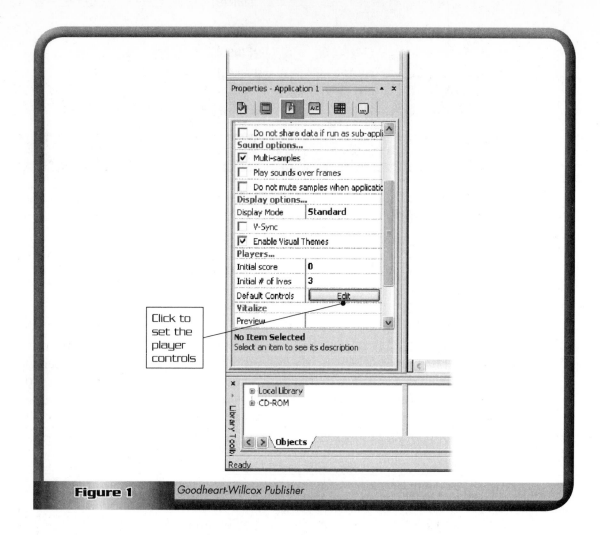

Click to set the player controls

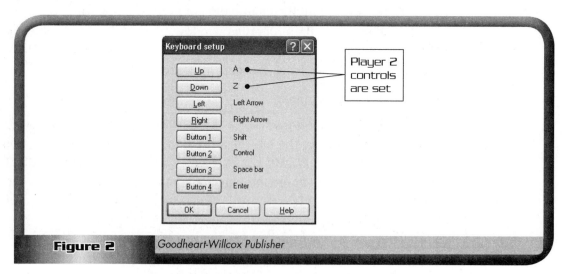

Player 2 controls are set

14. In the **Settings** tab of the **Properties** window, change the background color for the Level 1 frame to green.

15. Add two more frames.

16. Rename the third and fourth frames as Winner, Right and Winner, Left.

17. Change the background color for the Winner frames to green.

Adding Game Assets

Frame Editor

18. Display the Level 1 frame in the frame editor.

19. In the **Library Toolbar** window, expand the resource tree Library > Games > Miscellaneous. Double-click on the Bat and Ball library file, and drag the Bat object onto the frame, as shown in **Figure 3.** Notice how this object is a simulated 3D object.

20. Drag the Ball object onto the frame, and place it at the center (410,310). Notice how this object has a shadow, which helps to simulate 3D. Later in the game build, you will create improved artwork for the ball.

21. Insert a new counter object, place it in the top-right corner of the frame.

22. Using the **Properties** window, change the size of the counter to 30 × 45.

23. Name the counter Counter, Right-Hand Player.

24. Right-click the counter, and click **Clone Object** in the shortcut menu. Recall, a clone is a copy that can have different programming from the original.

25. In the **Clone Object** dialog box, click the **OK** button to accept the default values of two rows and one column.

26. Move the cloned counter to the top-left corner of the frame.

27. Rename the cloned counter to Counter, Left-Hand Player.

28. Select the Bat object, and in the **Size/Position** tab of the **Properties** window, change the angle property to 90. This rotates the bat so its long dimension is vertical.

29. In the **Movement** tab, change the **Movement** property to **Eight Direction**.

30. Click the **Directions** property, and in the pop-up window that is displayed, click the left- and right-hand blocks to remove the default arrows, and click the top and bottom blocks to add arrows, as shown in **Figure 4.**

31. Similarly, click the **Initial direction** property, remove the default arrow, and click the top block to add an arrow.

32. Rename the bat object as Bat, Right Hand.

33. Move the bat to the right-hand side of the frame.

34. Create one clone of the bat, and move the clone to the left-hand side of the frame.

35. Change the name of the cloned bat to Bat, Left Hand.

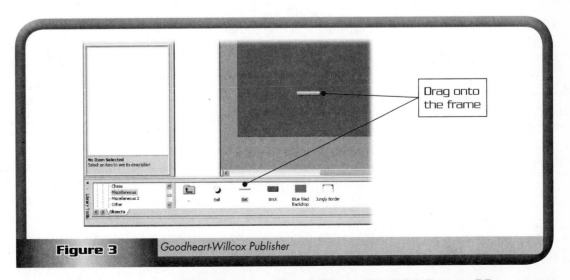

Figure 3   *Goodheart-Willcox Publisher*

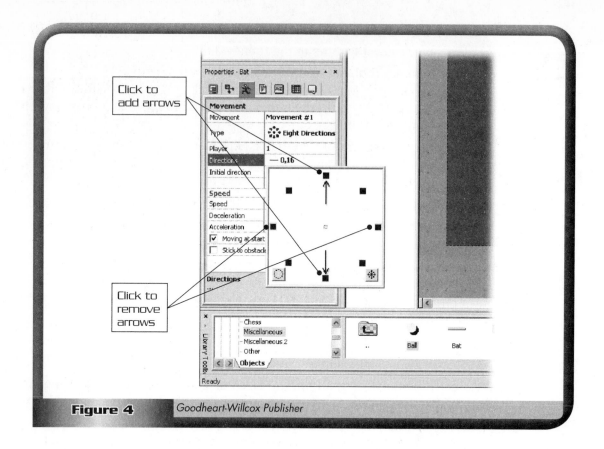

Click to add arrows

Click to remove arrows

Figure 4   Goodheart-Willcox Publisher

36. In the **Movement** tab of the **Properties** window for the left bat, click the **Player** property, and click **2** in the drop-down list. This assigns the Bat, Left Hand object to player 2.

37. Select the Ball object, and in the **Movement** tab of the **Properties** window, and change the **Movement Type** property to **Bouncing Ball**.

38. Set the **Initial direction** property to a random pattern for left and right movement, as shown in **Figure 5.**

39. Set the **Speed** property to 35.

Programming

The first programming will set the Ball object to bounce on the top and bottom edges of the frame. The pseudo code is:

> **IF** the ball leaves the scope to the top or bottom,
> **THEN** the ball will bounce.

After that, programming will be added to test if either player has missed the ball. This will be indicated by the ball leaving the play area to the left or right. The pseudo code is:

> **IF** the ball leaves the scope to the right,
> **THEN** destroy the ball
>> **AND** add one to player 2's score
>> **AND** create a new ball in the center of the frame.
> **IF** the ball leaves the scope to the left,
> **THEN** destroy the ball
>> **AND** add one to player 1's score
>> **AND** create a new ball in the center of the frame.

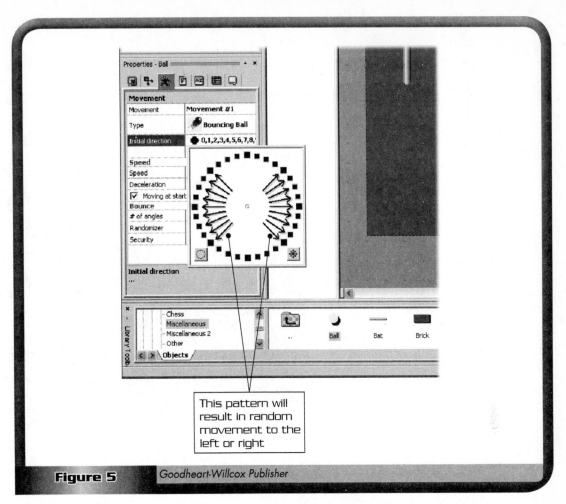

This pattern will result in random movement to the left or right

Figure 5   *Goodheart-Willcox Publisher*

Event Editor

40. Display the event editor for the Level 1 frame.

41. Add a new condition, and in the **New Condition** dialog box, right-click on the Ball object, and click **Position > Test position of "Ball"** in the shortcut menu.

42. In the **Test Position** dialog box that is displayed, click the top and bottom arrows pointing out of the frame area, and click the **OK** button.

43. Right-click in the Ball column, and click **Movement > Bounce** in the shortcut menu.

44. Add a new condition, and in the **New Condition** dialog box, right-click on the Ball object, and click **Position > Test position of "Ball"** in the shortcut menu.

45. In the **Test Position** dialog box that is displayed, click the right-hand arrow pointing out of the frame area, and click the **OK** button.

46. Right-click in the cell where the **Counter, Left-Hand Player** column intersects the **Line 2** row, and click **Add to Counter** in the shortcut menu. In the expression editor, enter 1, and close the expression editor. When the right-hand player (player 1) misses the ball, the left-hand player (player 2) receives a point.

47. Right-click in the cell where the **Create New Objects** column intersects the **Line 2** row, and click **Create object** in the shortcut menu.

48. In the **Create Object** dialog box, click the Ball object, and click the **OK** button. The frame editor is temporarily displayed, along with a different **Create Object** dialog box, as shown in **Figure 6**.

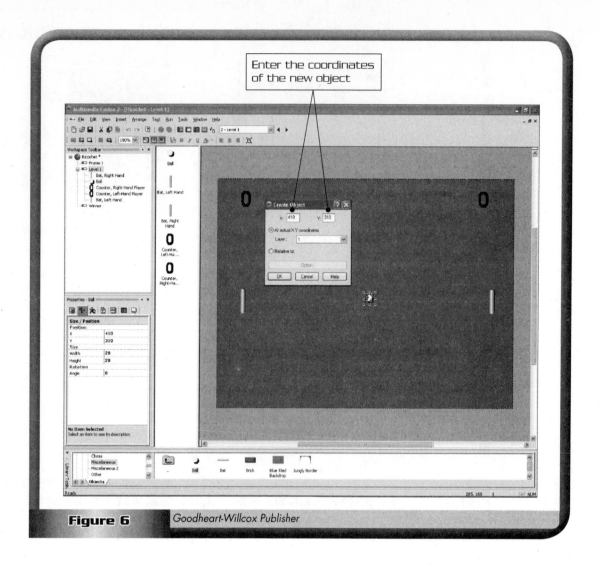

Enter the coordinates of the new object

Figure 6   *Goodheart-Willcox Publisher*

49. Click the **At actual X,Y coordinates** radio button, enter 410 in the **X:** text box, and enter 310 in the **Y:** text box. This will place the ball in the center of the screen, which is also the original location of the ball.

50. Click the **OK** button. The event editor is redisplayed.

51. Right-click in the cell where the **Ball** column intersects the **Line 2** row, and click **Destroy** in the shortcut menu. If the ball is not destroyed, it may eventually reenter the scope and cause an error.

52. Right-click on the number **2** for the second row, and click **Copy** in the shortcut menu. Since the programming for the ball leaving the left side of the scope is very similar to what was just programmed, starting with a copy and editing it is more efficient.

53. Right-click on the number **3** for the third line, and click **Paste** in the shortcut menu.

54. Double-click the condition statement on line 3. The **Test Position** dialog box is displayed in which the condition can be edited.

55. Click the right-hand arrow pointing out of the frame area to turn it off, and click the left-hand arrow pointing out of the frame area to turn it on. Close the dialog box.

56. On line 3, drag the check mark from the **Counter, Left-Hand Player** column into the **Counter, Right-Hand Player** column. When the left-hand player (player 2) misses the ball, the right-hand player (player 1) receives a point.

57. On line 3, delete the check mark from the **Counter, Left-Hand Player** column.

Using OR Logic

58. Create a new condition on line 4: **IF** the Ball object collides with the Bat, Right Hand object.

59. Right-click on the condition statement on line 4, and click **OR (logical)** in the shortcut menu.

60. Right-click on the OR (logical) statement, and click **Insert** in the shortcut menu, as shown in **Figure 7**.

61. In the **New Condition** dialog box, program this pseudo code: **IF** the Ball collides with Bat, Left Hand object. The condition now has the same meaning as **IF** the ball collides with either bat.

62. To complete the action on line 4, program this pseudo code: **THEN** the ball will bounce. This code already exists, so you can copy that check mark to be more efficient.

Run Frame

63. Test play the frame, and debug if needed. Check the controls for both players. Also, let the ball pass by each bat to make sure it regenerates and the correct score is added correctly.

If the respawning of the ball is not working properly, try deleting the two "create object" check marks and reprogramming them. An error has been reported with the create-object programming in some versions of MMF2 on certain operating systems.

Simulated 3D Ball

64. Launch PowerPoint.

65. Open the 3D Simulation file created in the last activity. Choose one of the simulated spheres on the first three slides that you feel will work in the game, and copy it.

Frame Editor

66. In MMF2, open the Level 1 frame in the frame editor.

67. Open the Ball object in the image editor.

68. Clear the existing image, and paste the ball from PowerPoint. When prompted, resize the canvas.

69. Set the background color as the transparency mask.

Transparency

Figure 7   *Goodheart-Willcox Publisher*

If you are having trouble setting the background color as the transparency mask, try closing the image editor and then reopening it. The background must be transparent for the **Crop** command to work, which you will use next. Similarly, you may need to close the image editor and reopen it if you are having trouble with the **Crop** command.

Crop

70. Click the **Crop** button. The image is automatically cropped to the edges of the image. Close the image editor.

71. Using the **Properties** window, change the size of the Ball object to 20 × 20, which is its original size.

72. Click the **Movement** tab in the **Properties** window, and enter 5 for the **Randomizer** property and 24 for the **Security** property. These settings will make the ball movement more realistic and allow the ball to free itself when stuck in a pattern.

73. Save your work, and test play the frame.

Run Frame

Victory Condition

The basics of a video game have been created, but there is no victory condition. In this game, the first player to reach a score of 9 is the winner. You need to add the programming for the game to recognize which player wins the game.

    IF Counter, Right-Hand Player equals 9,
    THEN jump to the Winner, Right frame.
    IF Counter, Left-Hand Player equals 9,
    THEN jump to the Winner, Left frame.

74. Display the event editor for the Level 1 frame.

75. On line 5, add a new condition, and in the **New Condition** dialog box, right-click on the Counter, Right-Hand Player object, and click **Compare to a value...** in the shortcut menu.

76. In the expression editor, enter 9, and close the expression editor.

77. Right-click in the cell where the **Storyboard Controls** column intersects with the **Line 5** row, and click **Jump to frame** in the shortcut menu.

78. In the **Choose a Storyboard Frame** dialog box, click the Winner, Right frame, and click the **OK** button, as shown in **Figure 8**.

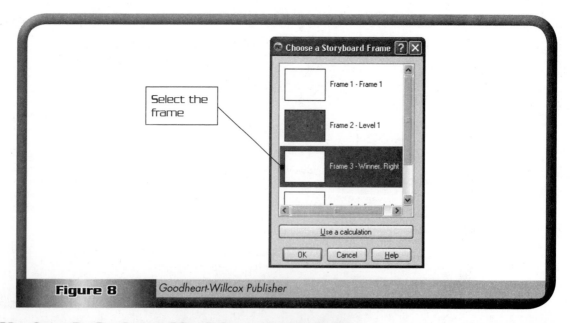

Figure 8   *Goodheart-Willcox Publisher*

79. Similarly, on line 6, program **IF** Counter, Left-Hand Player equals 9, **THEN** jump to the Winner, Left frame.

Frame Editor

80. Display the frame editor for the Winner, Right frame.

81. Insert a new static text object in the middle of the frame.

82. Double-click on the static text object, and enter Player 1 Wins!

83. Use the formatting tools on the **Frame Editor Toolbar** to change the font to a typeface that matches the theme of the game, change the size of the font to 72, and change the color of the font to contrast with the frame background.

84. Use the **Properties** window to change the background color of the static text object to match the background color of the frame. Also, remove the border around the static text object.

85. Use the sizing handles to resize the static text object so all of the text is visible.

86. Insert a new button object near the bottom of the frame.

87. Double-click on the button object, and enter Rematch.

88. In the **Properties** window, click the **About** tab, and change the **Name** property to Button_Rematch.

89. Click the **Icon** property, and then click the **Edit** button that appears, as shown in **Figure 9.** The **Edit Icon** dialog box is displayed, which is an image editor for the icon. The appearance of the button itself is *not* changed in this dialog box.

90. Fill the transparent background (checkerboard pattern) with red, and close the **Edit Icon** dialog box. This will allow the button to be easily identified later when programming. This change has no impact on gameplay and will not be visible to the player.

91. Similarly, insert another button, label it Quit, name it Button_Quit, and change the background of the icon to blue.

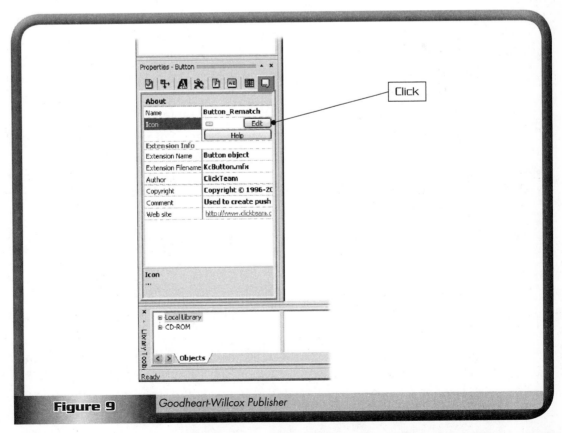

Figure 9 *Goodheart-Willcox Publisher*

Event Editor

92. Display the event editor for the Winner, Right frame.

93. On line 1, program this pseudo code: **IF** the **Rematch** button is clicked, **THEN** restart the application.

94. On line 2, program this pseudo code: **IF** the **Quit** button is clicked, **THEN** end the application.

95. Similarly, create the Winner, Left frame.

Title Slide

Before you can test play the game, the title frame needs to be created and programmed to launch the game. Earlier, you added the Title Page frame. Now it is time to finalize that frame.

96. Display the frame editor for the Title Page frame.

97. Apply the artistic and programming skills you have learned to create a decorative title slide. Be sure to add text that describes the user interface controls for each player.

98. Add three buttons to the frame, one each for **Beginner**, **Regular**, and **Advanced**. Program the **Beginner** button to jump to the Level 1 frame. The other two buttons will be programmed later after additional levels have been created.

Run Application

99. Save your work, and test play the game.

Levels

Storyboard Editor

100. Display the storyboard editor.

101. Right-click on the line number for the Level 1 frame (line 2), and click **Copy** in the shortcut menu.

102. Right-click on the line number for the next frame (line 3), and click **Paste** in the shortcut menu.

103. Repeat this to add one more copy of the Level 1 frame.

104. Rename the first copy to Level 2, and rename the second copy to Level 3, as shown in **Figure 10**.

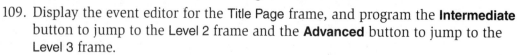
Frame Editor

105. Display the frame editor for the Level 2 frame.

106. Modify the properties of the ball to increase its speed. You may also need to increase the bat speed.

107. Display the frame editor for the Level 3 frame.

108. Modify the properties of the ball to increase its speed from what was set on the Level 2 frame. Also, decrease the length of each bat.

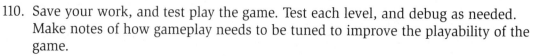
Event Editor

109. Display the event editor for the Title Page frame, and program the **Intermediate** button to jump to the Level 2 frame and the **Advanced** button to jump to the Level 3 frame.

Run Application

110. Save your work, and test play the game. Test each level, and debug as needed. Make notes of how gameplay needs to be tuned to improve the playability of the game.

Tuning

111. On all levels, program the bats to either wrap movement or stop if they go outside the scope to the top or bottom.

112. Set the order of the counters in the object stack to be behind the ball and bat objects. This will allow gameplay to be unobscured by the counters.

113. Add obstacles that the ball will bounce off of to increase the difficulty of gameplay and randomness of the ball movement.

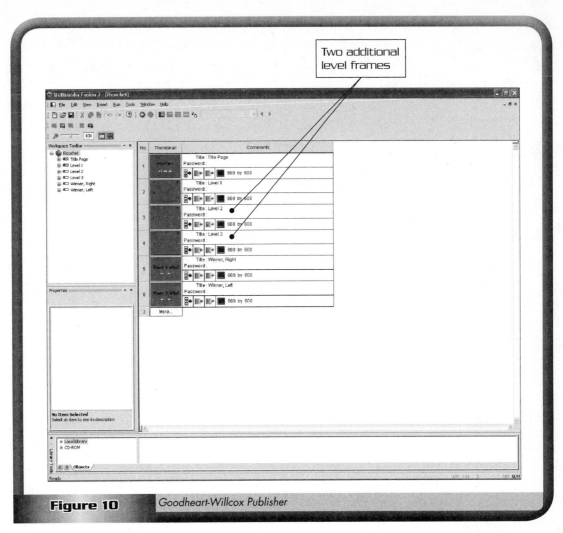

Two additional level frames

Figure 10   *Goodheart-Willcox Publisher*

114. Add simulated 3D objects as the bats. Try out different shapes like triangles and stars to create unusual ball movements.

115. Add obstacles in the game that, when hit with the ball, are destroyed and change the bats to shapes. Use animation directions to achieve the different shapes.

116. Set up bricks or other simulated 3D objects to activate game features like changing the ball speed or creating additional balls.

Window Size

The game currently is sized to run in an 800 × 600 window. This is too large for many tablets and smartphones. Also, since mobile devices come in many different sizes, the game needs to be able to adjust for the best fit.

117. Select the Ricochet application in the asset tree.

118. Click the **Window** tab in the **Properties** window.

119. Uncheck the **Menu bar** property. This will hide the menu bar that is displayed at the top of the game window.

120. Check the **Change Resolution Mode** property. This allows the resolution of the game to change, which is needed as screen size change.

121. Check the **Resize display to fill window size** property. This will expand or contract the game to fit inside the screen dimensions of the device on which the game is played.

Run Application

122. Save your work, and test play the game. Debug if needed.

Porting

123. With the Ricochet application selected, click the **Settings** tab in the **Properties** window.

124. If the Flash module has been purchased from Clickteam, click the **Build Type** property, and click the Flash option in the menu.

125. Compile the game, and submit it for grading according to the directions provided by your instructor.

Review Questions

1. Briefly describe how to make a game build a two-player game in MMF2.

_____

_____

_____

_____

2. What is the difference between a clone and a copy in MMF2?

_____

_____

_____

_____

3. Why must the ball be destroyed when it leaves the scope?

_____

_____

_____

_____

4. How were simulated 3D assets integrated into this game build?

_____

_____

_____

_____

5. What was added to this game build to balance player skill?

_____

_____

_____

_____

Activity 10-3
Three-Dimensional Modeling Tools

Objectives

Students will create three-dimensional models in a virtual world. Students will use 3D primitives to create complex objects. Students will apply materials to a 3D object and render the object.

Situation

The Really Cool Game Company has reviewed your work with simulated 3D objects and thinks you have the skills to start working in an actual 3D environment. You will be using open-source software called Blender (www.Blender.org) to build a basic 3D model. Mastering 3D modeling software requires much more than can be provided in this lesson, but the lesson will give you an idea if you have an aptitude for 3D art.

How to Begin

1. Launch Blender.
2. Click anywhere outside of the splash screen to close it. A default cube is displayed in the middle of the drawing window. Displayed on the cube are the *3D transform manipulator* and the 3D cursor. The manipulator is positioned on the center of the selected object or group of objects. It is used to *transform* (move, scale, or rotate) objects.
3. Click anywhere on the screen. The 3D cursor moves to any point you click in the drawing window. The *3D cursor* is used to position the creation of a new object.

Changing the View

Blender has several panels and windows that contain controls and tools for all attributes of the 3D model and animation. One of the most commonly used panels is the **3D View** panel. The tools in this panel control the way objects in the drawing window are displayed. The tools also give you the ability to edit objects. The current view is displayed in the top-left corner of the drawing window.

4. Locate the **3D View** panel at the bottom of the screen.
5. Click the **View** menu and select **Top** from the menu, as shown in **Figure 1.** This displays the top orthographic view.

In the top view, you are looking straight down on the XY plane. In other words, the computer screen is parallel to the XY plane. The Z axis projects perpendicular to the screen. It is important to note that the axes in Blender are aligned to the traditional Cartesian coordinate system. When looking at the top view, the +Y axis points to the *top* of the screen, not to the bottom of the screen as in Multimedia Fusion 2.

Moving Objects

6. Click the green arrow on the 3D transform manipulator and drag upward. This moves the selected object in the +Y direction. Dragging downward moves the selected object in the −Y direction.
7. Release the mouse to drop the object in the new location.

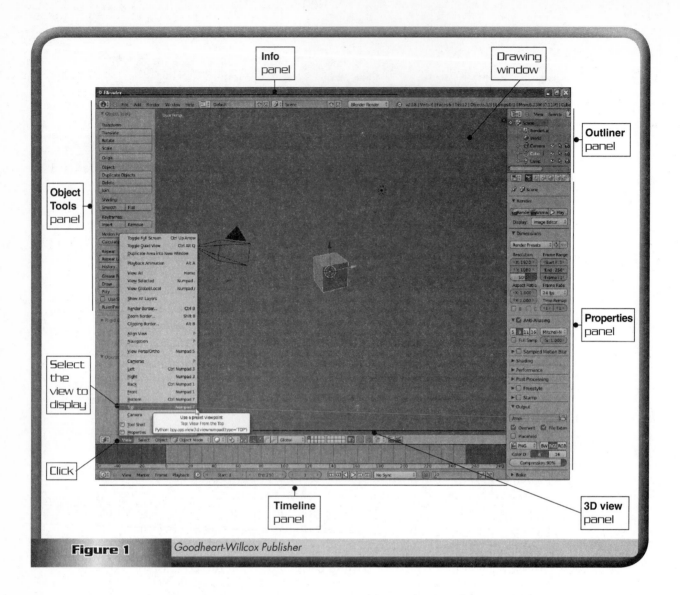

Info panel

Drawing window

Outliner panel

Object Tools panel

Properties panel

Select the view to display

Click

Timeline panel

3D view panel

Figure 1   *Goodheart-Willcox Publisher*

8. Press the [Ctrl][Z] key combination to undo the move.

9. Using similar steps, try moving the cube two grid spaces on the +X axis using the red arrow on the 3D transform manipulator.

10. Change the view to the right-side view.

11. Move the cube upward (+Z) using the blue arrow on the 3D transform manipulator. Notice that the grid remains aligned to the XY plane, so it is not visible in the right-side view.

As you move the object, it may appear as if the object is rotating as you drag it. This is not the case. The view is currently set to a perspective projection, and because of this you may see the sides of the cube as you drag it. In a perspective view, parallel lines recede to a vanishing point. If you toggle the view to orthographic projection (**View** > **View Persp/Ortho**), parallel lines remain parallel, and you will not be able to see the sides of the cube as you drag it.

Deleting Objects

An object other than a cube will allow you to better see the transforms applied. Before creating a new object, delete the default cube.

12. On the **3D View** panel, click **Select** > **Border Select**. This starts the selection tool that allows you to draw a border or box around an object to select it.

13. Move the cursor in the drawing window and notice the crosshairs that follow the cursor.

14. Click near the bottom-left edge of the cube, drag to draw a box around the cube, and release the mouse button. The selection box only needs to touch the object, not fully enclose it. The selected object is outlined.

15. Press the [Delete] key. A pop-up menu is displayed at the cursor location asking you to confirm the deletion. Click **Delete** in the menu to delete the object.

Adding a Mesh

16. Display the top view.

17. Click near the center of the grid to place the 3D cursor at that location. The location of the 3D cursor is where the mesh will be added.

18. On the **Info** panel, click **Add** > **Mesh** > **Monkey**. The mesh object is added to the drawing window and automatically selected.

Object

19. On the **Properties** panel, click the **Object** button. The properties of the selected object are displayed in the panel, as shown in **Figure 2**.

20. In the **Transform** area of the **Properties** panel, click in the top text box below **Location:**. This is the X value for the object's location. Enter 3 to set the X coordinate of the object.

21. Similarly, change the Y value to 4. The Y value is the middle text box under **Location:**.

22. Make sure the Z value is 0. The Z value is the bottom text box below **Location:**.

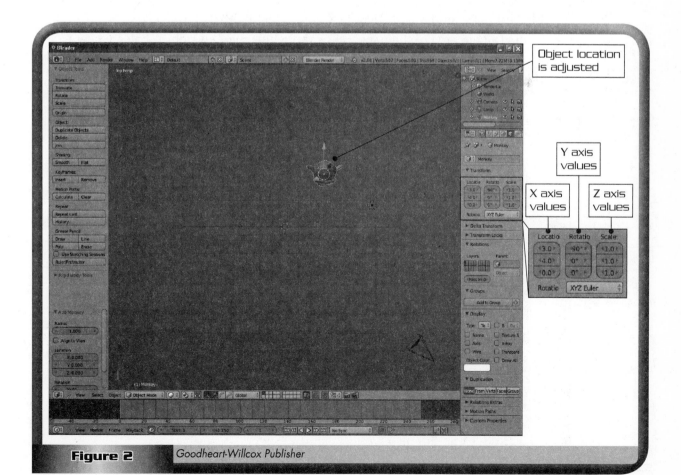

Figure 2   *Goodheart-Willcox Publisher*

Saving

The concept of saving in Blender is very similar to many other programs, but the process is not based on the familiar Windows save dialog box. Also, it is important to remember Blender does *not* autosave your work or ask if you want to save when you click the close button (X). If you exit Blender without performing a save, your work will be lost forever!

23. On the **Info** panel, click **File > Save As...** (once the file is saved, you can click **File > Save**). The save window is displayed, as shown in **Figure 3.**

24. Navigate to your working folder. The current folder is displayed on the top line.

25. Rename the default untiltled.blend to Monkey Business. The .blend extension is automatically added.

26. Click the **Save as Blender File** button to complete the save. The save window is closed and the drawing window is displayed. Look at the title bar to see that the correct file name and path are displayed.

Materials

The ability to work with materials is one of the most important aspects of 3D modeling. The materials are as important as the mesh, if not more important. A well-designed and applied material can often hide flaws in a mesh, but a perfect mesh cannot hide a poor-quality material.

Material

27. With the monkey mesh selected, click the **Material** button on the **Properties** panel. You may need to resize the panel in order to see the button.

28. Click the **New** button to add a new material to the project. The new material is named Material.001 and the default material properties are displayed in the panel, as shown in **Figure 4.**

29. Click in the material name text box, and rename the material as Purple.

30. In the **Diffuse** area of the panel, click the white color swatch. A color wheel is displayed.

31. Click on the color wheel to choose a purple color. Notice that both the monkey head and the preview sample change color to match your selection.

Monkey

32. On the right side of the material preview, click the **Monkey** button to change the preview from a sphere to a monkey head.

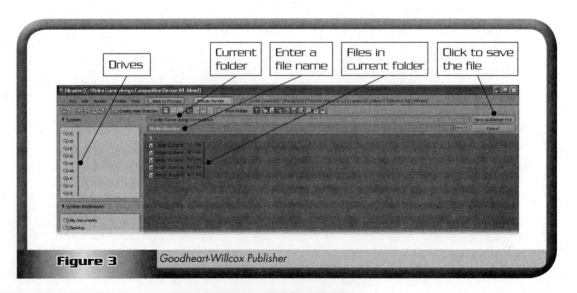

Drives Current folder Enter a file name Files in current folder Click to save the file

Figure 3 *Goodheart-Willcox Publisher*

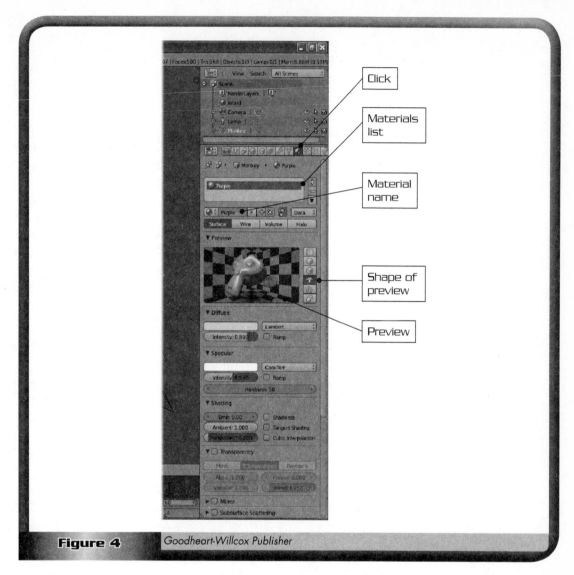

Figure 4   *Goodheart-Willcox Publisher*

33. Click the **Intensity** slider, and drag it left and right to change the intensity value. You can also click on the slider to activate a text box and enter a value. Set the intensity value to .500. Intensity is like a saturation value of the HSL model. An intensity of 0 is black (no color intensity). A value of 100 is the full color you selected.

Color Reflection

Below the diffuse color properties are the specular color properties. Most objects have a specular color that is white or near white based on the diffuse color. The hardness setting determines the size of the specular highlight. Hard objects with a smooth surface, like a billiard ball, have a small specular highlight. Soft objects or objects with a rough surface have a large specular highlight.

34. Click the color swatch in the **Specular** area of the panel.

35. In the color wheel, select a yellow color. Notice how the highlight on the material preview is now yellow instead of the default white.

36. Click on the **Hardness** label and enter 1 in the text box that is enabled. The material preview changes to show the specular color as the predominant color. This means the specular highlight is very large, indicating the material is soft or has a rough surface.

37. Change the hardness setting to 500. The material preview shows very few yellow highlights. This means the specular highlight is very small, indicating the material is very hard and smooth.

38. Change the hardness to 150. The highlights are medium in size.

Duplicating Objects

When making copies of objects Blender, they can be either independent of the original or linked to the original. A linked copy has all of its properties tied to the original object. Changing the properties on the original also changes the properties on the copy. An independent copy inherits properties from the original, but it is not linked. This means that changing the properties on the original object will *not* change the properties on the copy. For this lesson, you will create an independent copy.

39. With the mesh selected, click the **Duplicate Objects** button on the **Object Tools** panel. Without clicking, move the mouse. The copy moves relative to the cursor.

40. Left-click when the copy is where you want to place it. The new object is named the same as the original with .001 added to the end of the name. So, the copy you just created is named Monkey.001, as seen in tree in the **Outliner** panel.

41. In the **Outliner** panel, expand the tree for the Monkey and Monkey.001 objects. You will probably need to resize the panel to see the entire tree, **Figure 5.** Notice both monkey objects have the Purple material attached.

42. Click the Monkey.001 object in the tree so its mesh icon is highlighted to signal it the selected object. This is another method of selecting objects. You can also right-click on an object in the drawing window to select it.

43. Click the **Object** button in the **Properties** panel.

Object

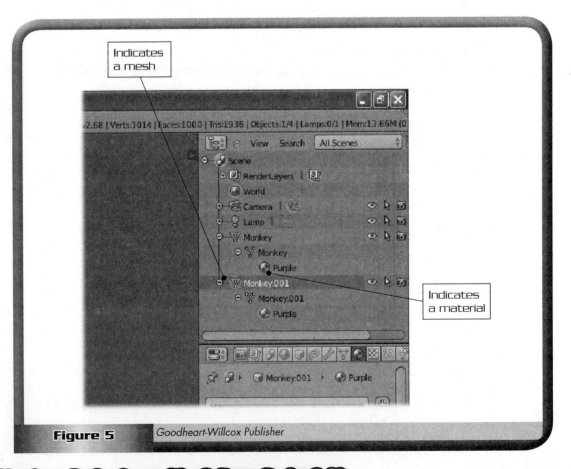

Figure 5   *Goodheart-Willcox Publisher*

44. Change the name of the object to Blue Monkey. Notice that the entry in the **Outliner** panel automatically updates.

Material

45. Click the **Material** button in the **Properties** panel.

46. Click the plus (+) button to the right of the material name (*not* the one to the right of the material list) to add a new material.

47. Using skills learned earlier, create a blue material named for the Blue Monkey object.

48. Change the position of the Blue Monkey object to (−3,4,0).

Rotating Objects

Rotation is revolution about an axis. If the top view is displayed, rotation will occur around the Z axis. Remember, in this view, the Z axis is perpendicular to the computer screen.

49. With the Blue Monkey object selected, click the **Rotate** button on **Object Tools** panel.

50. Move the cursor around the Blue Monkey object and the object will spin to follow the cursor. The angle of rotation is shown in the coordinate display on the **3D View** panel as you drag the mouse. Once you click to set the rotation, the angle is shown in the **Angle** text box in the **Object Tools** panel, as shown in **Figure 6.** This text box can also be used to enter an exact value.

51. Rotate the Blue Monkey object 180 degrees.

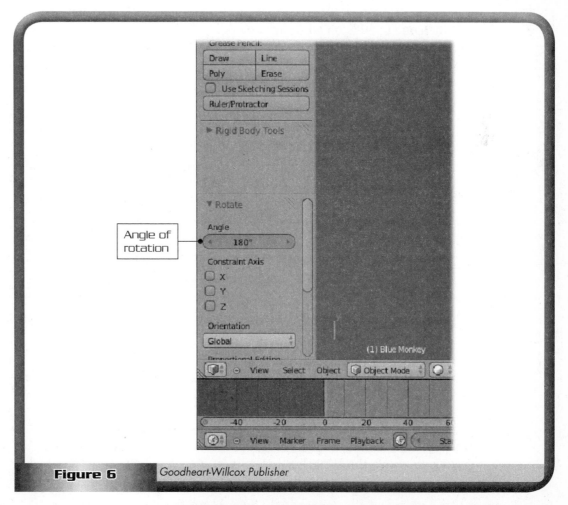

Figure 6   *Goodheart-Willcox Publisher*

52. Display the back view (**View** > **Back**). In this view, the Y axis is perpendicular to the screen, so you can rotate objects about this axis.

53. Click the **Rotate** button again, and rotate the Blue Monkey object 90 degrees about the Y axis.

54. Display the left view (**View** > **Left**). In this view, the X axis is perpendicular to the screen, so you can rotate objects about that axis.

55. Click the **Rotate** button again, and rotate the Blue Monkey object 180 degrees about the X axis. You have now rotated about all three axes.

56. Press the mouse wheel button and drag the mouse to free-rotate the view. The objects are not being rotated, only the view of them is being rotated.

57. Move the mouse around to see the monkey heads in different perspectives. Release the mouse wheel button to fix the view.

58. Hold the [Shift] key, press the mouse wheel button, and drag the mouse to pan the view. Release the mouse wheel button to fix the view.

Primitives

Blender has many built-in primitives. The monkey you have been working with so far is not considered a primitive. It is a prebuilt mesh. The 3D primitives in Blender are cube, circle, UV sphere, icosphere, cylinder, cone, and plane (although a plane does not have three dimensions).

59. Display the top view.

60. Move the 3D cursor to a point near the purple monkey.

61. In the **Info** pane, click **Add** > **Mesh** > **Cone** to place a cone primitive.

Object

62. In the **Properties** panel, enter .8 in the three text boxes below **Scale:**. This scales the cone to 80% on all three axes.

63. Using the 3D transform manipulator, move the cone to the top of the purple monkey's head, like a party hat. Use the mouse wheel to zoom the view. Move the cone on all three axes as needed, and display the front view, as shown in **Figure 7**.

64. Rename the cone object as Hat.

65. Create a yellow material and apply it to the cone.

Material

66. Using the border select tool (**Select** > **Border**), select both the purple monkey and the hat. You can tell both are selected by the border around the objects in the drawing window. Also, each object in the tree in the **Outliner** panel displays a circle over its icon.

67. In the **Object Tools** panel, click the **Join** button. This combines the Purple Monkey mesh and the Hat mesh. They are no longer separate objects. Only a single mesh remains.

68. With the new mesh selected, click the **Origin** button in the **Object Tools** panel.

69. In the menu that appears, select **Origin to Geometry**. This centers the local origin to the new mesh.

70. Rename the new mesh Monkey-Hat.

The location of the local origin is important since it is where rotation and scaling transformations are centered. If the local origin is off center, the object will rotate out of balance. In some cases, such as modeling a swinging hammer, this is what you want. A hammer rotates about a point near the bottom of the handle where it is grasped. That means the local origin needs to be at the base of the handle. To do this, you would move the 3D cursor to the point near the bottom of the handle, then select **Origin** > **Origin to 3D Cursor** in the **Object Tools** panel.

Come primitive
move into place

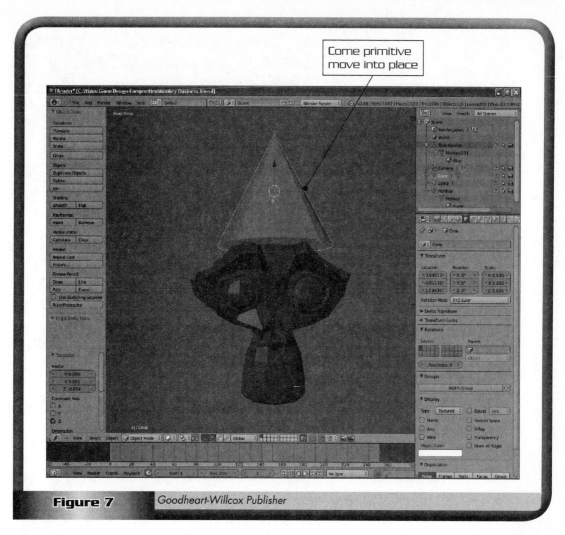

Figure 7   *Goodheart-Willcox Publisher*

Edit Mode

To this point, you have been working in *object mode.* This mode allows you to transform or alter the entire object. Sometimes you need to change only a part of an object. To do this, you need to switch to *edit mode.* In edit mode, the object is no longer covered in a material. It is displayed shaded with edges and vertices visible. Any selected edge or vertex can be altered in edit mode. You can choose a selection mode to select only vertices, only edges, or only faces.

71. On the **3D View** panel, click the **Mode** button (currently labeled **Object Mode**) and select **Edit Mode** from the menu, as shown in **Figure 8.**

Vertex Select Mode

72. Click the **Vertex Select Mode** button on the **3D View** panel.

73. Move the cursor to the point of the hat (cone) and right-click (not left-click) to select just that single vertex. The selected vertex is displayed in white. You can now move this point in any direction.

74. Drag the vertex upward to stretch out the hat. The hat changes shape because the edges are attached to the vertex.

Face Select Mode

75. Click the **Face Select Mode** button on the **3D View** panel. This allows you to select the faces of the object instead of the vertices.

76. Click **Select > Select/Deselect All** from the **3D View** panel to ensure no faces are selected. If everything is selected, choose the entry again so nothing is selected.

77. Draw a border selection box around the monkey's lower chin and mouth.

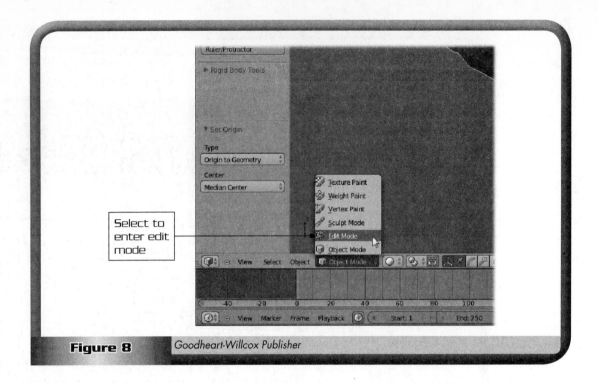

Select to enter edit mode

Figure 8 *Goodheart-Willcox Publisher*

78. Using the 3D transform manipulator, drag the selected faces down to stretch out the monkey's face.

79. Use the mouse wheel button to rotate the view. Notice that only part of the chin was selected, which has made a real mess out of the monkey, as shown in **Figure 9.** Features that are not visible, or are "behind" the visible features, were not selected.

80. Press the [Ctrl][Z] key combination to undo moving the faces.

Limit Selection to Visible

81. Click the **Limit Selection to Visible** button on the **3D View** panel to turn the button off. This is a toggle. The feature is off if the button is light colored and on if the button is dark colored.

82. Display the front view, and zoom and pan as needed to center the monkey and hat in the view.

83. Click **Select > Select/Deselect All** from the **3D View** panel to deselect all faces.

84. Create another selection set of the mouth and chin. This time, the back faces are selected in addition to the visible faces.

85. Move the selected faces down.

86. Zoom, pan, and rotate the view as needed to make sure the back faces moved with the visible faces. Then, display the front view, and center the monkey and hat in the view.

87. Switch to object mode to see the materials applied. Now, this is a purple monkey who is not having much fun at the party and is feeling bad with a long face.

Smoothing

Notice that the monkeys are still very rough looking. All of the polygons used to build the shape are still visible. These hard edges can be removed by smoothing the model. Smoothing is applied by object, not to the entire scene. Be sure you are in object mode before continuing.

88. Select the Monkey-Hat object.

89. Click the **Smooth** button in the **Shading:** area of the **Object Tools** panel. Notice how the polygons are no longer displayed. Instead, the mesh is smoothed.

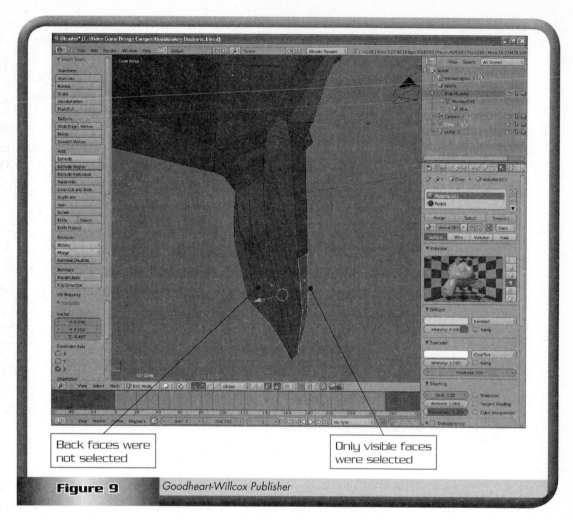

Back faces were not selected

Only visible faces were selected

Figure 9 Goodheart-Willcox Publisher

90. Click the **Flat** button in the **Shading:** area of the **Object Tools** panel. Notice how the mesh is again displayed as polygons.

91. Display the smoothed view of the Monkey-Hat object, as shown in **Figure 10**.

Extruding

Extruding is the process of taking a 2D object or feature and adding height to create a new volume. For example, a circle can be extruded into a cylinder. Additionally, a flat face on a mesh can be extruded to create a new feature on the mesh.

92. The Monkey-Hat object should have a Z value of 0; if not, change that now.

Use 3D Manipulator

93. Click the **Use 3D Manipulator** button on the **3D View** panel to turn off the 3D manipulator. You cannot click on the local origin with the manipulator displayed.

94. Left-click on the local origin of the Monkey-Hat object (the dot) to place the 3D cursor at that location.

95. Turn on the 3D manipulator.

96. On the **Info** panel, click **Add > Mesh > Circle**. A circle is added, centered on the 3D cursor. Notice that the circle appears as either an ellipse or a line, depending on the projection of the view. This is because in the front view you are looking at the edge of the circle.

Object

97. With the circle selected, use the **Properties** panel to scale it by 200 percent on the X and Y axes.

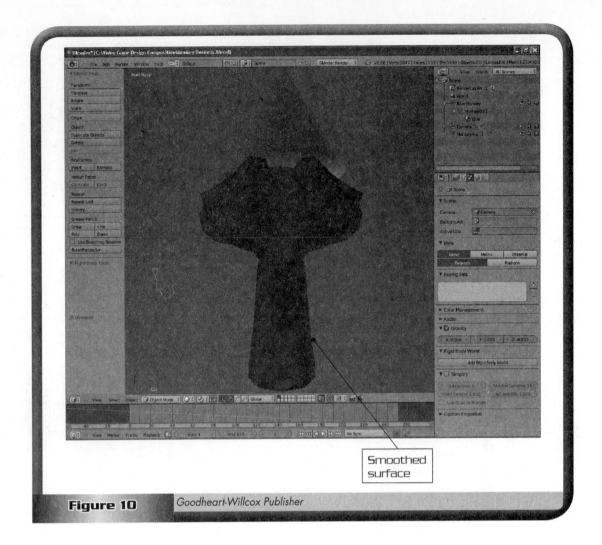

Smoothed
surface

Figure 10   *Goodheart-Willcox Publisher*

Vertex Select Mode

98. Change to edit mode, and click the **Vertex Select Mode** button in the **3D View** panel.

99. Select all vertices on the circle. You may wish to rotate the view to better see the circle.

100. In the **Object Tools** panel, click the **Extrude Region** button.

101. Move the cursor upward to extrude the circle. Hold down the [Ctrl] key as you drag to snap in increments. Extrude the circle four units straight up and click. After clicking, you can enter exact values in the X, Y, and Z text boxes that appear at the bottom of the **Object Tools** panel.

102. Change to the Top view. The extruded circle is a hollow tube, not a solid cylinder. When you extrude a circle, it does not have volume, but when you extrude a face, it is solid.

103. Switch to object mode and move the extruded circle so it is centered on the Monkey-Hat object.

104. Switch to the Front view and move the extruded circle down as needed so only part of the Monkey-Hat object is sticking out of the top, as shown in **Figure 11.**

105. Rename the extruded cylinder Barrel.

106. Save your work, and submit it for grading.

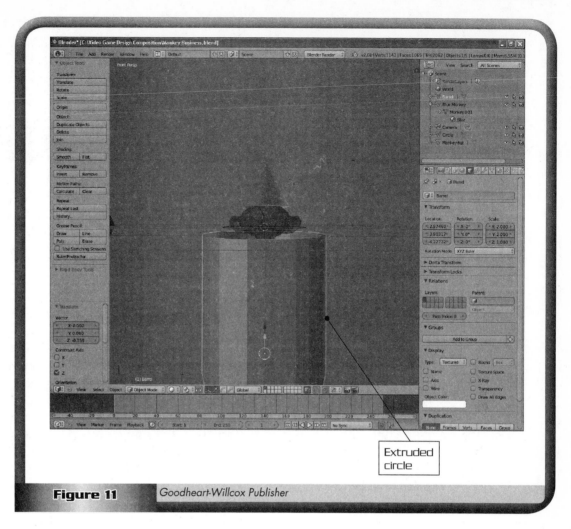

Extruded circle

Figure 11 | *Goodheart-Willcox Publisher*

Review Questions

1. Which Blender tool consists of a three-color representation of the axes and can be used to move a selected object?

   _____

2. Which Blender tool marks the location where a new mesh will be created in the scene?

   _____

3. Which material setting controls the size of the specular color?

   _____

4. List the three selection modes available when working in edit mode.

   _____

   _____

5. Describe the difference between a selection created with the **Limit Selection to Visible** button on and off.

   _____

   _____

   _____

   _____

Activity 10-4

3D Modeling Composition

Objectives

Students will use multiple extrusions to construct a complex object. Students will apply reflection and mirror qualities to a texture. Students will apply modifiers. Students will create visual effects. Students will use keyboard hot keys in the design process.

Situation

You have successfully completed basic training for 3D software. You can begin creating custom models and meshes. The Really Cool Game Company is building a 3D game based in medieval times. The scene will be in first person perspective and includes a night setting where a character will walk through the dark castle using only the light from a candle. Your job is to create a 3D candle to use in the game. The candle will be prominently displayed closest to the camera in first person view, so it needs to be of good quality.

This activity builds on the skills you acquired in the last activity. As you gain experience in 3D modeling, you will find that using keyboard hot keys to switch between functions is quicker than drilling down through menus. This lesson makes use of hot keys for functions you have already learned.

How to Begin

1. Launch Blender, and click out of the splash screen.
2. Delete the default cube from the scene.
3. Set the view to orthographic projection by clicking **View > View Persp/Ortho** in the **3D View** panel or pressing the [5] key on the number pad.
4. Place the 3D cursor in the center of the grid, if it is not already there.
5. In the **Info** panel, click **Add > Mesh > Cylinder**.
6. At the bottom of the **Object Tools** panel, click the **Cap Fill Type** drop-down list, and click **Triangle Fan** in the list. This adds a cap of the specified type to each end of the cylinder so it is not hollow.
7. At the bottom of the **Object Tools** panel, set the radius to 1.000 and the depth to 6.000. Depth is the height setting for the cylinder.
8. At the bottom of the **Object Tools** panel, set the X, Y, and Z location and rotation values to 0, as shown in **Figure 1.**
9. Save the file as *LastName_*Candle in your working folder.

Cupping the Top of the Candle

10. Press the [7] key on the number pad to display the Top view.
11. Click the **Shading** button, and click **Wireframe** in the menu, or press the [Z] key to toggle to a wireframe display.

Shading

12. Press the [Tab] key to toggle from object mode to edit mode.
13. Deselect all of the vertices by pressing the [A] key.
14. Right-click on the vertex in the center of the cylinder to select it.
15. Click **View > Toggle Quad View** or press the [Ctrl][Alt][Q] key combination to display four viewports, as shown in **Figure 2.** The quad view can help the designer see the scene from different views: Top, Front, Right, and the camera or a perspective view.

Name: _____

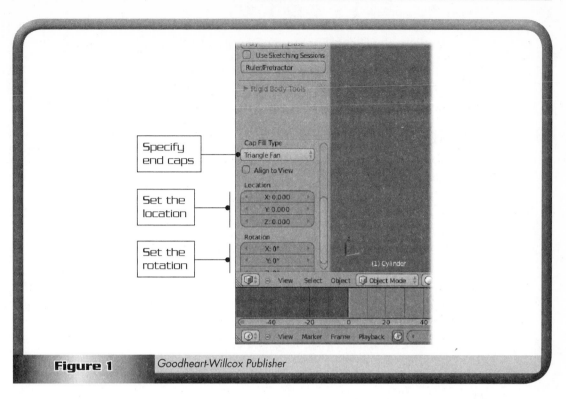

Figure 1   *Goodheart-Willcox Publisher*

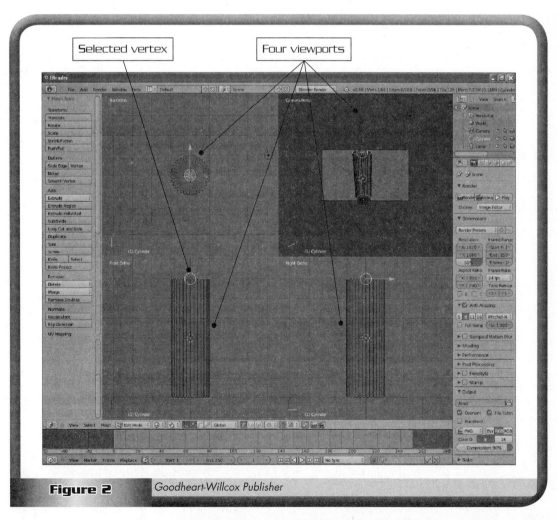

Figure 2   *Goodheart-Willcox Publisher*

16. Use the 3D manipulator to drag the top vertex down one unit. Enter the exact value in the **Object Tools** panel. The top of the candle is now cupped slightly.

17. Switch to object mode.

18. Switch to solid-shaded display.

19. Rename the object to Candle.

Tessellating the Mesh

Tessellating an object increases the number of vertices, edges, and faces. Increasing the available features allows for a finer refinement of the model, making it easier to change the shape of the candle.

Modifiers

20. With the candle selected, click the **Modifiers** button in the **Properties** panel, click the **Add Modifier** button to display a list of available modifiers.

21. Click **Subdivision Surface** in the **Generate** group of the list. This is a tessellation modifier.

22. In the **Properties** panel, click the right-hand arrow on the **View:** setting to see how the subdivisions change the shape of the candle. Notice how there is a big change from 1 to 2 and from 2 to 3, but higher values have little change on the object.

23. Enter 2 for the **View:** setting. This is the tessellation value that will be displayed in the drawing area.

24. Enter 3 for the **Render:** setting. This is the tessellation value that will be applied during rendering.

Removing the Bottom of the Object

Notice how the tessellation of the object has altered it so it bulges inward and is rounded at both ends. This is a nice effect for a stylized candle in a video game. It could be left like this, but if the bottom is removed so the bottom of the candle is flat, the object will look better because the rounding will be limited to the top where the wick and flame will be.

25. Toggle to edit mode. Notice how you can see the original mesh and the result of the tessellation inside of it.

Apply Modifier to
Editing Cage

26. In the **Properties** panel, click the **Apply Modifier to Editing Cage** button. The mesh is displayed with the effects of the modifier applied.

27. Toggle to a wireframe display.

28. On the **Object Tools** panel, click the **Loop Cut and Slide** button.

29. Move the mouse to the center of the depth (height) of the candle. A horizontal cut line appears on the object.

30. Click to set the cut line at the vertical center of the candle. Slide mode is entered, and you can drag the loop up or down.

31. Move the loop down to the bottom of the candle, and click to set the position. A loop of edges is added at that position. By adding this loop near the bottom of the candle, the effect of the tessellation is altered, and the rounding at the bottom of the candle is reduced.

32. Add another loop, and slide it toward the top to reduce the rounding at the top of the candle. You may want to leave some rounding to help provide a visual cue that the top of the candle is melting, as shown in **Figure 3.**

33. Click **Render > Render Image** on the **Info** panel or press the [F12] key to render the scene.

34. Press the [F11] key or click **Render > Show/Hide Render Image** to hide the rendering and return to the drawing window.

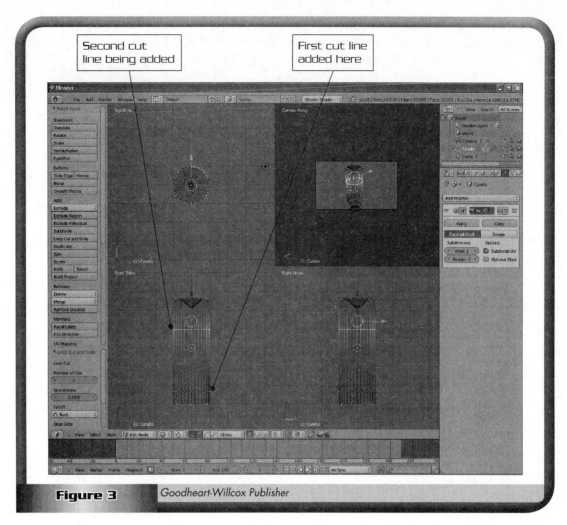

Second cut
line being added

First cut line
added here

Figure 3   *Goodheart-Willcox Publisher*

Adding Variety for Realism

A basic candle has been created, but it looks too computer generated. The sides are perfectly smooth, and the depression simulating the area where wax is burned is a perfect cone. In the real world, a candle would burn unevenly, so the depression would not be uniform.

35. Select a few vertices at the top of the candle. You can hold down the [Shift] key and individually select vertices or use a selection box.

36. Use the 3D manipulator to move the selected vertices downward and slightly outward. This will simulate a section of the candle that the flame deformed, as shown in **Figure 4.**

37. Render the candle to see the effect. Hide the rendering.

38. Similarly, add some more deformations at different locations around the top of the candle.

39. Render to see your result.

40. Refine the model as needed. Use the [Ctrl][Z] key combination to undo any errors.

Creating a Wax Material

Material

41. Toggle to object mode, and display a solid-shaded view.

42. With the candle selected, click the **Materials** button in the **Properties** panel.

43. Add a new material, and name it Red Wax.

44. Set the diffuse color to a medium red.

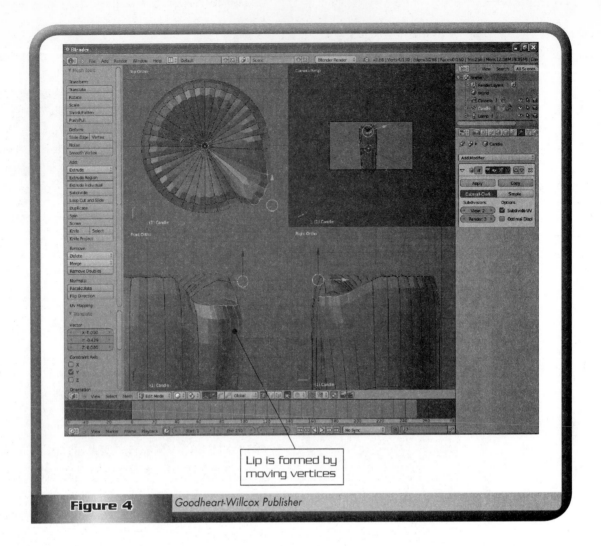

Lip is formed by moving vertices

Figure 4　　Goodheart-Willcox Publisher

45. Set the specular color to a medium-light yellow. Since the light produced by a candle flame is orange or yellow, the reflected light would be more yellow than white.

46. Set the hardness to 150 to reduce the size of the specular highlight.

47. Render the scene to see the result. Hide the rendering.

Adding a Wick

The candle still needs a wick to hold the flame. The wick will be a simple cylinder primitive added to the scene.

48. Toggle to edit mode and a wireframe view.

49. Select the vertex in the middle of the depression at the top of the candle.

50. Press the [Shift][S] key combination, and click **Cursor to Selected** in the shortcut menu that appears. This places the 3D cursor at the location of the selected vertex.

51. Toggle to object mode. If you remain in edit mode, the added mesh will become part of the existing mesh.

52. Add a cylinder mesh to the scene.

53. Change the radius to 0.05; depth to 2; location to 0,0,0; and rotation to 0,0,0. Add triangular fan end caps.

54. Change the name of the object to Wick.

55. Create a new material named Black, and adjust the material settings to create the wick material.

Creating a Holder

The candle still needs a holder so the player character can carry it. A simple plate for the candle to stand on is all that is needed.

56. Press the [Shift][S] key combination, and click **Cursor to Center** in the shortcut menu. This moves the 3D cursor to the scene origin, which is in the center of the candle.

57. Add a circle. This should be placed around the candle center.

58. Toggle to edit mode, and click the **Extrude Region** button in the **Object Tools** panel. The circle is extruded as one piece.

59. Press the [Z] key to constrain to the Z axis of movement. You do not need to hold it down, just press it once.

60. Extrude the circle 0.5 units.

61. Click the **Scale** button in the **Object Tools** panel, drag the mouse up to flare the circle, and click.

62. Enter 3 in the X, Y, and Z **Vector** text boxes in the **Object Tools** panel.

63. Click the **Extrude Region** button again, and extrude the mesh 0.05 units on the Z axis.

64. Click the **Extrude Region** button again, and extrude the mesh 0.1 units on the Z axis.

65. Scale the extrusion to 110 percent (1.1) on the X and Y axes.

66. Click the **Extrude Region** button again, and extrude the mesh 1.000 units on the –Z axis.

67. Scale the extrusion to 0 percent on the X, Y, and Z axes. This creates a point, as shown in **Figure 5**.

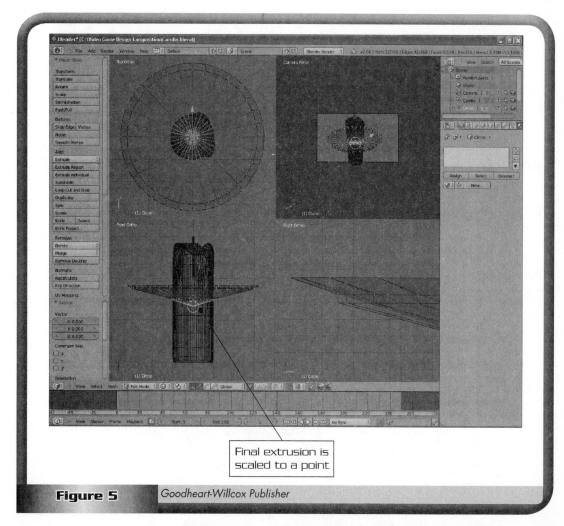

Final extrusion is scaled to a point

Figure 5   *Goodheart-Willcox Publisher*

68. Deselect all vertices.

69. Toggle to object mode, and display a solid-shaded view.

70. Name the new object Dish.

71. Move the object down on the Z axis so bottom of the candle is resting on top of the dish.

72. Add a new material named Brass, and define a material for a brass metal with a high reflective value.

73. Render the scene to see the result.

74. Fix any errors.

Melted Wax

For more realism, the model should include some wax that has dripped down onto the dish. This detail does not need to be very detailed, so a simple cylinder can be used. Mapping will be used to provide a texture simulating the randomness of wax that has dripped into the dish.

75. Snap the 3D cursor to the center of the scene.

76. Add a cylinder mesh, and name it Melted Wax.

77. Set the radius to 1.5 and the depth to 0.3. Add triangle fan end caps. Move the object down to rest on top of the dish.

Material

78. Select the Candle object, and click the **Materials** button.

79. Click the drop-down arrow next to the materials list, and click **Copy Material** in the menu, as shown in **Figure 6.**

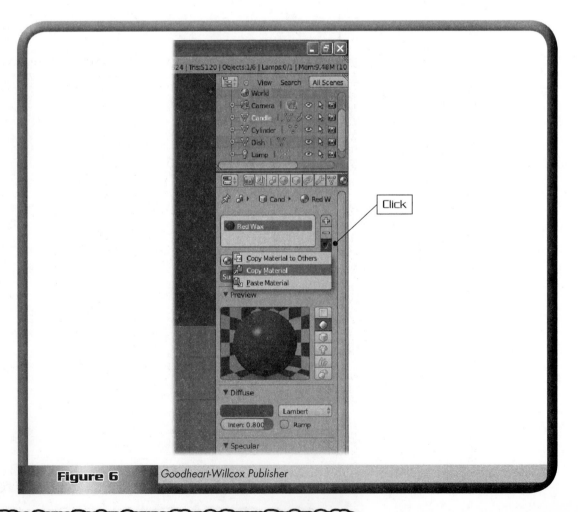

Figure 6   *Goodheart-Willcox Publisher*

80. Select the Melted Wax object, and click the **Materials** button.

81. Add a new material, and name it Melted Wax.

82. Click the drop-down arrow next to the materials list, and click **Paste** in the menu. This pastes the material definition of the copied material (Red Wax) as the material definition for this material (Melted Wax). However, the materials are not linked.

Texture

83. With the Melted Wax object selected, click the **Texture** button on the **Properties** panel. You may need to resize the panel to see the button.

84. Click the **New** button to add a texture. Name the new texture Melted Wax.

85. Click the **Type:** drop-down list, and click **Distorted Noise** in the list. Notice how the preview changes. Noise is a pattern of random waves.

86. Change the **Distortion:** setting to 3. Notice the noise pattern tightens.

87. Change the **Size:** setting to 0.35. This setting changes the size of each noise bump.

88. Render to see the result. The pattern is applied to the color, which is not the desired effect. This map should simulate a bumpy surface, so some settings need to be changed.

89. Make sure the Melted Wax object is selected and the **Texture** button is on in the **Properties** panel. Then, uncheck the check boxes in the **Diffuse** area.

90. Check the **Displacement** check box, and enter 0.25 in the text box, as shown in **Figure 7.** This applies the texture as a map that affects the geometry, which is similar to a bump map.

91. Render to see the result.

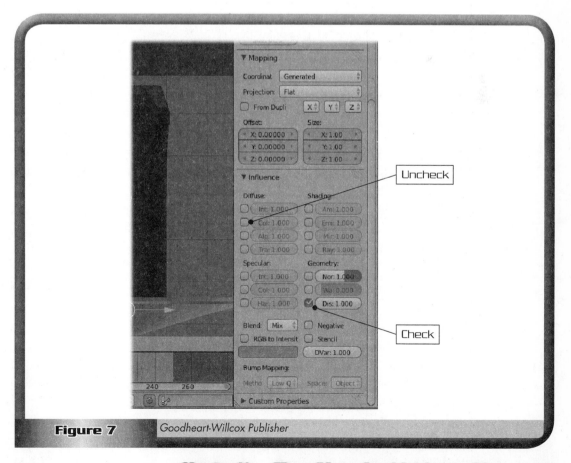

Figure 7   *Goodheart-Willcox Publisher*

Dish Base

The bottom of the dish is a point. This is not a problem when a character is carrying the candle. However, if the candle is set down, a player may wonder how a pointed bottom can allow the candle to be set down. The dish needs a flat base.

92. Snap the 3D cursor to the center of the scene.

93. Add a cylinder mesh.

94. Set the radius to 1.500 and the depth to 0.5. Add triangle fan end caps. Move the object down so the bottom point on the dish is inside the cylinder.

95. Name this object Base.

96. Copy the material definition of the Brass material on the dish, and paste it into a new material on the base. Name the new material Brass_Base.

97. Rotate the view to inspect all sides of the model for errors. Look for the candle or melted wax not touching the dish, or the dish protruding from the base.

98. Fix any errors.

99. Render to see the result.

Flame

The candle and holder look pretty good, but there is no flame. The candle should produce a yellow-orange ball of light from the wick. Basic lighting and a glow effect can simulate the illumination provided by the candle flame. Later, the candle flame can be animated for better realism.

100. Toggle to object mode, and select the Wick object.

101. Snap the 3D cursor to the selected object.

102. In the **Info** panel, click **Add** > **Mesh** > **UV Sphere**.

103. In the **Object Tools** panel, enter 0.5 in the **Size** text box. This is the diameter of the sphere.

104. Rename the object as Central Glow.

105. Move the sphere so it is centered on the top of the Wick object. The location does not need to be exact. It may help to switch to a wireframe view.

106. Add a material to the Central Glow object, and name it Halo.

107. Click the **Halo** button below the material name, as shown in **Figure 8.** This changes the material type from the default of surface to a halo.

108. In the **Halo** area of the **Properties** panel, enter 0.025 in the **Alpha:** text box. This controls the transparency of the material. Since this is a ball of light, it is mostly transparent.

109. In the **Halo** section, click the color swatch, and change the color to the same values as used for the specular color on the wax materials.

110. Change the **Size:** setting to 0.6. This determines the size of the particles that make up the sphere.

111. Change the **Hardness:** setting to 70 to dim the sphere and reduce the harsh outline.

112. Change the **Add:** setting to 0.4. This determines how much of the glow color is added to other objects in the same space.

113. In the **Halo Options:** area, check the **Texture**, **Shaded**, and **Soft** check boxes. The **Texture** option allows a texture to break up the surface. The **Shaded** option allows it to reflect light from other sources. The **Soft** option will soften the edges.

Texture

114. Click the **Texture** button.

115. Add a new texture, and name it Glow Cloud.

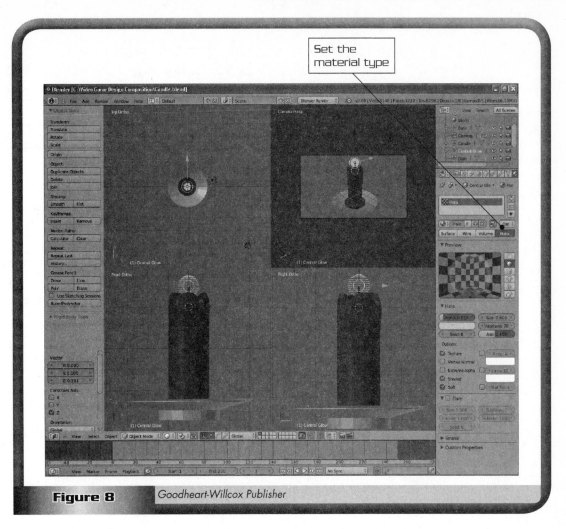

Set the material type

Figure 8   *Goodheart-Willcox Publisher*

116. Click the **Type:** drop-down list, and click **Clouds** in the list.

117. Click the **Hard** button in the **Noise:** area. This will disperse the glow more than if the **Soft** button is clicked.

118. Change the **Depth:** setting to 5.

119. In the **Influence** area, click the color swatch, and change the color to red. This will color the black part of the cloud texture red and apply gradient to the gray portions. The gradient will mix the yellow set earlier with red using the cloud pattern, making the perceived color more orange.

120. Render to see the results.

121. Save your work, and submit it for grading.

Review Questions

1. What is the hot key to toggle between object mode and edit mode in Blender?

   _____

2. What is the effect of a subdivision surface modifier in Blender?

   _____

   _____

   _____

   _____

3. Why would variety be added to a 3D model?

_____

_____

_____

_____

4. Briefly describe how to copy a material definition from one material to a new material.

_____

_____

_____

_____

5. Which material type is used in the model to simulate a flame on the candle?

_____

Activity 10-5
Lighting Theory and Camera Position

Objectives

Students will apply lighting theory to create triangle lighting for a 3D scene. Students will move the camera to set up a scene. Students will render a static scene and output it in different resolutions.

Situation

The creative director has reviewed your 3D work and believes you have the ability to do more. The candle created in the last activity needs to be properly lighted and rendered for an image to be used on the game box cover. You will need to apply basic triangle lighting to the scene to reduce shadows and provide the best presentation for a static image. During gameplay, the candle will include different animation and lighting, but for the game box cover, the scene needs to be set more like a photograph.

How to Begin

1. Launch Blender.
2. Open the *LastName_*Candle file from the last activity.
3. Save the file as *LastName_*Candle Rendering in your working folder.

World

The scene must have a background and a table on which the candle can be placed. For the background, you will use built-in features of Blender. First, create a table under the holder.

4. Snap the 3D cursor to the center of the scene.
5. In the Info panel, click **Add > Mesh > Plane**.
6. In the **Object Tools** panel, set the radius of the plane to 10.
7. Move the plane object down on the Z axis so it is just below the Base object.
8. Rename the object as Table.
9. Create a material for the Table object that is similar to wood. Use textures as appropriate.

World

10. In the **Properties** panel, click the **World** button. Displayed in the preview is the default gray background. This is the background that has appeared in the renderings you have done to this point.
11. In the **World** area of the panel, there are three check boxes: **Paper Sky, Blend Sky**, and **Real Sky**. You may need to resize the panel to see the entire label. Check only the **Blend Sky** check box.
12. In the **World** area of the **Properties** panel, check the **Blend Sky** check box. Notice the **Zenith Color:** swatch is activated and the preview shows a blend, or gradient, from the horizon color to the zenith color. See **Figure 1.** In Blender, the horizon, which is where the sky meets the ground, is the XY plane with a Z value of 0. The *zenith* is the top of the sky. The *nadir* is the bottom of the sky.

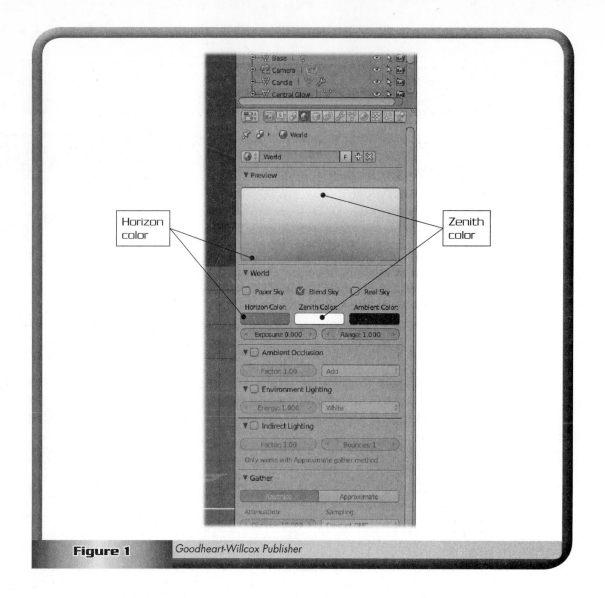

Figure 1   *Goodheart-Willcox Publisher*

13. Click the **Horizon Color:** color swatch and change to a medium-light blue.

14. Change the zenith color to white.

15. Render the scene to see how the background has changed. With the **Blend Sky** check box checked, the gradient starts at the bottom of the image and continues to the top of the image, regardless of the location of the XY plane. Clearly the background is too light, more like a bright sunny day than a nighttime scene in which a candle is needed.

16. Change the horizon color to a darker blue and the zenith color to black.

17. Render the scene again. The background is more appropriate for a nighttime scene.

18. In the **World** area of the **Properties** panel, click the **Ambient Color:** swatch, and change the color to a dark orange.

19. Render the scene. Notice how everything in the scene has an orange cast. Unless you set the color to a very dark shade of orange, the scene may even be washed out with orange. This obviously does not look realistic.

20. Change the ambient color to nearly black, such as R.001, G.001, B0. Alternately, change the color to black. The ambient color should always be almost black.

21. Near the bottom of the **Properties** panel, expand the **Stars** area and check the **Stars** check box.

22. Enter 8 in the **Size:** text box.

23. Enter 10 in the **Separation:** text box.

24. Render the scene. This rendering probably looks more like dots in the background than a night sky.

25. Experiment with settings for the stars to obtain a nice background, similar to the one shown in **Figure 2**.

Adding Lighting

To get the correct lighting, a photographer adjusts the lights to create highlights and shadows. In 3D modeling, the same thing must be done. In Blender, you add lamps and adjust the angle of illumination to achieve the best highlights and shadows. Shadows are an important part of any scene as they help ground the objects, or place them in context of depth in the scene.

26. Select and delete the existing point lamp. If you render the scene now, it will be entirely dark except for the flame and the background. There is no illumination provided to the objects in the scene.

27. Move the 3D cursor above the candle and flame. You do not need to be precise in its location.

28. On the **Info** panel, click **Add** > **Lamp** > **Spot**.

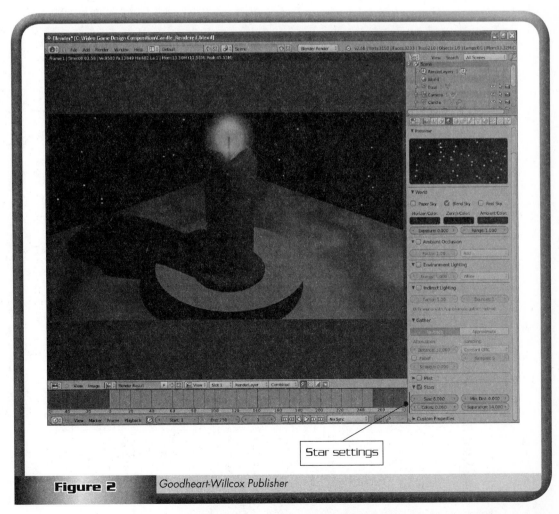

Star settings

Figure 2   *Goodheart-Willcox Publisher*

29. Move the lamp so it is close to the camera in the scene. The location does not need to be exact.

30. Click the **Object** button on the **Properties** panel.

Object Data

31. Enter 1.5 in the **Energy:** text box and 100 in the **Distance:** text box. You will likely need to adjust these values later to improve the illumination. The energy setting controls intensity, while the distance setting controls how far from the lamp illumination stops.

32. In the **Shadow** area, click the **Ray Shadow** button.

33. Click the **Object** button on the **Properties** panel.

Object

34. Using the **Rotation:** text boxes, rotate the lamp about the X and Y axes so the lamp points toward the candle at an angle, as shown in **Figure 3.** Adjust the position of the lamp as needed. This is the key light.

35. Add two more spotlights, and adjust their positions and settings to create a backlight and a fill light. Refer to Figure 10-6 in the textbook. The fill light should have an intensity of about one-half of the key light, and the backlight should have an intensity of about one and one-half of the key light.

Positioning the Camera

The default scene contains a camera. You now need to move it into a position to display an appropriate view of the scene. To position the camera, it helps to create a dummy object in the center of the scene. You can then use this object as a reference location to aim the camera.

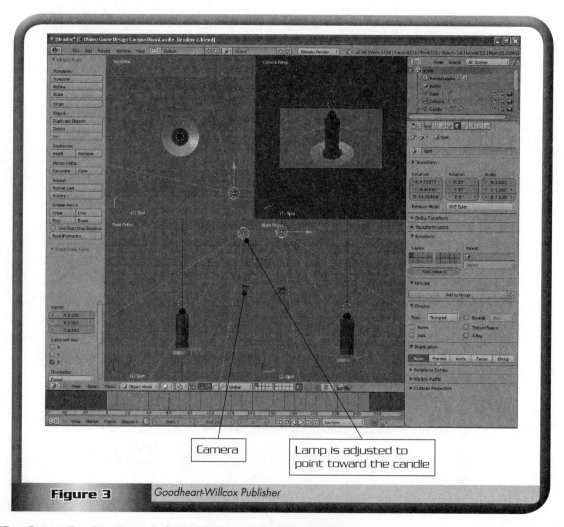

Camera

Lamp is adjusted to point toward the candle

Figure 3   *Goodheart-Willcox Publisher*

36. Add a small UV sphere in the dish near the bottom of the candle, and name it Camera Focus.

37. Select the existing camera.

Object Constraints

38. Click the **Object Constraints** button on the **Properties** panel.

39. Click the **Add Object Constraint** button, and click **Track To** in the menu.

40. Click in the **Target:** text box, and select the Camera Focus object in the menu, as shown in **Figure 4.**

41. In the **To:** area, click the **–Z** button.

42. Click the **Up:** button, and click **Y** in the menu.

43. Display the quad view, if not already displayed.

44. Move the Camera Focus object as needed until the candle and holder are completely visible in the Camera Perp view.

Rendering

In 3D modeling, the computer creates the rendering based on the scene set up by the artist. A computer rendering can be saved as a still image (picture) or an animation file that can be used in another application. Since the scene is not animated, you will be creating a still image. In order to use the artwork in a game or an illustration, as in this case, the scene needs to be rendered to an image file. Before rendering the scene, you need to exclude the dummy object from the rendering.

45. In the **Outliner** panel, click the restrict renderability icon (camera) for the Camera Focus object, as shown in **Figure 5.** The dummy object will not be rendered.

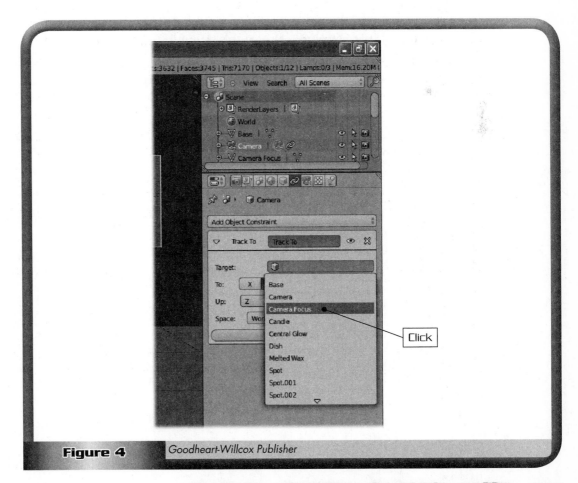

Figure 4   *Goodheart-Willcox Publisher*

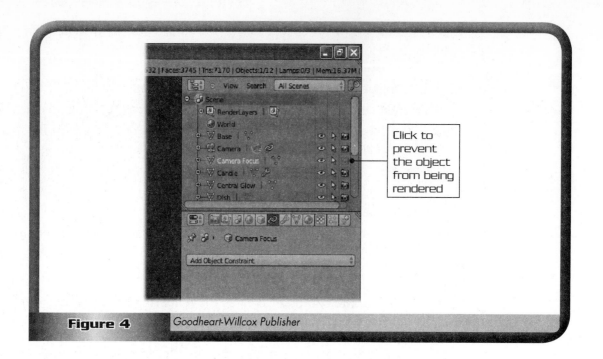

Click to prevent the object from being rendered

Figure 4   *Goodheart-Willcox Publisher*

Render

46. In the **Properties** panel, click the **Render** button. Various rendering settings for the scene are displayed in the panel.

47. Click the **Render Presets** button and choose **HDTV 1080p** in the menu that is displayed. The settings in the **Dimensions** area are filled in based on the selection. Notice the frame in the camera view.

48. Click the **Render Presets** button and choose **TV NTSC 4:3** in the menu. This is the format of older televisions. Notice the frame in the camera view changes to match the aspect ratio in the **Dimensions** area.

49. Enter 1200 in the **X:** text box and 900 in the **Y:** text box. This will create an image that is 3″ × 4″ at 300 dots per inch (dpi), which is a common resolution used for print images.

50. At the top of the **Properties** panel, click the button next to **Display:**, and click **New Window** in the menu. This sets the destination for the rendering as a new window.

51. Render the scene. The rendered image is displayed in a separate window.

52. In the new window, select **Image > Save As Image**, as shown in **Figure 6.** The window displays Blender's save interface.

53. Navigate to your working folder.

54. In the panel on the left, click the file type button, which is set to PNG by default, to display all of the available image file types.

55. Save another copy as *LastName*_Candle Cover_print.tif in TIFF format. This is a format commonly used in print publication.

56. The marketing department also wants a rendering for a television commercial. Save another copy of the rendering as *LastName*_Candle_HDTV.png in the correct size and in the PNG format. You will need to render the scene again at the new dimensions before saving the image file.

57. Save your work, and submit all image and Blender files for grading.

Name: _____

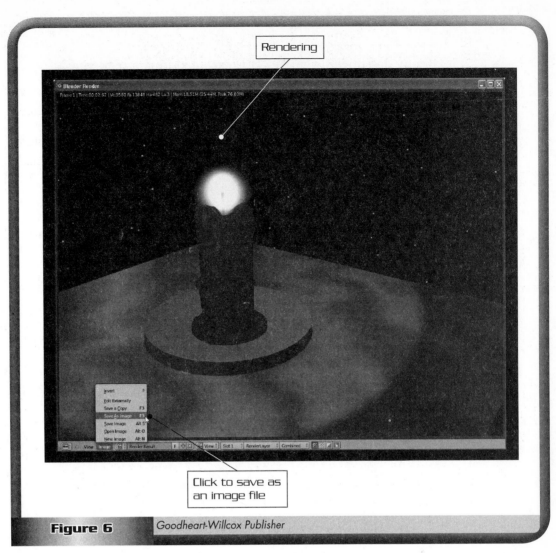

Rendering

Click to save as
an image file

Figure 6 | *Goodheart-Willcox Publisher*

Review Questions

1. What is the relationship between the horizon, nadir, and zenith?

   _____

   _____

   _____

   _____

   _____

2. What color should the ambient color be?

   _____

3. What are the names of the three lights used in triangle lighting?

   _____

   _____

   _____

4. What setting in Blender controls the intensity of a light (lamp)?

_____

5. Briefly describe how an object is excluded from a rendering.

_____

_____

_____

_____

Chapter 11
Animation Composition

Objectives

After completing this chapter, you will be able to:

- Create a frame-by-frame animation.
- Animate character lip movement to synchronize with spoken words using a standardized animation set.
- Enhance animation tweens by moving facial components for realistic effect.
- Manipulate facial landmarks in an animation to convey nonverbal communication.
- Implement a particle system in a 3D model.
- Create pose-to-pose animations for game assets.
- Animate 2D sprites to produce a particle system.

Goodheart-Willcox Publisher

iPi Soft, LLC

Gordana Sermek/Shutterstock.com

Name: _____

Date: _____

Class: _____

Bellwork

Day	Date	Activity	Response
1		Complete the anticipation guide and the K and W columns of the KWL chart for this chapter.	
2		Explain deceleration in terms of acceleration, velocity, displacement, and vector.	
3		Define *perception*.	
4		What translation has occurred if an object moves from coordinate position (0,5,0) to (0,5,10)?	
5		Explain the motion of an airplane caused by the rudder.	
6		What is an animation arc? Why is it important to video game animation?	
7		Explain conservation of energy and conservation of matter.	
8		Which property of animation allows a squished marshmallow to maintain conservation of matter? Why?	
9		What are the three key component areas used to categorize the principles of animation?	
10		List and explain two types of animation timing.	
11		What is an aura and how can it be used in game design?	

Day	Date	Activity	Response
12		How can a balloon help a beginning animator understand maintaining volume in animation?	
13		What is momentum?	
14		What is inertia and how is it demonstrated in animation?	
15		Describe how to apply solid drawing to digital animation.	
16		What are tweens?	
17		Describe how particle animation is created.	
18		How is hair created using particle animation?	
19		Describe the parent-child relationship for forward kinetics.	
20		Describe two ways motion-capture animation can be created.	
21		How is an explosion animation created?	
22		What is the purpose of chroma keying?	
23		Complete the L column of the KWL chart and the After Reading column of the anticipation guide with what you learned from this chapter.	
24		Speculate why animators would look at a sound waveform. What information and benefits from seeing the waveform could be obtained?	

Anticipation Guide

Directions

Before reading the chapter, read each statement in the table below. In the column titled Before Reading, write the letter *T* if you agree with the statement or *F* if you disagree with the statement. After reading the chapter, reread each statement in the table below. In the column titled After Reading, write the letter *T* if you agree with the statement or *F* if you disagree with the statement. Be prepared to justify your answers in a class discussion.

Before Reading	Statement	After Reading
	Vectors describe the direction of motion.	
	Kinetic energy is transformed into heat, light, sound, or other form of energy in a collision.	
	Straight-ahead action is done using keyframes and tweens.	
	Particle animation is used to create fire and hair in video games.	
	To create a lip sync animation, the artist must synchronize the facial movements with the spoken sounds.	

KWL Chart

Directions

Before reading the chapter, fill in what you already know about the topic in the K column and what you want to learn in the W column. After reading the chapter, review what you know and wanted to learn about the topic. Reflect on what you have studied and completed in this chapter. Fill in what you learned in the L column. Be prepared to justify your answers in a class discussion.

Topic: Animation		
K What you already *know*	**W** What you *want* to learn	**L** What you *learned*

Activity 11-1

Straight-Ahead Action

Objectives

Students will apply the principles of animation in a straight-ahead action. Students will use software to generate a frame-by-frame animation. Students will apply value to create depth and spatial relationship.

Situation

You have developed many great skills while working for the Really Cool Game Company. Having a spectrum of game-design skills makes you a valuable member of the team. To continue advancing your skills in game art, the company wants you to learn the basics of animation and integrate 2D animation into a video game. Your task is to complete straight-ahead action in a frame-by-frame animation for use in the pitch documents for a new video game.

How to Begin

1. Launch PowerPoint 2010.

2. Switch to a blank layout.

3. If the ruler is not displayed along the top and left side of the slide, right-click anywhere on the slide, and click **Ruler** in the shortcut menu.

4. Right-click on the slide, and click **Grid and Guides...** in the shortcut menu. In the dialog box that is displayed, check the **Display drawing guides on screen** check box, and close the dialog box.

5. Save the file as *LastName*_Squash-Stretch in your working folder.

Ball

The animation will consist of a ball and a shadow. As the frames progress, the ball will demonstrate the squash and stretch animation principle.

6. Draw an oval that is 2.5″ high by 2.5″ wide.

Oval

7. With the oval selected, click the dialog box launcher on the **Shape Styles** panel of the **Format** tab in the ribbon, as shown in **Figure 1**. The **Format Shape** dialog box is displayed. Keep this dialog box open for this lesson. Drag it around the screen as needed to keep it out of the way.

8. Click **Position** on the left side of the **Format Shape** dialog box.

9. Enter 0 in the **Horizontal:** and **Vertical:** text boxes. Also, click **Top Left Corner** in both **From:** drop-down lists.

10. Click **Fill** on the left side of the dialog box.

11. Create a radial gradient from the top-right corner using the settings shown in **Figure 2.**

12. Check the **Rotate with shape** check box.

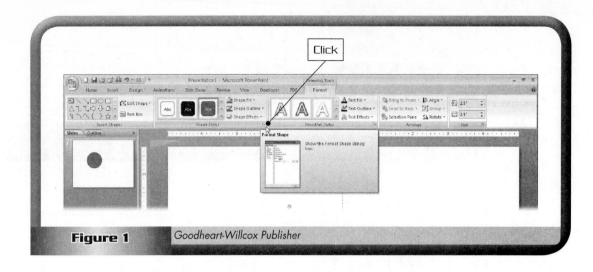

Click

Figure 1 *Goodheart-Willcox Publisher*

Stop	Position	Color
1	15%	R240, G240, B240
2	66%	R0, G0, B0
3	100%	R150, G150, B150

Figure 2 *Goodheart-Willcox Publisher*

13. Click **Size** on the left side of the dialog box. Enter −15 in the **Rotation:** text box. This positions the specular highlight of the ball to simulate a light source to the right and above the ball. This light location will produce a shadow below and to the left of the center of the ball.

14. Click **Line Color** on the left of the **Format Shape** dialog box, and click the **No line** radio button. Alternately, to create a more stylized ball, the line color could be set to black.

15. Add another oval that is 0.5″ high by 0.8″ wide.

Oval

16. Right-click on the oval, and click **Send to Back > Send to Back** in the shortcut menu. This will keep the shadow object behind the ball object as the animation is created.

17. Set the position of the shadow object as 0″ from horizontal and 7″ from vertical based on the top-left corner. This creates a shadow below the ball and to the left of the ball center, which is where the shadow should be based on the specular highlight on the ball.

18. Remove the line color from the shadow object.

19. Add a radial gradient from the center using the settings shown in **Figure 3.**

Stop	Position	Color
1	10%	R0, G0, B0
2	55%	R65, G65, B65
3	85%	R130, G130, B130

Figure 3 *Goodheart-Willcox Publisher*

Straight-Ahead Action

When animating straight-ahead action, you start at the beginning with the first frame, and create each additional frame one after the other until the animation is complete. The first frame of the animation is complete. Now you need to add the remaining frames in the animation.

20. Right-click on the thumbnail of the slide, click **Duplicate Slide** in the shortcut menu. This places an exact copy of the first slide as the second slide.

21. On slide 2, click and hold the horizontal guide, and drag it to the bottom edge of the ball. As you drag, the ruler position is displayed as help text. The bottom edge of the ball is 1.25.

22. Similarly, drag the vertical guide to the right-hand edge of the ball (2.50). The new positions of the guides will help position the ball on this animation frame.

23. Move the ball so it is centered at the intersection of the guides.

24. Drag the vertical guide to the left-hand edge of the ball (3.75).

25. Resize the shadow object to 0.6" × 1". As the ball moves closer to the surface, which is the bottom edge of the slide, the shadow will increase in size. This provides a spatial relationship between the ball and the surface on which the shadow appears.

26. Align the left-hand edge of the shadow object with the vertical guide, and the bottom edge of the shadow object with the bottom of the slide, as shown in **Figure 4.**

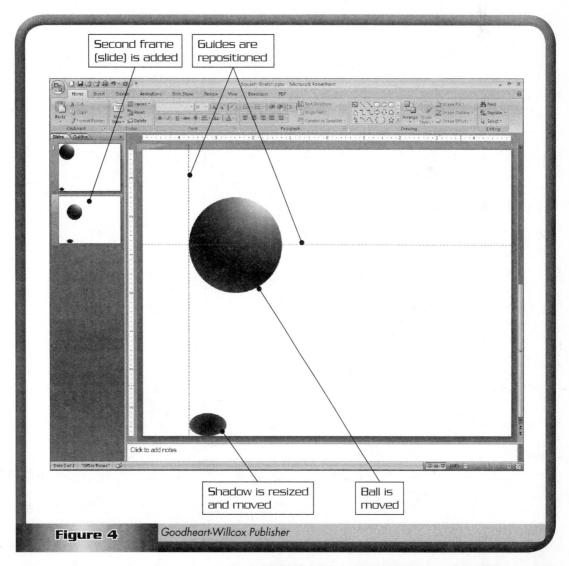

Figure 4   *Goodheart-Willcox Publisher*

Stretch Animation

As the ball moves downward, the animation principle of squash and stretch should be applied. Before the ball hits the surface, the squash and stretch will not be as pronounced as after it bounces off the surface. Refer to Figure 11-10 in the textbook.

27. Select the ball, and click **Size** on the left side of the **Format Shape** dialog box.

28. Uncheck the **Lock aspect ratio** check box.

29. Click the up arrow next to the **Height:** text box once. This changes the height setting to 2.6″.

30. Click the down arrow next to the **Width:** text box once to change the width to 2.4″. As the ball is morphed, any change in height should have an opposite change in width to maintain volume.

31. Duplicate slide 2.

32. On slide 3, reposition the guides below and to the right of the ball. The positions do not need to be exactly at the edges.

33. Move the ball to center it on the intersection of the guides.

34. Resize the ball object to 2.7″ × 2.3″ by clicking the up arrow on the **Height:** value up once and the down arrow on the **Width:** value down once.

35. Move the vertical guide to the left edge of the ball.

36. Resize the shadow object to 0.7″ × 1.2″ by clicking the up arrow on the **Height:** setting once and the up arrow on the **Width:** setting twice.

37. Align the left-hand edge of the shadow object with the vertical guide, and the bottom edge of the shadow object with the bottom of the slide.

38. Duplicate slide 3.

39. Using similar steps, create the fourth and fifth animation frames. Do not resize the ball object on slide 5. The ball will hang off the bottom edge on slide 5, as shown in **Figure 5.**

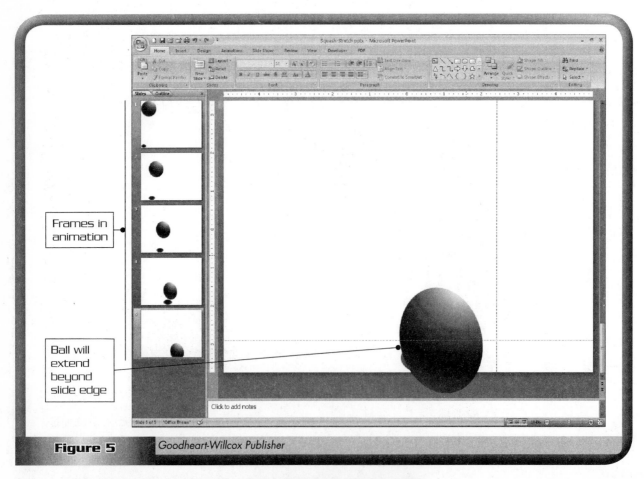

Frames in animation

Ball will extend beyond slide edge

Figure 5 *Goodheart-Willcox Publisher*

Squash Animation

The bottom edge of the slide is simulating the surface on which the shadow appears. At this point, a squash animation should begin as the ball bounces.

40. On slide 5, select the ball object.

41. Counting the number of clicks, click the down arrow next to the **Height:** text box until the bottom of the ball reaches the bottom edge of the slide. The setting should be 2.3″. Be sure to count the number of clicks.

42. Click the up arrow next to the **Width:** text box the number of times you counted in the previous step. The setting should be 2.7″. This maintains the volume of the object and creates a squashed ball.

43. Navigate to slide 1, and press the down arrow key to flip through the animation frames. Notice how the animation principle of squash and stretch has been applied and the spatial relationship of the shadow to the ball.

Follow-Through

The ball has hit the surface and begun to bounce. Now, follow-through needs to be created by bouncing the ball back up as it stretches out from the squash. Remember, the squash and stretch effect should be more pronounced after the bounce than before.

44. Duplicate slide 5.

45. Move the vertical guide to the right side of the ball. Leave the horizontal guide in its current location.

46. Change the size of the ball to 2.5″ × 2.5″.

47. Position the ball so its bottom is aligned with the bottom edge of the slide and its right-hand side is against the vertical guide. The idea is that the ball is springing back into shape after the squash, as shown in **Figure 6**. It is not being translated relative to its right-hand edge. This also provides some slow in and slow out at the point of the bounce.

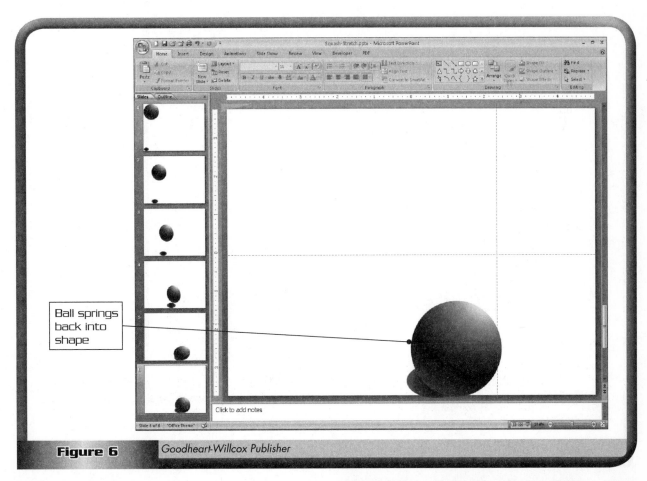

Ball springs back into shape

Figure 6   *Goodheart-Willcox Publisher*

Rebound

48. Duplicate slide 6.

49. Set the gridlines to touch the right-hand edge and top of the ball.

50. Center the ball at the intersection of the gridlines.

51. Increase the **Height:** setting by four clicks, and decrease the **Width:** setting by four clicks.

52. Change the **Rotation:** value to 35 degrees to apply the stretch in the direction of the bounce.

53. Click **Fill** on the left side of the dialog box, and uncheck the **Rotate with shape** check box. This is needed to move the specular highlight to match the direction of the light, as shown in **Figure 7.**

54. Resize the shadow object to 0.8″ × 1.5″.

55. Move the shadow object to the left-hand edge of the ball.

56. Duplicate slide 7.

57. Move the guides to the top and right-hand edges of the ball.

58. Center the ball at the intersection of the guides.

59. Decrease the **Height:** setting by one click, and increase the **Width:** setting by one click.

60. Move the shadow object to the left-hand edge of the ball.

61. Resize the shadow object to 0.7″ × 1.3″.

62. Add a blank slide as the ninth frame in the animation.

63. Click the slide 1 thumbnail, hold down the [Shift] key, and click the slide 9 thumbnail. This selects all slides in the presentation.

64. On the **Transitions** tab in the ribbon, check the **After:** check box on the **Timing** panel, and enter 00:00.1 in the text box. Also, uncheck the **On Mouse Click** check box.

65. Press the [F5] key to display the animation (slide show).

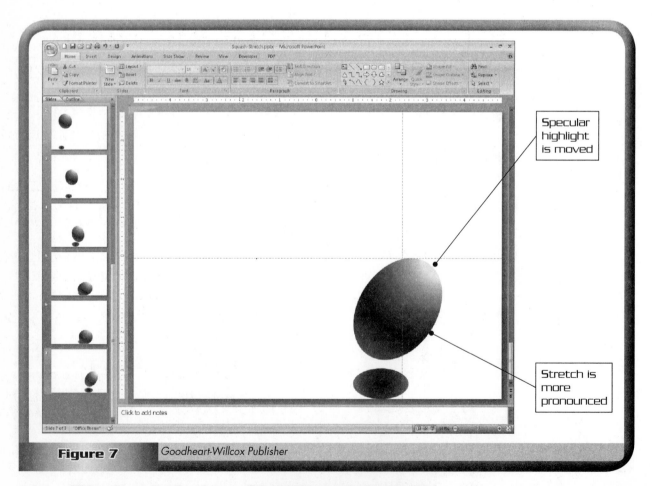

Specular highlight is moved

Stretch is more pronounced

Figure 7   *Goodheart-Willcox Publisher*

Name: _____

Skill Application

66. Start a new PowerPoint presentation, and change the layout to a blank slide.

67. Save the file as *LastName_*Bounce in your working folder.

68. Create a 1″ diameter simulated 3D ball using gradients of colors of your choice.

69. Create a background for the slide in a color that complements the color of the ball.

70. Create an animation where the ball drops straight down from the top of the screen and bounces at the bottom. Animate the ball bouncing four times, applying the animation principle of squash and stretch.

71. Add a shadow object, and animate it to reflect the position of the bouncing ball.

72. Set all slides to automatically advanced 0.10 seconds.

73. Click the **Set Up Slide Show** button on the **Set Up** panel in the **Slide Show** tab of the ribbon. In the **Set Up Show** dialog box that is displayed, check the **Loop continuously until Esc** check box, and close the dialog box.

74. Play the animation.

75. Save your work, and submit all files for grading.

Review Questions

1. Briefly describe how the guides were used to animate the action.

   _____

   _____

   _____

   _____

2. Describe what determines the position of the shadow object and why the vertical guide was positioned on the left-hand edge of the ball.

   _____

   _____

   _____

   _____

3. What was the purpose of the shadow object?

   _____

   _____

   _____

   _____

4. Why must an opposite change in the ball's width occur when the ball's height is changed?

   _____

   _____

   _____

   _____

5. On the last frame of the animation in which the ball is visible, its size is 2.8″ × 2.2″. If another frame is added after this frame, what would be the size of the ball?

   _____

Name: _____

Date: _____

Class: _____

Activity 11-2

Lip-Sync Animation

Objectives

Students will animate character lip movement to synchronize with spoken words using a standardized animation set. Students will record and edit voice and design a custom 2D character lip-sync animation. Students will create 2D keyframe poses for lip-sync animations.

Situation

The Really Cool Game Company wants your design team to create the lip-sync animations for a new handheld game. The game is for a very young audience. The dialogue in the game is between two characters and used to introduce new topics to the player. You have been assigned the task of creating the basic animation set and programming the animation. Additionally, you will need to record a vocal soundtrack and edit it as needed to produce the character dialogue.

A lip sync is a set of facial animations to match a standard set of sounds made by the character. A simple lip sync may be created in puppet style, where the mouth only opens and closes for each syllable of the word. A basic lip sync can be created from an animation set of about ten basic facial expressions. In many cases, this is sufficient to represent almost all the sounds in the English language. A basic lip sync allows for faster rendering than an advanced lip sync because fewer pixels change, which is important in low-power platforms such as handheld devices. It also allows for a faster build time because it is easier to create. An advanced lip sync may be created from an animation set containing over 100 different expressions.

How to Begin

1. Launch PowerPoint 2010, and open the *LastName*_Vector file created in Activity 9-2.
2. Save the file as *LastName*_Lip Sync in your working folder.
3. Delete all slides except for the first slide. There should be one slide left containing one of the characters.
4. Delete the name from the slide.
5. Delete the mouth object.
6. Duplicate slide 1.
7. Keep duplicating slides until there are a total of nine slides.

Lip Animation Set

Now, you need to create the basic lip animation set that will be used to make the character talk. A very basic animation set will be used for this character. It will consist of nine different facial expressions: resting; basic consonant; O; L; A; E and I; F and V; M, B, and P; and Q, R, U, and W. It can be helpful to stand in front of a mirror and watch your lips as you pronounce each one of these sounds, making note of how your lips form the sounds. The O sound is the first facial expression you will create, and it requires a big circle shape for the mouth.

Oval

Shape Fill ▾

Shape Outline ▾

Text Box

Moon

8. On slide 1, create an oval. Hold down the [Shift] key as you drag to create a circle. The circle should extend from just below the nose to just above the chin, as shown in **Figure 1.**

9. Fill the shape with black. Black is used to indicate the inside of the mouth.

10. Change the shape outline to a color appropriate for lips.

11. Change weight (thickness) of the outline to six points to give the lips some dimension.

12. Insert a text box in the upper-right corner of the slide. Enter O in the text box, and change the size to about 50 points.

13. Create a moon shape, rotate it 90 degrees, and change its dimensions to match the inner curvature of the circle. Fill the shape with white with no outline. This shape will be teeth.

14. Display the guides, if not already displayed, and move them to the middle of the character's mouth.

Consonant Pose

For this basic-lip sync animation set, a basic consonant pose will be used for most of the letters. The mouth shape should look like the character is pronouncing the letter T. Think about how your lips change shape from an O sound to the sound of a consonant. The corners of your mouth are wide, and your lips are open just a bit.

15. On slide 2, create a flowchart terminator shape centered on the guides. The height and width should be set to create a mouth that is consistent with the mouth on slide 1.

Flowchart: Terminator

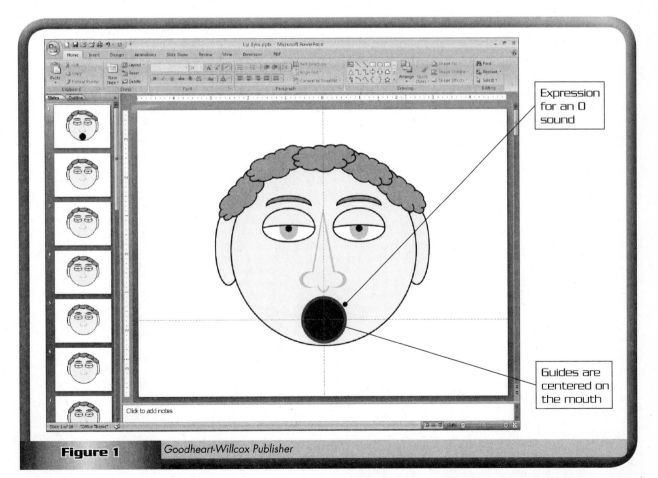

Figure 1 *Goodheart-Willcox Publisher*

Moon

Text Box

16. Format the shape with the colors and line thickness used on slide 1.

17. Create a moon shape, and format it to create upper teeth as on slide 1. There will be some black above the corners of the shape, as shown in **Figure 2.** This is okay for a basic animation.

18. Insert a text box in the upper-right corner of the slide. Enter Consonant in the text box, and change the size to about 50 points.

Resting Pose

19. Copy the terminator shape on slide 2, navigate to slide 3, and paste the shape.

20. Change the height of the shape so there is no space between the lips. It is okay if a thin line of black is visible.

Text Box

21. Insert a text box in the upper-right corner of the slide. Enter Rest in the text box, and change the size to about 50 points.

F and V Pose

Notice how your lips are formed when you pronounce the letter F. Your lips are basically closed with your top teeth overlapping your bottom lip. This expression is similar to the basic consonant expression created earlier.

22. Copy the terminator and moon shapes on slide 2, navigate to slide 4, and paste the shapes.

23. Adjust the height of the terminator shape until the lips are nearly closed, but leave some space for the teeth.

24. Move the terminator shape so it is centered on the guides.

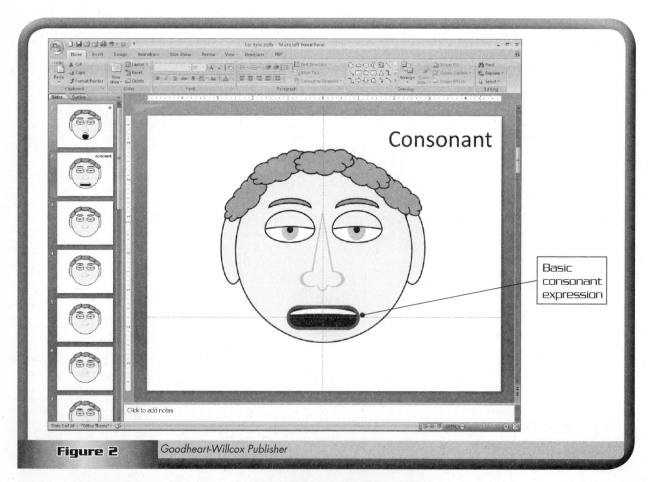

Figure 2   *Goodheart-Willcox Publisher*

25. Move the teeth, and adjust them to fit between the lips. The bottom of the teeth should touch the bottom lip, as shown in **Figure 3.**

26. Insert a text box in the upper-right corner of the slide. Enter F and V in the text box, and change the size to about 50 points.

E and I Pose

Notice how your lips are formed when you pronounce the letter E. The corners of your lips curl back and your mouth is midway open.

27. Copy the terminator and moon shapes on slide 2, navigate to slide 5, and paste the shapes.

28. Widen the mouth, and close it slightly.

29. Center the mouth on the guides.

30. Adjust the teeth to match the new size of the mouth.

31. Insert a text box in the upper-right corner of the slide. Enter I and E in the text box, and change the size to about 50 points.

A Pose

Notice how your lips are formed when you pronounce the letter A. Your mouth is midway open, the corners of your mouth are slightly in, and your tongue is forward in your mouth.

32. Copy the terminator and moon shapes on slide 2, navigate to slide 6, and paste the shapes.

33. Narrow the mouth slightly, and open it a bit farther.

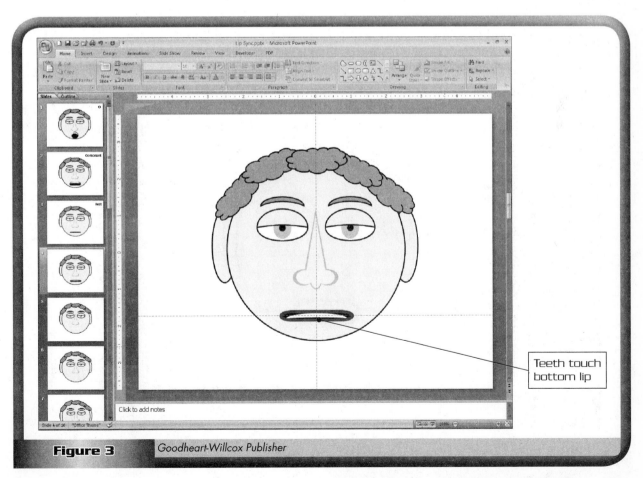

Teeth touch bottom lip

Figure 3   *Goodheart-Willcox Publisher*

34. Center the mouth on the guides.

35. Adjust the teeth to match the new size of the mouth.

Flowchart: Delay

36. Create a flowchart delay shape, and rotate it 90 degrees. Fill the shape with light red with no outline. This will be a tongue, as shown in **Figure 4.**

Text Box

37. Insert a text box in the upper-right corner of the slide. Enter A in the text box, and change the size to about 50 points.

L Pose

Notice how your lips are formed when you pronounce the letter L. Your mouth is midway open, and your tongue is touching the roof of your mouth. This is similar to the A facial expression, but with the tongue in a different position.

38. Copy the terminator, moon, and delay shapes on slide 6, navigate to slide 7, and paste the shapes.

39. Rotate the tongue 180 degrees.

40. Extend the tongue upward to touch the teeth.

Text Box

41. Insert a text box in the upper-right corner of the slide. Enter L in the text box, and change the size to about 50 points.

B, M, and P Pose

Notice how your lips are formed when you pronounce the letter M. Your lips touch each other and curl back into your mouth.

42. Copy the terminator shape on slide 2, navigate to slide 8, and paste the shape. This will be used as a reference, and then deleted.

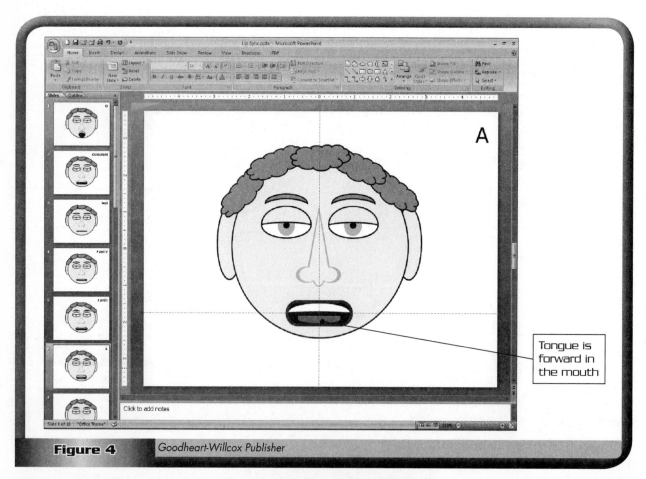

Figure 4   *Goodheart-Willcox Publisher*

Video Game Design Composition Software Design Guide

Heart

43. Create a heart shape. Fill it with the lip color with no outline.

44. Resize the heart so it is the same width as the mouth and about one-quarter as high.

45. Align the top of the heart shape with the horizontal guide. This will be the bottom lip.

46. Delete the terminator shape.

47. Copy the heart shape, flip it vertically, and align it to the horizontal guide, as shown in **Figure 5.** The lips should just touch or overlap slightly.

48. Create two ovals to complete the corners of the mouth.

49. Create an oval, fill it with black with no outline, and place it behind the lips.

50. Insert a text box in the upper-right corner of the slide. Enter B, M, and P in the text box, and change the size to about 50 points.

Text Box

Q, R, U, and W Pose

Notice how your lips are formed when you pronounce the letter R. Your lips curl forward in a small circle. This is similar to the facial expression for the O sound.

51. Copy the oval and moon shapes on slide 1, navigate to slide 9, and paste the shapes.

52. Reduce the size of the lips, but keep them in a circle.

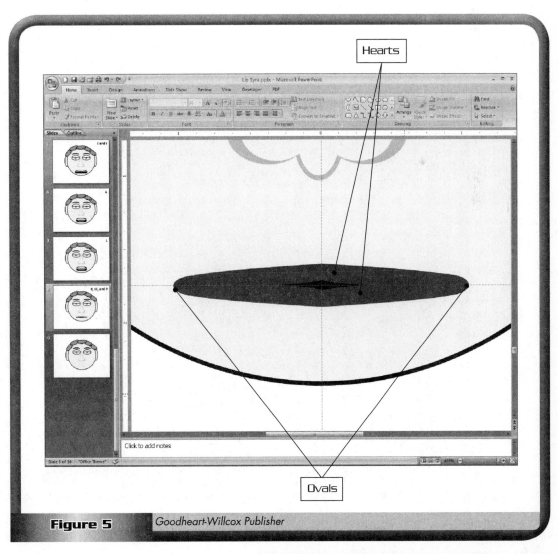

Figure 5 *Goodheart-Willcox Publisher*

53. Adjust the teeth to match the lips. They should have very little height, as teeth are barely visible in this facial expression.

Text Box

54. Insert a text box in the upper-right corner of the slide. Enter Q, R, U, and W in the text box, and change the size to about 50 points.

Exposure Sheet

The basic facial expressions are complete. The next step to create the *exposure sheet*, or *dope sheet*. An Exposure sheet shows the key poses and how long the pose will need to be viewed in the animation sequence. This sheet sets up the path of animation and the timing.

55. Hide the guides.

Slide Sorter

56. Click the **Slide Sorter** button on the **Presentation Views** panel of the **View** tab in the ribbon. This displays a view of all slides on one screen, which will function as the exposure sheet for this activity, as shown in **Figure 6**.

57. Starting with the upper-left slide, arrange the slides to have the character say *hello*. Drag and drop slides to arrange them, and copy and paste slides as needed. Refer to **Figure 7** for the order of slides.

58. Delete any unused slides.

59. Save the file as *LastName_* Lip Sync_Hello. Saving as a copy preserves an unaltered copy of the facial expressions.

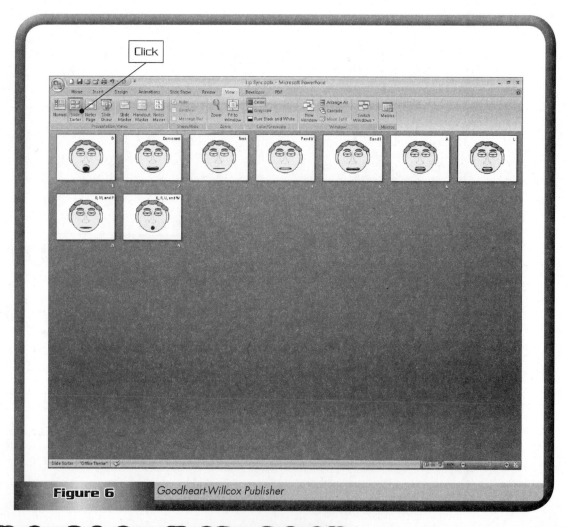

Figure 6   *Goodheart-Willcox Publisher*

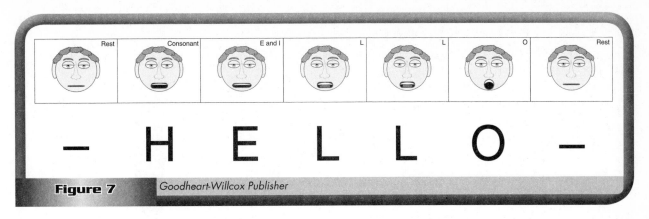

Figure 7 *Goodheart-Willcox Publisher*

Advancing Exposures

Each frame in the animation needs to be set to advance automatically. This is in preparation for the sound engineering that will add an audio track.

60. Select the first slide .

61. On the **Transitions** tab in the ribbon, check the **After:** check box on the **Timing** panel, and enter 00:00.1 in the text box. Also, uncheck the **On Mouse Click** check box.

62. Enter 00.1 in the **Duration** text box.

63. Click the **Apply to All** button to make all slides have the same settings.

64. Press the [F5] key on your keyboard to preview the animation timing. If needed, alter the **After:** setting to slow down or speed up the playback. You may need to alter this setting again after engineering the sound for the animation.

Sound Engineering

With the facial animation completed, it is time to record the soundtrack. In the normal production sequence, all dialogue is recorded before the animations are created. It is much easier to match the animation to the dialogue instead of the other way around. For this basic animation, however, it will be easy to make adjustments if needed.

65. Make sure the microphone is installed, and launch Audacity.

66. Record yourself speaking *hello.*

67. Trim the waveform to remove the head and tail as needed.

68. Export a WAV file named Hello to your working folder.

69. Close Audacity.

Importing Sound

70. In PowerPoint, double-click the thumbnail for slide 1 to display the slide in the normal view.

71. Click the **Audio** button on the media panel of the **Insert** tab in the ribbon.

72. Browse to your working folder, and select the Hello.wav file.

73. If a dialog box appears asking how you want the sound to start in the slide show, click the **Automatically** button.

74. If the dialog box does not appear, select the speaker icon, and click the **Animations** tab in the ribbon. In the **Timing** panel, click the **Start:** drop-down menu, and click **With Previous** in the menu.

75. Drag the speaker icon off the slide so it will not show during the animation, as shown in **Figure 8.**

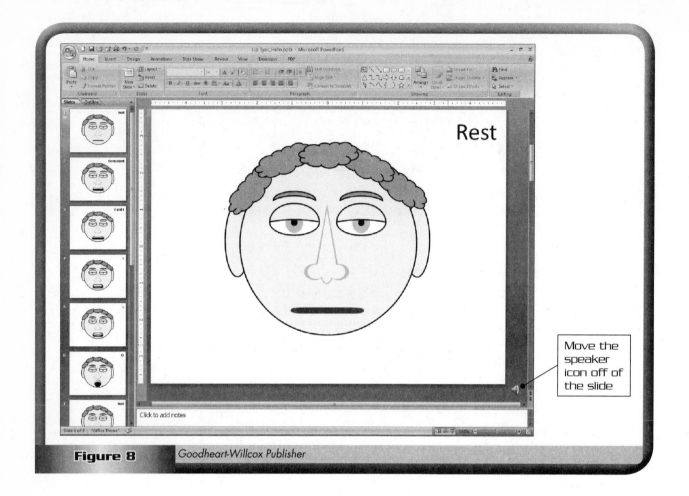

Figure 8   *Goodheart-Willcox Publisher*

 76. Click the **Animation Pane** button on the **Advanced Animation** panel of the animations tab in the ribbon.

77. Click the drop-down arrow next to Hello.wav in the **Animation Pane**, and click **Effect Options…** in the menu. The **Play Audio** dialog box is displayed.

78. In the **Stop playing** area of the **Effect** tab, click the **After:** radio button, and enter 999 in text box. This is to prevent the sound from stopping after the first slide or the slide not advancing until after the sound has finished playing. The specific number is not important as long as it is high enough to prevent an error.

79. Close the **Play Audio** dialog box.

80. Press the [F5] key to play the lip-sync animation.

Exposure Timing

Now that the lip-sync animation plays, the duration of each key pose needs to be tuned to match how long each letter is spoken.

81. On each individual frame, alter the **After:** setting until the lip movement matches the sound.

82. Add ten rest frames at the end of the animation.

83. Delete the text frames from all frames.

84. Save your work, and submit all files for grading.

Review Questions

1. Why does a basic lip sync render faster than an advanced lip sync?

   _____

   _____

2. How can a single primitive (shape) in PowerPoint be used as a mouth and lips?

   _____

   _____

   _____

   _____

3. Describe the difference between the facial expressions for O and R.

   _____

   _____

   _____

   _____

4. Describe what PowerPoint feature was used as the exposure sheet.

   _____

   _____

   _____

   _____

5. What PowerPoint setting is altered to adjust the timing of the animation to match the audio track?

   _____

   _____

Activity 11-3

Lip-Sync Enhancement

Objectives

Students will create a 2D lip-sync animation. Students will enhance animation tweens by moving facial components for realistic effect. Students will synthesize captioning and read-along timing.

Situation

The Really Cool Game Company has reviewed your first lip-sync animation. It liked the character and wants to see an advanced lip-sync animation. Your task is to create a lip-sync animation for a complete statement including captioning.

How to Begin

1. In PowerPoint, open the original *LastName_* Lip Sync file, and save it as *LastName_* Lip Sync_Statement in your working folder.
2. Launch Audacity.
3. Record this statement: Hello, my name is *YourName*.
4. Trim the waveform to remove the head and tail as needed.
5. Export the sound as a WAV file named **Statement**.

Statement Lip Sync

In the previous activity, the timing of the lip-sync animation was achieved by adjusting the amount of time each slide was displayed. Another way to adjust the timing of the lip-sync animation is increasing the number of frames for a given facial expression. In this method, the expression frames added to form the words are the keyframes. Any frames added to adjust the timing are the tweens, and the process of adding those frames is tweening.

6. In PowerPoint, display the slide sorter.
7. Copy and paste the key facial expressions as needed for the recorded statement. Use the I facial expression for Y. Include a rest frame between each word, as well as at the beginning and end.
8. Set the slides to advance automatically with no time after each frame.

9. Insert the Statement.wav audio track into the animation.
10. Add copies of expression slides where needed to adjust the timing of the animation to match the audio track.

Facial Animation

Once the animation is synchronized to the audio track, other facial movements can be added to help improve the realism of the animations. For example, when a person speaks, he or she usually maintains eye contact with the audience. To achieve this, the eyes make slight adjustments, called *eye hop*. Eye hop can also be used for a moving hold. Additionally, an *expressive animation* allows the audience to receive nonverbal information from the character. For example, by moving or tilting the eyebrows, information can be sent to the audience.

11. At the beginning of each word, move the pupils and irises upward, as shown in **Figure 1.** Make the movement occur over two frames.

12. On a third fame, move the pupils and irises halfway back to their original positions. This creates three frames of animation for the eye hop.

13. For the word hello, animate the eyebrows to rise up and back down as the word starts.

14. For your name, animate the eyebrows to tilt inward and back to normal as your name starts.

Caption and Read-Along Timing

The game designers want to have read-along captions included for all lip-sync animations. Captions allow the audience, which is very young, to see words as they are spoken. This will help the cognitive development of the audience.

Rectangular Callout

15. On the frame that begins the word hello, add a rectangular callout shape.

16. Move the callout to the top-left corner of the slide.

17. Drag the diamond at the end of the callout tail to the corner of the character's mouth, as shown in **Figure 2.**

18. With the callout selected, and enter Hello, my name is *YourName*. The text appears in the middle of the rectangular box.

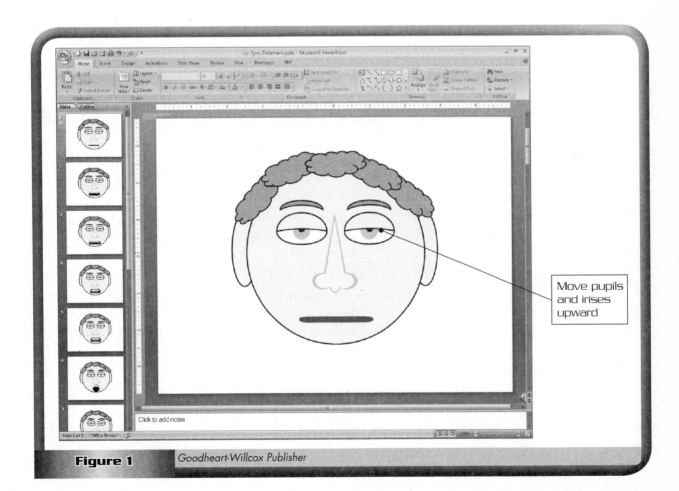

Figure 1 *Goodheart-Willcox Publisher*

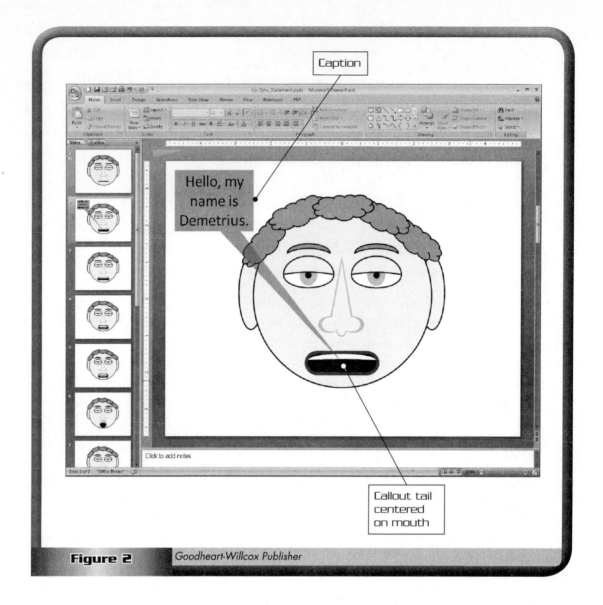

Figure 2   *Goodheart-Willcox Publisher*

19. Change the font size so the words are large enough to read easily, and select a font color of your choice.

20. Set the fill and outline colors to your choice, but set the fill color to 50 percent transparent. The transparency will allow the caption to be visible without obscuring the character.

21. Copy the callout, and paste it on every frame in the animation set.

22. Change the font color of the words to match the audio track as the animation progresses. For example, on slides for which the word hello is played on the audio track, change the font color of the word hello in the caption. You can either change the color by word or by letter.

23. Test the animation, and debug as needed.

24. Save your work, and submit it for grading.

Review Questions

1. Why is eye hop important to an animation?

   _____

   _____

   _____

   _____

2. What type of information is provided to the audience by expressive animation?

   _____

   _____

   _____

   _____

3. Why would a character's eyebrows move upward when saying hello?

   _____

   _____

   _____

   _____

4. Briefly describe how captions were added to this lip-sync animation in PowerPoint.

   _____

   _____

   _____

   _____

5. How is the caption timed to the animation and audio track?

   _____

   _____

   _____

   _____

Name: _____

Date: _____

Class: _____

Activity 11-4

Exposure Sheets

Objectives

Students will synthesize emotional expressions in a 2D animation. Students will manipulate the eyes and other facial landmarks to convey nonverbal communication.

Situation

The Really Cool Game Company's art director has commented on the lip-sync animations you created. Although the lip movement and sound match well, the character lacks realistic emotion. The art director wants you to complete an emotionally expressive character for the game in development. The character will be a simple block-type model that can be used to demonstrate facial landmarks. *Facial landmarks* are reference points on the face. These landmarks are typically around the eyes, nose, mouth, and ears. The facial movements used for speech and expressions change the distance between these landmarks. Before design work will be done on the in-game characters, you need to produce a mock-up exposure sheet based on the block-type character and submit it for approval.

How to Begin

1. Launch PowerPoint 2010.

2. Switch to a blank presentation.

3. Insert various shapes to construct the basic character shown in **Figure 1.** Make the overall size 7″ × 7″. You may alter the design to suit your preferences. This is a normal or nonexpressive state for the character.

4. Insert a text box at the top of the slide, and enter Normal.

5. Save the file as *LastName*_Expression Sheet in your working folder.

Eyelid and Mouth Landmarks

This simple character will not have many facial landmarks. Only a few landmarks can still effectively show emotion. In this example, the eyelids, eyebrows, pupils, and mouth will be used to show the range of expression animations.

6. Duplicate the first slide twice so there are three slides in total.

7. On slide 2, change the text to Happy.

8. Replace the mouth shape with a moon shape. This simulates the corner landmarks on the mouth moving up, along with the middle landmarks on the mouth moving down.

9. Move the top eyelid rectangle down just a bit, and the bottom eyelid rectangle up a bit more to partially cover the pupils. When a character smiles, the eyelids close a bit, and the bottom eyelid landmarks move more than the top eyelid landmarks.

10. On slide 3, change the text to Sleepy.

11. Move the bottom eyelid rectangle up a bit, and move the top eyelid rectangle down so it covers the top half of the pupil.

Face-colored rectangles function as eyelids

Figure 1   *Goodheart-Willcox Publisher*

12. Make the mouth almost completely closed.

13. Select the top eyelid rectangle, and use the up and down arrow keys to move the eyelid. You can see how changing the facial landmarks for just the top eyelid can make the character wake up and fall asleep.

Pupil Landmark

14. Duplicate slide 3.

15. On slide 4, change the text to Awake.

16. Move pupils down so they are between the top and bottom eyelids. Notice how a simple shift in the pupil landmark creates a completely different expression.

17. Duplicate slide 4.

18. On slide 5, change the text to Sad.

19. Move the pupils down so they are half covered by the bottom eyelid.

20. Duplicate slide 5.

21. On slide 6, change the text to Shy.

22. Move the pupils so they are between the top and bottom eyelids and to the right, as shown in **Figure 2.**

23. Duplicate slide 6.

24. On slide 7, change the text to Embarrassed.

25. Move the pupils to the left.

26. Duplicate slide 7.

27. On slide 8, change the text to Guilty.

28. Move upper eyelid open a bit more, move the pupils to the upper-left corner of the eyes, and open the mouth wider.

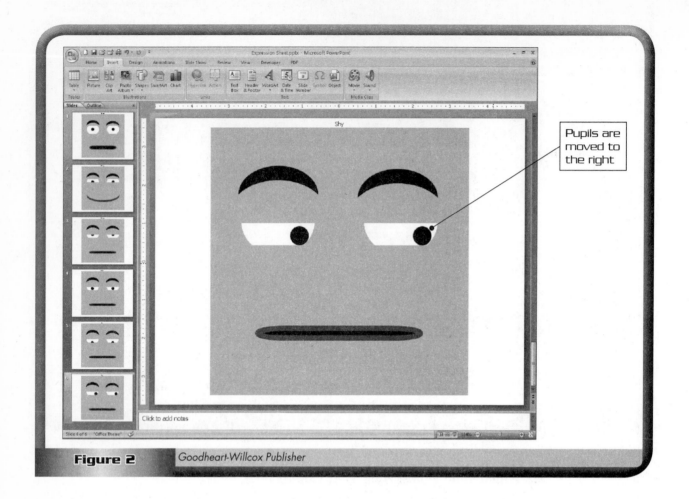

Figure 2   *Goodheart-Willcox Publisher*

Eyebrow Landmarks

Moving the eyebrows up and down and changing their angle will also produce different emotional expressions. To make a face more menacing or angry, the eyebrows typically slant down. To show happiness or surprise, the eyebrows typically slant up. During excitement, the eyebrows often lift.

29. Duplicate slide 8.

30. On slide 9, change the text to Excited.

31. Raise the eyebrows to near the top of the character's head. Also, rotate each eyebrow outward slightly.

32. Open the eyes wider, and move the pupils to the center of the eyes.

33. Duplicate slide 9.

34. On slide 10, change the text to Upset.

35. Angle the eyebrows down toward the center of the face. Also, move the eyebrows downward closer to the eyes.

36. In PowerPoint, display the slide sorter. This view functions as the expression sheet for this activity.

37. Make note of any expressions that are too similar to other expressions, and modify the expressions as needed.

Slide Sorter

Combining Landmarks

To this point, the facial expressions have been created for the most part by moving one landmark. By moving several landmarks for each emotional expression, almost any needed facial expression can be created.

38. Using the specifications given in **Figure 3,** create additional expressions by changing the appropriate landmarks.

39. Save your work, and submit it for grading.

Review Questions

1. How many landmarks were used in this activity, and what are they?

   _____

   _____

2. What landmarks were moved to change the sad expression into the shy expression.

   _____

   _____

3. Describe how eyebrow landmarks can be used to create a menacing expression.

   _____

   _____

   _____

   _____

4. How can the expression sheet, which in this activity is the slide sorter view, be used to identify expressions that need to be modified?

   _____

   _____

   _____

   _____

   _____

5. Speculate why moving several landmarks can allow for almost any needed facial expression.

   _____

   _____

   _____

   _____

   _____

Slide #	Expression	Top Eyelid	Bottom Eyelid	Pupil	Eyebrow	Mouth
11	Anger	1/4 down	1/4 up	Center	Tilt down	Flat
12	Surprise	Open	Open	Enlarge	Tilt up	Open full
13	Innocence	Open	Open	Top, right	Tilt up slightly	Small O like whistling
14	Sneaky	Almost closed	Almost closed	Center, left	Flat	Flat
15	Yelling	Almost closed	Almost closed	Center, down	Tilt down	Open full

Figure 2   *Goodheart-Willcox Publisher*

Activity 11-5

3D Particle Animation

Objectives

Students will implement a particle system in a 3D model. Students will create a realistic fire animation based on a particle system.

Situation

The Really Cool Game Company's creative director has contacted the lead artist about the 3D candle you created in Activity 10-4. The artist was impressed with how quickly you were able to create quality game art. The creative director feels it is time to increase your experience with game animation using advanced 3D tools. Your task is to modify the candle from Activity 10-4 with a particle system to create a realistic flame.

How to Begin

1. Launch Blender.
2. Open the *LastName*_Candle Rendering file saved in Activity 10-5. This is the file that contains the candle, table, and background.
3. Save the file as *LastName*_Candle Flame in your working folder.

Emitter and Material

A particle system requires an emitter to generate the particles. The *emitter* is simply an object from which the particles are created. The particles will create the flame.

4. Select the Central Glow object.
5. Press the [Shift][S] hot key combination, and click **Cursor to Selected** in the shortcut menu to move the 3D cursor to the center of the selected object.
6. Delete the Central Glow object.
7. Add a circle object, and name it Flame Emitter. In Blender, any object can be used as an emitter for a particle system.
8. Scale the Flame Emitter object to about 50 percent on all axes.
9. Click the **Material** button in the **Properties** panel.
10. Add a new material, and name it Flame Color.

Material

11. Change the material type to a halo.
12. In the **Halo** area, enter 0.25 in the **Alpha:** text box.
13. Click the color swatch, and change the color to a medium yellow.
14. Set the size to 0.5.
15. Set the hardness to 40.
16. Enter 1 in the **Add:** text box.
17. Click the **Texture** button.

Texture

18. Add a new texture, and name it Flame Marble.
19. Set the type to marble, as shown in **Figure 1**.

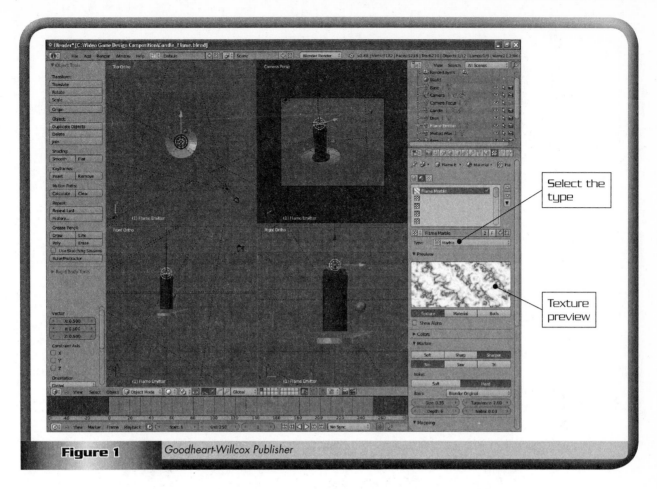

Select the type

Texture preview

| Figure 1 | Goodheart-Willcox Publisher |

20. Click the **Sharper** and **Hard** buttons to refine the pattern. Notice how the preview changes.

21. Enter 0.35 in the **Size:** text box.

22. Enter 6 in the **Depth:** text box.

23. Enter 7.6 in the **Turbulence:** text box.

24. In the **Mapping** area, enter 0.3 in the **Y Size:** text box and 0.2 in the **Z Size:** text box. These settings determine how the texture is positioned on the object.

25. In the **Influence** area, click the color swatch, and set the color to a dark orange.

26. Render the scene.

Flame Particles

There is not much of a flame at this point. So far, you have created an object not that different from the Central Glow object created in Activity 10-4. This object serves as the emitter from which particles will be generated, but it will also provide the material to the particles. Now, you will add a particle system to create the flame and give it some movement. There are many settings for a particle system: how many particles are emitted and over what time, particle size, randomness, and the forces that drive the particles. The particle system is automatically linked to the animation timeline.

27. In the **Timeline** panel at the bottom of the screen, enter 100 in the **End:** text box, as shown in **Figure 2.** Since the start time is one by default, this sets the total number of frames in the animation.

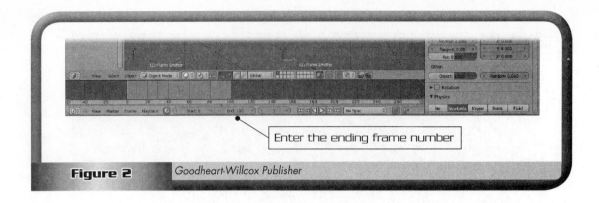

Enter the ending frame number

Figure 2   *Goodheart-Willcox Publisher*

Particles

28. With the Flame Emitter object selected, click on the **Particles** button in the **Properties** panel.

29. Add a new particle system, and name it Candle Flame.

30. Enter 300 in the **Number** text box. This is the "amount" of particles.

31. Enter –300 in the **Start:** text box. This is the frame on which particles will begin to be generated. By setting the starting frame to before the first frame of the animation, the particles will be moving on the first frame.

Play Animation

32. Click the **Play Animation** button on the **Timeline** panel to see the particles in the viewport. The particles are emitted from the object and fall straight back down due to the gravity setting, as shown in **Figure 3.**

Particles fall downward

Figure 3   *Goodheart-Willcox Publisher*

Jump to First Frame

33. Stop the animation by clicking the pause button, and return to frame 1 by clicking the **Jump to First Frame** button.

34. In the **Properties** panel, enter 100 in the **End:** text box. This is the frame on which the emitter stops generating particles.

35. Enter 25 in the **Lifetime:** text box. This means each particle will disappear after 25 frames. Adjusting this value will alter the height of the flame.

36. In the **Velocity** area, enter 0.105 in the **Random:** text box. This will cause some random particles to be emitted at a different speed than others.

37. In the **Field Weights** area, enter –0.1 in the **Gravity** text box. The negative value allows the particles to go upward instead of downward. Adjusting this value will also affect the flame height.

Play Animation

38. Play the animation, and notice the difference in how the particles move.

39. Stop the playback, and return to frame 1.

Jump to First Frame

40. In the **Render** area of the **Properties** panel, uncheck the **Emitter** check box. If this is checked, the object used as the emitter will be rendered. In some cases, this may be desired.

41. Render an image of the first frame. Notice how the particles have created a realistic flame, as shown in **Figure 4.**

Flame Animation

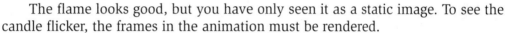

Render

The flame looks good, but you have only seen it as a static image. To see the candle flicker, the frames in the animation must be rendered.

42. Click the **Render** button in the **Properties** panel.

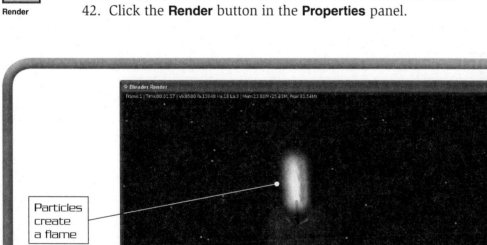

Particles create a flame

| **Figure 4** | *Goodheart-Willcox Publisher* |

43. Set the resolution to 640 × 480 pixels at 100%.

44. In the **Output** area, set the file type to **AVI JPEG**.

45. Click on the file browser button to the right of the output path. Blender's file-saving interface is displayed.

46. Navigate to your working folder, and name the file Candle Burning.

47. Click the **Accept** button to close the file-saving interface.

48. In the **Properties** panel, click the **Animation** button in the **Render** area. The animation begins rendering. It may take a few minutes for all frames to render.

49. Using Windows Explorer, navigate to your working folder, and double-click on the AVI file to play the video.

50. Save the Blender file, and submit all files for grading.

Review Questions

1. What is an emitter in Blender?

2. From where is the material for particles obtained?

3. How do you ensure that particles exist on the first frame of the animation?

4. How can the height of the candle flame be adjusted? Describe two methods.

5. What must be done to see the candle flicker?

Activity 11-6

Animation Integration

Objectives

Students will animate 2D game objects for use in a playable video game. Students will create pose-to-pose animations for game assets. Students will create straight-ahead action for game assets.

Situation

The Really Cool Game Company has received great feedback from the prototype *Frog Crossing* game. The players liked the game, but felt like there was nothing different from other versions of this game. To differentiate the game from other copies, the creative director wants to try a level that has the frog swimming through the obstacles to get from one side to the other. This would provide different gameplay and immersion from other *Frogger* clones. Your task is to create the animation for this gameplay.

How to Begin

1. Launch PowerPoint, and open the *LastName_*Frog Art file created in Chapter 9.
2. Save the file as *LastName_*Frog Animation in your working folder.
3. Ungroup both the frog and the shadow frog (the black frog). It should be completely ungrouped, with any subgroups also ungrouped.
4. Drag a selection box around all parts of the body, including the eyes, spots, and shadow.
5. Select and group all parts of one front leg. Repeat this for the other front leg and then each back leg.
6. Bring the body to the front of the object stack. There will be a shadow line around the body, which will help provide depth to the animated character, as shown in **Figure 1.**
7. Duplicate slide 1.

Articulation

With the front and back legs of the frog as separate groups, the frog can be articulated to make an animation. This will be straight-ahead action because each frame is created in order instead of by keyframing.

8. On slide 2, select the body group, and press the down arrow key once. This moves the body group closer to the center of the slide.
9. Select the right-hand front leg group, and rotate it about 30 degrees to the left. This brings the fingers near the top edge of the slide.
10. Move the leg toward the body as needed to reattach it to the body.
11. Adjust the left-hand front leg group using the same techniques.

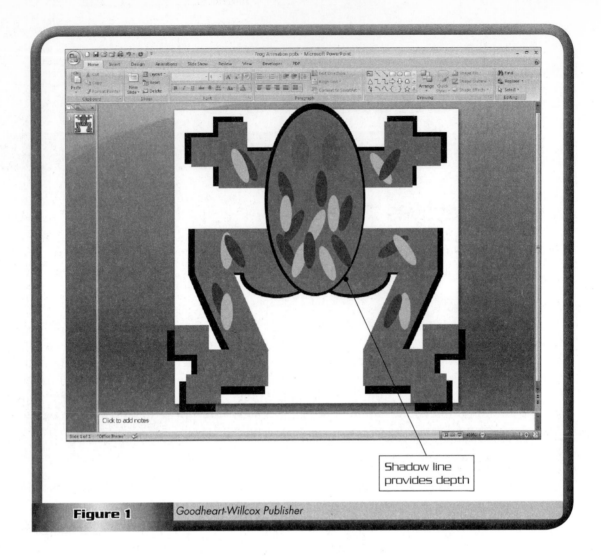

Shadow line provides depth

Figure 1   *Goodheart-Willcox Publisher*

12. Select the right-hand back leg group, and rotate it about 10 degrees to the right.

13. Move the leg toward the body as needed to reattach it to the body.

14. Adjust the left-hand back leg using the same technique.

15. Duplicate slide 2.

16. On slide 3, select the body group, and press the down arrow key once.

17. Rotate the front legs an additional 10 degrees, and move the legs as needed to reattach them to the body, as shown in **Figure 2**. Do not adjust the back legs.

Finishing Animation

You have created three animation frames. These frames are one-half of a single swimming stroke for the frog. From here, it is a simple process to complete the animation.

18. Right-click on the slide 2 mini slide, and click **Copy** in the shortcut menu.

19. Right-click below the slide 3 mini slide, and click **Paste** in the shortcut menu.

20. Similarly, copy slide 1, and paste it as slide 5.

21. Use the up and down arrow keys to scroll through the animation.

22. Refine any movements that are too sharp between frames.

23. On each slide, group all of the frog parts and the background object.

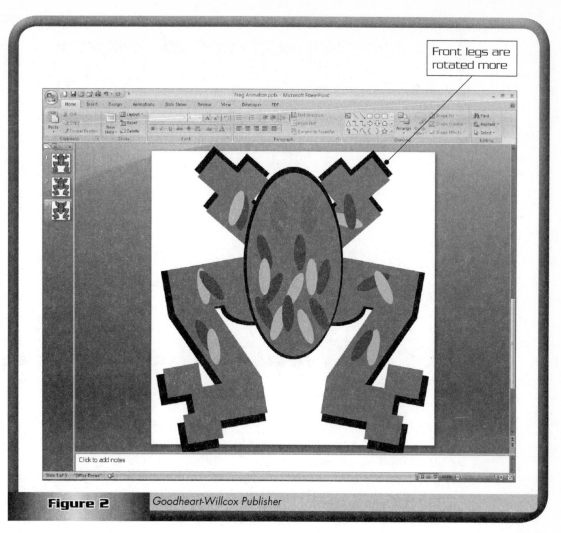

Front legs are rotated more

Figure 2   Goodheart-Willcox Publisher

Integrating into the Game

So far, the animation has articulation, but there is no translation. It is as if the frog is swimming in place. The translation will occur in the game. The same animation will be used in the game for both jumping on land and swimming in the water.

24. Launch MMF2, and open the Frog Crossing w Art game from Chapter 9.

25. Save the file as *Lastname_*Frog Crossing w Swimmer in your working folder.

Storyboard Editor

26. Display the storyboard editor, copy Level 1, and paste it at the bottom, as shown in **Figure 3.**

27. Rename the new level as Swimming Level.

28. Display in the frame editor for the Swimming Level.

Frame Editor

29. Right-click on the Avatar object, and click **Clone Object** in the shortcut menu.

30. In the **Clone Object** dialog box, enter 2 in the **Rows** text box and 1 in the **Columns** text box, and click the **OK** button.

31. Rename the clone Avatar_Swimmer.

32. Move the original Avatar object outside the scope. This object and its programming will be implemented later.

33. Move the Avatar_Swimmer object to position (288,448). This is where the original Avatar object was located.

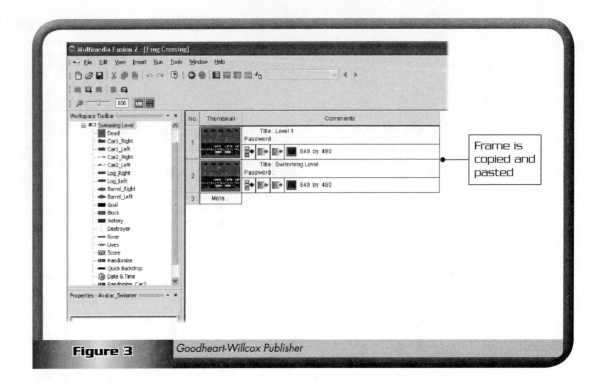

Goodheart-Willcox Publisher

34. Open the Avatar_Swimmer object in the image editor.

35. Select the Up animation for the Stopped animation set. You should see the single animation frame for the frog in this animation.

Clear

36. Clear the image.

37. In PowerPoint, copy everything on slide 1, return to the image editor in MMF2, and paste the image. When prompted, resize the canvas.

Paste

38. If needed, set the transparency color to the background color of the image, but this should already be set since the same background color was used in PowerPoint.

Transparency

39. Right-click on Frame 1 in the **Frames** tab, click **Copy** in the shortcut menu, right-click again, and click **Paste** in the shortcut menu. This adds the copy as Frame 2.

40. Select Frame 2, clear the image, and paste the image from slide 2 in PowerPoint.

41. Similarly, paste images from PowerPoint to create Frame 3, Frame 4, and Frame 5.

42. Click the **Play** button to see the animation. The preview plays very quickly.

43. Click the **Direction Options** tab in the image editor, as shown in **Figure 4**.

44. Change the **Speed:** setting to 20. This controls the frame rate, or how quickly the frames advance.

45. Check the **Loop** check box. This specifies that the animation will play continuously.

46. Click the **Play** button to see the animation repeat continuously. You may notice the frog seems to step to one side while jumping. This is an issue with the hotspot.

47. Click to the **Frames** tab, and select Frame 1.

View Hot Spot

48. Click the **View Hot Spot** button, and move the hotspot to the center of the frame.

49. Similarly, move the hotspot on each animation frame.

50. Play the animation. Fix any frames that still have the frog misaligned by refining the hotspot location.

51. Select all five frames of the animation, and copy them.

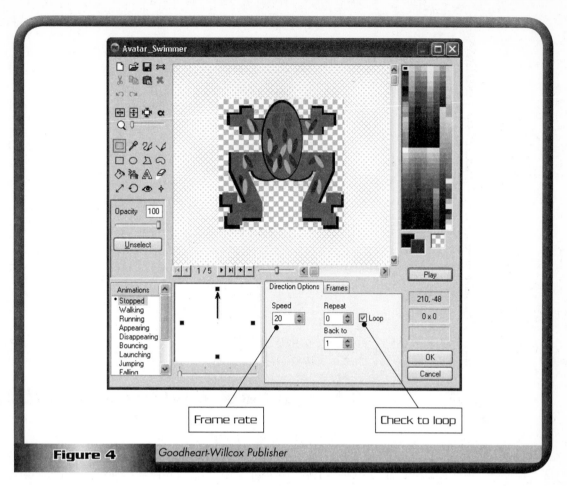

Figure 4 *Goodheart-Willcox Publisher*

52. Select the Right animation, and paste the copied frames.
53. Delete the original frame.
54. Rotate all frames 90 degrees to the right.
55. Change the frame rate to 20 and loop the animation.
56. Similarly, change the Down and Left animations.
57. Close the image editor.
58. Change the size property of the avatar to its original size of 32 × 32.
59. Move the avatar to its original position. Since the hotspot is changed, the original coordinates are no longer accurate.

Swimming Gameplay

The frog animation is always jumping. This does not match the current gameplay. The static image of the frog is best for jumping from one place to another. This animation best matches the swimming action desired, but a frog would not swim across a road. The road needs to be changed to water.

60. Open the backdrop object (road) in the image editor.
61. Fill the entire image with blue to simulate water, and close the image editor.

Fill tool

62. Select the Avatar_Swimmer object, and click the **Movement** tab in the **Properties** window.
63. Change the **Movement Type:** property to **Eight Direction**, as shown in **Figure 5.**
64. Change the **Speed:** property to **25.** Since the frog is in water, it will move slower.

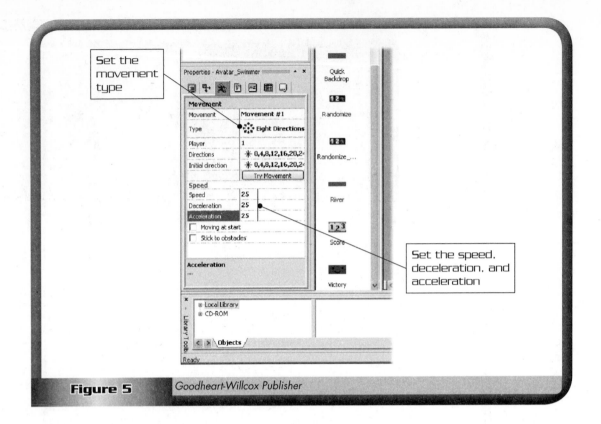

Set the movement type

Set the speed, deceleration, and acceleration

65. Change the **Deceleration:** property to 25. It will take longer to stop in water.

66. Change the **Acceleration:** property to 25. It will take longer to get started in water.

67. Uncheck the **Moving at start** check box.

68. Click the **Try Movement** button in the **Movement** tab. Try bumping into the edges to see how the acceleration and deceleration settings affect the movement. Also try moving diagonally. Close the window when done testing.

Updating the Destroyed Animation

The animation for when the avatar is destroyed needs to be recreated on the new object, but it needs to be changed to reflect the new gameplay. In the new animation, the frog will spin and sink under the water. This animation will be a pose-to-pose animation since keyframes will be used.

69. Display the Avatar_Swimmer object in the image editor.

70. Copy Frame 1 in the Up animation for the Stopped animation set.

71. Display the Disappearing animation set, and paste the copied frame. Frame 1 will be first and second keyframes for this animation.

72. Right-click on Frame 1, and click **Rotation** in the shortcut menu.

73. In the **Make One-Turn Rotation** dialog box, enter 8 in the **Number of frames in the turn:** text box, as shown in **Figure 6.** This tells the MMF2 to create six tweens between the first and second keyframes.

74. Click the **Clockwise** radio button. This is important for realism because in the northern hemisphere water spins clockwise as it goes down the drain.

75. Click the **OK** button to close the window and create the tweens.

76. Click the **Direction Options** tab, and check the **Loop** check box.

77. Click the **Play** button to preview the animation. Notice that the frog rotates around the hotspot, so the rotation appears to be around the tip of the frog's nose.

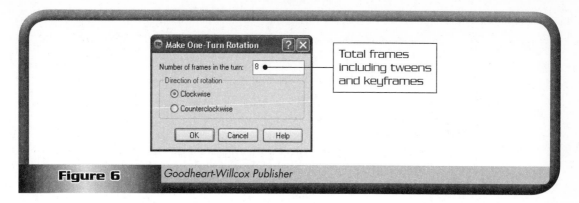

Figure 6   *Goodheart-Willcox Publisher*

View Hot Spot

78. On each frame of the Disappearing animation, move the hotspot to the center of the frame.

79. Preview the animation. Notice how the frog now spins about the center of its body, which is more appropriate.

80. On the **Direction Options** tab, uncheck the **Loop** check box. This animation will only play once.

81. On the **Frames** tab, right-click on Frame 8 in the Disappearing animation, and click **Zoom** in the shortcut menu. This function allows an animation to be created that enlarges or reduces the frames using keyframes. The Frame 8 is the second keyframe in the animation, but the first keyframe for the second part of the animation.

82. In the **Insert Resized Frames** dialog box, enter 0 in the **Final Width** and **Final Height** text boxes, as shown in **Figure 7.** This will create a keyframe with the image reduced to zero. Note: if you are having trouble entering 0 in both text boxes, try unchecking the **Proportional** check box.

83. Enter 8 in the **Number of frames:** text box. This will add a third, ending keyframe to the animation. The final keyframe will have no image, and there will be six tweens between the second keyframe and the final keyframe, each with a gradually reduced image.

84. Click the **OK** button to create the tweens. There should be a total of 16 frames, including the spinning frames.

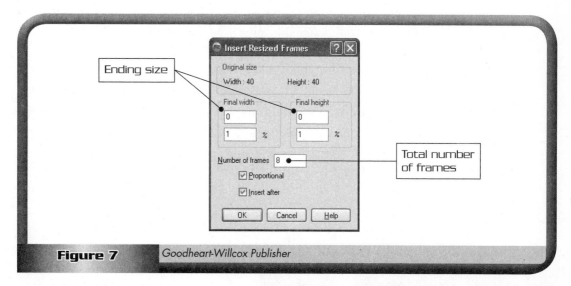

Figure 7   *Goodheart-Willcox Publisher*

85. Copy Frame 16, and paste it as Frame 17.

Clear

86. Clear the image on Frame 17. This is to ensure the last frame of the animation is blank.

87. Preview the animation.

88. Close the image editor, and save your work.

Skill Application

The gameplay, art, and programming must be modified to fit the new animated avatar. Programming similar to that associated with the original Avatar object must be added to the new Avatar_Swimmer object. Also, the original Avatar must be programmed to appear once the player arrives at the middle area. Additionally, the road has been changed into a river, so objects must be modified to match the new gameplay.

89. Replace images for the car and truck objects with images of boats, alligators, or other obstacles that fit the theme. Use the PowerPoint files you created in Chapter 9 as the basis for creating these objects so they will be the same sizes as current objects.

90. Add the programming necessary to destroy the Avatar_Swimmer object and reset the player to the start if the object collides with an obstacle in the lower river:

> **IF** the Avatar_Swimmer object collides with a Group.Bad object,
> **THEN** play a sound,
>> **AND** destroy the Avatar_Swimmer object
>> **AND** subtract 1 from the lives
>> **AND** create an Avatar_Swimmer object at the starting position.

91. Add an active object named Middle Grass that is stretched to cover the grass area below the logs and barrels. Color the object green to match the grass.

92. To switch the player character from the Avatar_Swimmer object to the Avatar object, program the following pseudo code. The Y value of 235 is a good point where the swimmer is almost all the way on the Middle Grass object, but not into the second river. The Avatar object must be aligned for tile based, the Avatar_Swimmer object repositioned so the destroy animation does not appear, and then the Avatar_Swimmer object destroyed to prevent an error.

> **IF** the Y coordinate of the Avatar_Swimmer object is equal to 235,
> **THEN** create an Avatar object at the location of the Avatar_Swimmer object
>> **AND** set the Y position of the Avatar object to 224
>> **AND** set the position of the Avatar_Swimmer object to −154,−100
>> **AND** destroy the Avatar_Swimmer object.

93. Add programming needed so the original Avatar object is destroyed if it collides with the lower water and add an Avatar_Swimmer object is created at the starting point.

94. Create animations for sinking logs and barrels.

95. Add lily pads and other Group.Good objects that can be randomly generated.

96. Add sounds for the swimming frog and others needed to match gameplay.

97. Test play the game, and debug it as needed.

98. Save your work, compile an EXE file, and submit it for grading according to the directions provided by your instructor.

Review Questions

1. Which type of action was created for the articulation animation, and what made it that type?

   _____

   _____

   _____

   _____

2. Describe the process of integrating the artwork created in PowerPoint into the game in MMF2.

   _____

   _____

   _____

   _____

3. Why was it necessary to adjust the hotspot of the animation after the artwork was imported into MMF2?

   _____

   _____

   _____

   _____

4. Describe how the basic gameplay was altered in this game build.

   _____

   _____

   _____

   _____

5. How were keyframes used when the destroyed animation was created for the swimmer frog?

   _____

   _____

   _____

   _____

Activity 11-7

2D Particle Animation

Objectives

Students will generate custom sprites for a sprite sheet. Students will animate sprites to produce a particle system. Students will apply value and tone to particles. Students will program a particle system using vector-direction controls.

Situation

The Really Cool Game Company requires game art for a new game where the player is a firefighter who puts out fires with a fire hose. The game concept requires fire animation in a 2D game environment. A particle system will generate the fire. Additionally, the water from the fire hose will be generated by a particle system that is aimed using the mouse. Your job is to create a proof of concept for the particle systems for the fire, water, and smoke. For testing purposes, each of these will be programmed to aim toward the mouse. Other designers will later use these animations in gameplay as needed.

How to Begin

Rectangle

Oval

1. Launch PowerPoint 2010, and switch to a blank layout.
2. Create a rectangle that is 3″ × 3″ with a black fill and outline.
3. Create an oval that is 3″ × 3″ with no outline.
4. Align the circle so it fits perfectly inside the black square.
5. Select the oval, and open the **Format Shape** dialog box.
6. Click **Fill** on the left, and click the **Gradient fill** radio button on the right.
7. Click the **Preset colors:** drop-down list, and click Fire in the list.
8. Click the **Type:** drop-down list, and click Radial in the list
9. Click the **Direction:** drop-down list, and click From Center in the list.
10. Leave the **Format Shape** dialog box open.
11. Save the file as *LastName_*Fire Sprites in your working folder.

Sprite Sheet

A *sprite sheet* is a collection of animation frames shown on a single sheet. These can be transferred into a game engine as a single image or as individual frames.

12. Make three copies of the oval and rectangle so there are four total of each.
13. Select the oval in the first set, and in the **Format Shape** dialog box, set the transparency for all gradient stops to 25 percent.
14. For the oval in the second set, set the transparency for all gradient stops to 50 percent.
15. For the oval in the third set, set the transparency for all gradient stops to 75 percent. The transparency settings will allow more value to blend the flame particle as it fades, as shown in **Figure 1**.
16. Group each oval with its corresponding black rectangle. These four groups will be individual frames of the animation.

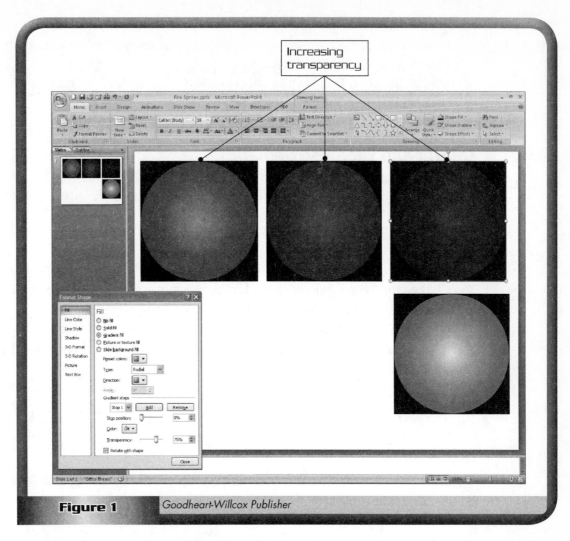

Figure 1 *Goodheart-Willcox Publisher*

Importing Sprites

For 2D particle animation, the lifespan of the particle is controlled by the number of sprite frames and the frame rate. This is different from how a 3D particle system functions, as you saw earlier in this chapter.

17. Launch MMF2, and save the file as *LastName*_Fire Particles in your working folder.

18. Set the background color for Frame 1 to black.

19. Add an active object named Flame anywhere on the frame.

20. Display the object in the image editor, and delete Frame 1 from the Stopped animation set.

21. Select the Right animation in the Disappearing animation set.

22. Copy the image with no transparency from the sprite sheet in PowerPoint and paste it as Frame 1. Resize the canvas.

23. Copy and paste Frame 1 three times for a total of four frames.

24. Replace the Frame 2 image with the 25% transparency image.

25. Replace the Frame 3 image with the 50% transparency image.

26. Replace the Frame 4 image with the 75% transparency image.

27. Set the hotspot to the center for all frames.

28. Copy and paste Frame 1.

View Hot Spot

29. Drag the pasted frame so it becomes Frame 2.

30. Similarly, copy each frame so there are two frames for each sprite, as shown in **Figure 2.** This creates a longer animation.

31. On the **Direction Options** tab, set the speed to 30 with no looping or repeating.

32. Close the image editor.

33. Resize the Flame object to 40 × 40.

Emitter and Vector Movement

The animated particles need to be generated from an emitter to create the simulated flame. The emitter can be any object, as the particles are generated relative to that object. The flame will travel in a vector that is set by the position of the mouse.

34. Add an active object named Emitter near the center of the frame. The default image can be changed later.

35. Select the Flame object, and click the **Movement** tab in the **Properties** window.

36. Change the **Type** property to **Vector**. Vector movement causes the object to travel in a straight line based on the vector that is provided.

37. Enter 400 for the **Speed** property and 0 for the **Direction** property.

38. In the **Gravity/Acceleration** area, enter 0 for the **Strength** property and **Direction** property. The flame will not be affected by gravity.

Special Movement Controller

The vector movement needs a controller to set the direction the vector will be produced. A special type of object is used in MMF2 as the movement controller.

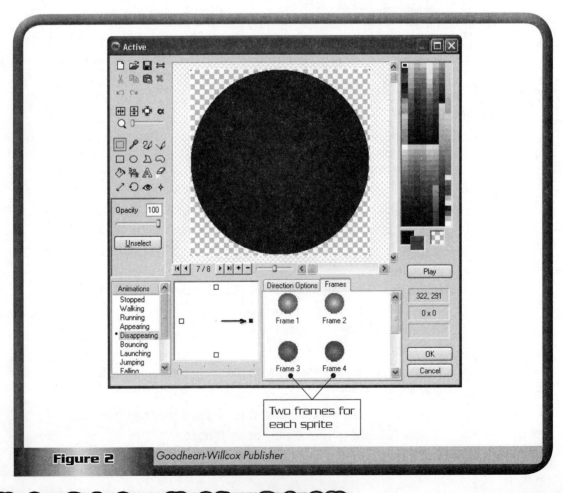

Figure 2   *Goodheart-Willcox Publisher*

39. Insert a new Clickteam movement controller object. In the **New Object** dialog box, this object is located in the **Movements** category, as shown in **Figure 3.** This object holds values that can be called later.

40. Drag the movement controller object outside of the scope so it will not be visible during gameplay.

Programming

This build is a proof of concept. The programming required is fairly simple, as you are only creating an effect.

41. Display the event editor, and add a new condition.

42. In the **New Condition** dialog box, right-click on the mouse/keyboard icon, and click **The mouse > Repeat while mouse key is pressed** in the shortcut menu.

43. In the dialog box that is displayed, click the **Left button** radio button, and click the **OK** button. This specifies that the condition will be true while the left mouse button is pressed.

44. Add an event to create a Flame object at (0,0) relative to the Emitter object.

45. Right-click in the cell where the **Clickteam Movement Controller** column intersects the **Line 1** row, and click **Set object** in the shortcut menu. In the dialog box that is displayed, select the Flame object. This will apply the movement settings from the controller to the Flame object.

46. Right-click in the same cell again, and click **Vector movement > Direction > Set direction toward point** in the shortcut menu. This command needs to point the vector in the direction of the mouse. The X coordinate is set first.

47. In the expression editor, enter XMouse. This means the current X coordinate of the mouse pointer location.

48. Click the **OK** button to close the expression editor, and a new expression editor is displayed for entering the Y coordinate.

49. Enter YMouse, and close the expression editor.

50. Right-click in the cell where the **Clickteam Movement Controller** column intersects the **Line 1** row, and click **Vector movement > Direction > Set direction toward angle** in the shortcut menu. The angle of the vector needs to be set.

Event Editor

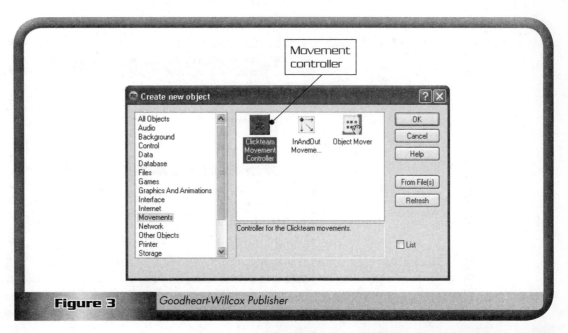

Figure 3 *Goodheart-Willcox Publisher*

51. In the expression editor, click the **Retrieve data from an object** button.

52. In the **New Expression** dialog box, right-click on the Clickteam Movement Controller object, and click **Vector movement** > **Get Direction** in the shortcut menu. This adds code to the expression editor, and a portion of the code is highlighted.

53. With the >fixed value< portion of the code highlighted, click the **Retrieve data from an object** button.

54. In the **New Expression** dialog box, right-click on the Flame object, and click **Retrieve Fixed Value** in the shortcut menu.

55. The code in the expression editor should read VEC_Dir("Clickteam Movement Controller", Fixed("Flame")). Click the **OK** button to close the expression editor window.

Run Frame

56. Test play the frame. The particles should follow the cursor as long as the left mouse button is held down. If a particle appears at the beginning of the frame, move the particle outside the scope in the frame editor.

Effect Options

Right now, the particles do not create a good illusion of a flame. This is because an animation effect still needs to be added. In MMF2, effects are used to control how each new image component is added to the animation. In this case, only the new portion of the image needs to be created for the flame. This will eliminate the bottoms of the animated particles to make it all appear as one piece. An add effect is used to achieve this.

Frame Editor

57. Display the frame editor, and select the Flame object.

58. Click the **Display Options** tab in the **Properties** window.

59. Click the **Effects** property to display the **Edit** button, and then click the button. The **Effects** dialog box is displayed, as shown in **Figure 4**.

60. Expand the tree for the Standard group, and click **Add**. Then, click the **OK** button to close the dialog box.

61. Save your work, and test play the frame.

Run Frame

Refinement

The flame looks much better now. However, it is missing some resizing to taper the end of the flame as it goes farther from the emitter.

62. Open the Flame object in the image editor.

63. Select Frame 2, and click the **Size** button.

Size

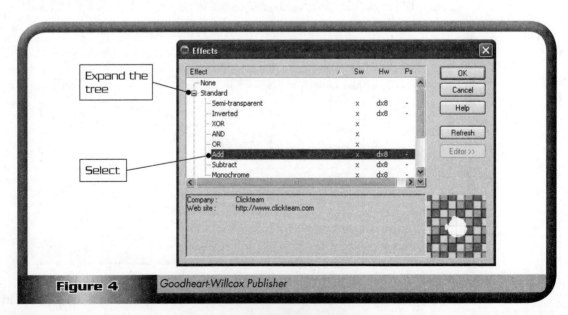

Figure 4   *Goodheart-Willcox Publisher*

Name: _____

64. Check the **Proportional**, **Stretch**, and **Resample** check boxes, as shown in **Figure 5.** This ensures the fire ball is not stretched out of proportion and that the resizing is applied to the image, not the canvas.

65. Enter **38** in the width (**w**) text box. Since the **Proportional** check box is checked, the height is automatically set to 38 as well.

66. Click the **Apply** button to fix the setting.

67. Similarly, change the size of the remaining frames as shown in **Figure 6.**

68. Close the image editor.

69. Save your work, and test play the frame. The flame should now be tapered as its particles travel from the emitter, as shown in **Figure 7.**

Run Frame

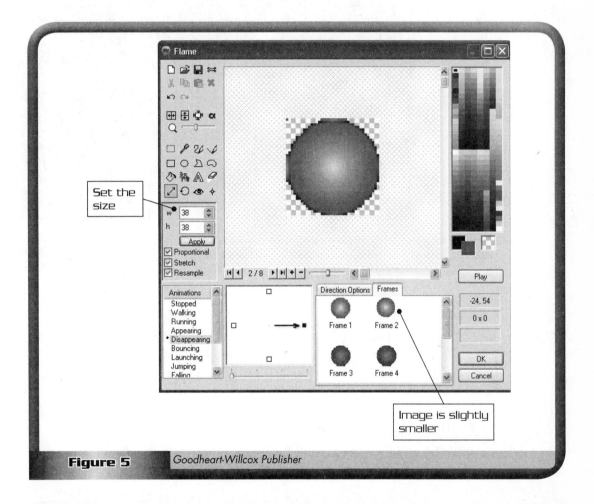

| Figure 5 | Goodheart-Willcox Publisher |

Frame	Size
Frame 3	36
Frame 4	34
Frame 5	32
Frame 6	30
Frame 7	28
Frame 8	26

| Figure 6 | Goodheart-Willcox Publisher |

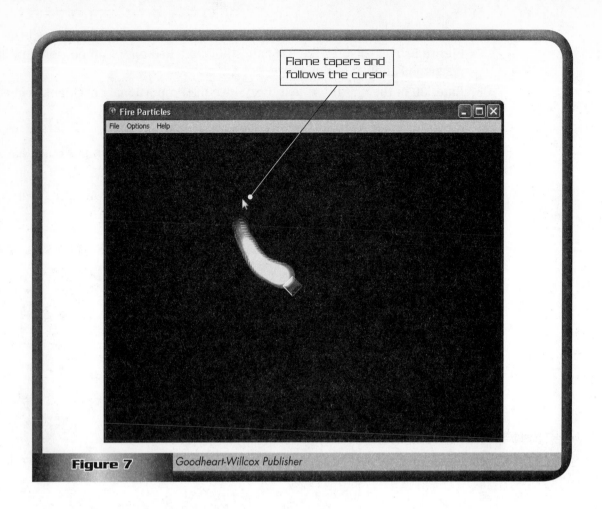
Flame tapers and follows the cursor

Figure 7   *Goodheart-Willcox Publisher*

Skill Application

70. Add a new frame to the game, and create a particle system to generate smoke. Change the background color as needed for contrast.

71. Add a new frame to the game, and create a particle system to generate water from a fire hose. Change the background color as needed for contrast.

Review Questions

1. Why was a black fill used for the rectangle in PowerPoint?

_____

_____

_____

_____

2. What is a sprite sheet?

_____

_____

_____

_____

3. Briefly describe how sprites are used in this activity to simulate the fading of the flame.

_____

_____

_____

_____

4. Why is an emitter object needed in this 2D particle system?

_____

_____

_____

_____

5. What is the purpose of the movement controller object?

_____

_____

_____

_____

Chapter 12
Programming Composition

Objectives

After completing this chapter, you will be able to:

- Design a programming array to store and compare values.
- Explain the theory behind binary code.
- Use a game engine to design a programming array to store and compare values.
- Program game assets using a Visual Basic script editor.
- Work as a team to solve problems.

Ronald Caswell/Shutterstock.com

Goodheart-Willcox Publisher; images: Klich Boin/Shutterstock.com, DM7/Shutterstock.com, Ecoimages/Shutterstock.com

Goodheart-Willcox Publisher; images: gregiith/Shutterstock.com, diversepixel/Shutterstock.com

Name: _____

Date: _____

Class: _____

Bellwork

Day	Date	Activity	Response
1		Complete the anticipation guide and the K and W columns of the KWL chart for this chapter.	
2		What is a computer bit, and how does it relate to a computer byte?	
3		Summarize what binary is.	
4		How is a compiler used?	
5		How is syntax used to create a programming sentence?	
6		Compare and contrast object attributes and object properties.	
7		How are methods similar to verbs?	
8		Why would a programmer choose one programming language over another?	
9		What is the distribution cost for an XNA developer selling through the app hub?	
10		Evaluate the name of the variable Direction. What data would you expect the variable to hold and why?	
11		What is the difference between an integer variable type and a single variable type? Which variable type would a programmer select to add a decimal value to a long variable?	

Day	Date	Activity	Response
12		What does it mean if a variable is declared?	
13		What is an array, and how does it access data?	
14		How does programming in modules help organize a script?	
15		Describe the shape of a decision symbol in a flowchart. Can the decision symbol contain more than a Yes and No branch?	
16		What is the role of a comment in a computer program?	
17		How does using paper made from sugar cane help the environment?	
18		Why does a computer programmer intercalate the code?	
19		What is meant when an algorithm is said to be elegant?	
20		What is recursion?	
21		How does inertia apply to motion?	
22		How does a ship resist the force of gravity pulling it to the bottom of the sea?	
23		Complete the L column of the KWL chart and the After Reading column of the anticipation guide with what you learned from this chapter.	
24		Speculate a character would be able to jump very high in a game. Describe three possible reasons why jumping very high would be realistic.	

Name: _____

Date: _____

Class: _____

Anticipation Guide

Directions

Before reading the chapter, read each statement in the table below. In the column titled Before Reading, write the letter *T* if you agree with the statement or *F* if you disagree with the statement. After reading the chapter, reread each statement in the table below. In the column titled After Reading, write the letter *T* if you agree with the statement or *F* if you disagree with the statement. Be prepared to justify your answers in a class discussion.

Before Reading	Statement	After Reading
	Computer programming uses many syntax elements found in spoken languages like English.	
	Pseudo code is the actual computer code used in Visual Basic programming.	
	The number 4.25 is an integer variable.	
	A **Do While** command is a type of loop command.	
	Physics must be applied in the video game exactly as it functions in the real world.	

KWL Chart

Directions

Before reading the chapter, fill in what you already know about the topic in the K column and what you want to learn in the W column. After reading the chapter, review what you know and wanted to learn about the topic. Reflect on what you have studied and completed in this chapter. Fill in what you learned in the L column. Be prepared to justify your answers in a class discussion.

Topic: Computer Programming		
K What you already *know*	**W** What you *want* to learn	**L** What you *learned*

Name: _____

Date: _____

Class: _____

Activity 12-1
Array Programming

Objectives

Students will design a programming array to store and compare values. Students will work with strings to customize gameplay. Students will program recognition of multiple victory conditions.

Situation

Some of the games The Really Cool Game Company creates involve complex arrays. These arrays store player data and, in RPGs, character dialogue. To help you learn the function of arrays in programming, you will begin by building a two-player game of *Tic-Tac-Toe*. This will be a proof of concept build. When testing proves the functioning, the game will be built in a game engine.

How to Begin

1. Launch Microsoft Excel 2010.
2. Highlight columns A through H.
3. Right-click on a highlighted column header, and click **Column Width...** in the shortcut menu.
4. In the **Column Width** dialog box that is displayed, enter 11, and click the **OK** button.
5. Similarly, highlight rows 1 through 14, and set the row height to 55.
6. Save the file as *LastName_*Tic-Tac-Toe Array in your working folder.

Labels and Cell Borders

![Merge & Center]

7. Enter the labels shown in **Figure 1.** For locations specified as a range, highlight the range and click the **Merge and Center** button on the **Alignment** panel of the **Home** tab in the ribbon.

All Boarders

8. Highlight the ranges in **Figure 2,** click the drop-down arrow on the **Font** panel of the **Home** tab in the ribbon, and click **All Borders** in the drop-down menu. Borders will help bring attention to areas of the game map.

Array Data

In this game, the array will be a mirror image of the game map. The array will transform the input of the X and O players from the game map into a binary number system that the computer can manipulate. A simple **IF**...**THEN**...**ELSE** event is used to do this. The pseudo code for the upper-right square is:

  IF a player inputs X in cell B2,
  THEN the array B10 value equals 1
  ELSE
    IF the player inputs O in cell B2,
    THEN the array B10 value equals 10
    ELSE the value equals 0.

Location	Label Text	Text Format	Text Color
B1:D1	Tic-Tac-Toe	Arial, size 26	Black
F1:H1	Type X Player's Name Below	Arial, size 12	Black
F3:H3	Type O Player's Name Below	Arial, size 12	Black
B5:C5	Winner:	Arial, size 22	Black
D5	*leave blank*	Arial, size 36	Red
D6	*leave blank*	Arial, size 36	Red
B2:D4	*leave blank*	Arial, size 50	Black
A8	Array Programming	Arial, size 28	Black
B9	Y1	Arial, size 28	Black
C9	Y2	Arial, size 28	Black
D9	Y3	Arial, size 28	Black
A10	X1	Arial, size 28	Black
A11	X2	Arial, size 28	Black
A12	X3	Arial, size 28	Black
E9	Raw Test	Arial, size 10	Black
F9	Refined Array	Arial, size 10	Black
G9	Victory Test	Arial, size 10	Black

Figure 1   *Goodheart-Willcox Publisher*

Location	Merge and Center
B2:D4	No
B10:D12	No
F2:H2	Yes
F4:H4	Yes

Figure 2   *Goodheart-Willcox Publisher*

Insert Function

9. Select cell B10, and click the **Insert Function** button on the **Formula Bar** above the column headers. The **Insert Function** dialog box is displayed, as shown in **Figure 3.**

10. In the **Search for a function:** textbox, enter if, and click the **Go** button. This will locate the **IF** logical test.

11. In the **Select a function:** list, select **IF**, and click the **OK** button. The **Function Arguments** dialog box is displayed, as shown in **Figure 4.**

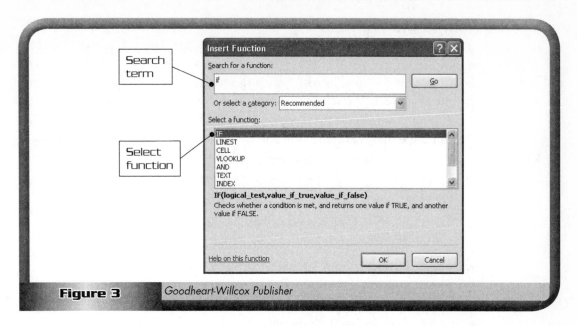

Figure 3   *Goodheart-Willcox Publisher*

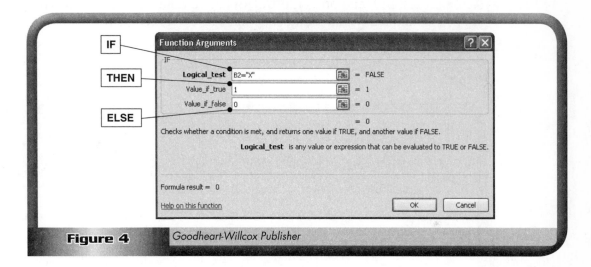

Figure 4   *Goodheart-Willcox Publisher*

12. Click in the **Logical_test** text box in the dialog box, and then click cell B2 in the spreadsheet. The cell name (B2) is added to the text box. The entry in this text box is the **IF** part of the logic statement.

13. At the end of the **Logical_test** text box, enter ="X". The letter X is a string, and strings must be enclosed in quotation marks. This completes the argument: **IF** the value in cell B2 is equal to X.

14. In the **Value_if_true** text box, enter 1. The entry in this text box is the **THEN** part of the logic statement and executed when the **IF** statement is true.

15. In the **Value_if_false** text box, enter 0. The entry in this text box is the **ELSE** part of the logic statement and executed when the **IF** statement is false. Later, this will be edited with for the **ELSE IF** statement.

16. Click the **OK** button to close the dialog box and insert the formula into cell B10.

17. Enter the letter X in cell B2. This can be either uppercase or lowercase. Notice that the array position B10 has a value of 1.

18. Enter the letter O in cell B2. Notice that the array position B10 has a value of 0. This value will be 0 for any value in cell B2 other than the letter X.

Compound Formula

So far, you have created an **IF**…**THEN**…**ELSE** statement. You will now modify the programming to create an **IF**…**THEN**…**ELSE IF** statement.

19. Click cell B10 to select it. Notice the formula is =IF(B2="X",1,0). A comma separates the **IF**, **THEN**, and **ELSE** portions of the statement. Also notice how parentheses are used to contain parts of the statement.

Insert Function

20. Click the **Insert Function** button to open the **Function Arguments** dialog box.

21. Click in the **Value_if_false** text box, and delete the value.

22. Enter IF(B2="O",10,0). This means **ELSE IF** the value in cell B2 is equal to O, **THEN** set the value of the cell B10 to 10 **ELSE** set the value of cell B10 to 0.

23. Click the **OK** button to close the dialog box and update the formula (programming).

Relative Copy

Relative copying can be used to quickly fill in the formulas for the rest of the array. In *relative copying,* the cell references inside a formula change according to the relative location of the copy to the original.

24. Select cell B10, and press the [Ctrl][C] key combination to copy its content. The cell is outlined with a marquee to indicate its content is the source for copies, as shown in **Figure 5**.

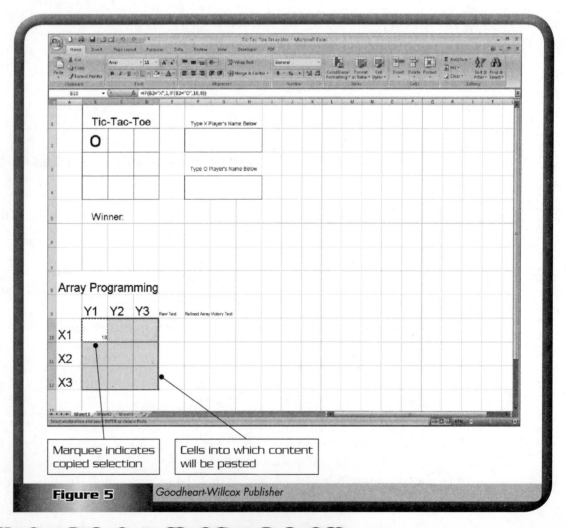

Marquee indicates copied selection

Cells into which content will be pasted

Figure 5   *Goodheart-Willcox Publisher*

25. Highlight the range B10:D12, and press the [Ctrl][V] key combination to paste the copied content.

26. Press the [Esc] key to end the coping process.

27. Click cell C12 to select it. Notice how the original formula changed to =IF(C4="X",1,IF(C4="O",10,0)).

28. Fill the game map (B2:D4) with Xs and Os to test that all the cells in the array will hold a value of 1 or 10. If a space in the game map is left empty or contains a value other than X or O, the corresponding cell in the array should hold a value of 0.

Raw Testing for Victory

The game must test for all possible victory conditions. When a player wins, his or her name will be displayed as the winner. The array data will be used to calculate when a player has won and which one won. By totaling the values in row, columns, and diagonals, a winner can be determined.

29. Click cell A13 to select it. This cell is where the raw test for diagonal victory will be calculated using the **SUM** method. In Excel, a function is a method.

30. Enter the formula =SUM(B12,C11,D10). This finds the sum of the three cells.

31. In cell B13, enter the formula =SUM(B10:B12). Notice that a range of cells is specified to create a raw test for vertical victory.

32. In cell C13, enter the formula =SUM(C10:C12).

33. In cell D13, enter the formula =SUM(D10:D12).

34. In cell E13, enter the formula =SUM(B10,C11,D12). This is a test for diagonal victory.

35. In cell E12, enter the formula =SUM(B12:B12). This is a raw test for horizontal victory.

36. In cell E11, enter the formula =SUM(B11:B11).

37. In cell E10, enter the formula =SUM(B10:B10).

Refining the Test

The raw test provides a total, but these totals need to have meaning added to determine if a given total meets the victory condition. In this game, player X wins if the sum of the three cells in the raw test is 3 ($1 + 1 + 1$). Player O wins if the sum is 30 ($10 + 10 + 10$).

38. In cell F10, create a formula to match this pseudo code:

> **IF** the value in cell E10 equals 3,
> **THEN** enter 1
> **ELSE**
>> **IF** the value in cell E10 equals 30,
>> **THEN** enter 10
>> **ELSE** 0.

39. Similarly, program cells F11, F12, A14, B14, C14, D14, and E14 to test if player X wins (3) or player O wins (30).

Testing

By adding all of the cells for the refined array test, a winner can be determined. If there is a winner, one of the cells in the refined test array will display either 3 or 30, and all other cells in the refined test array will display 0.

40. In cell G10, use the **SUM** method (function) to create a formula to add all of the cells in refined test array: F10, F11, F12, A14, B14, C14, D14, and E14.

41. Enter X in each of the cells in the top row of the game map (B2:D2), and clear all other cells in the game map. Notice that the victory test (G10) equals 1 for player X winning, as shown in **Figure 6.**

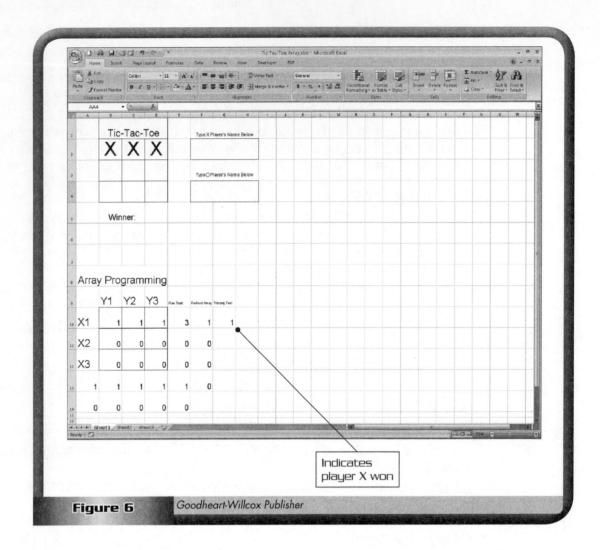

Figure 6

Goodheart-Willcox Publisher

42. Replace each X with O. Notice that the victory test equals 10 for player O winning.

43. Test each victory condition possible using only three Xs or three Os on the game map.

44. Debug if needed.

Glitch

There is a slight glitch in the victory condition that occurs when a player completes a win from two directions at the same time. This is a level C bug, but can be easily fixed.

45. Add an X in cells B2, C2, D2, D3, and D4. Notice that the victory test total is 2. There is no winner for a result of 2.

46. Replace each X with an O. Notice the victory test total is 20. There is no winner for a result of 20.

47. To fix the glitch, program this pseudo code in cell H10:

> **IF** the value in cell G10 equals 2,
> **THEN** enter 1
> **ELSE**
> > **IF** the value in cell G10 equals 20,
> > **THEN** enter 10
> > **ELSE** enter the value in cell G10.

48. Save your work, and test to see if the glitch is fixed. The value in cell H10 should be 1, 10, or 0.

Programming with Strings

The players will enter their names in the text fields next to the game map. The game will determine who has won and display the winner's name, as shown in **Figure 7.** Remember, strings must be contained in quotation marks.

49. In cell D5, program this pseudo code:

> **IF** the glitch fix (cell H10) indicates player X wins,
> **THEN** display the text Player X Wins!
> **ELSE**
>> **IF** the glitch fix (cell H10) indicates player O wins,
>> **THEN** display the text Player O Wins!
>> **ELSE** display the text None.

50. In cell D6, program this pseudo code:

> **IF** the glitch fix (cell H10) indicates player X wins,
> **THEN** display the contents of the cell containing the name of player X (cell F2)
> **ELSE**
>> **IF** the glitch fix (cell H10) indicates player O wins,
>> **THEN** display the contents of the cell containing the name of player O (cell F4)
>> **ELSE** display the text None.

51. Test all possible victory conditions for both players.

52. Debug if needed.

53. Save your work, and submit the file for grading.

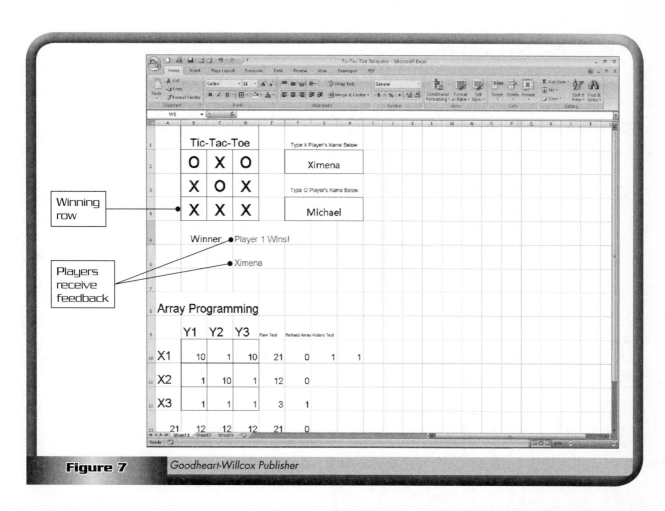

Figure 7 *Goodheart-Willcox Publisher*

Review Questions

1. Briefly describe how the array in this activity is a mirror of the game map.

   _____

   _____

   _____

   _____

2. What is the formula entered in Excel for **IF** the value in cell D8 is equal to Yes, **THEN** display Okay?

   _____

   _____

   _____

   _____

3. Describe how relative copying is used in this activity to improve efficiency in programming the array.

   _____

   _____

   _____

   _____

4. Why is a refined test of the array data needed?

   _____

   _____

   _____

   _____

5. What special consideration must be given to strings when they are included in programming?

   _____

   _____

   _____

   _____

Activity 12-2

Tile-Based Prototyping

Objectives

Students will format and resize cells in a spreadsheet. Students will use the formula wizard in Excel to help write logical formulas. Students will use multiple tabs and exchange data between worksheets. Students will apply conditional formatting. Students will explain the theory behind binary code.

Situation

The Really Cool Game Company wants a prototype *Battleship*-style game designed as a single-player game. Your job is to develop formulas using a spreadsheet to test the concept of the features that will be used in the graphical user interface (GUI). Other programmers will create the fully functional single-player game.

How to Begin

1. Launch Microsoft Excel.
2. Double-click the tab labeled Sheet 1 to enable editing of the name.
3. Enter Game Frame as the new name of the tab.
4. Similarly, rename Sheet 2 as Map and Sheet 3 as Ships.
5. Save the file as *LastName*_Battleship GUI in your working folder.

Formatting

6. Click the Game Frame tab to activate it.
7. Click the A column heading to highlight the entire column, hold, and drag to the M column heading to select columns A through M.
8. Right-click anywhere in the selection, and click **Column Width...** in the shortcut menu.
9. In the **Column Width** dialog box that is displayed, enter 3, and click the **OK** button. The width of the selected columns is changed.
10. Similarly, select columns N through Z, right-click, and click **Hide** in the shortcut menu. The columns are still there, they just have a width of zero and are not visible, as shown in **Figure 1.**
11. Select columns AA through AM, and change the column width to 3.
12. In cell A1, enter Firing Field. Format the text as 16 point bold.

Fill

13. Change the fill color of cell A1 to green.

Font Color

14. Change the text color of cell A1 to white.
15. Select the range of cells A1:M1.

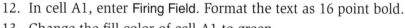

16. Click the **Merge and Center** button on the **Alignment** panel of the **Home** tab in the ribbon.
17. Change the border of the merged cells to a thick box.

Borders

18. Select the range of cells A2:M20, and change the border to all borders.
19. With this range of cells still selected, change the border to a thick box. The thicker frame is applied to the outside of the selection.

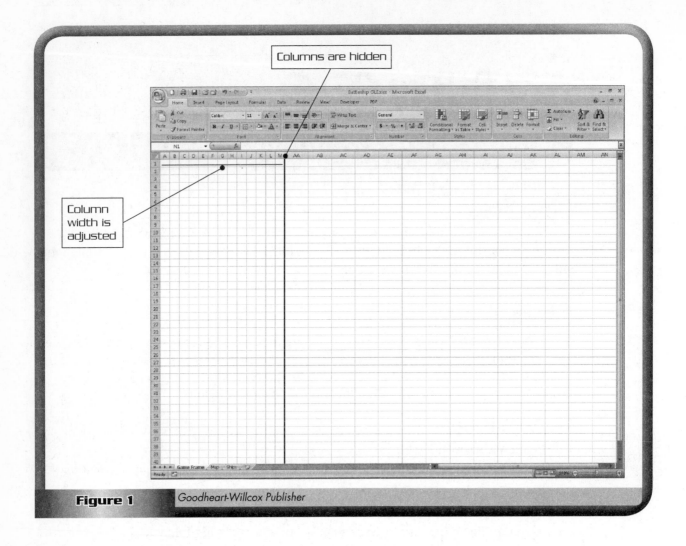

Columns are hidden

Column width is adjusted

Figure 1

Goodheart-Willcox Publisher

20. Select the range of cells A1:M20, and press the [Ctrl][C] key combination to copy the selection.

21. Click in cell AA1 to make it active, and press the [Ctrl][V] key combination to paste the copied content. Press the [Esc] key to end the copy.

22. Click in cell AA1, and change the text from Firing Field to Hits and Misses.

23. Click the select all button at the upper-left corner of the spreadsheet to select the entire worksheet, as shown in **Figure 2.**

24. Copy the contents of the worksheet.

25. Click the Map tab to make it current.

26. Click cell A1 to select it, and paste the copied content. The Game Frame worksheet is copied into the Map worksheet.

27. Similarly, copy the Game Frame worksheet into the Ships worksheet.

Modifying and Placing Ships

28. Click the Ships worksheet to make it active.

29. Change the text Firing Field to Ship Placement.

30. Highlight columns AA through AM, right-click anywhere in the selection, and click **Delete** in the shortcut menu. This removes the Hits and Misses grid.

31. In the Ship Placement grid, place the ships (as text) the opponent will try to sink as specified in **Figure 3.** These are the positions for testing. Later, the ships will have to be repositioned to play the game.

Name: _____

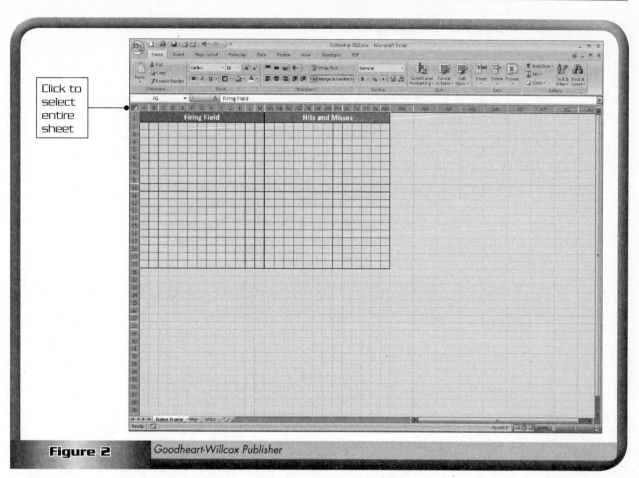

Figure 2   *Goodheart-Willcox Publisher*

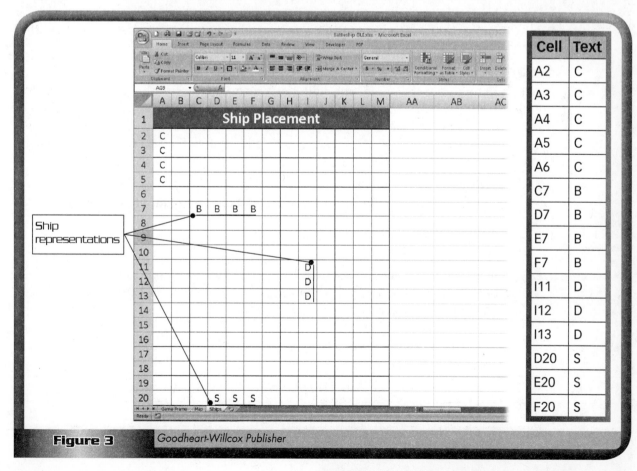

Figure 3   *Goodheart-Willcox Publisher*

Understanding Binary Code

Binary code is the basis for all computer programming. It uses the number 1 to indicate yes and 0 for no. In some cases, a programmer will want to test if many conditions are true, or yes. To do this easily, a response will be programmed to add together by changing the place values. For example, in this game build, if you want to test a cell to see if where a ship segment is located in it, program a binary representation of 1 for yes (a segment is in that cell) or 0 for no (a segment is not in that cell). This provides a binary result of either 1 or 0 to test if there is a segment in a cell. Later, programming is added to test if the player has selected a cell. This response is programmed as 10 for yes and 00 for no. The tens place now holds the binary test for selecting a cell. Ultimately, you are trying to see if the cell contains a ship segment *and* has been selected. If the binary tests are added, the results and meaning shown in **Figure 4** are created. Complete the table below with binary representation for each condition.

Test 1	Binary	Test 2	Binary	Test 3	Binary	Test 4	Binary	Total	Meaning
Yes	1	Yes	10	Yes	100	Yes	1000	1111	YYYY
No	0	No	00	No	000	Yes	1000	1000	YNNN
Yes	1	No	00	Yes	100	No	0000	0101	
Yes		Yes		No		Yes			
								0111	
								1001	
									NNYY
									NNNN

Creating Binary Number Fields

To help program the game, you will convert the text to numbers. This conversion will be based on binary code such that if there is a ship segment in a cell it will display 1 and if not it will display 0.

32. Click the Map worksheet to make it active, and change the text Firing Field to Ship Positions in Binary.

33. Click cell A2 to select it.

34. Click the **Insert Function** button to display the **Insert Function** dialog box.

Insert Function

Player Selected	Binary for Selected	Segment in Cell	Binary for Segment	Total Binary	Binary Meaning
Yes	10	Yes	1	11	Yes, Yes
No	00	Yes	1	01	No, Yes
Yes	10	No	0	10	Yes, No
No	00	No	0	00	No, No

Figure 4   *Goodheart-Willcox Publisher*

35. Click the **Or select a category:** drop-down list, and click **Logical** in the list. This filters the displayed functions to only logical functions.

36. In the **Select a function:** list, click **IF**, and then click the **OK** button. The **Functions Arguments** dialog box is displayed.

37. Click in the **Logical_Test** text box, then click the **Ships** tab (worksheet), and click cell A2, as shown in **Figure 5.** The formula built in the text box is Ships!A2.

38. Click at the end of the formula, and enter an equals sign and two quotation marks so the formula reads Ships!A2="". The formula is testing **IF** cell A2 is blank. Empty quotes means nothing is entered in the cell, or it is blank. Look to the right of the text box, and notice Excel reports the statement is false. Since the letter C is entered in cell A2, the cell is not blank, and the formula evaluates to false.

39. Click in the **Value_if_true** text box, and enter 0. This means **THEN** set the value to zero, which converts empty cells to 0 in the binary field.

40. Click in the **Value_if_false** text box, and enter 1. This means **ELSE** set the value to one, which converts filled cells to 1 in the binary field.

41. Click the **OK** button to set the formula. Cell A2 on the Maps worksheet should display 1.

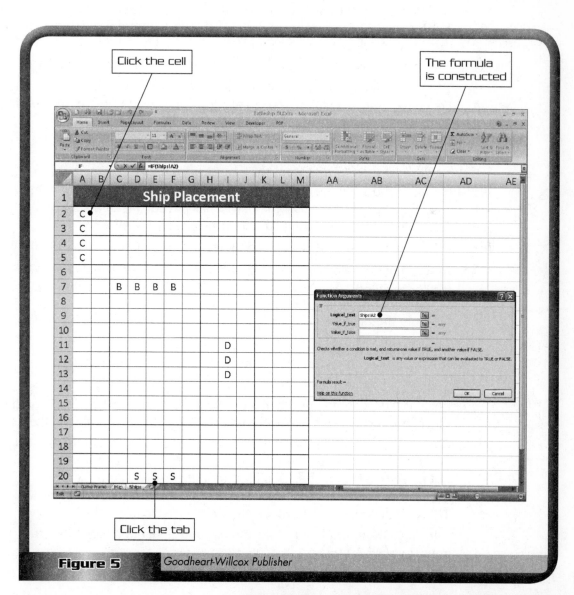

Figure 5   *Goodheart-Willcox Publisher*

42. On the Map worksheet, select cell A2, copy it, select the range of cells A2:M20, and paste the copied content. Press the [Esc] key to end the copying.

43. Examine the displayed values in the grid and compare them to the grid on the Ships tab. Notice how all the blank spaces in the grid on the Ships tab are shown as 0s on the Maps tab, and cells containing a letter are shown as 1s.

44. On the Ships tab, enter a space in cell M20. The cell looks empty, but display the Maps tab. Notice cell M20 displays 1. A space is a character just like a letter. Always take care to properly delete the ships.

45. Delete the space from cell M20 on the Ships tab.

Programming for Hits and Misses

46. Click the Game Frame. The player will be typing in Xs in the Firing Field grid to try and hit the hidden ships.

47. Enter the letter X in cell M2.

48. Click the Map tab, and change the text Hits and Misses to Shot Taken in Binary.

Insert Function

49. Click cell AM2 to select it, and click the **Insert Function** button. A formula needs to be constructed to convert the player's Xs into binary so the game can properly display hits and misses.

50. Build a formula for this pseudo code: **IF** cell M2 on the Game Frame tab contains an X, **THEN** display 10 **ELSE** display 0. If you program the formula correctly, 10 should be displayed in cell AM2 on the Map tab.

51. Use relative copying to copy the content of cell AM2 to the range AA2:AM20.

52. Test your work by adding some random Xs in the Firing Field grid on the Game Frame tab and checking to make sure 10 is displayed in the corresponding cell on the Map tab.

Compound Formulas

In spreadsheets, formulas can be combined to make *compound formulas.* A compound formula will be used to display hits and misses. Another compound formula will be used to check if the player has already taken a shot in a given location.

53. Click the Game Frame tab, and enter the letter X in cell A2.

54. Click cell AA2, and click the **Insert Function** button, and select the **IF** function.

Insert Function

55. In the **Function Arguments** dialog box, click in the **Logical_test** text box, and enter Map!A2+Map!AA2=11. This compound formula is testing if there is a ship segment in the cell (1 from the Ship Position in Binary grid) and if the player has taken a shot (10 from the Shot Taken in Binary grid).

56. Click in the **Value_if_true** text box, and enter X.

57. Highlight the formula in the **Logical_test** text box, and copy it.

58. Click in the **Value_if_false** text box, and paste the formula.

59. Click at the beginning of the **Value_if_false** text box, and enter (IF(at the beginning. The open parentheses tells Excel a second **IF** condition is starting in the formula.

60. Click at the end of the **Value_if_false** text box, change 11 to 10, and enter „O", ""). The formula in this text box should be: (IF(Map!A2+Map!AA2=10,"O", "")), as shown in **Figure 6.** Be sure letter O is used, not a zero. The entire formula constructed in the dialog box means **IF** cell A2 on the Map tab plus cell AA2 on the MAP equals 10, **THEN** set the value to O, **ELSE** set the value to nothing.

61. Click the **OK** button to close the **Function Arguments** dialog box. An X should appear in cell AA2.

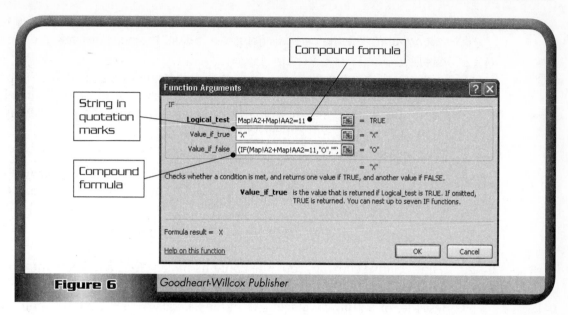

Figure 6   *Goodheart-Willcox Publisher*

62. Using relative copying, copy the contents of cell AA2 on the Game Frame tab, and paste into the range AA2:AM20 on the Game Frame tab to fill in the rest of the Hits and Misses grid. The random Xs you placed earlier in the Firing Field grid should be reflected as Xs and Os on the Hits and Misses grid.

Conditional Formatting

The game is functional at a basic level, but it can be made better. To make each hit easier to see, you will program the game to color those cells in red. Conditional formatting will be used to achieve this. *Conditional formatting* is when the formatting of a cell is based on a condition being true or false.

63. Click the Game Frame tab, and select cell AA2. The value in this cell is X because the player entered an X in cell A2, which is a hit.

Conditional Formatting

64. Click the **Conditional Formatting** button on the **Styles** panel of the **Home** tab in the ribbon, and click **New Rule...** in the drop-down menu. The **New Formatting Rule** dialog box is displayed, as shown in **Figure 7**.

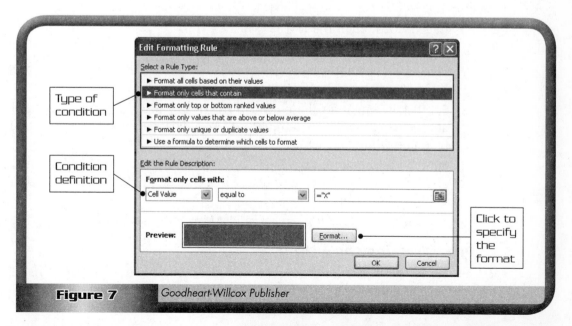

Figure 7   *Goodheart-Willcox Publisher*

65. In the **Select a Rule Type:** list at the top of the dialog box, click **Format only cells that contain**. The dialog box changes to reflect the options available for that selection.

66. In the **Format only cells with:** area, click **Cell Value** in the left-hand drop-down list, **equal to** in the middle drop-down list, and enter X in the right-hand text box. Do not include the quotation marks around the X. This is not specifying a string, rather a value that will appear in the cell.

67. Click the **Format...** button. A standard Windows formatting dialog box is displayed.

68. Change the font and fill colors to red. Using the same color for the text and the background effectively makes the X invisible so the player only sees a red block.

69. Click the **OK** button to close the formatting dialog box, and then click the **OK** button to close the **New Formatting Rule** dialog box. Cell AA2 should be a solid red block.

70. Using relative copying, copy the contents of cell AA2, and paste into the range AA2:AM2.

71. Test the formatting by placing Xs in the Firing Field grid. Any hit should be reflected as a red block in the Hits and Misses grid. Misses should be reflected as Os. This is a much better interface for the player.

Heads-Up Display (HUD)

Some player statistics need to be added to inform the player. Before continuing, however, you probably have noticed as cells were copied and pasted that the original formatting of borders has been altered. Reformat the borders on all tabs to match the original formatting set at the beginning of this game build, and then follow the instructions for adding a HUD.

72. Click the Game Frame tab.

73. Enter Player Statistics in cell A22.

74. Select the range of cells A22:AM22, and click the **Merge and Center** button.

Borders

75. Change the font to 16 point, bold, and white, and change the fill to black.

76. Select the range of cells A23:AM23, and change the border to all borders.

77. In cell A23, enter the text Shots.

78. In cell F23, enter the text Hits.

79. In cell K23, enter the text Misses.

80. In cell AC23, enter the text % Hits.

81. In cell AH23, enter the text % Miss.

82. Merge and center these ranges of cells A23:B23, C23:D23, F23:G23, H23:I23, K23:L23, M23:AA23, AC23:AD23, AE23:AF23, AH23:AJ23, and AK23:AL23.

83. Set the alignment for these cells to right: A23, F23, K23, AC23, and AH23. These are the merged cells containing text. Also, change the fill to black and the font to bold and white for these cells.

84. Set the alignment for these cells to left: C23, H23, M23, AE23, and AK23. These are the merged cells without text. Also, change the fill to yellow and the font to bold for these cells.

85. Fill cells E23, J23, AB23, AG23, and AM23 with black, as shown in **Figure 8.**

Programming the HUD

The visual design of the HUD is complete, but it is not yet functional. Each of the yellow cells needs to be programmed to display game statistics. For example, cell D23 needs to report how many times the player takes a shot.

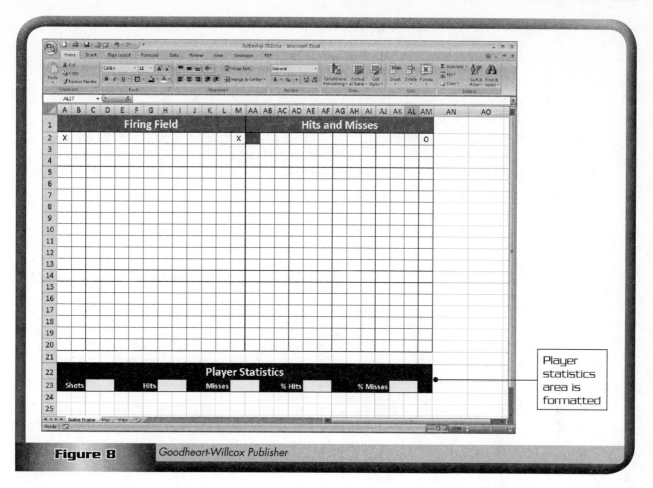

Figure 8 *Goodheart-Willcox Publisher*

Insert Function

86. Select cell C23 on the Game Map tab, and click the **Insert Function** button.

87. In the **Insert Function** dialog box, click **Statistical** in the **Or select a category:** drop-down list.

88. In the **Select a function:** list, click **COUNTA**, and click the **OK** button. This function is a method that counts the number of cells in a range that are *not* empty. Each time the player fills in a cell to take a shot, it will increase the count.

89. In the **Functions Arguments** dialog box, click in the **Value 1** text box, and then in the spreadsheet select the range of cells A2:M20.

90. Click the **OK** button to close the **Function Arguments** dialog box.

Insert Function

91. Select cell H23, and click the **Insert Function** button.

92. In the **Insert Function** dialog box, click **Statistical** in the **Or select a category:** drop-down list, click the **COUNTIF** function in the **Select a function:** list, and click the **OK** button. This function counts the number of cells in a range that meet a specified condition.

93. In the **Functions Arguments** dialog box, click in the **Range** text box, and then in the spreadsheet select the range of cells AA2:AM20.

94. Click in the **Criteria** text box, and enter "X". The quotation marks must be used.

95. Click the **OK** button to close the **Function Arguments** dialog box.

96. Similarly, program cell M23 to count the Os in the Hits and Misses grid.

Percent Style

97. Click in cell AE23, and enter the formula =H23/C23. This formula means the number of hits divided by the number of shots taken. To display the result as a percentage, click the **Percent Style** button on the **Number** panel in the **Home** tab of the ribbon.

98. Similarly, enter a formula in cell AK23 to calculate the percentage of misses.

Programming a Lookup Table

The game looks great, but there is one more improvement before the concept can be fully tested. The player needs to be given a rank based on his or her performance in the game. A lookup table will be created for this.

99. In cell A24 on the Game Frame tab, enter the text Rank.

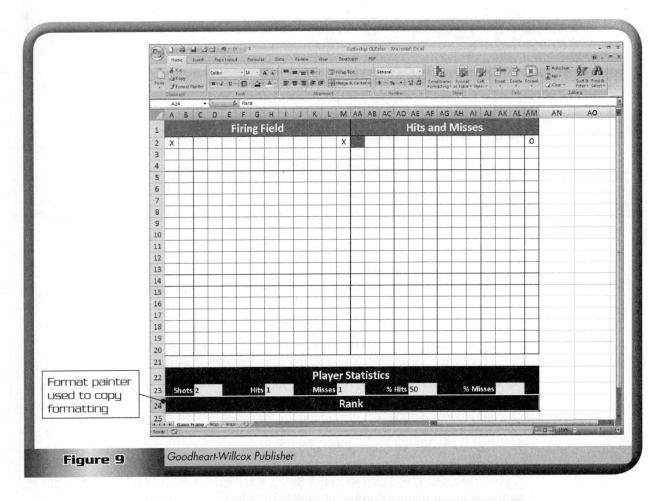

100. Select cell A22, click the **Format Painter** button on the **Clipboard** panel, on the **Home** tab of the ribbon, and click cell A24. The format painter reformats cells to match the donor cell (A22) without changing the information contained in the destination cell (A24), as shown in **Figure 9.**

101. Similarly, format cell A25 to match cell A24.

102. Enter the text as specified in **Figure 10.** These are labels to keep track of what is going to be programmed.

Figure 9   *Goodheart-Willcox Publisher*

Cell	Text
A27	All Hit
A28	Rank
F27	Binary
H27	String
L27	Rope
M27	String

Figure 10   *Goodheart-Willcox Publisher*

103. Merge and center cells F28:G28, F29:G29, F30:G30, F31:G31, H28:I28, H29:I29, H30:I30, and H31:I31.

104. In cell C27, create a formula for this pseudo code: **IF** the number of hits equals 17, **THEN** display 100 **ELSE** display 0. While there are only 14 possible hits in this prototype, the finished game will have 17 possible hits.

105. Enter the data specified in **Figure 11.** This creates the lookup table that will be used to choose the correct rank for the player.

106. Copy the range of cells G28:G31, click cell M28, and paste.

107. Merge and center cells K28:L28, K29:L29, K30:L30, K31:L31, M28:AA28, M29:AA29, M30:AA30, and M31:AA31.

108. Enter 30 in cell C28. This a test value for setting the rank. Later, this will be programmed to be automatically calculated.

109. Enter 1 in cell K28.

Insert Function

110. In cell K29, use the **Insert Function** tool to build a formula for this pseudo code: **IF** the value in cell C28 is greater than or equal to 30, **THEN** display the value 10 **ELSE** display the value 0. The formula should be: =IF(C28>=30,10,0).

111. Similarly, create a formula in cell K30 for this pseudo code: **IF** the value in cell C28 is greater than or equal to 40, **THEN** display the value 100 **ELSE** display the value 0.

112. Similarly, create a formula in cell K31 for this pseudo code: **IF** the value in cell C28 is greater than or equal to 50, **THEN** display the value 1000 **ELSE** display the value 0.

113. Merge and center the range of cells K32:L32, and enter the formula =SUM(K29:K31).

Programming the Rank

The resulting total shown in cell K32 is called a rope. A *rope* is used to stagger the place values of formulas so that when added together, a unique binary number is the result that can be matched up to a lookup table. In this case, if the rope is 111, the rank should be captain. If the rope is 1, the rank is ensign. Now that the lookup table and rope are complete, cell A25 can be programmed to display the rank. A placeholder cell will be used as part of the process.

Insert Function

114. Click cell AG28 on the Game Frame tab, and click the **Insert Function** button.

115. In the **Insert Function** dialog box, click **Lookup & Reference** in the **Or select a category:** drop-down list.

116. In the **Select a function:** list, click the **VLOOKUP** function, and click the **OK** button. This function is a method that retrieves data from a lookup table.

117. In the **Function Arguments** dialog box, click in the **Lookup_value** text box, and enter K32, as shown in **Figure 12.** This specifies to search the lookup table for the value of cell K32.

118. Click in the **Table_array** text box, then in the spreadsheet select the range of cells F28:I31. This range contains the values of the lookup table. The labels are not part of the lookup table data.

F28	F29	F30	F31	H28	H29	H30	H31
1	11	111	1111	Ensign	Officer	Captain	Admiral

Figure 11   *Goodheart-Willcox Publisher*

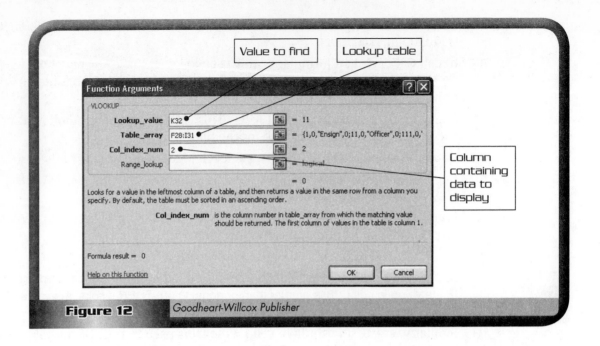

Figure 12   *Goodheart-Willcox Publisher*

119. Click in the **Col_index_num** text box, and enter 2. This means the value to be displayed is contained in the second column of the table. The second column of the lookup table contains the string to be displayed.

120. Click the **OK** button to finalize the formula.

Cell AG28 should be displaying Officer, however it is displaying 0. This is because the **VLOOKUP** function does not recognize merged cells as a single cell. So, when the range of cells F28:I31 was selected, what appears to the eye to be two columns is seen as four columns (F, G, H, and I) by the **VLOOKUP** function. Since what the **VLOOKUP** function sees as the second column is blank, the value displayed is 0. In order to correct this, cells will be unmerged and the data shifted.

121. Click cell F28, and click the **Merge and Center** button to unmerge the two cells.

122. Similarly, unmerge cells F29, F30, F31, H28, H29, H30, and H31.

123. Move the content in cell H28 to cell F28.

124. Similarly, move the content in cell H29 to cell F29, H30 to F30, and H31 to F31. Cell AG28 should now display Officer.

125. In cell A25, create a formula for this pseudo code: **IF** the value in all hits cell (C28) is greater than zero, **THEN** display the correct rank string (AG28) **ELSE** display "Complete Game to Receive Rank".

126. Test the ranking feature by changing the value of cell C28. Each rank from ensign to admiral should be displayed by entering 20, 30, 40, and 51 as the test numbers.

127. When the functionality tests properly, enter this formula in cell C28: =AE23*C27. This is the percentage of hits multiplied by all hits.

Hiding Programming and Repositioning the Fleet

The game is functional, but there is a lot of programming visible to the player. It is an easy process to hide the programming so the player will not see it. Then, the ships need to be repositioned for gameplay.

128. Select rows 27 through 32 on the Game Frame tab.

129. Right-click anywhere on the selection, and click **Hide** in the shortcut menu. The programming is no longer visible to the player, as shown in **Figure 13**.

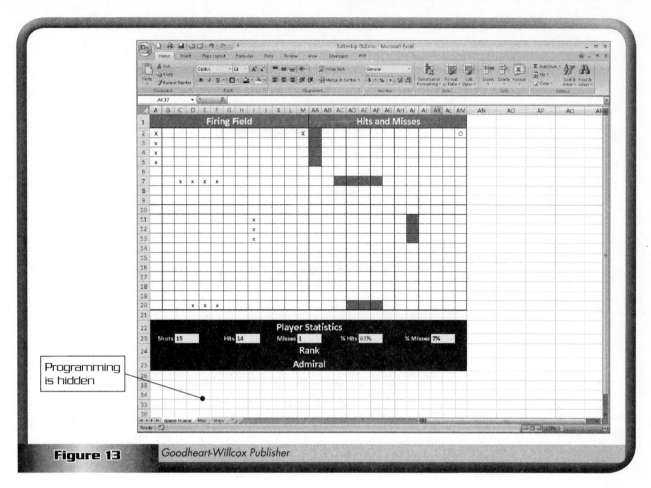

Figure 13   *Goodheart-Willcox Publisher*

130. Click the Ships tab.

131. Place five ships as specified in **Figure 14.** Place the ships in random locations, but remember each ship must be a straight line of cells either vertically or horizontally. Notice that the carrier is one cell longer than in the test version.

Protecting Data and Distributing the Game

Before the game is tested by others, the data needs to be protected. This is needed to prevent changes that will damage the programming. To do this, the worksheets will be locked and formulas hidden.

132. Click the Ships tab, select columns A through M, right-click, and select **Hide** in the shortcut menu. This hides the ship locations from the player.

133. With the Ships tab active, click the **Protect Sheet** button on the **Changes** panel of the **Review** tab in the ribbon.

134. In the **Protect Sheet** dialog box, check the **Protect worksheet and contents of locked cells** check box, as shown in **Figure 15.**

Ship Type	Carrier	Battleship	Destroyer	Submarine	Patrol Boat
Symbol	C	B	D	S	P
Cells Occupied	Five	Four	Three	Three	Two

Figure 14   *Goodheart-Willcox Publisher*

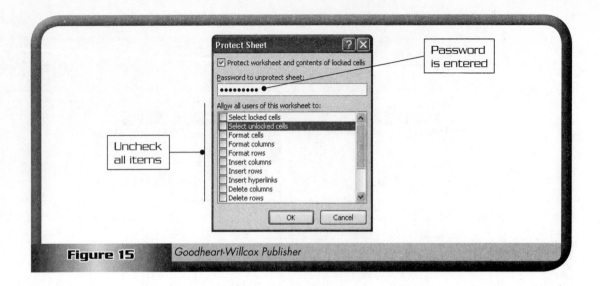

Figure 15   Goodheart-Willcox Publisher

135. Click in the **Password to unprotect sheet:** text box, and enter your last name. Letter case matters.

136. In the **Allow all users of this worksheet to:** list, uncheck each item.

137. Click the **OK** button. You are prompted to reenter the password before the sheet is locked. Password protecting the sheet adds a level of security that prevents the player from unhiding the columns on the sheet to expose the ships.

138. Similarly, click the Map tab, hide columns A through AM, and password to protect the sheet.

139. Save the file, then perform a save as and save it as *LastName_*Battleship Game in your working folder.

140. Distribute the Battleship Game file to a classmate as directed by your instructor. Have your classmate provide constructive criticism of your design.

141. Play the game designed by a classmate, and provide constructive criticism of his or her design.

142. Save your work, and submit all files for grading.

Review Questions

1. Describe the meaning of 1 and 0 in binary code.

_____

_____

_____

_____

2. What is the purpose of creating the Map sheet in this game build?

_____

_____

_____

_____

3. Describe conditional formatting.

_____

_____

_____

_____

4. When the lookup table was initially created, cells were merged. The **VLOOKUP** function does not recognize merged cells as a single cell, so the merged cells were unmerged and the data moved. What is another way this error could have been corrected?

_____

_____

_____

_____

5. Describe security features of this game build to prevent a player from cheating or accidentally breaking the game.

_____

_____

_____

_____

Activity 12-3

Tile-Based Tic-Tac-Toe

Objectives

Students will use a game engine to design a programming array to store and compare values. Students will program strings and paragraph-based dialogue. Students will retrieve array data for comparisons. Students will program interactivity zones to create tile-based games.

Situation

The Really Cool Game Company has reviewed the proof of concept design for *Tic-Tac-Toe* created in Activity 12-1. It has approved the project. Now your task is to implement an array into a tile-based game using the Multimedia Fusion 2 game engine. You must include subroutines in the programming to allow functionality in the game to switch between player X turn and player O turn and determine the winner.

How to Begin

Frame Editor

Grid Setup

1. Launch MMF2, and name the new application Tic-Tac-Toe.
2. Save the file as *LastName*_Tic-Tac-Toe Game in your working folder.
3. Display Frame 1 in the frame editor.
4. Change the grid to 50 × 50.
5. In the **Library** window, expand the tree Local Library > Backgrounds > Tiles > Small Backdrop Tiles, and insert a gray background tile, such as Tile 58, onto the game frame.
6. Resize the tile to 100 pixels × 100 pixels.
7. Move the tile to (0,0), and then copy and paste the tile to form a grid that is three tiles across and three tiles down, as shown in **Figure 1**.
8. Insert a red tile onto the game frame, and resize it to 100 pixels × 100 pixels.
9. Open the red tile in the image editor, and, using the tools in the image editor, add a large X to the tile.
10. Insert a blue tile onto the game frame, and resize it to 100 pixels × 100 pixels.
11. Open the blue tile in the image editor, and add a large O to the tile.

Strings

To begin setting a series of events for one player turn, start by inserting a string. A series of text messages will be displayed to the player, and these are strings.

12. Insert a new string object in the blank area near the top of the game frame. The string object is located in the Text category in the **Create New Object** dialog box.
13. Resize the object to 300 pixels wide by 65 pixels high, and set the location to (335,0).
14. Rename the object to String_PlayerTurns.
15. With the string object selected, click the **Settings** tab in the **Properties** window, and click the default string Text for the **Paragraph 1** property.

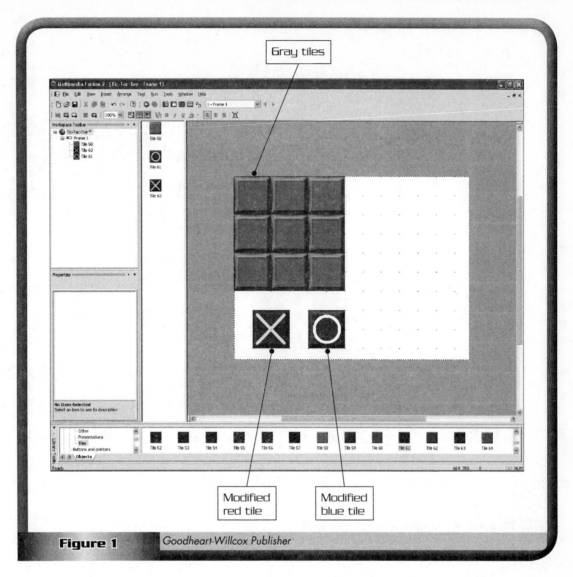

Figure 1   *Goodheart-Willcox Publisher*

16. Enter Player X Turn as the new string.

17. Click the **New** button below the **Paragraph 1** property to create a second paragraph property (**Paragraph 2**).

18. Change the **Paragraph 2** property to state Player O Turn. Use the capital letter O, not a zero.

19. Click the **Text Options** tab in the **Properties** window, and double-click the **Font** property to open the **Font** dialog box.

20. Change the font size to 36, and close the **Font** dialog box.

21. Insert a new static text object below the String_PlayerTurns object, and change the text to read Click a gray space to insert your mark. Resize the object to display all of the text, and remove the border.

22. Insert a new string object, resize it to 300 pixels wide by 100 pixels high, and set its location to (335,215).

23. Change the font size of the string to 36.

24. Add three paragraphs to the string: No Winner, Player X Wins!, and Player O Wins!, as shown in **Figure 2.**

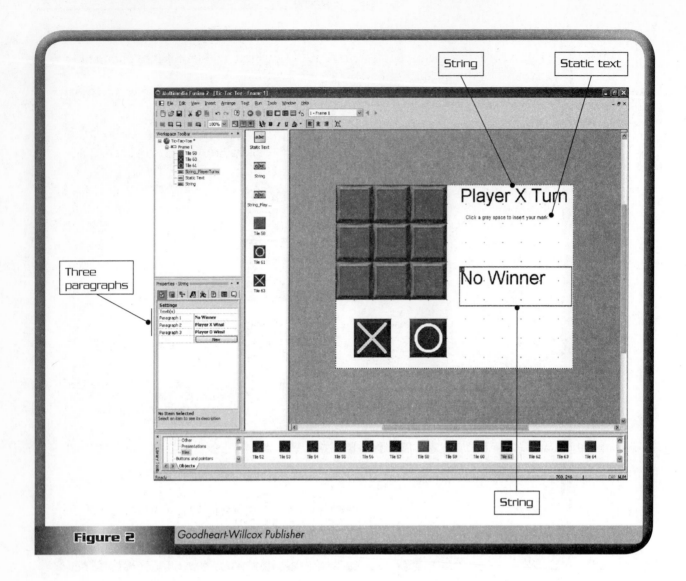

Figure 2   *Goodheart-Willcox Publisher*

GUI and Array

The game needs one button for player interaction. This will allow for resetting the game. Additionally, game data will be stored in an array, which must be created.

25. Insert a new button object, and name it Reset Button.

26. Change the size of the button to 200 pixels wide by 100 pixels high, and set the location to (385,100).

27. Enter Reset Game as the display text, and change the font size to 24.

28. Insert a new array object somewhere outside of the scope. The array object is located in the Data category in the **Create New Object** dialog box.

29. Name the array object Victory_Array.

30. With the array object selected, click the **Settings** tab in the **Properties** window.

31. Enter 3 in the **X dimension** and **Y dimension** properties and 1 in the **Z dimension** property. This creates an array that mirrors the three by three construction of the game map.

32. Click the **Type of array** property, and change the property to **Number array**. This is important so the numbers stored in the array will not be stored as text.

Global Variables

The basic game layout is created. A global variable will be used to change the gameplay mode to switch from one player to another.

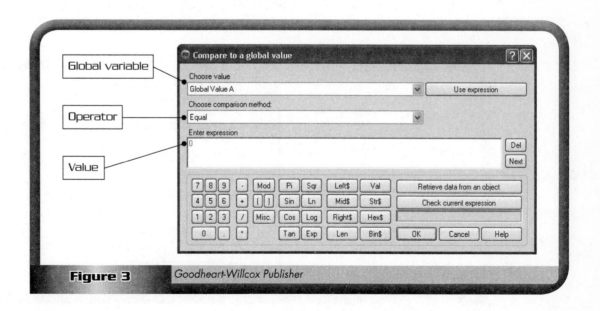

Event Editor

33. Display the event editor.

34. On line 1, insert a comment that states Is Player O Turn.

35. On line 2, add a new condition. In the **New Condition** dialog box, right-click on the **Special** icon, and click **Compare to global value** in the shortcut menu. The expression editor is displayed, as shown in **Figure 3**.

36. Make sure **Global Value A** is selected in the **Choose value** drop-down list, the **Equal** operator is selected in the **Choose comparison method:** drop-down list, and 0 is entered in the text box. Click the **OK** button to close the expression editor.

37. On line 3, add a new condition, and program this pseudo code: **IF** the value of global variable **A** is equal to 1. When global variable **A** is set to 1, it is player O's turn.

38. Create a subroutine named Player X Turn. Review Activity 7-3 if you do not recall how to do this.

39. Create a subroutine named Player O Turn.

40. On line 2, add this pseudo code: **THEN** activate the Player X Turn subroutine **AND** deactivate the Player O Turn subroutine.

41. On line 3, add this pseudo code: **THEN** activate the Player O Turn subroutine **AND** deactivate the Player X Turn subroutine.

42. Right-click on the number for line 4, and click **Insert > A new event** in the shortcut menu to add an event above the first subroutine. Program this pseudo code: **IF** the player clicks the **Reset** button, **THEN** restart the application.

Placing an X on the Map

Player X will be able to place an X square in any empty space on the game map. The value of this move will be stored in the array.

43. On line 6 in the Player X Turn subroutine, add a new condition, and program this pseudo code: **IF** on Player X Turn subroutine activation, **THEN** deactivate the Player O Turn subroutine.

Figure 3   Goodheart-Willcox Publisher

44. Right-click in the cell where the **Line 6** row intersects the **String_PlayerTurns** column, and click **Set paragraph...** in the shortcut menu.

45. In the **Set Paragraph** dialog box, click the first paragraph, and click the **OK** button, as shown in **Figure 4.** This adds the pseudo code **AND** display paragraph 1 for the String_PlayerTurns object to line 6.

46. On line 7, program this pseudo code: **IF** the player clicks on a gray tile, **THEN** create a red tile at 0,0 relative to the position of the gray tile **AND** destroy the gray tile.

Zones

A zone can be designated as a trigger. This trigger will listen for a mouse click in the zone and adjust the global value to switch from player X's turn to player O's turn.

47. On line 8 in the Player X Turn subroutine, add a new condition.

48. In the **New Condition** dialog box, right-click on the keyboard and mouse icon, and click **The Mouse** > **User clicks within a zone** in the shortcut menu.

49. In the dialog box that is displayed, click the **Left button** radio button, click the **Single click** radio button, and click the **OK** button. The frame editor is temporarily displayed, along with the **Zone Setup** dialog box.

50. In the **Zone Setup** dialog box, enter 0 in the left-hand **Horizontal** text box and 300 in the right-hand text box, as shown in **Figure 5.** Enter the same values in the two **Vertical** text boxes.

51. Click the **OK** button to set the zone and return to the event editor. The pseudo code for this is: **IF** the player clicks anywhere in the game map zone.

52. On line 8, program this pseudo code: **THEN** change the value of global variable **A** to 1. When player X clicks on the game map to make a move, the game will switch to player O's turn.

Error Avoidance

What if player X clicks on a space where there is already an X or an O? The game will switch to player O's turn without placing an X. The game should remain player X's turn when this error occurs. Only one line of code is needed.

53. On line 9 in the Player X Turn subroutine, program this pseudo code: **IF** the player clicks on an X tile **OR** an O tile, **THEN** set the value of global variable **A** to 0.

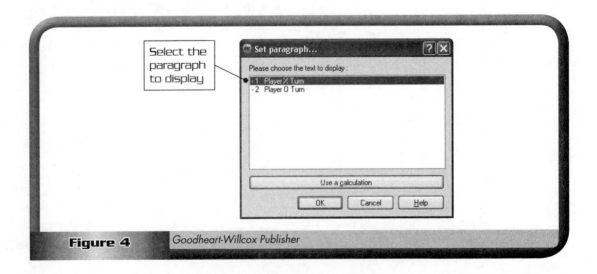

Figure 4   *Goodheart-Willcox Publisher*

Name: _____

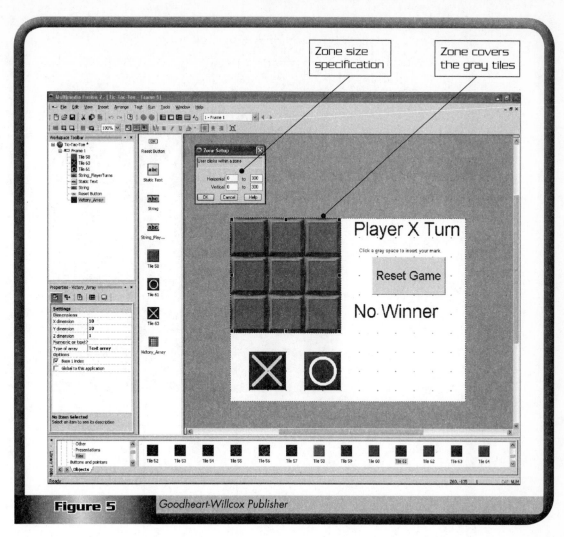

Zone size specification

Zone covers the gray tiles

Figure 5   *Goodheart-Willcox Publisher*

Storing Values in an Array

When player X makes a move, the value 1 needs to be stored in the array. This is similar to the functionality of the proof-of-concept game created in Excel. However, unlike the Excel array, the programmer is unable to view the array and values. To keep track of the array, many programmers use graph paper or a spreadsheet to record and label the array indexes so they can keep track of what is in the array.

54. On line 10 in the Player X Turn subroutine, add a new condition, and program this pseudo code: **IF** the player left-clicks in the zone **AND** the player left-clicks on the gray tile X1,Y1. A new zone must be defined to fully cover the individual tile, as shown in **Figure 6.**

55. Right-click in the cell where the **Line 10** row intersects the **Victory_Array** column, and click **Write > Write Value to XY** in the shortcut menu. The expression editor is displayed.

56. Enter 1 in the expression editor, and click the **OK** button. A new expression editor is displayed.

57. As this is the X1 position of the game map, enter 1, and click the **OK** button. A new expression editor is displayed.

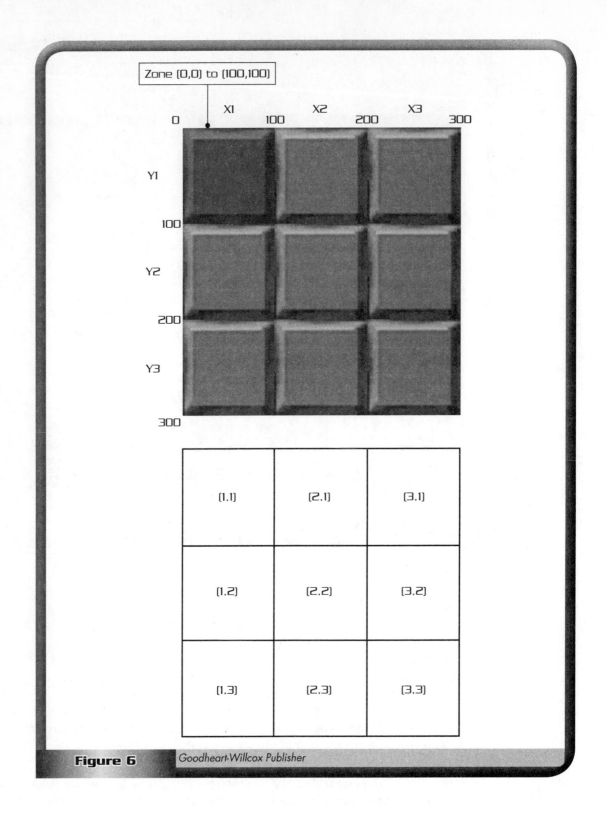

Zone (0,0) to (100,100)

	X1	X2	X3
	[1,1]	[2,1]	[3,1]
	[1,2]	[2,2]	[3,2]
	[1,3]	[2,3]	[3,3]

Figure 6   *Goodheart-Willcox Publisher*

58. As this is the Y1 position of the game map, enter 1, and click the **OK** button. This completes the programming to set the value of the X1, Y1 position of the array to 1, as shown in **Figure 7.**

59. Similarly, add programming to place the value 1 in the array for the remaining eight zones of the game map. To improve programming efficiency, you can drag the existing check mark and then edit it as needed.

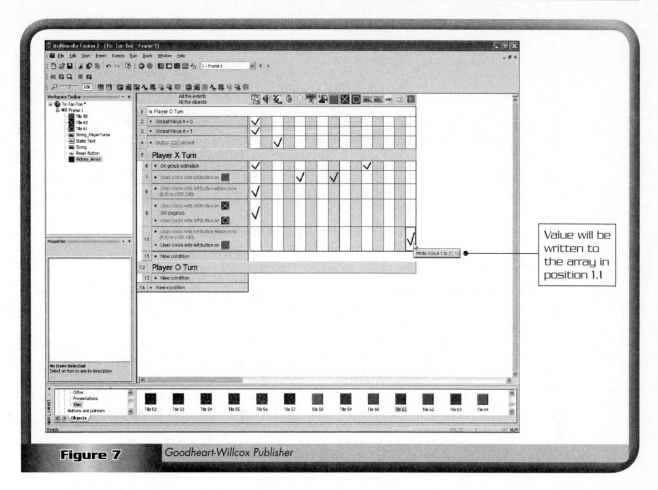

Value will be written to the array in position 1.1

Figure 7   *Goodheart-Willcox Publisher*

Player O Turn

The programming for the Player X Turn subroutine is complete. Now, programming needs to be added to the Player O Turn subroutine.

60. Copy all the programming lines from the Player X Turn subroutine by clicking on the first line (line 6), holding down the [Shift] key, and clicking the last line (line 18). Then, right-click on the selection, and click **Copy** in the shortcut menu.

61. Paste the copied code into the Player O Turn subroutine by right-clicking on the first line in the subroutine (line 21), and clicking **Paste** in the shortcut menu.

62. Edit the code in the Player O Turn subroutine as needed to place an O tile when the player clicks and to switch the game mode to player X's turn.

63. In the Player O Turn subroutine, modify the code for the array so the value 10 is placed in the array.

Run Application

64. Save your work, and test play the game. Check if the game places the X and O tiles properly and switches modes. Make sure to test the clicking error handling and reset button as well. Debug if needed.

Victory Condition Testing

The values stored in the array need to be tested to determine the winner. When a winner is determined, the correct string text must be displayed to the players.

65. At the end, which should be line 35, add a comment that states Victory Condition Programming.

66. On line 36, add a comment that states Top Row Test.

67. On line 37, add a new condition. In the **New Condition** dialog box, right-click on the **Special** icon, and click **Compare two general values** in the shortcut menu. The expression editor is displayed.

68. Click in the top text box, delete the existing value, and click the **Retrieve data from an object** button.

69. In the **New Expression** dialog box, right-click on the **Victory_Array** object, and click **Read value from XY position** in the shortcut menu. A string of code is added to the top text box in the expression editor, as shown in **Figure 8.**

70. Replace >X Offset< with 1, and replace >Y Offset< with 1. The expression should read ValueAtXY("Victory_Array", 1, 1). This tells MMF2 to read the value in the X1, Y1 position of the array.

71. Make sure the comparison method is **Equal**, and enter 1 in the bottom text box. Close the expression editor. This tests **IF** the value in the X1, Y1 position of the Victory_ Array object is equal to 1.

72. Complete the programming on line 37 to match this pseudo code to test if player X has filled the top row of the game map:

> **IF** the value in the X1, Y1 position of the Victory_Array object is equal to 1,
> > **AND** the X2, Y1 position of the Victory_Array object is equal to 1,
> > **AND** the X3, Y1 position of the Victory_Array object is equal to 1,
> **THEN** destroy the gray tiles
> > **AND** display paragraph 2 of the victory condition string (Player X Wins!).

73. On line 38, program this pseudo code to test if player O has filled the top row of the game map:

> **IF** the value in the X1, Y1 position of the Victory_Array object is equal to 10,
> > **AND** the X2, Y1 position of the Victory_Array object is equal to 10,
> > **AND** the X3, Y1 position of the Victory_Array object is equal to 10,
> **THEN** destroy the gray tiles
> > **AND** display paragraph 3 of the victory condition string (Player O Wins!).

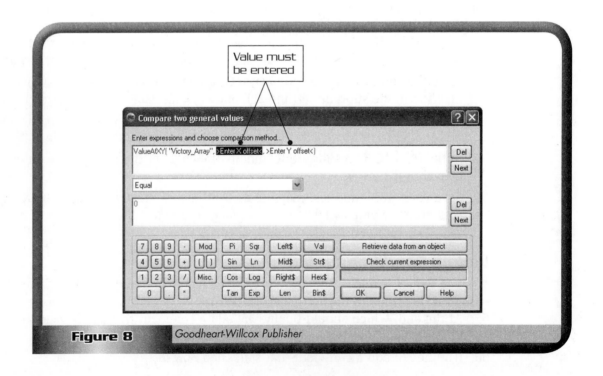

Figure 8   Goodheart-Willcox Publisher

Name: _____

74. Similarly, add the programming needed to test if player X or player O has filled the middle row, bottom row, left-hand column, middle column, right-hand column, left diagonal (top-left to bottom-right), and right diagonal (top-right to bottom-left). Copy and paste programming to increase your efficiency. Add a comment before each test to indicate what the programming does.

75. Test play the game.

Run Application

75. Save your work, compile an EXE file, and submit it for grading according to the directions provided by your instructor.

Review Questions

1. Describe how strings are used in this game build.

_____

_____

_____

_____

2. What are the dimensions of the array created in this game build, and why were those dimensions used?

_____

_____

_____

_____

3. Describe how a global variable is implemented in this game build.

_____

_____

_____

_____

4. What are the two applications of zones in this game build?

_____

_____

_____

_____

5. Interpret the meaning of this code: ValueAtXY("Car_Config", 5, 8).

_____

_____

_____

_____

Activity 12-4

Visual Basic Script Programming

Objectives

Students will use custom assets in game design. Students will use original art to customize design. Students will program game assets using a Visual Basic script editor. Students will use a game engine to create a custom pinball game.

Situation

The Really Cool Game Company uses the Visual Pinball game engine for designing pinball games. These games are able to play on a PC as well as being uploaded into a virtual pinball game. The virtual pinball game is a standalone game that uses a video playing field to simulate the real-world movement and physics of a mechanical pinball machine. All of the devices used in a mechanical pinball machine are available in the virtual pinball game.

How to Begin

1. Launch Visual Pinball, and maximize the window if needed.
2. Select **File** > **New** to begin building a new pinball game. A blank pinball template is displayed in the main window.
3. Click **File** > **Save As...**, and save the game as *LastName*_Pinball Sample in your working folder.
4. Click the **Play** button to render the 3D environment.

5. Use the left and right [Shift] keys to control the flippers.
6. Press and hold the [Enter] key to pull the plunger, and release the key to launch the ball.
7. Test the basic physics and movement of the game environment. Close the window when finished exploring the basic functionality of the pinball machine.

Heads-Up Display

Default physics and a layout are included in the template. Your task is to add custom features to make a playable game.

8. Click the **Options** button. This is a toggle that displays and hides the **Options** panel on the right-hand side of the interface, as shown in **Figure 1**.

9. Click the **Backdrop** button to view the backdrop. The backdrop is the HUD for the game. Notice the black box. This is the score area for player 1.
10. Click the **Backdrop** button again to return to the game-environment view.

Game Objects

Visual Pinball has many standard objects that are used in most pinball games. These game objects can be placed, resized, customized, and programmed.

11. Click the **Bumper** button. The cursor changes to indicate a bumper can be inserted.

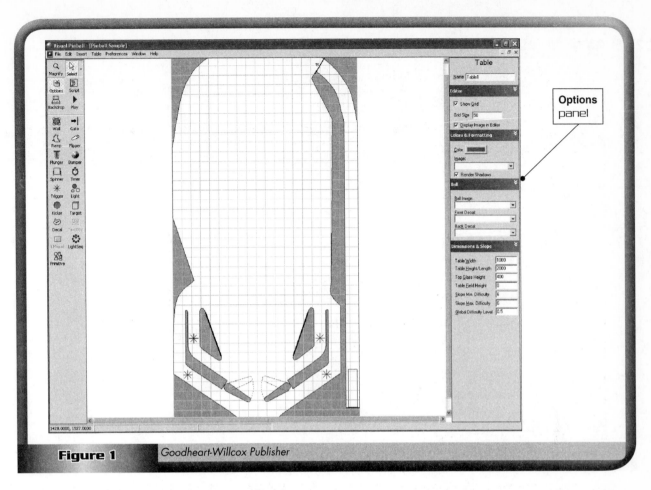

Figure 1   *Goodheart-Willcox Publisher*

12. Click near the top of the game environment to add a bumper. The **Options** panel displays properties for a bumper.

13. Add two additional bumpers to the top of the game environment. Notice that each bumper is given a unique name, as shown in **Figure 2.** Once a bumper has been added, it can be selected and dragged.

14. Select the first bumper, and change the color to blue using the settings in the **Options** panel.

15. In the **State** area, click **LightStateOn** in the **State** drop-down list, and check the **Flash When Hit** check box. This means the bumper will be illuminated when the game starts and flash when the bumper is hit.

16. Select the second bumper, change the color to orange, and set the light state to off.

17. Select the third bumper, change the color to red, and set the light state to blinking.

18. Play the game, and test the bumpers.

Score

The bumpers work, and you can manipulate the ball with the flippers, but the game has not been programmed to keep score. To do this, the programming script must be modified. Visual Basic is very easy to read and understand. It uses **IF**…**THEN** programming you have seen as pseudo code in previous activities. Visual Basic is an *object-oriented language,* which means the programming is based on objects that have properties and methods.

19. Select the first bumper, and click the **Script** button. A new window is opened that contains the Visual Basic script, as shown in **Figure 3.**

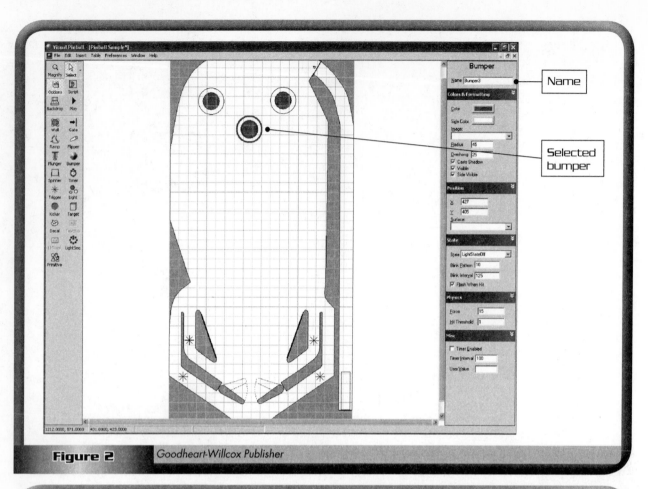

Name

Selected bumper

Figure 2   *Goodheart-Willcox Publisher*

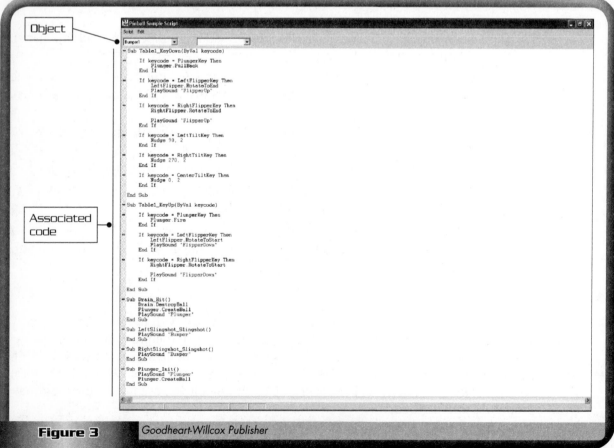

Object

Associated code

Figure 3   *Goodheart-Willcox Publisher*

20. Make sure **Bumper1** is selected in the left-hand drop-down list. This is the object to which the code is attached. If you renamed this object, choose the correct name.

21. Click the right-hand drop-down list, and click **Hit** in the list. This is the event that will be programmed. Notice at the bottom of the window that a new sub, or subroutine, has been added:

```
= Sub Bumper1_Hit( )
End Sub
```

Variables

Before the score can be changed, it needs to be added as a variable to the script. In most programming languages, a variable must be declared as a data type. A *data type* is the kind of information the variable will hold. Some variables will hold numbers and others will hold characters (text). There are many data types. Visual Basic allows a variable to be declared as a variant data type. *Variant* is an automatic data type and can be a number or character. In Visual Basic, if you do not specify the data type it will automatically be variant type. Other common data types for Visual Basic and most other programming languages are shown in **Figure 4.** All of the variables used in the pinball game will be the **Variant** type. The Visual Basic script (VBS) in this program does not accept explicit data type declarations. Each game asset has a predetermined **Variant** data type.

Data Type	Data	Range	Description	Example
Integer	Whole number	–2,147,483,648 and 2,147,483,647	Number values up to four bytes.	X = 543210987
Short	Whole number	–32768 and 32767	Number values up to two bytes.	X = –12345
Long	Whole number	A very large number.	Number values up to eight bytes.	X = 1234567890111213
String	Character	Any number of characters.	Holds text only shown in "quotation". Numbers entered into a string variable are text and not numbers, meaning they cannot be used in calculations unless first converted.	X = "hello world" X = "4" X = "anything"
Boolean	True/false	On or off state only.	Used to check if something is true, active, or enabled or not.	X = true
Single	Decimal number	Short decimal values.	Number with decimal value up to four bytes; single precision floating point.	X = 3.14159
Double	Decimal number	Long decimal values.	Number with decimal value up to eight bytes; double precision floating point.	X = 12345.1234567890

Figure 4 *Goodheart-Willcox Publisher*

The game score should change by adding the points from an asset hit by the ball. To add the score as a variable, some code must be manually entered, starting after the Bumper1_Hit subroutine.

22. Click at the end of the End Sub line for the Bumper1_Hit subroutine, and press the [Enter] key twice to leave a blank line.

23. Enter '*********** Adding Score Variable and Formula. The apostrophe indicates the line is a remark or REM statement. A REM statement is not part of the functioning code. The comments you added to MMF2 game builds are REM statements.

24. Press the [Enter] key to start a new line, and enter Dim Score. This declares a variable named **Score** and prepares it for accepting data.

25. Press the [Enter] key twice to leave a blank line, and enter Sub AddScore(points). This begins a new subroutine named AddScore. The statement in parentheses is a named parameter for the subroutine; in this case, points.

26. Press the [Enter] key to start a new line, and press the [Tab] key to *intercalate* the code.

27. Enter Score=Score+points. This is a recursive formula because the **Score** variable uses itself to solve for its new value. Visual Basic is case sensitive, so be sure to exactly match the case of the letters.

28. Press the [Enter] key, press the [Tab] key, and enter ScoreText.Text=FormatNumber (Score,0,–1,0,–1). This code sets the **Text** property of the object named **ScoreText** to the variable **Score** and formats the text. The **ScoreText** object is the default text box in the game backdrop.

29. Press the [Enter] key to start a new line, and enter End Sub. This ends the subroutine. The Sub and End Sub lines are not indented as part of the intercalating process.

30. Press the [Enter] key, and add the REM statement '*********Adding Score Ends Here.

31. Click on the blank, indented line in the Sub Bumper1_Hit ( ) subroutine, and enter AddScore(10). This calls the AddScore subroutine, and the parameter is assigned a value of 10. Remember, the AddScore subroutine has a parameter named points, which is used in the formula Score=Score+points. The value 10 is used in this formula and added to the current score. The completed code is shown in **Figure 5**.

32. Click the **Script** pull-down menu, and click **Compile** in the menu. This compiles the code so the game engine can use it.

33. Close the script window.

Play

34. Test play the game. Check that the score increases by 10 when the Bumper1 object is hit.

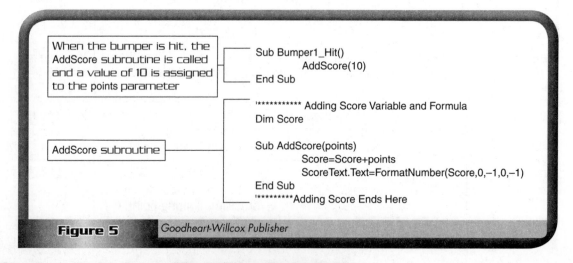

When the bumper is hit, the AddScore subroutine is called and a value of 10 is assigned to the points parameter

```
Sub Bumper1_Hit()
        AddScore(10)
End Sub
```

AddScore subroutine

```
'*********** Adding Score Variable and Formula
Dim Score

Sub AddScore(points)
        Score=Score+points
        ScoreText.Text=FormatNumber(Score,0,–1,0,–1)
End Sub
'*********Adding Score Ends Here
```

Figure 5 *Goodheart-Willcox Publisher*

Name: _____

Copy and Edit Scripting

The code you added is basically the same as what is needed for the other bumpers. Copying, pasting, and editing the code is more efficient than programming each subroutine from scratch.

35. Open the script window.

36. Select the three lines in the Sub Bumper1_Hit ( ) subroutine, and press the [Ctrl][C] key combination to copy the code.

37. Click at the end of the Sub Bumper1_Hit() subroutine, press the [Enter] twice to leave a blank line, and press the [Ctrl][V] key combination to paste the code.

38. Change the name of the subroutine to Sub Bumper2_Hit(), and change the parameter value to 15.

39. Similarly, create a subroutine named Sub Bumper3_Hit() with a parameter value of 20.

40. Compile the script, and close the script window.

41. Test play the game. Check that the scoring works properly for each bumper.

More Scoring

The AddScore( ) subroutine will work for any game asset, not just the bumpers. You will now add scoring to the game for the built-in slingshots. The slingshots are located just above the flippers.

42. Open the script window.

43. Locate the LeftSlingshot_Slingshot( ) subroutine, click after the PlaySound "Bumper" line, press the [Enter] key to start a new line, and press the [Tab] key to intercalate the code.

44. Enter AddScore (5). Hitting the left slingshot with the ball will score five points.

45. Similarly, program the right slingshot to score five points. The completed code is shown in **Figure 6.**

46. Compile the script, and close the script window.

47. Test play the game. Check that the scoring works properly for each slingshot.

Textures

The pinball game has functional gameplay, but it could use a little style. You will now add textures to game assets to create a visually interesting game environment.

48. Using clipart, sample photos, or the Internet, locate a free-use image of wood flooring, and save it as Wood.jpg in your working folder.

49. Click the **Table** pull-down menu, and click **Image Manager...** in the menu. Before a texture can be applied in Visual Pinball, it must be imported using the **Image Manager** dialog box, as shown in **Figure 7.**

50. Click the **Import** button, browse for the Wood.jpg image file, and open it.

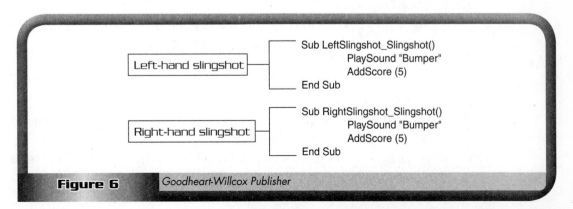

Figure 6   *Goodheart-Willcox Publisher*

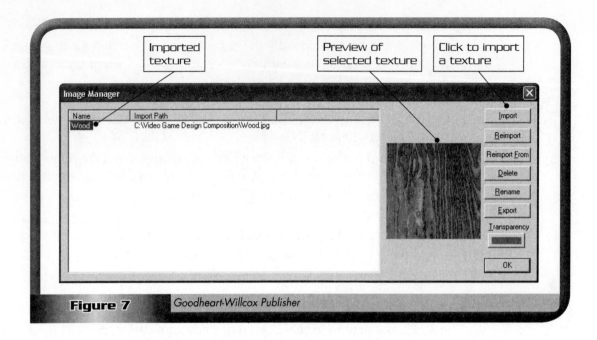

Imported texture

Preview of selected texture

Click to import a texture

Image Manager

Name | Import Path
Wood | C:\Video Game Design Composition\Wood.jpg

Import
Reimport
Reimport From
Delete
Rename
Export
Transparency

OK

Figure 7   *Goodheart-Willcox Publisher*

51. Close the **Image Manager** dialog box.

52. Click the **Options** button if the **Options** panel is not already displayed.

Options

53. Click anywhere off of the table in the main window to ensure no object is selected. The **Options** panel should have the label **Table** at the top to indicate the displayed options are for the entire table.

54. In the **Color & Formatting** area, click the **Image:** drop-down list, and click the wood image that was imported.

55. Test play the game. See how the texture is placed on the table.

Play

Flipper Modification

Manufacturers of mechanical pinball games often customize the flippers to add to the pinball action and appearance of the game. You will now do the same for this pinball video game.

56. Click the left-hand flipper to select that object.

57. Using the **Options** panel, change the flipper color to green.

58. Change the rubber color to red.

59. Change the rubber thickness to 4.

60. Change the right-hand flipper to match the left-hand flipper.

61. Test play the game. See how the changes are applied to the flippers.

Play

Gate Asset

A gate allows the ball to pass one way and not the other. Basically, it flips up in one direction only. You will now add a gate to the game.

62. Click the **Gate** button.

Gate

63. Position the gate at the top of the game next to the left-hand bumper.

64. In the **Options** panel, change the rotation of the gate to 45 degrees. Notice the arrow on the gate indicating which direction the ball can pass. It should be pointing toward the top of the game.

65. Move the bumpers to positions similar to what is shown in **Figure 8** to make a row with gaps large enough for the ball to move through, but not around the gate and bumper.

Play

66. Test play the game. See how the gate functions.

Name: _____

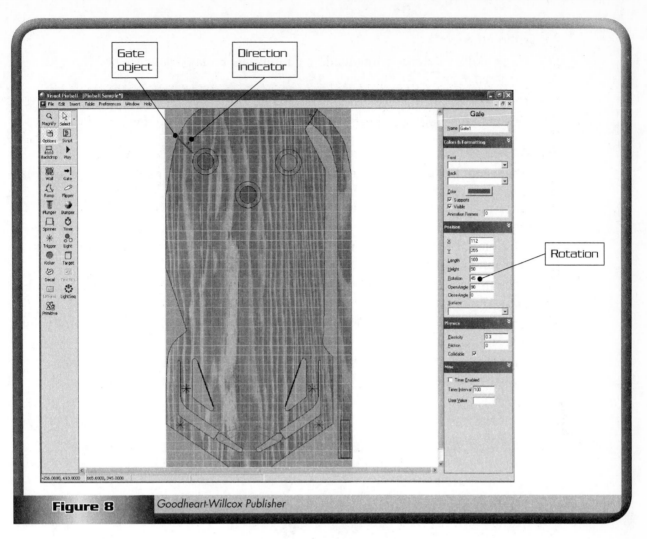

Figure 8   *Goodheart-Willcox Publisher*

Sound Engineering

The game is functional, but you may have noticed the bumpers do not have any sound associated with them. The prebuilt objects, like the flippers and slingshots, are already programmed to play sounds. In the next set of steps, you will learn how to use the sound manager to upload sounds and edit the programming to allow sound for each bumper.

67. Using clipart, sample photos, or the Internet, locate a free-use WAV file of a ding or bell, and save it as Bumper_Hit.wav in your working folder. If the file is not in the WAV format, it must be converted to WAV to be used in Visual Pinball.

68. Similarly, locate a laser-type sound to be played when the gate is triggered, and save it as Gate.wav in your working folder.

69. Click the **Table** pull-down menu, and click **Sound Manager...** in the menu. The **Sound Manager** dialog box functions similar to the **Image Manager** dialog box.

70. Import the Bumper_Hit.wav and Gate.wav sound files, and close the **Sound Manager** dialog box.

71. Open the script window.

72. Locate the Sub Bumper1_Hit() subroutine, click at the end of the AddScore(10) line, press the [Enter] key to start a new line, and press the [Tab] key to intercalate the code.

73. Enter PlaySound "Bumper_Hit". This code tells the game engine to play the sound file whenever the bumper is hit by the ball. Any code between Sub Bumper1_Hit() and End Sub will be processed whenever the Bumper1 object is hit by the ball.

74. Copy and paste this line of code into the Sub Bumper2_Hit() and Sub Bumper3_Hit() subroutines.

75. Using skills you have learned, add a subroutine to play a sound when the gate is triggered.

76. Compile the script, and close the script window.

77. Test play the game. See how the sounds have improved the game.

Map Design

The layout of the wall for the game map can be changed. The wall is the glass that appears over the top of the gameplay area.

78. Click the **Options** button if the **Options** panel is not already displayed.

79. Click on anywhere on the light gray areas of the game map to select the wall. A dark blue border indicates the areas of the wall. The red circles are control points that can be moved to change the wall dimensions.

80. Click the control point to the left of the left-hand bumper to select it. The control point settings are displayed in the **Options** panel.

81. Check the **Smooth** check box in the **Options** panel. This changes the control point to a smooth curve.

82. Drag the control point to create a smooth turn past the bumper, as shown in **Figure 9.** Move other control points as needed to create a good curve.

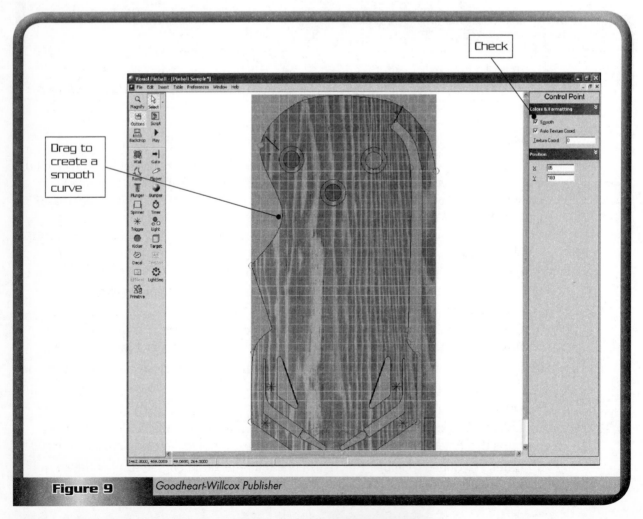

Figure 9   *Goodheart-Willcox Publisher*

83. Select the wall, and change the **Top Color** and **Side Color** settings to yellow.

84. Check the **Top Visible** and **Side Visible** check boxes so the top and side will be visible during gameplay.

85. Select each of the gray areas of the wall, and change the top and side colors to match.

86. Modify the wall to create a custom game map that is playable.

87. Add more objects for the ball to interact with, and add the programming needed to adjust the player score.

88. Test play the game, and debug as needed.

89. Save your work, and submit all files for grading.

Review Questions

1. What makes Visual Basic an object-oriented language?

   _____

   _____

   _____

   _____

2. What is a data type?

   _____

   _____

   _____

   _____

3. Describe the **Variant** data type.

   _____

   _____

   _____

   _____

4. What is used in Visual Basic to indicate the line is a REM statement?

   _____

5. How is code intercalated?

   _____

   _____

   _____

   _____

Activity 12-5

Programming Team

Objectives

Students will work as a team to solve problems. Students will work as a team to create a thematic video game design.

Situation

The Really Cool Game Company believes that you and your team can make an excellent game using the Visual Pinball software. The tasks assigned to your team are to brainstorm ideas, research components and designs, and design a quality pinball game using your school as the theme. The project is green lighted only to the proof-of-concept stage. When your team's proof of concept is approved, it will need to develop the custom game art, gameplay, and features needed to build a prototype game. The target audience is high school students.

How to Begin

1. Form into teams as directed by your instructor. All work must be done as a team.
2. Decide team roles based on the expertise, skill, and desire of the team members.
3. Research machine construction, gameplay, and components for pinball machines.
4. Brainstorm a thematic design for the team's game.
5. Explore the objects, components, and controls available in the Visual Pinball software.

Interactivity

6. Determine the important elements of the game and gameplay that the team feels are needed to entertain the target audience. Record these decisions in a list in a word processor document.
7. Add story elements such as characters, rooms, and bonuses.
8. Design triggers, kickbacks, and other gameplay elements to match the theme of the game.
9. Design locks and unlocks for the player to achieve.
10. Explore adding puzzle elements to the game, such as light patterns or other clues to rewards.
11. Explore adding strategy elements to the game, such as ball captures for multiball gameplay.
12. Explore adding multiple flippers or other interactivity elements to give the player more control over the environment.

Design

13. Create a world design document to show the layout of the game map.
14. Add the gameplay elements to the Visual Pinball software to create a proof-of-concept game.

Presentation

15. Assemble a proof-of-concept game.

16. Prepare a pitch presentation for the class. Make sure to explain the story and thematic elements of the game and any unique selling points of the game.

17. Describe or demonstrate the gameplay and unique features of the game.

18. Solicit comments from the class.

Reflection

19. As a team, reflect on the constructive criticism received from the class.

20. Integrate improvements to the design as needed from presentation comments.

21. Obtain the green light from your instructor to build the prototype.

Building the Prototype

22. Discuss the time deadline and how to best meet it.

23. Create a Gantt chart or PERT diagram to prioritize tasks and find dependencies.

24. Assign tasks as needed to maximize fast tracking with tasks done in parallel.

Programming

25. Program the scoring, functions, and other interactions of gameplay.

26. Modify the parameters and settings for each object to achieve the desired gameplay.

27. Test programming and scripts in a separate game build before adding them to the prototype game.

Art

28. Develop game art appropriate to the theme.

29. Place game art on the game map.

Sound

30. Create sound effects appropriate to the theme of the game.

31. Program the sounds to play as needed.

Tuning and Evaluation

32. Review the list of important elements for the team's game.

33. Evaluate how well the team feels that it has achieved the important elements.

34. Create an evaluation rubric from these elements for others to evaluate the game during testing.

Testing

35. Have other students play, test, and evaluate the game with the rubric the team created.

36. Review the evaluation rubrics.

37. Modify the game as needed.

38. Save the game.

39. Review the game and evaluation results with your instructor.

40. Save your work, and submit all files for grading.

Chapter 13
Simulation Composition

Tanja/Shutterstock.com

Ruslan Rizvanov/Shutterstock.com

PhotoStock10/Shutterstock.com

Name: _____

Date: _____

Class: _____

Bellwork

Day	Date	Activity	Response
1		Complete the anticipation guide and the K and W columns of the KWL chart for this chapter.	
2		What is the purpose of a simulation?	
3		What parameters would be tested for a paper-airplane simulation?	
4		List ways to reduce the amount of electronic waste in the environment.	
5		Describe how crowd funding works.	
6		Compare and contrast an ecosystem with a simulation system.	
7		How does chaos theory effect a simulation?	
8		How can perception be simulated in a virtual environment?	
9		How does a complex simulation allow an entity to select the most important goal?	
10		List six simulation models.	
11		What is a capture suit, and in what type of simulations would it be used?	

Name: _____

Day	Date	Activity	Response
12		What are the three components needed to sustain a system?	
13		What is queuing, and how is it important to a simulation?	
14		How is concealment data stored in automobiles and airplanes?	
15		How is exposure data related to the HUD of a video game?	
16		What are the five stages of applied event modeling?	
17		Define *event exploration*.	
18		What is an extensible framework?	
19		Complete the L column of the KWL chart and the After Reading column of the anticipation guide with what you learned from this chapter.	
20		Speculate what would happen to the right-rear section of the vehicle frame shown in textbook Figure 13-3. Analyze the simulation data, and suggest possible actions that could be undertaken to avoid damage to the right-rear of the vehicle.	

Anticipation Guide

Directions

Before reading the chapter, read each statement in the table below. In the column titled Before Reading, write the letter *T* if you agree with the statement or *F* if you disagree with the statement. After reading the chapter, reread each statement in the table below. In the column titled After Reading, write the letter *T* if you agree with the statement or *F* if you disagree with the statement. Be prepared to justify your answers in a class discussion.

Before Reading	Statement	After Reading
	Graphics for simulations are higher quality than video games.	
	Simulation entities are programmed with the five senses.	
	A hearing simulation may use a particle simulation to take the place of sound.	
	Heuristics involves learning by trial and error.	
	Automated simulations evaluate queuing to determine the cost of things waiting in line.	

KWL Chart

Directions

Before reading the chapter, fill in what you already know about the topic in the K column and what you want to learn in the W column. After reading the chapter, review what you know and wanted to learn about the topic. Reflect on what you have studied and completed in this chapter. Fill in what you learned in the L column. Be prepared to justify your answers in a class discussion.

Topic: Computer Simulations		
K What you already *know*	**W** What you *want* to learn	**L** What you *learned*

Activity 13-1

Artificial Intelligence: Maze AI

Objectives

Students will design and program artificial intelligence for entities. Students will program a simulation that includes entity movement and thinking.

Situation

Since video game design and simulation design share many of the same mechanics, the Really Cool Game Company is branching out into the simulation market. It wants you to get a foundation in simulation design so you can work on both video game and simulation projects. The first project involves creating artificial intelligence for an entity and a maze the entity must solve. The entity must navigate the maze and find the goal object without interaction from the player. This simulation is like the basic mouse-in-a-maze experiment in which the mouse must find the cheese.

How to Begin

1. Using PowerPoint or other graphics program, create a maze similar to the one shown in **Figure 1**. Use only right-angle turns and no curves. Evenly space the walls so the path is the same width throughout the maze. Create a maze that requires up, down, right, and left movement to solve, but do not create dead ends except for the very end of the maze.

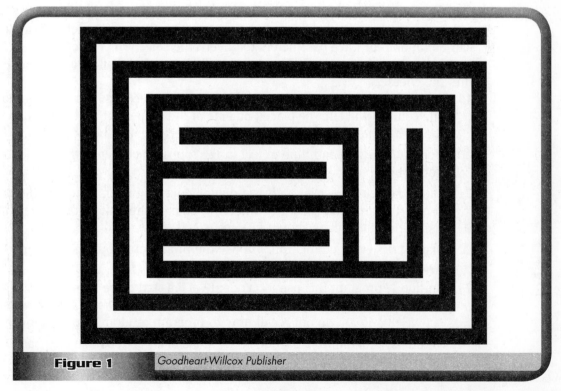

Figure 1   *Goodheart-Willcox Publisher*

Frame Editor

Clear

Paste

Transparency

2. Group the objects, and copy the image.

3. Launch MMF2, and start a new application.

4. Rename Frame 1 as Sightless Entity, and display the frame editor.

5. Insert a new backdrop object anywhere on the frame.

6. Open the backdrop object in image editor.

7. Clear the default image, and paste the copied maze image. Resize the canvas.

8. Set the transparency color to the color of the path, and close the image editor.

9. Rename the object as Maze 1, and set its size to 640 pixels × 480 pixels (the size of the frame).

10. Click the **RunTime Options** tab in the **Properties** window, and change the **Obstacle type** property to **Obstacle**.

11. Save the file as *LastName_*Maze AI in your working folder.

Entity and Goal

This game will have an entity to act as the mouse in the maze. Artificial intelligence will be programmed for this entity. A goal needs to be placed at the end of the maze for which the entity will search.

12. Insert a new active object at the start of the maze, and name it Entity 1.

Clear

Hotspot

Hotspot

13. Change the size of the object to 10 pixels × 10 pixels, and move the object to the center of the pathway. You may need to turn off snap if it is on.

14. Open the object in the image editor, clear the image, and fill it with black.

15. Change the hotspot to the center of the image.

16. Insert a new active object at the end of the maze, and name it Goal.

17. Change the size of the object to 20 pixels × 20 pixels. The size can be smaller if the path in your maze is not 20 pixels wide.

18. Open the object in the image editor, clear the image, and fill it with red.

Programming Random Action and the Objective

For entities that have artificial intelligence (AI), the entities do not really think, rather the programmer creates choices from which the entity selects. This selection can be random or have parameters to govern the selection. The choices for the entity in this level will be random. The mouse will have to bump its way around the maze to find the cheese.

19. Insert a new counter object on top of the Goal object, and name it Direction Counter. The counter will later be placed outside of the scope, but it needs to be visible to check that the programming is working correctly before being hidden.

20. Insert a new date and time object in the top-right corner of the frame. Insert it as a clock object.

21. Edit the clock properties so it is a digital clock, is in stopwatch mode, and displays hours, minutes, and seconds. If needed, change the font color so the clock is visible on the wall, as shown in **Figure 2.**

Event Editor

22. Display the event editor. You will use the programming skills developed in this class to program the game.

23. On line 1, program this pseudo code: **IF** at the start of the frame, **THEN** set the direction counter to choose from four random numbers **AND** start the stopwatch. Refer to Activity 8-4 if you do not recall how to program random numbers for the counter.

24. On line 2, program this pseudo code: **IF** the entity collides with the goal, **THEN** stop the stopwatch **AND** destroy the entity.

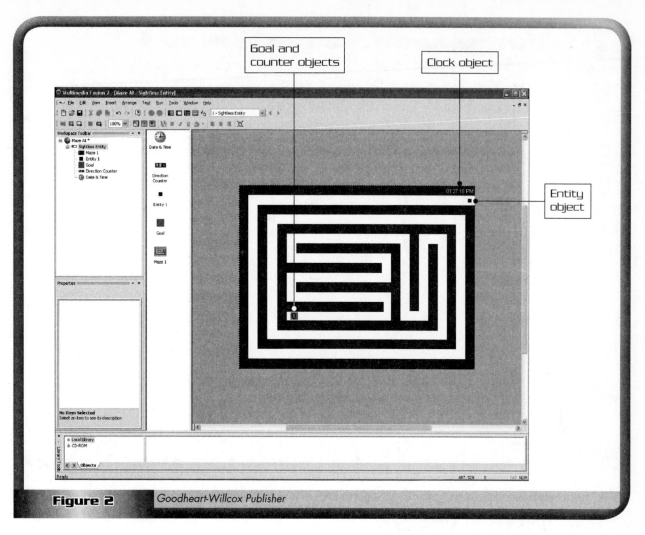

Figure 2   *Goodheart-Willcox Publisher*

25. On line 3, program this pseudo code: **IF** the direction counter equals 0.
26. On line 4, program this pseudo code: **IF** the direction counter equals 1.
27. On line 5, program this pseudo code: **IF** the direction counter equals 2.
28. On line 6, program this pseudo code: **IF** the direction counter equals 3.
29. After line 6, create four subroutines, and name them Up, Down, Right, and Left, as shown in **Figure 3.**
30. On line 3, program this pseudo code: **THEN** activate the Right subroutine **AND** deactivate the Up, Down, and Left subroutines.
31. On line 4, program this pseudo code: **THEN** activate the Up subroutine **AND** deactivate the Down, Right, and Left subroutines.
32. On line 5, program this pseudo code: **THEN** activate the Left subroutine **AND** deactivate the Up, Down, and Right subroutines.
33. On line 6, program this pseudo code: **THEN** activate the Down subroutine **AND** deactivate the Up, Right, and Left subroutines.
34. On line 2, program this pseudo code: **THEN** set the counter to 9. This will stop the movement of the entity as the counter is outside of the range specified. In effect, this is adding **AND** stop the movement of the entity to the existing code.

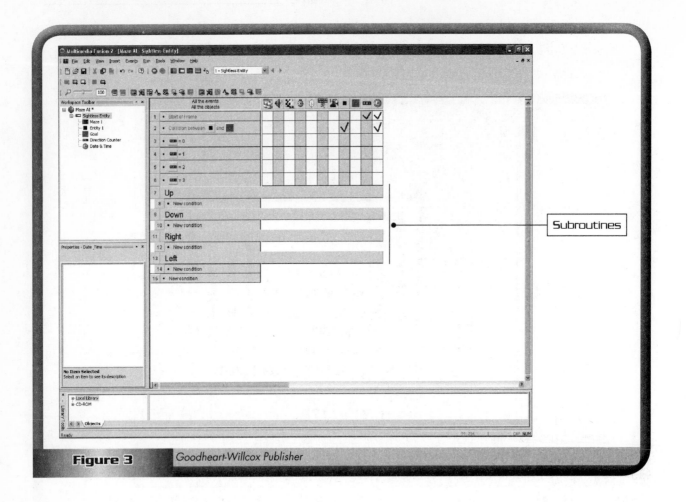

Figure 3   Goodheart-Willcox Publisher

Directional Movement

The movement of the entity can be programmed using tile-based movement, like in the frog-crossing game, or vector movement, like in the 2D particle animation. To reduce the processing load on the computer, tile-based movement will be used.

35. In the Up subroutine group, program the following pseudo code: **IF** always, **THEN** set the position of the entity to −10 pixels relative to its own Y coordinate.

36. Similarly, program movement for the Down, Left, and Right subroutines. All movement should be either positive or negative 10 pixels relative to the entity's current position.

Collision Detection

As the entity moves through the maze, it will run into the walls. On colliding with a wall, it will then randomly select a new direction of travel. The entity must be told to back away from the wall it ran into and change its direction.

37. Add a new condition to the Up subroutine, and program this pseudo code:

IF the entity is overlapping a backdrop object,
THEN set the Y coordinate of the entity to +12 pixels relative its current position
AND set the counter to a random choice from four numbers.

38. Similarly, program movement for the Down, Left, and Right subroutines to move away from the collision direction by 12 pixels and choose a random direction, as shown in **Figure 4.**

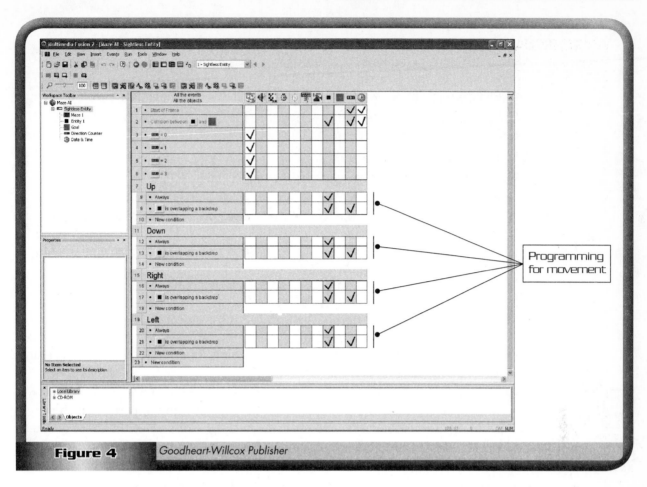

Figure 4   *Goodheart-Willcox Publisher*

Running the Simulation

This simulation is for a very energetic mouse trying to find the cheese. The simulation is ready to run. Watch the entity try to solve the maze, and see how long it takes.

39. Test play the frame. Whoops! Did the mouse run away?

Run Frame

40. Add a new backdrop object as an obstacle to close the entrance to the maze.

41. Save your work, and test play the frame.

Simulated Eyesight

Did you find yourself cheering for the little guy? Did he frustrate you, getting so close and then running all the way back to the start? Maybe some eyes will help the entity navigate the maze. At least it will stop running into things. Line-of-sight sensors will be used to simulate eyesight.

42. Copy the Sightless Entity level, and name the copy Sighted Entity.

43. Display the frame editor for the Sighted Entity frame, and insert a new active object named Left Sensor.

44. Change the size of the object to 35 pixels × 5 pixels. The 35 pixels should be about one-third of the width of the path, so adjust this as needed.

Clear

45. Open the object in the image editor, clear the image, and fill it with green. Also change the hotspot to the center.

Hotspot

46. Create three clones of the object, and name them Right Sensor, Top Sensor, and Bottom Sensor.

Chapter 13   Simulation Composition   **485**

47. Rotate the top and bottom sensors 90 degrees.

48. Place the entity against one wall and the correct sensor against the entity, as shown in **Figure 5.** Make sure the sensor is long enough to overlap the wall opposite the entity is touching. This is the line of sight. If the line of sight is too short to overlap the opposite wall, then the eyes will not have much value.

49. Change the size of each sensor so it overlaps the opposite wall, but does not extend through to the other side.

Event Editor

50. Display the event editor.

51. Above the first subroutine, program this pseudo code:

> **IF** always,
> **THEN** set the position of the Left Sensor object to –20 pixels relative to the position of the entity
>> **AND** set the position of the Right Sensor object to 20 pixels relative to the position of the entity
>> **AND** set the position of the Top Sensor object to –20 pixels relative to the position of the entity
>> **AND** set the position of the Bottom Sensor object to 20 pixels relative to the position of the entity.

52. Drag this programming line to the top so it becomes line 1. This is a housekeeping step to help organize the code.

Run Frame

53. Test play the frame. Make sure the sensors are following the entity. There will appear to be a slight lag or bounce between the sensors and the entity, which is due to how MMF draws the objects and normal. Does the entity solve the maze quicker?

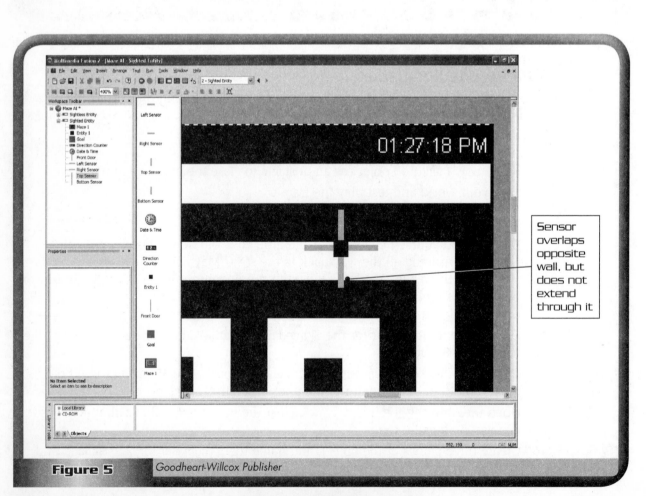

Sensor overlaps opposite wall, but does not extend through it

Figure 5   *Goodheart-Willcox Publisher*

Decision-Making

You probably noticed that the line-of-sight sensors do not help the entity solve the maze any quicker than without the sensors. This is because the entity is not making any decisions based on the line-of-sight sensors. The entity needs to be programmed to have some basic artificial intelligence that allows it to make a decision to find an open path. A counter is used to store directional data. If building a larger simulation in MMF2, these data could be stored using flags, alterable values, arrays, or other data-storage devices.

54. Copy the Sighted Entity level, and name the copy AI Entity.

Frame Editor

55. Display the frame editor for the AI Entity frame, and insert two new counter objects outside the scope. Name these objects Counter Right Collision and Counter Top Collision.

Event Editor

56. Display the event editor. The counters will be programmed using binary logic, where true is a value of 1, and false is a value of 0, as shown in **Figure 6**.

57. Above the first subroutine, program this pseudo code: **IF** the Right Sensor object is overlapping a backdrop object, **THEN** set the Counter Right Collision object to 1.

58. Add a new event, and program this pseudo code: **IF** the Top Sensor object is overlapping a backdrop object, **THEN** set the Counter Top Collision object to 1.

59. Add a new event, and program this pseudo code: **IF** the Right Sensor object is **NOT** overlapping a backdrop object, **THEN** set the Counter Right Collision object to 0.

60. Add a new event, and program this pseudo code: **IF** the Top Sensor object is **NOT** overlapping a backdrop object, **THEN** set the Counter Top Collision object to 0.

61. Locate the existing event for **IF** at the start of the frame, and program this pseudo code: **AND** set the Counter Right Collision object to 0 **AND** set the Counter Top Collision object to 0.

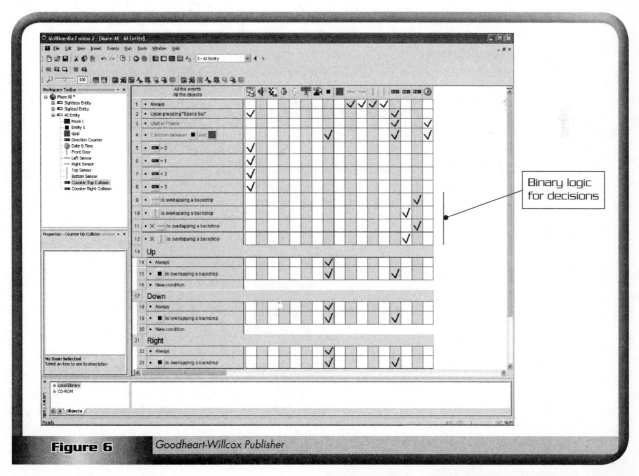

Figure 6 *Goodheart-Willcox Publisher*

Movement Choice

The artificial intelligence you are programming will make a fixed choice instead of a random choice. When the entity is traveling upward, the logic is that if it hits a wall, the entity will check to see if there is a wall on the right. If there is a wall on the right, it will choose to move left. If there is not a wall on the right, it will choose to move right. The directional values for this simulation, which are determined by the Direction Counter object, are shown in **Figure 7.**

62. In the Up subroutine, locate the existing event for **IF** the entity is overlapping a backdrop object, and program this pseudo code **AND IF** the Counter Right Collision object is equal to 1.

63. For this event, edit the action for the Direction Counter so its value is set to 2. In essence, this tells the entity to move left, because when this counter's value is 2, the Left subroutine is activated.

64. For this event, add actions to set the Counter Top Collision and Counter Right Collision objects to 0. This readies the counters for another line-of-sight sensing.

65. Copy this event, and paste it as the next line of programming in the Up subroutine. This new line will be the decision if a wall is on the right of the entity

66. Edit the copied event to match this pseudo code:

> **IF** the entity is overlapping a backdrop object
>> **AND** the Counter Right Collision object is equal to 0,
>
> **THEN** set the Y coordinate of the entity to +12 pixels relative to its current position
>> **AND** set the Direction Counter object to 0
>>
>> **AND** set the Counter Top Collision object to 0
>>
>> **AND** set the Counter Right Collision object to 0.

67. Similarly, add programming to the Down, Right, and Left subroutines so the entity will move in the opposite direction if a wall is sensed.

68. Save your work, and test play the frame. The entity should quickly solve the maze. Debug as needed.

Skill Application

69. Add an active object to the simulation, locate an image of a mouse, and change the image for the active object to the mouse.

70. Create an animation frame for each of the four directions, and edit the mouse image as appropriate.

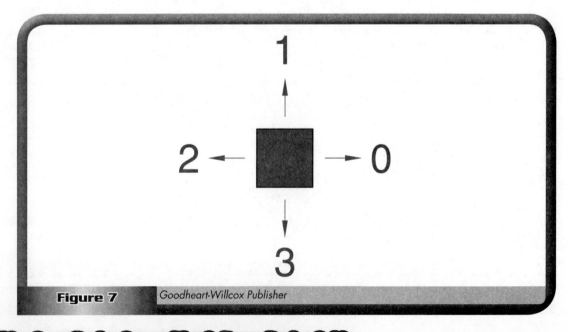

Figure 7   *Goodheart-Willcox Publisher*

71. Add programming so the mouse object is always in the exact location of the entity.
72. Add programming so the mouse image displayed corresponds to the direction the entity is moving.
73. Add programming to make the entity and all sensors invisible.
74. Tune and refine the mouse animation and positioning to fit inside the maze.
75. Move the Direction Counter object outside of the scope so it is not visible during the simulation.
76. Locate an image of cheese, and change the image for the Goal object to the cheese image.
77. Save your work, compile an EXE file, and submit it for grading according to the directions provided by your instructor.

Review Questions

1. Complete the table for three trial runs for the Sightless Entity level and AI Entity level. What is the average time it takes the artificial intelligence to solve the maze in each type of AI?

Trial	Sightless Entity Time	AI Entity Time
1		
2		
3		
Average		

2. What is the motivation of the entity in this simulation?

_____

_____

_____

_____

3. Describe how eyesight is programmed into this simulation.

_____

_____

_____

_____

4. Describe how a counter is used in this simulation to store directional data.

_____

_____

_____

_____

5. Speculate why programming AI with logical choices is better for a video game than random choices.

_____

_____

_____

Activity 13-2

Artificial Intelligence: Seeing and Tracking AI

Objectives

Students will program artificial intelligence to create a one-player game with a competitive computer player. Students will modify artificial intelligence systems to match player skill and escalate gameplay.

Situation

The Really Cool Game Company has received positive feedback from the *Ricochet* game created in Chapter 10. The only negative comment has been the lack of a one-player version. Making a one-player version of this game requires the designing and implementation of an artificial intelligence system. You have been assigned this task.

How to Begin

1. Launch MMF2 and open the *Ricochet* game created in Chapter 10.
2. Save the file as *LastName*_Ricochet AI in your working folder.
3. Display Level 1 in the frame editor.

Frame Editor

Searching Movement

The left-hand bat will be controlled by the computer as a "thinking" player. To achieve this, the bat will be given virtual eyes to scan the game map. If the eyes find the ball, then the bat will follow the movement of the eyes to hit the ball.

4. Using the **Properties** window, change the **Type** property in the **Movement** tab for the Bat, Left Hand object to **Static**. This removes the player 2 controls.
5. Add a new active object in the middle of the frame, and name it **AI Eyes**. This will be the sensor that locates the ball.
6. Change the size of the object to 400 pixels × 10 pixels, as shown in **Figure 1.**
7. Open the object in the image editor, change the image to a solid square filled in the color of your choice, and move the hotspot to the left-center position.

Hotspot

8. Using the **Properties** window, change the **Type** property in the **Movement** tab for the AI Eyes object to **Bouncing Ball**.
9. Set the **Initial direction** property to positions 8 and 24 only.
10. Enter 20 for the **Speed** property.
11. Click the **# of angles** property, and click **8** in the drop-down list.
12. Enter 0 in the **Randomizer** and **Security** properties. This will make the AI Eyes object move only up and down to scan for the ball.

Placing the Eyes

The AI Eyes need to be attached to the Bat, Left hand object. This is done programmatically, similar to how the sensors were attached to the entity in the last activity.

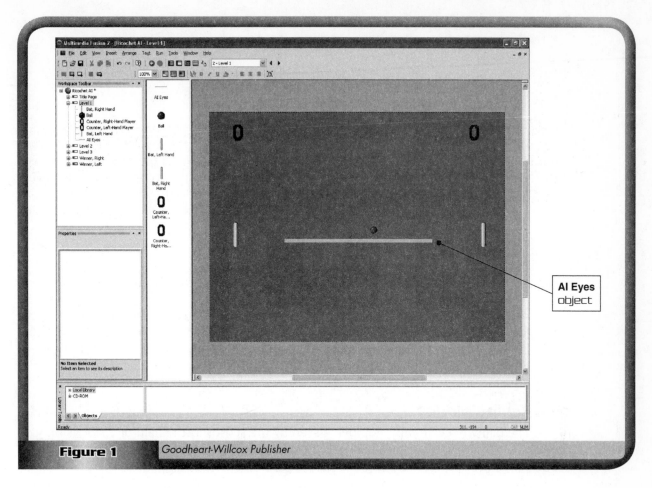

AI Eyes object

Figure 1 *Goodheart-Willcox Publisher*

Subroutines will be used to switch from search mode to follow mode when the eyes find the ball.

Event Editor

13. Display the event editor for the Level 1 frame, add a new comment on the last line of programming that states AI Eyes Tracking.

14. Below the comment, program this pseudo code: **IF** at the start of the frame.

15. On the next line, program this pseudo code: **IF** the Ball object overlaps the AI Eyes object.

16. On the next line, create a subroutine named Following.

17. Below the Following subroutine, create a new subroutine named Searching.

18. In the Following subroutine, program this pseudo code:

   IF always,
   THEN set the Y coordinate of the left-hand bat to the Y coordinate of the AI Eyes object
      AND set the X coordinate of the AI Eyes object to the X coordinate of the left-hand bat.

19. Copy this event, and paste it in the Searching subroutine.

20. In the **IF** at the start of the frame line below the comment, program this pseudo code: **THEN** activate the Searching subroutine.

Run Frame

21. Play the frame. Check that the left-hand bat follows the motion of the AI Eyes object and the AI Eyes object is attached to the left-hand bat. The AI Eyes object and left-hand bat very quickly move out of the scope because the programming to make the AI Eyes object bounce has not been added.

22. In the Searching subroutine, program the following pseudo code. Refer to **Figure 2**.
    IF the AI Eyes object leaves the play area on the top or bottom,
    THEN the AI Eyes object will bounce.
23. Save your work, and test play the frame. Make sure the AI Eyes object and left-hand bat stay on the frame.

Following the Eyes

When the sensor finds the ball, it must then follow the movement of the ball. The left-hand bat will be in following mode when this occurs. When the sensor cannot see the ball, then the left-hand bat will be in searching mode. The two modes are achieved by activating or deactivating the correct subroutine.

Run Frame

24. Locate the programming line for **IF** the Ball object overlaps the AI Eyes object, and add this pseudo code:
    THEN activate the Following subroutine
            AND deactivate the Searching subroutine.
25. Add a new event in the Following subroutine, and program this pseudo code:
    IF the AI Eyes object is overlapping the Ball object,
    THEN set the Y coordinate of the AI Eyes object to the Y coordinate of the Ball object.
26. Save your work, and test play the frame. See what happens when the sensor finds the ball. Also, you may notice a problem with the bouncing of the sensor at the top or bottom of the frame. Note, the scoring will not work properly because the frame is being played, not the application.

Switching Modes

The ball will eventually stop being seen by the sensor as the field of vision is only 400 pixels by 10 pixels. This allows the human player a chance to score as the left-hand bat will sometimes be searching and miss the ball.

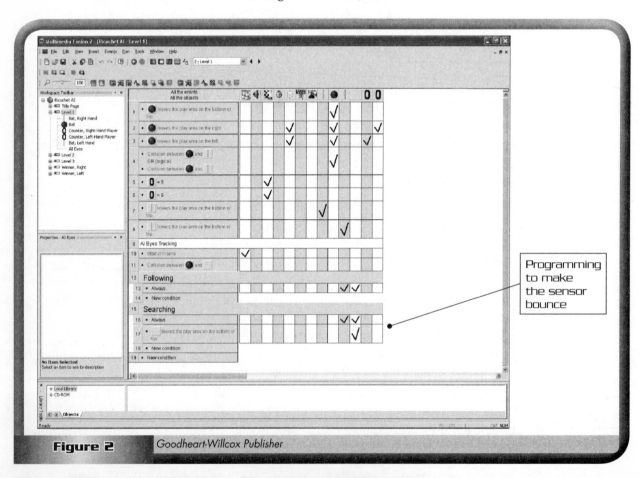

Programming to make the sensor bounce

Figure 2   *Goodheart-Willcox Publisher*

27. Add a new condition to the Following subroutine, and program this pseudo code:

> **IF** the AI Eyes object is **NOT** overlapping the Ball object,
> **THEN** activate the Searching group of events
> > **AND** deactivate the Following group of events.

Preventing Conflicts

It is good practice to make sure subroutines are properly activated and deactivated. This will also correct the bouncing error you may have experienced during testing.

28. Add a new condition to the Following subroutine, and program this pseudo code:

> **IF** this subroutine is activated,
> **THEN** deactivate the Searching group.

29. Add a new condition to the Searching subroutine, and program this pseudo code:

> **IF** this subroutine is activated,
> **THEN** deactivate the Following group.

Run Frame

30. Drag each of these two new lines of code to the top of their respective subroutines, as shown in **Figure 3.**

31. Save your work, and test play the frame.

Tuning

The artificial intelligence is working. Now the AI Eyes object needs to be made invisible during gameplay.

Run Application

32. In the Following and the Searching groups, locate the **IF** always condition, and program this pseudo code: **AND** make the AI Eyes object invisible.

33. Save your work, and test play the application. Play the beginner level, as that is the only level with AI.

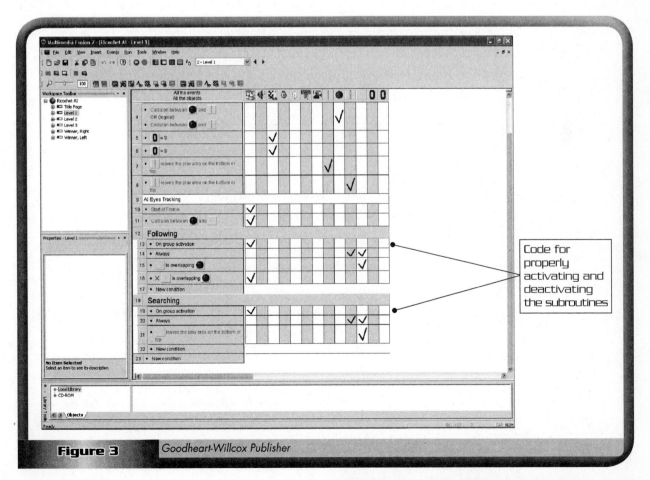

Figure 3 Goodheart-Willcox Publisher

34. Debug the Level 1 frame as needed. This frame should be completely error free at this point.

Skill Application

35. Modify the Level 2 (intermediate) and Level 3 (advanced) frames to include AI.

36. Adjust the settings and size of the sensor to match the difficulty of each level.

37. Add buttons to the Title Page frame to allow the player to choose one-player or two-player gameplay.

38. Copy the three level frames, and modify each to create two-player levels, as existed in the original *Ricochet* game.

39. Save your work, compile an EXE file, and submit it for grading according to the directions provided by your instructor.

Review Questions

1. Why was the sensor object wide, but thin, and why did it not extend across the entire scope?

   _____

   _____

   _____

   _____

2. Describe how the AI moves the left-hand bat in this game.

   _____

   _____

   _____

   _____

3. How are subroutines used in programming the AI for this game build?

   _____

   _____

   _____

   _____

4. Why is the sensor made invisible during gameplay?

   _____

   _____

   _____

   _____

5. How did you modify the sensor to make the AI more challenging on the second and third game levels?

   _____

   _____

   _____

   _____

Name: _____

Date: _____

Class: _____

Activity 13-3

Artificial Intelligence: Thinking AI

Objectives

Students will program an entity with artificial intelligence to simulation computer thinking and choice. Students will program an array to create perception for an entity to make the best choice. Students will program entity motivation to defend an attack. Students will program entity navigation to place game objects in the correct locations.

Situation

The Really Cool Game Company has received positive feedback for the *Tic-Tac-Toe* game created in Chapter 12. The company would like your team to program AI for the game so it can be played in one-player mode. The AI must determine the best location for the computer player's move. As you brainstorm ideas for the AI, keep in mind the skills you have used throughout your training. You can use any technique to create the AI. This can include items such as sensors, array totals, good-bad-neutral qualifiers, randomizing, counters, and more. The most important move in the game is the first move. Other moves are reactions to either block the opponent or risk strategies to win.

How to Begin

1. Form into teams as directed by your instructor.
2. Play a few rounds of tic-tac-toe with your teammates. Each time you play, construct a flowchart or use case on a blank sheet of paper or in a word processing document.
3. Determine strategies for winning and blocking based on the use case, and record the strategies and moves.
4. As a team, brainstorm ways to create a perception system for the AI. Decide if you will use sensors, array totals, good-bad-neutral qualifier groups, counters, or a combination. Record all of your ideas.
5. As a team, brainstorm ways to create a navigation system for the AI. This will determine how to place the O tile in correct locations on the game map. The computer player will always be O, and the human player will always have the first move. Record all of your ideas.
6. As a team, brainstorm ways to create a motivation system for the AI. This must include a blocking strategy and a winning strategy. Your team may decide to design an aggressive motivation for the AI to win or a blocking strategy for the AI to always tie. Motivation can also be used to allow for more or less difficult gameplay. Record all of your ideas.

Preparing to Program AI

7. Launch MMF2, and open the *Tic-Tac-Toe* game created in Chapter 12.
8. Save the file as *TeamName*_Tic-Tac-Toe Game AI in your working folder. You may want to create several copies for each team member to attempt new programming and test. Keep a clean copy so when testing proves the programming works, a final version will be programmed from the clean copy without errors or unused lines of programming.

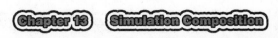

9. Copy and paste Frame 1, and rename it as AI Frame.

10. Display the event editor for the AI Frame.

11. Modify the programming of the AI Frame as needed to implement the perception system to detect the position of the X player. Remove any unneeded programming from the original two-player version of the game.

AI Navigation

The functioning of the game for the first player X move (the human player) is basically the same as the main gameplay. The only difference is switching to a subroutine that will allow the computer to select an appropriate space to defend the strategy to counter player X's move. The existing Victory_Array object or other sensory system can be used to sense where the player X move was made. The AI will have a predetermined location on the game map to place the O tile for the start of the game based on the location of the first X tile. You may need to construct multiple subroutines and global variable activations to achieve full navigation.

12. Using the use case, design and program the navigation system to place an O tile in the best location for the AI to make its first move.

13. Add programming to allow the player X (the human player) to take a turn after the first turn was taken by the AI.

14. Add programming to switch to an AI subroutine and make the next appropriate move for the AI. This will likely involve a new perception system to detect the second move of player X and to test if blank spaces are available. Try to avoid strictly random placement of the O tiles; that is not AI. Implement your team's thoughts as programming to achieve a blocking or attacking strategy.

AI Motivation

Determine if you are using a blocking or attacking strategy to motivate the AI. A sensory system must be constructed to detect if the AI will scan to fill an empty space for victory or scan to detect the patterns from the use case that must be blocked to prevent a player X victory. Use the existing Victory Array object, sensor objects, counters, or other method of detecting the near-win patterns. If a pattern has more than one position option, use a randomizing element for the AI to make a choice.

15. Review the notes from your team discussions.

16. Construct a system to determine the perception for the AI. Include pattern recognition needed to understand the player X strategy that does not include an opportunity to win or block. This may also include random location selection when there is no logical location to place the O tile.

Tuning

With gameplay functional, the team must test the AI systems to make sure it will work in all use case scenarios. Any bugs discovered in tuning must be rated and corrected as appropriate.

17. Construct a system to detect the X and O positions and test for victory.

18. Display the correct string values for player turn and victory.

19. Test play and note any errors. Debug as needed.

20. Save your work, compile an EXE file, and submit it for grading according to the directions provided by your instructor.

Review Questions

1. Describe the navigation systems your team developed for the AI and why these were appropriate.

   _____

   _____

   _____

   _____

2. Describe the motivation systems your team developed for the AI and why these were appropriate.

   _____

   _____

   _____

3. Describe the perception systems your team developed for the AI and why these were appropriate.

   _____

   _____

   _____

4. What game objects were used to determine when player X was near victory?

   _____

   _____

   _____

5. How did the AI system understand how to place the O tile to achieve victory?

   _____

   _____

   _____

Activity 13-4

HITL Simulation

Objectives

Students will evaluate a discrete-event simulation as to real-world physics and application. Students will evaluate a human-in-the-loop (HITL) simulator as to the inductive logic and heuristics. Students will evaluate the iconic logic value from success and failures revealed in design and testing.

Situation

The Really Cool Game Company would like to build an engineering simulator to test rocket technology. This simulator will save time and money for the client by allowing virtual testing of expensive equipment. Additionally, it will eliminate the risk of explosions and crashes into populated areas found with real-world testing. The Really Cool Game Company has found an existing simulator and would like your team to evaluate the performance and value of the software. Your evaluation will help the company make decisions on the design for its own simulation build.

How to Begin

1. Form into teams as directed by your teacher.
2. Launch the Kerbal Space Program demo, and click the **Start Game** link on the main screen.
3. On the **Start Game** menu, click the **Training** link.
4. Select the Construction Basics tutorial, as shown in **Figure 1.**
5. Complete the tutorial to create the spacecraft in the vehicle assembly plant.
6. When the new components are unlocked, review the available components and the benefits each provides to the project.
7. Click the **Exit** button to end the tutorial and return to the main menu.

Exit

Human in the Loop

Flight of the spacecraft requires a human in the loop to control aspects of flight. This simulation has a tutorial covering flight controls.

8. Complete the Flight Basics tutorial.
9. Launch the spacecraft, and refine your skills at piloting the craft.
10. Evaluate the inductive logic obtained through repeated attempts to navigate the spacecraft.
11. Identify five critical thinking and learning skills developed from inside the system. Describe how the simulation system induced learning for each.

Iconic Logic

12. Watch a classmate play the two tutorials in the simulation.
13. Evaluate the modifications made and the piloting skills during flight.

Name: _____

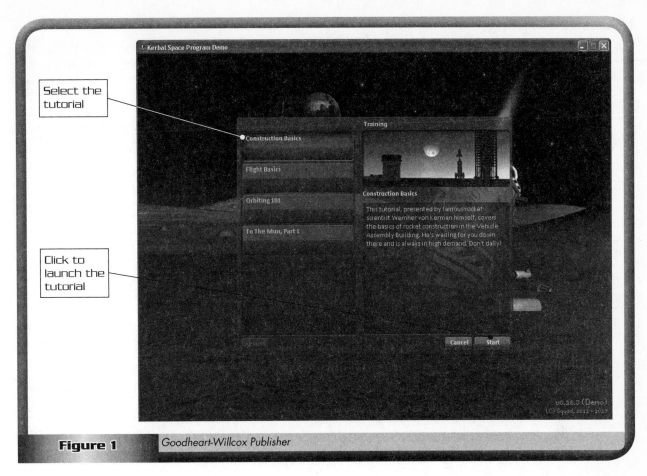

Select the tutorial

Click to launch the tutorial

Figure 1   *Goodheart-Willcox Publisher*

14. Ask questions to get a better understanding of what the player is doing, what the player is trying to achieve, and why they are doing it that way. Do *not* try to give advice or direct the player to use other tactics.

15. Evaluate the iconic logic aspects of the simulation.

16. List five critical-thinking and learning skills demonstrated by the classmate interacting with the system. Evaluate if each was an intended outcome of the simulation.

17. For each intended outcome, describe why this is an important intended learning outcome.

18. For each unintended outcome, describe changes to the simulation system that could reduce the unintended outcomes.

Evaluations and Recommendations

19. Using the data collected from personal experience and observation, evaluate the software and make recommendations as to what The Really Cool Game Company should do to pursue making a spacecraft assembly and flight simulator.

20. Assemble your team to review each team member's findings and observations.

21. Brainstorm possible improvements and modifications to include in the simulation.

22. Discuss the learning goals for the simulation and what you believe would be the most beneficial features to the game.

23. Create a PechaKucha style presentation to summarize the team's results and recommendations.

24. Present the team's results and recommendations to the class, and answer questions.

Heuristic Learning

25. Research what is needed to build a working rocket capable of achieving the goal of landing on the moon. This includes thrust, gravity, fuels, components weight, component materials, and more. Cite your reference materials.

26. Write a summary of your research.

27. Evaluate the research, and create a spacecraft Kerbal Space Program demo to match.

28. Speculate what contributed to any failure of the attempt.

29. Write a hypothesis statement to predict the cause and effect relationship responsible for the failure.

30. Make changes to the spacecraft that will test the hypothesis.

31. Record your results.

32. Evaluate your results and make a new prediction of what modifications will produce the required rocket design.

Review Questions

1. What was the purpose of using a trial-and-error simulation to determine the functional capabilities of each component?

2. How could a test flight be made into a discrete-event simulation?

3. Describe how heuristic learning helped you decide on the components used in the rocket.

4. List five critical thinking and learning skills developed from inside the system.

5. Describe how the simulation system induced learning for each critical thinking and learning skill.

Activity 13-5

Video Game Design Simulation

Objectives

Students will apply skills and knowledge in a video game design business simulation. Students will apply heuristic learning to the business of running a video game design studio. Students will practice decision-making skills and summarize inductive learning obtained through the simulation.

Situation

The Really Cool Game Company believes you have the skills and knowledge to run a division of the company. To test this assumption, it wants you to participate in an entrepreneurial simulation of a startup video game design studio. You and your team should carefully evaluate each decision made in the simulation and the impact it will make on productivity and profitability. Other teams will be competing against you, and the company will compare your team's performance against the other teams. Be prepared to defend all decisions made in the simulation.

How to Begin

1. Form into teams as directed by your instructor. Initially, each student in the team will individually evaluate the simulation.
2. Launch the Game Dev Tycoon Demo software, click anywhere on the splash screen to start the tutorial.
3. Read the instructions in the tutorial, clicking the **OK** button to advance to each new screen.
4. The first task is to create a company name, input your name, and modify the avatar, as shown in **Figure 1.**
5. Complete the tutorial to gain an understanding of the features and functions in the simulation.

Team Simulation

6. Working with your team, start a new simulation and record your result on the form provided by your instructor. To start a new simulation, press the [Esc] key, and click **New** in the menu.
7. Record all decisions made during the month.
8. Reflect on your decisions for each month of the simulation, and record your thoughts.
9. Explain the rationale for your decisions to upgrade, hire, fire, and so on.
10. Evaluate if each decision was the best possible and if making a different decision would have increase productivity, profitability, customer volume, and fan volume.
11. Take screen captures for each month of the simulation, and paste the screens in a PowerPoint presentation.

Team Presentation

12. Refine the team presentation to include information on the decisions, the results you were attempting to achieve, and how the decisions matched the attempt.
13. Use the template form provided by your instructor to record important decisions.
14. Make a class presentation, and respond to feedback.

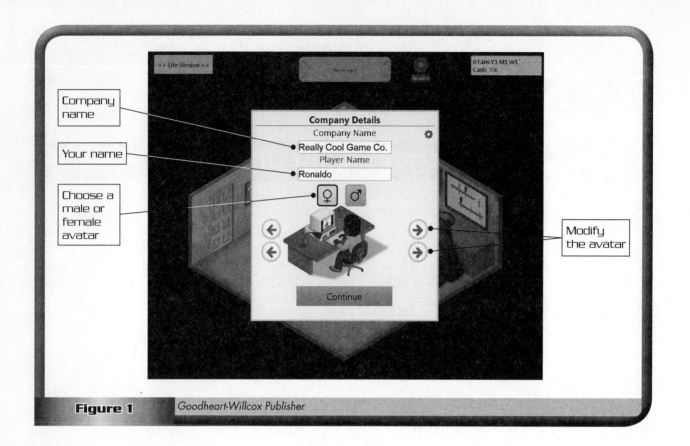

Company name

Your name

Choose a male or female avatar

Modify the avatar

Company Details

Company Name

Really Cool Game Co.

Player Name

Ronaldo

Continue

>> Lite Version <<

No Project

0 Fans Y1 M1 W1
Cash: 70K

Figure 1   *Goodheart-Willcox Publisher*

Capstone Project

Objectives

After completing this chapter, you will be able to:
- Use game design documents to create a production plan for a video game build.
- Use computer tools to create video game programming and artwork.
- Create a playable video game with a game engine.
- Create animated objects in a video game.
- Add sound and music to a video game.
- Test a completed video game.
- Explain the roles of various members on a video game design team.
- Explain the role of team building on a video game design team.
- Describe how video game design teams conduct scheduling and communication.
- Explain how scheduling and budget impact a video game design team.
- Conduct written and verbal communication in context of a video game design team.
- List terminology related to the video game design industry.
- Engage in constructive criticism.
- Demonstrate appropriate interpersonal and personal workplace skills.
- Engage in teamwork to solve problems.
- Identify personal strengths and weaknesses.
- Analyze various aspects of a game, such as rules, gameplay, and longevity of design.
- Create design plans.
- Create character sketches.
- Create storyboards.

Activity 1

Design Submission

Objectives

Students will demonstrate mastery in the design process from conception to production. Students will develop design plans, character sketches, documentation, and storyboards for a proposed video game. Students will construct an original creation for a video game used in education. Students will use software tools to aid in the design and construction of the video game. Students will give and receive feedback on a video game design.

Situation

The Really Cool Game Company wants to enter a game to compete in an indie-developer competition. All design teams in the company will be creating games for the competition. Teams will manage themselves and the development budget. The game can be: 1) an educational game for grades K–6 that teaches skills in the areas of math, science, language arts, history, or technology; or 2) a game addressing current environmental issues and sustainability of resources.

Team Budget and Expenses

The following list shows the cost of various items. You must keep track of all costs associated with your game build.
○ Question answered by the instructor/specialist: $500 each
○ Salary of each team member: $100/day
○ Vacation day for an employee (an absence or off-task day): $150/day
   There is no charge if the employee (student) is on a field trip or a nondisciplinary main office visit; subject to review and verification by the instructor. Students who are off-task can be assigned a vacation day by the instructor for this behavior. Warning of vacation day charge may be given prior to actually expensing the day to the student either on the same day or any prior day.
○ Dispute arbitration by instructor: $500 each
○ Document resubmission fee: $200 each
○ Employee termination severance cost: $3,000 each
○ Specialist fee for help by an employee (student) from another group: Negotiate the amount before help begins; fee must be approved by the instructor. The fee is credited to the budget of the group from which the employee came.

Grading

200 points	for team budget (this can be a negative number; each point costs $10)
200 points	for documents
100 points	for 10-minute presentation
400 points	for game based on peer evaluations
100 points	for written game review
1000 points	maximum total

Time Schedule

- **Concept stage**

Concept approval:	2 days
Concept presentation to class prep and performance:	3 days
Design document approval:	3 days

- **Construction stage**

Build:	_____ days

- **Tuning stage**

Tuning:	_____ days

Total project days requested by team:	_____ days

Team Budget

$10,000 + $1,000 for each team member: _____
For example, team with four employees will have a budget of $14,000.

How to Begin

1. Use Microsoft Word or other word processing program to create a high-concept document to propose your game idea. Address the letter to your instructor with your school address. Your instructor's job title is Director of New Products for the Really Cool Game Company.

2. Print out and turn in the document to your instructor for review. Only written concepts will be reviewed and approved, so do not talk to your instructor!

3. When the Director of New Products approves the team's concept, prepare a presentation to propose the concept to the class. If your idea is not approved by the class, submit a new high-concept document until you receive the green light. The presentation should include the following points.

   - Request the time (amount of days) needed for each of the stages of production. This usually depends on the number of team members you have and the complexity of the game design. Your instructor and classmates will ultimately determine how many days they feel your team will need to complete the initial design.
   - Determine a launch date for the product and reasons why this would be the best day to begin selling the game.
   - Request a budget (amount of money) needed to complete the project and create a CD or upload it to the Internet.
   - Set a selling price for the game, explain the distribution plan, and determine the dollar amount that must be earned to break even on the build. The break-even point is where the expenses (salaries and design costs) equal the amount earned from sales.
   - Determine the total number of games that must be sold to reach the break-even point.
   - Break down your projections between the normal retail distribution and any alternative distributions used to determine sales volume and profitability.
   - Determine how much profit (not sales) is expected 12 months from the launch date.

Written Game Review

Each team will write an unbiased game review as a critic for the games from other teams. Game reviews will be graded based on biased/unbiased, features described, and information provided for other users.

Name: _____

Date: _____

Class: _____

Activity 2

Design Planning

Objectives

Students will demonstrate mastery in the design process from conception to production. Students will develop design plans, character sketches, documentation, and storyboards for a proposed video game. Students will construct an original creation for a video game used in education. Students will use many software tools to aid in the design and construction of the video game. Students will give and receive feedback on a video game design.

Situation

The Really Cool Game Company has approved your team's concept for the competition and provided a provisional budget. Your team will complete the industry-standard planning documents to finalize the ideas generated in the concept stage (Activity 1) before beginning the game build.

How to Begin

1. Assemble your team and brainstorm ideas for each document.

2. Use the ideas from your high-concept document created in Activity 1 to lead your team discussion on each of the documents needed.

3. Complete world design, storyboard, game script, and character documents. When all documents are complete, the Director of New Products will need to review your documents before any member of the team can begin the build.

4. Schedule a time with the Director of New Products to discuss the documents and receive approval.

5. Keep all approved documents in a folder for your team. You must have your documents present before your instructor will answer any questions during the game build.

Activity 3

Game Build and Tuning

Objectives

Students will demonstrate mastery in the design process from conception to production. Students will develop design plans, character sketches, documentation, and storyboards for a proposed video game. Students will construct an original creation for a video game used in education. Students will use software tools to aid in the design and construction of the video game. Students will give and receive feedback on a video game design.

Situation

The Really Cool Game Company has approved your team's design documents and returned them to you. Begin the construction stage of the game build. Remember to test along the way to ensure a high-quality product. Pacing your work is important as your team must stay within the budget and time schedule.

How to Begin

1. Your team's project manager will assign duties for each team member, including duties for the project manager.
2. Use 001 Game Greator, Multimedia Fusion 2, Microsoft Paint, Microsoft PowerPoint, Adobe Photoshop, Audacity, and any other programs available to aid in the creation of the game.
3. Equipment such as a digital camera or microphone must be signed out according to the schedule and procedures for the class. Do not wait until the last day to use the equipment shared by the class. It may not be available at that time and your schedule will not be met.
4. Work together to complete the tasks and problem solve to overcome design obstacles.
5. Review the expenses and fees charged in the team budget and expenses section.
6. For each day, track budget expenses on the budget-planning form or use spreadsheet software.

Team Budget and Expenses

- Question answered by the instructor/specialist: $500 each
- Salary of each team member: $100/day
- Vacation day for an employee (an absence or off-task day): $150/day
  There is no charge if the employee (student) is on a field trip or a nondisciplinary main office visit; subject to review and verification by the instructor. Students who are off-task can be assigned a vacation day by the instructor for this behavior. Warning of a vacation-day charge may be given prior to actually expensing the day to the student either on the same day or any prior day.
- Dispute arbitration by instructor: $500 each
- Document resubmission fee: $200 each
- Employee termination severance cost: $3,000 each
  A terminated group member will receive a copy of the game build and design documents from his or her team and must complete the game build on his or her own.
- Specialist fee for help by an employee (student) from another group: Negotiate the amount before help begins; fee must be approved by the instructor. The fee is credited to the budget of the group from which the employee came.

Name: _____

Date: _____

Class: _____

Activity 4

Evaluation

Objectives

Students will evaluate an original game build for the key elements. Students will complete a five-star review and provide constructive criticism. Students will demonstrate knowledge of bias by creating original biased and unbiased user reviews. Students will give and receive feedback on a video game design.

Situation

The Really Cool Game Company needs to promote your game and has asked your team to write a biased review and five-star rating. Additionally, you will need to obtain an unbiased review of your game from each team.

How to Begin

1. Play your team's game, and take note of all positive features of the game.

2. As a team, compare notes, brainstorm, and complete a biased, five-star review for the game.

3. As a team, write a biased game review and a biased critic review using Microsoft Word or other word processing program.

4. Provide a copy of your team's game to each of the other teams in the class.

5. Each of the other teams will create an unbiased, five-star review and critical review for your team's game. In evaluating games from other teams, stick to the facts when pointing out flaws. Be careful; biased/unbiased is part of the grade. Your team cannot show bias or the team grade will be reduced.

6. Print out your unbiased reviews and give each team the appropriate copy.

7. Place the reviews in order shown below, staple them or assemble electronically, and turn in to the Director of New Products (instructor).
   - Five-star review, biased
   - Critic review, biased
   - Five-star reviews, unbiased
   - Critic reviews, unbiased

Name: _____

Reviewed by: _____

Review type: Biased ❏   Unbiased ❏

Copy this page as needed for all reviews.

Team name:	
★ ★ ★ ★ ★	**Overall rating**
★ ★ ★ ★ ★	Quality of rules
★ ★ ★ ★ ★	User interface
★ ★ ★ ★ ★	Navigation
★ ★ ★ ★ ★	Performance
★ ★ ★ ★ ★	Play
★ ★ ★ ★ ★	Artistry
★ ★ ★ ★ ★	Longevity
★ ★ ★ ★ ★	Player interactions
★ ★ ★ ★ ★	Plot complexity
★ ★ ★ ★ ★	Rewards

Pros: _____
_____
_____

Cons: _____
_____
_____

Review Comments
_____
_____
_____
_____
_____
_____
_____

Activity 5

Job Evaluations

Objectives

Students will critique the quality and quantity of their contributions to the team. Students will assess themselves and other team members as to job performance. Students will explain the role they played on the team and the division of labor needed to complete a high-quality video game design.

Situation

Companies routinely evaluate employees to see who is doing the best job. Sometimes, these reviews are used to give promotions or bonuses to those who work hardest and create the best ideas.

The Really Cool Game Company has approved a budget request to give your team a bonus. To assign the bonus in a fair manner, it has asked each team member to provide input regarding the cooperation and performance of each member.

How to Begin

1. The Director of New Products will tell each team the total bonus amount available for the team. The amount will vary from team to team, but has no reflection on the quality of the final product.

2. Complete a project job performance review form for yourself as a self-evaluation of your work on this project with this team. Be honest!

3. Complete a project job performance review form as an evaluation for each member of your group. Be honest! You may be asked to explain your evaluation and the scores and bonus you gave.

4. Assign each group member a bonus amount. The bonus amount does not have to be equal for each group member. Assign a larger bonus to people you feel contributed the most and a smaller bonus to those who did the least. The sum of all bonuses cannot exceed the total bonus amount.

5. Staple together all project job performance review forms that you completed or assemble them electronically.

6. Give the stapled packet or electronic files to your team's project manager.

7. The project manager will turn in the evaluation packet to the Director of New Products.

Name: _____

Project Job Performance Review

Group name: _____

Period: _____

Group member's name: _____

Job title: _____

Copy this page as needed for all evaluations.

During the time spent working with your team, you have been able to see the strengths and weaknesses of each team member and yourself. Use the scale below to evaluate each team member on the character traits listed.

Attributes	Very Weak									Very Strong
	0	1	2	3	4	5	6	7	8	9
Imagination										
Technology awareness										
Logic competence										
Mathematics competence										
Aesthetic competence										
Presentation skills										
Listening skills										
Compromise										
Writing skills										
Research skills										
Responsibility										
Dependability										
Punctuality										
Positive attitude										
Initiative										
Respect for self										
Respect for others										
Professional dress										

Total performance score: _____

Total bonus budget amount: _____

Bonus amount requested for this employee: _____

To the best of my ability, I affirm that the above performance review reflects a true and unbiased opinion of the evaluated employee's work habits. All issues related to friendship have been excluded and no bargain or compensation was obtained to influence this evaluation.

Signature of evaluator: _____

Evaluator's name (print your name): _____

Date: _____

Peer Evaluation

Each team must play and evaluate the other teams' games and complete a five-star rating and critique on each game. These evaluations will be used to award points for the build for that team. The instructor will also evaluate the game. Your review must contain similar scores and *not* show favoritism and bias as bias will lower your team's score on the written game review.

Written Game Review

Each team will write an unbiased game review as a critic for the games of the other teams. Game reviews will be graded based on biased/unbiased, features described, and information provided for other users.

Team Grading

200 points	for team budget (this can be a negative number; each point costs $10)
200 points	for documents
100 points	for 10-minute presentation
400 points	for game based on peer evaluations
100 points	for written game review
1000 points	maximum total

Personal Grading

1000 points	for team grade
500 points	for group member performance reviews
500 points	for instructor performance review
2000 points	maximum total